Strokes

Inside the Fascinating, Mysterious World of Handwriting Analysis

Martin J. H. Povser

Revised Edition

iUniverse, Inc.
New York Bloomington

Strokes Revised Edition
Inside the Fascinating, Mysterious World of Handwriting Analysis

Copyright © 2009 by Martin J. H. Povser

iUniverse books may be ordered through booksellers or by contacting:

iUniverse
1663 Liberty Drive
Bloomington, IN 47403
www.iuniverse.com
1-800-Authors (1-800-288-4677)

ISBN: 978-1-4401-0106-9 (pbk)
ISBN: 978-1-4401-0107-6 (ebook)

Printed in the United States of America

iUniverse rev. date: 5/19/2009

This book is dedicated to
Ruth Ackerman Grim Leestma
whose grace and wisdom has
disarmed skeptical writers
and uplifted worried ones
for 58 years

Contents

Introduction

Why We Write

This is a book you've never seen before, even if you are a handwriting analyst. Allan Grim says, "I wish I had it when I started as an analyst." Grim and I are Graphoanalysts. We look for personality traits in handwriting from rules of the International Graphoanalysis Society. Developing his practice, Grim realized the public little understood handwriting analysis. He thought the media, critics, and skeptics, and even some handwriting analysts distorted it, mostly from ignorance. He wanted to convey to the public that his subject was a legitimate technique and a practical tool. He also knew it lacked a comprehensive study of its validity, which hindered its acceptance by psychology.

When he surveyed the handwriting analysis books, he was surprised how many existed. He reviewed many and found they usually listed handwriting strokes and their meaning for the writer's personality. They inserted some striking uses for the technique and added a slim history. Virtually all announced the subject is scientific, citing no authority and ignoring any knock on its legitimacy. Missing were issues that stimulated the public and analysts. Can you disguise your writing from analysis? How can you analyze the writing of someone whose style varies? Some of them no book discussed; others only briefly. Can printing be analyzed? Is doctors' writing different from the rest of us? Once in a while magazines and newspapers featured articles on the subject. As expected they conveyed only the core items repeated for years. The public's information was narrow and shallow.

Grim wondered why no book took you inside with an analyst to capture his challenges and struggles, especially analyzing, and facing critics. What does an analyst do first when he sees a sample? How does he handle the person insisting he analyze their writing on the spot? A few years ago, Sheila Lowe, an accomplished analyst from California, published a book in the Idiot's Guide series. Her volume on handwriting analysis is outstanding, says

1

Grim. It continues to sell and was updated in 2007. True to Idiot's Guide books the information is worthwhile but elementary. Hers is comprehensive but much of it is this-stroke-means-that personality trait. History, schools, analyses, legal and ethical issues, starting a business, and other topics appear. Yet Grim believes her book lacks many topics he and the public yearn for. Why isn't graphology more widely accepted? Can writing of Asians and Africans be analyzed? And one you especially won't find in these partisan treatises: What sound points do the critics make against it?

Without answers to his questions, he explored his chosen subject and read diverse materials, keeping notes of information he wanted to remember for himself and to pass on to other analysts. He also retained them for his teaching, articles, speeches, consulting, and seminars to enlighten the public and his fellow analysts. After years filling notebooks, in 2004 he again surveyed the inventory of books. No one had written that book he longed for. He decided it was time for him to write it.

Grim looked around to find an analyst with whom he could ride shotgun and narrate their experiences as part of the book. He also wanted to see if his were typical and if he could be objective writing about another analyst. He realized that no one nearby had the background he sought. The only one who seemed to qualify was Grim himself. He had a big problem with that. Although he doesn't think he is shy, he considers himself self-conscious. He says he does not like to talk about himself. I know from handwriting analysis that these people don't enjoy opening up about themselves. They don't like making a scene. They shrink from public displays. You will learn about this in these pages. Do you also wonder if this is shown in his handwriting? Read on. Grim also said he was repulsed that this might be seen as a memoir or an autobiography. That would put him at the center and he could not allow that.

Enter Martin Povser

To free him from his dilemma he approached me to be the writer of the book. I told him logically he must do the writing and to rejoice narrating all his experiences, good and bad. But he was adamant some other analyst must write it. They would write about all the areas he wanted covered, including his exploits. Somehow that would give him the separation and detachment he could tolerate. He knew I was a veteran analyst and thought I was a half-decent writer. He wasn't sure about his own skills for a lengthy book. He had been a lawyer for thirty years crafting soulless documents, except for the persuasion built into rational argument. He had plenty of notes for the text of the book but claims he couldn't inject them with vibrancy or imagination. With work he thought I could. Most of all he would not have to write about himself as a person.

Reluctantly I said I would be his author. Although Grim considered my writing passable, he wanted the book to be "presentable." The topic could be daunting to write with respectful heft. To ensure it he insisted I read some books on good writing and some classic literature too. Reluctantly I read a lot of his particular requests, including fiction like *Moby Dick* and *The Good Earth* and non-fiction like *The Perfect Storm* and *Seabiscuit*. Through all my reading renowned literature and books on good writing as well as endless hours of writing and revising this book, I'm a much better writer. I don't know if I'm a good writer, just further advanced. How good I am is up to you and the critics.

Although I believe it's essential to understand our literary partnership and the book's style, I relate the next steps reluctantly. When I showed him my first draft of the book, he recoiled. He had asked me to write a serious book about the subject from his notes, thoughts, sources, and experiences. He knew my writing style could be different but he remarked, "Where did you get that off-the-wall Tom Wolfe kind of stuff?" I wasn't sure to be flattered or censured. I said it came from the many moments of evolving into an improved writer and my individual style emerging from dormancy. Partly I was inspired by a book called *Spunk and Bite* by Arthur Plotnik. It arouses you to unlock the door to creative freedom, rush out and prance and jump about with fresh and appealing word combinations, not tired and flat ones.

I knew that if Grim had written the book, it would be a heady, dignified text. He was not aware that I had developed an offbeat, unusual manner of writing. We argued over my distinctive style and it became tense. Neither gave in. Finally I told him he could write it himself or he could get someone else to do it. He said it was too far along to switch authors. He wanted to get it done once and for all. We were into the second year and only trudging forward.

Because it blankets so many areas, Grim still goaded me to make it a compelling read. Whatever he does, Grim is exacting. In this instance someone else was doing his work. Thus, his own standards held a tight leash for my efforts. Bothered that I jar people with my "creative eccentricities," he fretted that the readers would be turned off by the odd style in a book intending to inform and convince the public about the merits of an already-battered subject. If this book was to elevate the subject's esteem, its form and content needed credibility, he reminded me often. I was firm and told him don't expect any changes to the book he wanted. I told him the book is not a series of goofy phrasings. I thought I was striking a balance between the style and the substance. Much of it follows conventional style, yet I think the text is lively while being instructive.

We fought some more. I told him I can't help myself and finally I wasn't going back for him. "Elvis and Ray Charles were true to their singular styles. That's a prime part of what made them great performers," I insisted. I wanted to follow my inner voice yearning for expression on the page. Grim finally gave in and I could stop taxiing on the runway and take off for my flight to fancy. He also trusted my knowledge of the subject and my ability to read his notes and convert them into stimulating prose. In yielding, he conceded that the subject can be dry and obscure. With my gusto and wallop throughout the book, it could be more appealing.

Groundbreaking

Grim sought an engaging book that gives people a deeper and more realistic view of handwriting analysis. It is distinctive in a few ways. Except for chapter headings, the book has no samples of handwriting within the text. That is not just ground-breaking for a handwriting book. That is earth-shaking. Grim explains that he "intended it to be about handwriting analysis, not the analysis of handwriting." He wanted reflection, not vivisection. A few instances occur where strokes are illustrated for their trait meanings. Since I had to describe the stroke, it was challenging to convey how a stroke looks knowing readers won't see it on paper. He also wanted to emphasize that it is not a how-to-analyze book or this-stroke-means-that book. A heaping stack of those exist and many should be censured for their incorrect statements on meanings. If you want to know what all those squiggles and curlicues mean, you can buy those books.

Grim didn't want this to be a question-and-answer book either. Yet all the questions he deems important and those that people ask about the most are woven through the text, rather than posed as queries. In a way the book is everything you always wanted to know about handwriting analysis but didn't know whom to ask. But without the questions and with questions you haven't thought of yourself. If you had, you would yearn for the answers. Can you analyze writing that was copied from another's style? He also believed analysts themselves were uninformed in some areas. Those were inserted in the book. One is the different ways people try to disguise their handwriting to avoid a proper analysis. Another is graphotherapy—altering your strokes to better your personality.

You might think this book is a brief for handwriting analysis. It is not. We thought a great advance was to include the major arguments for and against the validity of handwriting analysis. Prior books hardly ever discuss these. They especially avoid the adverse comments of outsiders. *The Write Stuff*, a 1992 book edited by the Berenstein brothers, was a scholarly attempt to assemble the arguments for and against handwriting analysis and cite some of the research. It had some leading experts and was technical and heartless. Some of that book's criticisms are inserted in this book. Since we are partial to handwriting analysis, you will note a bias toward the subject's being accepted as a serious scientific topic. In a spirited dialogue between us, Grim explains what it is and why it is superior to all other psychology tests or techniques that try to draw out personality. For this reason alone psychologists should be grabbing this book for their shelves.

If you think the book is mostly a memoir about Grim's handwriting analysis experiences, you'll be surprised. Most of it's about handwriting analysis itself. Grim doesn't even appear as a character to observe or talk about until the fifth chapter, where you join him only in his classroom teaching the subject. Yes, Grim appears in Chapters 1 and 2, but only to chat with me explaining graphology basics.

In the first two chapters I introduce you to the subject, beginning in grade school where you first encountered handwriting. I explain what it is and how it differs from other handwriting disciplines. Grim insisted on a history because he has never seen a really good one. Most are scanty and skip important people and signposts of progress. In Chapter 3 I tried to provide a thorough but non-boring history. It's not that long because the subject doesn't have a vast history. Mixed with it in early years we discuss the evolution of handwriting itself. You will be amazed to learn that many famous and brilliant minds in history believed in handwriting analysis. Two of them are featured in the history—Aristotle and Confucius, both of whom lived centuries before Christ. Yes, handwriting analysis is that old. But there is little to recount until the 19th century.

If you want to know about the research on handwriting analysis, we name sources with details. Because his story is so enthralling, one researcher, Milton Bunker, has his own chapter. Founder of Grim's school of handwriting analysis called Graphoanalysis, he was incited to probe why he couldn't conform his handwriting to his teacher's instruction. It's a gripping mystery whose solution you will discover by reading the chapter. You will also learn of his extraordinary research and his impact on the subject's growth.

Grim wanted the many practical uses for handwriting analysis to be included. In general the public doesn't realize all the marvelous ways this subject provides vital information to people to understand themselves and others they must deal with in their lives. Each of the significant ways is illustrated with intimate anecdotes. Even the minor uses are discussed. Some uses are personal (learning about that guy a lady met on the internet), some commercial (helping businesses discover a good worker), and some involve nations applying it to evaluate enemies.

Analysts are bombarded with an array of questions about handwriting. The most popular questions involve doctor's handwriting, printing, illegible signatures, and the serial killer one. All of these are discussed with their own chapter, except for the serial killer question. That is discussed in the segment about profiling of people, especially wicked ones.

No book has fully laid out how the law applies to handwriting analysis. As never before we expound on it in a serious but non-technical way. The major issues are explained and conclusions reached on their influence: Does handwriting analysis invade your privacy? Is it an infringement of the writer's copyrights to his own writing? Can an analysis report defame the writer? Addressed are the recent federal laws on discrimination as applied to personality tests in hiring employees. In addition, many people are unclear what distinguishes handwriting analysis from forensic analysis. Can both of their experts testify in court? Must you get the consent of the writer to analyze his handwriting? We also advise analysts on avoiding legal problems, especially aiding businesses in selecting employees.

Povser's Writing Style

Now you are reading Allan Grim's words. Marty Povser has asked me to tell you about his writing style. It wasn't what I knew when he began this book. He says it evolved after many re-writes and his true self intruding on the pages and refusing to leave. I tried to evict this pesky demon. Povser's already told you we had a battle over his transformation and I lost. Now I can only hope you appreciate this provocative subject without having to hold your nose from Povser's prose. Since I allowed him to retain his odd style and it still troubles me, I feel a duty to inform you about it. Call it a warning.

It is not easy to describe his manner of writing. He uses a collection of irreverent, amusing, goofy ways to design and deploy his words. You can call it eclectic, a smorgasbord of verbal victuals some tasty and some an acquired taste. He not only seizes every food item in the supermarket, he runs out to a gourmet shop for more. Povser writes as if no one will read his book or is indifferent to his words' impact. Maybe he concocted these verbal gyrations to entertain himself and if the reader wants to join in the mirth, grab a knife and fork and a comfortable chair. Although sometimes he uses old techniques, they often saunter with new steps. Povser surprises you with his peculiar methods. Some you've seen before. For others he directs them into new paces. He throws in a few you haven't seen before and where he gets them I don't know. Let me give you an idea what you'll be reading.

His new mode suggests Tom Wolfe, the white-suited fop who skated on to the cultural ice in the 1960's with a series of articles and books all with names long and hard to recall but for their odd resonance, like Mau-Mauing the Flak-Catchers and The Tangerine Flake Orange-Colored Streamline Baby. The later ones seem to calm down but always carried more meaning than you knew. The Right Stuff, The Bonfire of the Vanities, and A Man in Full. The early names are weird as are his texts. He didn't invent New Journalism or Creative Non-Fiction but may be its most-fabled practitioner. This writing genre began in the 1950's and features the writer injecting himself into a work, often using casual and playful words, and sometimes blurring the line between fact and fiction.

But Wolfe is only a guide for fathoming what Povser does. His way of imparting his thoughts is to refuse to be hamstrung by the boundaries of conventional writing and escape to artistic freedom. Maybe to the point of abuse. His point of view is to be talking to YOU as if he were sitting down next to you as an intimate companion and explaining handwriting analysis knowing you will understand because you are close friends. He even scolds you as he feels necessary to understand this splendid topic. If he senses you may not be getting it, he seems to want to slap you around. Like Cher, not General Patton. In one spot where he wonders outloud if he is repeating himself, he says, "Good. It's important. Maybe now it will sink in." Conversational tone is not new of course but he thinks it helps with understanding this esoteric topic.

He starts by taking you back to grade school and reminds you what you did with pencils and crayons to learn handwriting. But he doesn't allow you a respectful interval to introduce his shocks of wordplay. On the first page of the book he blitzes you with the sprightly and the silly. You get fresh onomatopeia, telling similes, an endless adjective, and crafty word companions. Yes, I know this doesn't give you detail. You will have to discover it yourself by reading the book. However, your patience has earned you a jelly bean of example here. He spells a familiar word his own way. "Properly" becomes "prahperlay," suggesting Rex Harrison in *My Fair Lady* as Povser cites the demanding way you learned penmanship from your elementary teacher.

For the rest of the book here is a try at explaining some more. He saves a full-sentence description for a noun by wedging it into a prolonged adjective of words before the noun. The words are usually jammed together without spacing or dashes. For instance, in a chapter on the decline in penmanship instruction in schools, he laments its effect on children who live in this "zoomboomdoomtomb world." You know they will suffer for their whole frantic, volatile lives. In describing how my mind allegedly creates an energetic, imaginative classroom for my students, he sees me as having a "pennsylvanialotterypingpongballsonair mind." I never knew.

He will do as he pleases with words of his choosing. Oh, what choices. How writers wrote before is his command to try something different. If he can't find the right word, he devises his own. New words are called "neologisms" Hardly new as a concept, each are rare cultural artifacts. Povser renders them common. He claims he only creates them because nothing else would fit and his thesaurus failed him. Employing new words is risky. You must hope the reader understands your meaning. Povser is confident you can decipher them from the context. Try your mental de-coding ring on this one to see. In discussing the emotional state of someone who just got jilted by their girlfriend or their employer, he couldn't call up a word that expresses their anger, anxiety and rejection together. Not that he had to do it in one swoop. He tries "bortsnoggled."

That is word-fashioning. He also wants to re-format word locations for the thought conveyed. In the section on law, under the right of privacy he says it is "the right to be left alone." Guess where the word "alone" appears?

Povser has developed a crush on words. Yes, he adores them but it's beyond mere affection. He's possessive and controlling. He pounds and molds them into varieties, some old, some new, some bold, some irrepressibly blue, some endless, and some who-knew? In Chapter 1 he says the word Graphoanalysis "can be a real mouthful." Except he spells that last word "moufruw," the way it would sound with your mouth full. When he has me flitting from one little story to another, he says, "Grim wants to anec another dote." This is his try at clever word economy. Should he be arrested for verbal abuse? Not for making the public chuckle while trying out a new form of Scrabble.

He likes to mix and match words. Nouns become verbs and other parts of speech cross-gender too. He says that handwriting analysis is a subject "woodpeckered from scorn." He has "alexanderpopeian concern" that people with little knowledge of the subject try to apply it. His puns are his fun. Though a traditional comic device, they might be misplaced in a stately volume about a subject vying for acceptance. Povser says he doesn't care. He needs to rhumba and bunnyhop where his dancing shoes lead him. In the chapter where he discusses my attack on the deceased forensic authority Albert Osborn for frowning on handwriting analysis, Povser asks, "Why does Grim want to beat a dead force?" In the chapter on how the analysis of handwriting is done, Povser illustrates the wild strokes on capital letters the vain deploy. He begins with a question: "What do these abominable showmen strokes show about their creator?"

Povser takes a monumental chance to inform you about this subject and trying to entertain you along the way. When you just want to digest the information, his jazzy word riffs may turn you off. If you say cut the verbal comedy, please, I will understand. Since he hopes the book will enhance his subject's repute, he is also risking more disrespect for handwriting analysis. This was one of my pleas to him for restraining his language. If you're asking the public for more slack, its response to prancing prose may be, "No. If you want credibility, reform your words, take your message seriously, and present the subject with dignity."

I was upset and he knew it but I couldn't coax him back to what he called his "old, dreary" writing manner. Nothing I tried worked. He said he must be he. "Gravity is for Issac Newton, not me," he quipped. I shuttered but, after regaining my composure, I smiled. He pocks the book with stabs at wit as well. He begins the chapter about altering handwriting (like disguising it so it can't be analyzed) with a hommage to deception: "Things are not always what they seem. Toupées, tissue-stuffed bras, and Rock Hudson. And now, say it ain't so, Pluto." In the history of handwriting analysis chapter he applauds the Phoenicians for instituting the alphabet: "You recall those Phoenician letters from your dictionary. Always the first one on the page for each letter, they look drunk and disoriented. To their glorious breakthrough we owe a big, wet muwah today. We have honored them by creating a new soup, spelling bees, and a dim TV game show."

Refusing to give in to me, Povser has spoken. And now he has written. Often he writes as if tomorrow his fingers will fall off or his brain will curdle and he's done as a writer. He can't help his figures of speech and especially his analogies. His metaphors must not just punch in and out; they must let us know they are doing their job by parading their prowess. In discussing how children leave their penmanship instruction and go to their unique writing styles, he says: "When we left second grade and ultimately flopped into the chaise longue of our own methods, we had to erect them from somewhere." In a passage describing how youths can learn about themselves in their own writing, he declares: "Unknown potential can appear and the young person can learn to rappell up the craggy wall of success." Where he introduces the idea of rhythm in handwriting strokes he declares: "Rhythm is the feng shui of writing strokes."

Now you have some examples of Povser's writing gestures. Maybe too many already but plenty are left. You can find them in your spelunking through the book. They lurk around every page like hanging bats, asleep but primed to awaken, shriek and dart everywhere, invading your complacency, After a while you are alert and eager for them, or you dread their arrival.

These last few years have tried me and my principles. I knew I couldn't write this book as Povser did. But have I made the right decision to let him caper and frolic? I think so. Is the subject stimulating without need for a surge from colorful writing? I think so too. Still, I think Povser's frisky word-plays boost the book to a more enjoyable blend of information and presentation. I believe you can grin and sometimes guffaw even as you digest the vital facts and sober wisdom he imparts on this captivating subject. For that I praise him and thank him.

In handwriting there are no slips of the pen

Sigmund Freud

Elementary school classroom in Kutztown, Pennsylvania, around 1940

As we toiled through the grades the letters stared at us from above the blackboard as a constant reminder of our solemn duty to draw the strokes according to Palmer.

Chapter 1

Starting from Scratch

Why Can't We Write like We Learned in School?

In the whole living human race there are not two individuals who have the same handwriting, just as there are not two identical oak leaves in existence.

**Noted Czech graphologist
and researcher Robert Saudek**

Birds don't do it and bees don't either. Chimps come nearest with their rowdy fingerpainting. Looking for food, chickens lay down their "scratch," which we borrow to describe awful human writing. Honestagod, somewhere they give elephants giant pens for their trunks to coil around and bohhhmmp and wohhhmmp at what must be vast writing pads. No one knows if they're doing artwork or their memoirs. With memoirs their legendary recall should yield rich detail. You will find little to enjoy, however. Their lives are boring as a 3 of Clubs.

When we slap the silliness out of this, we realize we are God's only creatures with lofty reasons to mark a surface. The prime one is to record our thoughts by what we call handwriting. Before entering school some of us tried it on our sidewalk, driveway, or even our ohGODnoyouDIDN'T wallpaper. Your mom then guided you into etch-a-sketching, maybe followed by TV-off writing drills. You whined your way through them but when school started you hopped in feeling like a hare among mere tortoises.

In school we learned how to do it prahperlay. Unlike a chimp, we weren't supposed to jab, whip, and flail anyway we want. Penmanship taught us the correct way to compose words on paper. It was Palmer Method for most of us and Zaner-Bloser for the rest. In the 1960's the progressive D'Nealian arrived for a few. Miss Pringle handed out pencils or crayons and told you to hold them *this* way. She ordered us to print letters and numbers on lined tablets of woody paper. Twenty-six letters, capitals, smalls, and the ten numbers enclosed our initial instruction. After the UPandDOWNandOVERandAROUND tedium of printed letters, we stepped up to script. We gleamed skipping rope, certain we had reached adult country. As we toiled through the grades, the letters stared at us above the blackboard, reminding us of our solemn duty.

You are now an adult and you still write with your hand, although less and less, you say. If you glance at the writing of other people, you find a radical change between then and now. Writing has lost its way. You and your friends don't seem to understand. This manner of handwriting was built to last until they pull the pen from your shaky hand after your death-bed will signing. The purpose was not only the discipline of dreary drills. It was also for the writer's duty—let the reader know his thoughts without having to squint. Palmer's writing method was an efficient way to write and easy on your hand and wrist. Fast forward to the present. After learning the model method, where are most of us? Not even close. After we left second grade and no one followed us out the door, we proclaimed our own styles. Today we caper in giddy freedom from Miss Pringle's commands.

Okay, some of your later teachers seemed to care. They insisted you resolve your rogue writing, or print. You smothered a groan and wondered why. Did you understand they actually wanted to read your theme and your test answers? Very few of us write close to what we learned in grade school. Since those who do are hard to find, we admire them. Trying to recall the copybook letters starts up that Robert Klein weeeuuuu music, and dry ice vapors drift by to obscure our memory. Yes, we all have an *idea* how they looked. Ask anyone what was schoolbook writing style and they can pick it out of a lineup. Getting us to prolong that model was tough. After Second Grade we should have kept it as a friend, not heaved it to the trash.

Consider what you've done. By erecting a barrier between yourself and your reader, they wince, as they can't unscramble your writing. You may know what you wrote but the rest of us don't. The troubling irony is that we are all writers and we are all readers. Thus, no respect from either side. Yes, some of us will protest this claim. You swear your style is fine and readable. Go to the head of the shameful class. For the rest of us our writing is legible but much is jumble and clutter. We are a flock of sheep who have gone astray. The absorbing question is why none of us baaaas to return to the fold. We know what we scrawl is often illegible. On occasion even a person with passable writing will have a signature that reads Mfflgzorch Bitlebrg. Dismayed by our writing's look, what are we doing about it? Just as Claude Rains in *Casablanca* when someone said gambling was going on at Rick's Café, we seem shocked, then carry on. This is the appalling depth we have reached. Few of us write as we learned in grade school, our writing stinks, and somehow we can't or won't change it.

Some people think they know why and they aren't alarmed. These people are called graphologists or handwriting analysts. This distinctive group believes we each write uniquely for a weighty reason: we have separate personalities. When we take our pen to paper our brain is directing our hand to draw only strokes reflecting our personality traits. Behold that word "strokes." When your pen touches the paper you begin with a dot. Usually quick and barely perceptible, the dot disappears into a line that sweeps up and down and around drawing strokes that have rollercoastered since grade school. The analyst surveys the writing and arrives at a sequence of traits from the strokes' form. To do a comprehensive analysis he looks at more than the strokes. Other aspects of the writing reveal personality too. The size, slant, rhythm, thickness, and the baseline and the zones the letters create reflect inner qualities. Even the spacing between the words and lines, and the spacing and placement of the margins are considered. All of these convey data to the analyst about the writer's nature . If a stroke or a space exists, an analyst can mine nuggets of your being from it. No part of the page escapes the analyst's judgment. Everything you do with your pen on paper sends a message about you.

Most of our strokes are so embedded in our style of writing that we barely reflect how we sculpt them. We grab the pen and focus on content, not technique. As our reliable strokes escort us wherever we go, we release them to the world and they foxtrot as we taught them with an occasional puzzling misstep. Since our personality traits are fairly consistent, our fingers obey by creating regular symbols. True, we are hopelessly human and fallible and sometimes nervous and sometimes angry and we don't always repeat the strokes. Yet analysts know we construct them steadily and often enough to be discerned as our basic qualities of character. When your spouse ambles across your driveway to the car, each step varies in some way. Yet each step forms a pattern telling you who it is. Same with handwriting. True, our human strokes differ word from word but are similar enough to insert into cubbyholes as personal traits.

Perhaps you always thought your lines on paper were just your way of doing it, maybe subtle defiance of your schooling, but nothing more. Some of it you thought about; some you just slalomed your own snowy gates. You twisted your signature to cryuncle at its matchless allure, or you molded your other strokes into some irreverent flair. When you took time to ponder that ink on paper, nothing much rose to mind. Maybe you considered Was it readable? Many of us scribble on paper with little strain at legibility, especially our signatures. We taunt the hapless reader with, "If you can't read my writing, that's *your* problem."

If you ask a handwriting analyst, it is *our* problem. The most offensive act with pen on paper is to write illegibly. In the main we write so others can read it. Many of us forget that. Worse, most illegible writers don't reform their writing to be legible. Is that rude and arrogant? Is North Dakota above South Dakota? For those who confess their writing is unreadable, and they should change it—How many actually do? Outrageously few.

———

Describing what's at work between our brain, our hands, and a pen isn't easy. We all know about a force called personality. What we don't realize is how magnetic it is. Remember that catch phrase from a few years ago, "The Devil made me do it?" It was slang for skirting blame where you acted out of character. You meant you just couldn't help it. When you press most of the chicken-scratchers they're stumped over their motive. Clueless and shoeless, do they need chicken soup for their solace? Why would they do this? Here is where wise analysts rush in to save these fools from treading around with their guilt, indifference or ignorance. Oh, sure, anyone who writes one way can change it as long as they concentrate. But it isn't easy, as you learned a few paragraphs ago. Start with the analysts' gospel that we each have unique mode of writing because we each have different personalities. When you spiraled into scrawl, you didn't do it on purpose. Who would do that on purpose? Yes, some know they draw rash lines. They deserve our disdain. When you know we can't read your writing, and you refuse to correct it, hold out your wrist for this ruler. For the others we should just take pity. They know they are doing it but they know not why they do it, say analysts. Still another group claims they write their way for some overt, sensible reason. Analysts believe these people deceive themselves. Though they may think otherwise, their motivation lies beneath the surface. For all these people, no matter how poorly they write or how steadfast is their adopted style, the source is inside their skull. They just don't realize it and the rest of us don't seem to either.

Try changing your writing on purpose. You cannot do it without a struggle. It takes work and constant attention. You have to crease your face and draw each stroke precisely. While you try, your personality does more than squawk. It resists. It's unseen power hand-wrestles you into its schemes. Your hand is harassed until you revert to your assigned style. Knowing this should snuff the scrawler's guilt. Their wandering has found a reason. They are not alone; we all drift and loiter in some way. Handwriting analysis supplies this giant truth: It's just our character exposed in the strokes on the paper. Take it in stride and don't change anything, except alter your Jackson Pollock writing features into a Keith Haring. Yes, it will be slamming against the fortress of your personality. But readability comes first and personality will have to yield to it. You will feel the pressure of your personality and live with it. Constantly it will remind you that handwriting is not just random but the result of its unseen might demanding tribute on the paper.

As a human act handwriting beckons several players to demonstrate their teamwork. The lead-off hitter is our brain, specifically the left side in the cerebral cortex. Here is the logical and verbal part of our thinking. As personal technology it's the word processing software for our computer mind. From that brain's left side we think in words and examine parts of the whole. Our right side handles our feelings, sensory images, the total picture, and the intuitive. From that command center our reflexes, our coordination, our memory, and our eyesight collaborate to spread the signals to our muscles and nerves in our wrist and fingers. They assume the duty of sweeping the pen through its paces. This may all be a long-delayed review of your health class in high school. Here is where you are jack-in-the-boxed with an unfamiliar notion. Those handwriting strokes stream from our personality assigning impulses to our cerebral cortex, which sends them to those nerves and muscles directing the hand holding the pen. Seemingly casual strokes are the basis for the familiar symbols in our letters. But they are hardly casual. Since the personality you have is different from everyone else's, your symbols appear as only your personality insists.

Draw any strokes on your tablet and you convey information in two ways: the content of the words and the style of the letters themselves. If you can read and comprehend the words, the content is public and recognizable. The style is something else. Although it's observable, its meaning is hidden in plain sight from you but an analyst can uncover it. Your own writing exposes the inner you silently squealing itself to the gleeful analyst grateful he can learn these intimacies. He is a member of an exclusive club with special access into anyone brave enough to write when he is around. When he spies a new piece of writing, an honorable analyst will stifle the impulse to rub his hands together. He takes his duty seriously, humbled by a revealing report that instantly unlocks secrets of a person recording his thoughts on the page. An analyst can't just avert his eyes. When a writing appears, the stroke meanings leap off the page into his curious mind instantly recording the writer's character. Can you blame him? A married man and his wife walk down the street passing a gorgeous woman. When his wife heaves an eyeful of daggers at him for looking, can he delete that visual delight from his memory?

———

Handwriting, penmanship, handwriting analysis, graphology, Graphoanalysis, forensic documents and calligraphy. To grasp handwriting's kinship to personality, you must gaze at these members of the family tree. Extending from its trunk, these words may be new to you or confusing to you. To enlighten you on their meanings and clarify their links to each other, I call on Allan K. Grim, Jr., a former lawyer, a professional Graphoanalyst, and a long-time colleague in handwriting analysis. We meet at a local restaurant, where he orders a regular Coke in a French drain of ice. I have decaf coffee, muddy, and pucker-up sugar.

"Can we start in the beginning," I ask.

"What's the beginning for you?" Grim replies.

"Okay, what is graphology?"

"It's the study of all writing. That's the basic dictionary concept."

"You mean it's not just about analyzing handwriting?"

"No. Handwriting analysis is actually a part of it. Handwriting analysts also study writing but they look for personality traits."

"Then what's the relationship between handwriting analysis and graphology?"

"Think of a business corporation. Graphology would be the corporate parent itself and handwriting analysis would be one of its divisions."

"That puts graphology on top of handwriting analysis, like it's something larger and covering more. I've heard they're considered almost the same thing."

"I can understand why. Over many years and a kind of evolution, graphology has become synonymous with handwriting analysis. People within the field use the terms interchangeably.

"So handwriting analyst is just another name for graphologist?"

"Yes. It's as if there was a father and a son and after many years the son became a brother. The father was graphology and the son was handwriting analysis. Going back to that corporate analogy, think of the subsidiary eventually merging into the parent corporation so it no longer exists as a separate entity."

"What brought this change over the years?"

"I'm not sure actually. It probably occurred because no one could devise a better name for handwriting analysis. If you try to say the words fast, you can't. Graphology is only four syllables whereas you-know-what is seven. When a word especially an important one is more than three syllables, people are irked and want to shorten it. It's part of our high-speed modern culture. Analysts will use either but graphology can be said faster. Unfortunately it too has more than three syllables.

"But you're a Graphoanalyst? How does that fit in with those two long terms?"

"I'm a handwriting analyst from a specific school called Graphoanalysis, which was founded by a Milton Bunker in 1929."

"Okay, a Graphoanalyst is also a graphologist and also a handwriting analyst but a special kind of those two.

"Yeah."

"I've heard you call people outside your school graphologists. For instance, you will say he is not a Graphoanalyst. He is speaking graphology, which is unproven."

"That's true. We tend to call a person a graphologist if they are analyzing handwriting and don't follow Graphoanalysis doctrines. It's sort of like this. We believe in our doctrines because Bunker was supposed to have tested them with real people and their handwriting over about two decades. Many non-Graphoanalysts hold beliefs both untested and varied. We think of ourselves as Catholics, and graphologists as heretics. We are the true religion. Graphoanalysts believe they cleave to only legitimate doctrines that their founder Bunker or others have established through countless surveys of handwriting."

"Well, aren't there some graphologists who think they hold established beliefs too?"

"Yes, there are some and with good credentials."

"Do you view them as heretics?"

"No, we see them as maybe at least good fellow Christians. They don't desire to be Graphoanalysts. It's somewhat like a Lutheran saying he doesn't want to be a Catholic. They differ with Graphoanalysts on fundamental points."

"Can't you all just get along."

"Not for now. The too-too twains are not about to meet; no golden spike is to be struck.

"Haven't you even tried to unite?"

"Ecumenical efforts have been launched from sincere analysts of both stripes. Yet the schism remains, just as with Protestants and Catholics. Getting along with people of good will in different camps is one thing. When the doctrines are incompatible, combining members into one large group is another."

"What would bring them together?"

"Probably comprehensive research of handwriting and what each aspect of it means. If those results were respected by all graphologists and the psychology community, we could meet under one, big, happy tent.

"I know handwriting also involves other areas aside of evaluating for personality. Penmanship, for instance."

"Yeah, penmanship instructs schoolchildren to draw strokes according to idealized models, like the Palmer Method. The students' styles, we believe, eventually evolve into their special way of writing that diverges from what they were taught. That's where we graphologists come in. When children morph into their unique forms we think they are making a statement about their actual character. Having to follow the school model prevented them from doing that. Now they are free to be themselves."

"What about calligraphy?"

"That is an artistic technique growing in the later years of the last century. It is beautiful stylized writing."

"What more is there?"

"Graphology as a generic term for all writing has under its umbrella an area known as Questioned Documents, Forensic Documents, Disputed Documents, or Suspect Documents.

"You mean four different ways of approaching a writing?"

"No. These are four names for the same discipline."

"What do you call people who do it?"

"Questioned Document Examiners or any of the other adjectives with Examiner following it.

We call their discipline QD for short and their practitioners QD's.

"They do court work, don't they?"

"Yeah. These experts determine whether a certain person actually signed their name to a document, like a will or a check, or wrote an anonymous letter. In court cases they testify as experts on the authenticity of a signature or other writing specimen.

"I've read about people who examine anonymous letters like bomb threats. Who does that?"

"These people do that too if it's handwritten. It involves the identity of handwriting, such as a 'poison pen' letter or a ransom note."

"What's that 'poison pen' letter?"

"Someone will handwrite a nasty letter threatening or criticizing the recipient or someone they know. Examiners handle any matter where handwriting is an issue, except to glean any personality traits. That is left to graphologists, also known as handwriting analysts, who are often avoided by the Examiners because Examiners consider themselves bonafide scientific experts. They want to stay pure because they testify in court and the law is very sensitive about having scientific foundations for its experts in court. Examiners deem graphologists as unscientific and will stay clear to evade any guilt-by-association."

"QD's analyze handwriting and so do graphologists. But the difference is that QD's aren't looking for personality traits, just whether the writing was done by someone in particular?"

"Right."

"And graphologists also analyze writing but to find only personality traits, not if a certain person wrote it or not."

"You got it."

QD Examiners support their often technical work with mechanical and technological aids. In the old days their sole device was a magnifying glass. With amazing precision their devices can determine the age of ink, paper, the kind of ink, and impressions made on paper. One machine can detect at the bottom of a pile of twenty papers an impression made at the top. Another blows carbon particles across a sheet with writing on it and impressions from another sheet above it. Soon the black particles line up to the strokes indented in the paper. They are now very readable. Take a writing where a portion is now unreadable from many cross-out lines. A device will erase the cross-outs and expose the words underneath, now readable. They use other equipment and materials which allow them to go beyond the writing to gauge a document's authenticity. In the 1990's a type-written document surfaced that showed a secret trust set up by John Kennedy for Marilyn Monroe's mother. When analyzed, the type font was found to be invented only after the date on the document. Kennedy's legacy was preserved from further erosion.

Those new to handwriting analysis stumble often saying the word Graphoanalysis. It can be a real mroufuw. After hearing it once, they may utter it with colliding syllables. Saying it right often takes a few tries with sympathetic help from an analyst. Graphoanalyst Allan Grim has been introduced at a talk with a syllable added to it. Some people will pause trying to say it. Grim says the way to remember it is to think of that Freud topic, psycho-analysis and stick a dash in the middle of it like so. It has the same number of syllables and the last four are the same as in Graphoanalysis. You merely have to pause slightly after the initial two syllables "Grapho," then just say that familiar word "analysis" and you're done. As a term handwriting analysis is pleasant to the ear. But its length annoys you, and trying to say it quickly is floomping through mud. Some graphoanalysts call themselves graphologists because it is slightly shorter and slightly easier to say fast. That only tends to blur the line between graphology and Graphoanalysis. These two approach handwriting differently, although many of their beliefs are shared. (See further elaborations in later chapters) To the public they seem the same when their names are used interchangeably. This causes confusion that remains unresolved.

Handwriting analysis suggests it deserves scientific respect. Up until now it hasn't earned it. If analysts want to come a-knockin' at the door of approval from the authorities, they must be presentably spiffy. There are standards to meet. Grim believes that handwriting analysis should be let into psychology and given a locker with its name on it. His sainted subject has a blunted nose from psychology's chronic door-slamming.

"If it was allowed in, where would you place it within psychology?" I ask.

"I would call it a hybrid," he answers. "It's astride a personality assessment test and a technique, such as a projective technique."

"How could it be a projective technique? Don't they need a stimulus, such as a vague image, to draw out the actual person as he expands on what the picture is about?"

"No, I think there are projective techniques that come from within. It's called "emitted" or something. Those blotchy images in the Rohrschach come from outside. This comes from inside their mind."

"Well, how can it be a personality test too?"

"It's also a personality assessment test simply because its intent is to reveal personality traits."

"To be a test, shouldn't there be questions asked?"

"Most of the traditional ones ask questions of the test taker. We are familiar with those from school and elsewhere. The questions relate to areas of personality, such as, "I have thoughts that I would like to hurt myself," or "I enjoy mingling with people," or "I cry easily." Questions like that. The test taker agrees or disagrees with the statement."

"It just seems hard to imagine it's one of those categories."

"It has to be by default as far as I know. Either it's a projective technique or personality assessment test or technique. I see it as part of both."

Whatever it is, Grim's subject demolishes the competition, he maintains. Hear him out. Handwriting analysis measures the whole person while the others can determine only parts. It is simpler, quicker, and cheaper to administer. All you need is a writer with a piece of blank paper and a pen and a table to write on and a chair to relax in. It doesn't invade your privacy, it shows the real person, not the public image, and it's harder to cheat.   A few people are always reluctant, stubborn, or shy about taking a personality test or technique. Getting them to hand over a sample of their writing should be simple and easy. Handwriting analysis is distinctive for this segment of society, as it pries open the stuck doors to themselves. They don't imagine they're fessing up about their private misery. They are just owning up to one of their common public acts, their handwriting. Unaware it spreads tales about themselves, they are startled when they see the analysis. Our handwriting is the best kept secret about our best kept secrets.

"I want to make it more public for everyone and have it be a common experience by immersing the subject into our culture," Grim announces. "It will enable us to know our true selves and then act on that knowledge for our own good.   After that we can use it to evaluate others or help others to know themselves as well."

Most of us have written our whole lives while others eavesdropped. Or we wrote and they saw our handwriting soon after. We didn't mind if anyone saw it before or after we wrote it. The writer of any document might protest if he has to give up one he intended only himself or someone specific to see. A diary or notes for a personal matter. That's fine. We won't look at that one. Where it's warranted, a right to privacy of our writing deserves respect and freedom from intrusion. (More of this later in a chapter on the law and graphology) Ask him to do another sample that is neutral. Having to provide a sample of writing intimidates very few of us. Even better for the nervous is that you can mail it in or deliver it.   No need to appear in front of an analyst as heartless judge. Know that analysts want originals if possible. A fax or other technology of the moment will do as long as it can fairly reproduce your writing. Many will analyze with only a copy but will grumble about it. Copies can be blurry and especially distort the pressure of the pen on the paper. If your sample was written in haste, not your usual calm style, no problem most of the time. If you are available and willing, just write another one.

When matched against traditional psychology tests handwriting analysis doesn't just compete as an equal. It outdoes them. The other traditional tests can take a long time, especially the battery of tests that have separate purposes. They can last hours if not into the next day. Then the responses must be tabulated and interpreted, and the findings reported. An accomplished handwriting analyst can take the person's writing, say a page or two, and within ten minutes start writing up a comprehensive outline of their personality.

———

A common phrase in recent decades is body language. We've seen it applied in many of the acts we do everyday that convey information about us. We might put our finger on our nose as we try to fib to a friend. We fail to realize our hand placement was telling our friend we shouldn't be believed. An old man teeters down the sidewalk while a gang of ruffians observes he is any easy mark for a mugging. They may not know it but they are applying what they know of body language. Handwriting is also expressive behavior, a form of body language, a gesture by the hand. The familiar ones, walking, shaking hands, sitting positions, and others are readily observable but disappear in an instant. Not so with handwriting, which survives long as you keep the paper it's written on. This is a boon to psychologists and others who want to retain the item to evaluate later.

Body language is not new, even as a concept within handwriting analysis. In the 1930's and thereafter Gordon Allport, the distinguished Harvard professor of psychology, studied handwriting as expressive behavior. Noting how handwriting was superior, he wrote, "Most self-expression is too fleeting and difficult to record for study. Since writing can be preserved on paper, it provides a permanent record of the individual's total personality with all its parts working together in dynamic action." Since the writing need not be studied while it's occurring, an analyst can work on it when he's ready. Writing from different times in the person's life can and should be used. No matter when prepared, it reveals change and trauma in your life. Your writing provides a graphic video of your fluid personality in freeze-frame. What you wrote a year ago captured your personal disposition at that time in your life. That was you then in your slog across the muddy soccer field of life. Consider the knowledge you could gain from a character snapshot of you or someone else at any time of their lives. That is just what handwriting gives you.

Although other psychology tests and techniques possess some of these features, none can claim all. Only a few can claim more than a couple. Handwriting's power is invisible and subtle in revealing the full dimensions of human beings. For its ability to cage all the best features of a psychology test or technique, Grim roars that it is king of its social science jungle among tests and techniques in psychology.

Some psychology tests solicit intimate information about the test taker. Many people can guess the inquiry's purpose. They can distort the answer as they see fit. Sure, someone can learn the rudiments of handwriting analysis and twist their obliging strokes into a favorable review of their character. If you stoop to that, shame on you. Do you want the truth about yourself or not?

Since many people among us are untrustworthy or clueless, they cheat on a personality test but do it badly. Others are too slow under their hat to get it. More naïve and earnest than anything, their answers come ashore inaccurate. If the question is whether they enjoy parties, their response may be about having fun or drinking rather than their socializing, which was the question's focus. With handwriting you don't need to know anything about yourself. You just need to be able to write naturally and freely. What the naked strokes disclose about you is all the analyst needs. With personality tests the individual taking the test can react to any question as his self-respect can bear. He may think he doesn't want anyone knowing he hates parties because of a disabling shyness. So how reliable can his answer be to that question, "Do you enjoy going to parties?"?

All these perks give handwriting analysis an edge in objectivity. Some analysts deem it the most objective of all personality tests or techniques. Another salient attribute enables it to sneak through our lives almost unnoticed. Very few know what it reveals. It's complicated and mystifying, two benefits that minimize cheating. Unless you know handwriting analysis, you don't know what you're handing the analyst when you write your sample. Aside from analysts, few really know how it works and what those strokes mean. This also aids its objectivity. You might say an individual could learn stroke meanings and seek to fool the analyst. Does this doom the analysis? Or does an antidote exist? As in football, says Grim, a defense can be mounted for every offense. Handwriting analysis has its ways of countering deception. When analysts ask for the sample, they make sure it is done in front of them and at a fast pace. Not rushed but rapid enough to lessen the schemer's ability to con their way through all the strokes. So many strokes exist that a ploy will lack time to be clever enough. The analyst has another advantage. Those manipulated strokes, which are parts of letters, are only a portion of what the analyst scans. Margins, spacing between words and lines, slant, size, thickness, direction of lines, rhythm, and other aspects are also important. Even with some knowledge of these, the shrewd writer shouldn't succeed. Forcing the writer into a speedy sample with many markers to confront should defeat anyone with a working knowledge of handwriting analysis.

Imagine yourself in 1690's New England. Could you be a handwriting analyst and analyze the writing of those forlorn ladies hanged as witches? Yes, says handwriting analysis. Imagine you are a member of Ghengis Khan's twelfth century Golden Horde, those Mongolian monsters who terrorized people from China in the East to Eastern Europe in the West. You don't spend all your time plundering. You want to be a handwriting analyst too. Could you ply your trade so many centuries ago in far off lands? Yes, says handwriting analysis. The information that writing gives us is timeless and universal. You can analyze the writing of historical figures often shrouded by their public image. See if Edison's persistence appears in his writing. Evaluate any patterns of evil in the writing of Hitler and Stalin. Do the writings of the assassins Booth, Oswald, Ray, and Hinckley have common strokes? Does Lincoln's writing show his greatness, his sense of humor and his depression? What about the inpenetrable Greta Garbo and the wonder about the real Johnny Carson?

Wherever you are in the world you can apply graphology to the native writing and language. No matter what word or sentence they're in, common strokes signify the same about the personality across cultures. In Costa Rica, Siberia or India, living today or yesterday, the native strokes disclose the same trait meanings. Certainly exceptions and variations exist. Regional, cultural and ethnic styles will mold the writing of their residents. A notable example is Germany's sharp and rigid script. You see many German scripts and immediately you can tell where the writer comes from. To properly assess foreign writing, an analyst must account for their demands of style, their mores and their traditions. Their powerful influence cannot be ignored. Some languages are written from right to left, in picture images, and in other ways. You would think this skews or rebuffs any try at assessing the writing, especially its slant. Nuh uh. Research has shown that in languages where writing goes from right to left, the rules on the meaning of the slant of the writing don't change. Whether its right-to-left lines of Arabic or Japanese, the meanings are the same as for American left-to-right style. The Chinese characters standing for whole words or concepts make no difference. If you are someone who believes that human nature is the same throughout the world and for all time, handwriting may provide you burly support.

Writing from different times and places can muddle an analysis. Two important factors merge to do it—how important and how useful the writing was in the culture. If you take a broad view of American history you can see the impact on writing. Until we began thumbing our sniffly noses at authority in mid-twentieth century, we followed our school instruction. Teachers stood strict and steady, particularly where they had to educate a jungle gym full of youngsters at one time in a single drafty room under a leaky red roof. We respected this rigid pomp of writing as it gave us the comfort of consistency in our waterpump, coal stove, and hickory-stick lives. We also depended on it because it was central in our communications. Before technology almost dodoed it with typewriters, telephones, and telegraphs, pen on paper was our primary means of recorded expression. As the twentieth century took its Mister Toad's Wild Ride our writing drifted onto the dusty, stony shoulder by scrapping the school models. In the foamy Sixties it revved up, and laid some Firestone rubber with many of us defying authorities and tradition. With its increasingly personal look and balky but improving ballpoint pens in hand, our writing lost its reliable structure. Anxiety from the stresses of modern society jarred many of us into choppy, roaming writing. Schools vaselined the slide to insolence by reducing or shedding penmanship drills. Many of us now write poorly and we wonder what it means. Secretly we suspect it reflects our inner turmoil, betraying the emotional pounding we are taking as we try to survive in a hostile world. Analysts would say our suspicions are correct. For those trying to keep their strokes rushing like the mighty Colorado, he sees instability. Our white-water-raft ride down the rapids of today may be the primary reason our writing has declined so much since grade school. It may further account for the epidemic of printing as the leading style of choice for young people. Some experts surmise that printing is a regression to legible writing to counter the chaos of their script styles. (More on this later in the chapter on printing.)

So many cultures in the world and so many different languages, customs and values. It's hard believing we write in patterns that mean the same for each personality. Nevertheless analysts are convinced of it, one of the improbable notions that jack up skeptics' eyebrows even higher on their rutted foreheads. Analysts also never tire of declaring that everyone's writing is unique and our personalities are complex. Is it possible two people in this wide world have the same handwriting styles? Analysts would clamor to have them meet, compare notes, not just handwritten ones, but personality ones. Identical writing means they should have identical personality traits, assert analysts. However, it's not likely these two people exist. The answer to the question generates googly odds that it's a certainty. In fact, it can be stated plainly. The esteemed Czech analyst, Robert Saudek, announced it in the early part of the twentieth century. He had moved to England and performed some respectable experiments on handwriting.

Spurning a calculator or a massive survey, he expressed it this way: "In the whole living human race there are not two individuals who have the same handwriting, just as there are not two identical oak leaves in existence."

Many writing styles are similar but when examined up close, complete identical patterns vanish. Grim emphasizes you have to distinguish between identical and similar. Yes, many are similar but the strokes don't xerox each other like the Rockettes. Blame it on our bossanova humanity. We aren't perfect; we have nerves and unsure dexterity. No analyst has seen any that matched up line by line. That doesn't mean there weren't any. It's a big world and we have a lot of history. Another angle is to take yourself as a guinea pig. You write your signature all the time. You can do it in your sleep or during sex. Of course you can. Write your signature, then, without peeking, write it again. Is it identical? Okay, try it again. You may peek and laser your eyes on it too. Even if you write one below the other and keep an eye on the first one, they won't be alike. Now for some serious googly numbers. A wise person calculated that the odds of two signatures of one person alone written freehand (not traced and not copied) looking exactly alike were one in 931 quintillion. How they knew that and who they were are lost in the smog of sloppy record-keeping.

Aristotle, the eminently rational Greek philosopher 2,300 years ago, wrote, "Handwriting is a symbol of speech and speech is a symbol of mental experience. Just as all men do not have the same speech sounds, so do all men not have the same writing." Our writing selves differ so vastly those numbers shouldn't seem so astronomical, especially when you realize what is counted in reaching those numbers. Margins around the writing, the spacing between lines and the words and the letters, the size of the writing, slant, thickness of the strokes, rhythm of the writing, relative size of the three areas of writing, that is, the upper area (the space from the top of the small letters upward), middle area (the space from the baseline, which is the imaginary line underneath the small letters to the top of the small letters), and the lower area (the space from the baseline downward). Even the isolated strokes within letters, such the cross bar and the stem of the letter t can be made several ways. The International Graphoanalysis Society has over a hundred strokes that relate to separate traits of personality. Thus, a seamstress lady from Colonial Delaware could have written the exact way you do in every respect, except that she drew her t bars short on the stem and you made them long. That would be picking nits but enough to say you and she did not have the same writing style. Almost identical but no cigar.

Analysts tell you they focus on strokes not letters. However, they know that a few letters contain particular traits not found elsewhere in other letters. The small letter e, by itself, discloses how willing the writer is to receive the views of other people. A narrow e means not very well ("close-minded"), the normal oval e means you are typically tolerant of other's thoughts, a wide e shows you are very accepting ("broad-minded"), and a very wide e show you are too accepting, which analysts convert to its more familiar name—gullibility. You might be thinking this could lead to an infinite number of traits because every degree the stroke changes could yield another trait. It's not that absurd. The difference must be significant. The analyst will judge when one stroke ends and the next begins. The dividing line between each trait isn't dark but analysts develop a knack to distinguish one from another. After centuries analysts have cultivated standards, reaching consensus on boundaries between separate traits. If you're viewing this as illusory, consider it this way. Say you're at a wedding reception watching some guy dancing. As a non-dancer you can tell instantly if he is a. Fred Astaire, b. pretty good, c. not bad, d. could be better, e. This guy should sit down, f. Please, I can't watch anymore, and g. complete klutz. That would give you seven variations a non-dancer can make in a casual look. Where one becomes the other is a matter of opinion. Same with analysts, but the differing results of their judgments will be small. They have over a hundred strokes to find and blend.

The letter t is more fertile than the letter e. It supplies a steamer trunk of strokes full of an antiquesroadshow of traits. You wonder why this is so since a t has only a stem, the line rising from the baseline, and a cross-bar, the line intersecting the stem. Customarily when we form a cursive t we begin with a lead-in stroke and finish the t with a lead-out or ending stroke. Also a cursive t usually has a stroke that retraces its stem as it descends to the baseline. This retraced stem can yield different traits. Whether it is split open slightly or drawn like a teepee or the lines are straight or curved or bulge into a loop, each conveys a separate trait. The stem's height provides at least four different traits. The cross-bar gives several, including it lengths, its placement before, on or after the stem, curved up like a bowl, or down like a sad mouth, or wavy or upward or downward, or pointy, and more. The array of strokes seems overwhelming. Not really. Only a few other letters have strokes and traits special to them. Somehow the t has gone forth and multiplied its effect on personality. In time budding analysts bloom and become familiar with all the variations. If they forget any they can reach for their frayed trait books and refresh their memory.

1. Dear Mom & Dad,
2.   Thanks to you I went and paid all my bills yesterday
3. got everyone's dress material (for the bridesmaids) and am
4. now sending you Mrs Jones invitation list. I feel
5. like I've done everything I'm supposed to and now
6. all I have to do is send my invitations and find
7. a job and apartment. What a relief I feel inside.

DIANNE'S WRITING BEFORE HER ACCIDENT

1. Dear Mom & Dad,
2.   Thanks to you I went and paid my bills yesterday,
3. got everyone's material (for the bridesmaids) and am
4. now sending you Mrs. Jones invitation list. I feel
5. like I've done everything I'm supposed to and now
6. all I have to do is send my invitations and find

DIANNE'S WRITING FOUR YEARS AFTER HER ACCIDENT

A compelling illustration of the link between the mind and personality traits is the story of Dianne Kalal. The top specimen of her handwriting was written a few weeks before she was to be married. The bottom one was written four years later after she was in an auto accident and wound up a quadriplegic. She wrote the bottom one with her bicep propelling the pen connected to a device strapped to her forearm. The two samples are remarkably similar. How we write is not random. Rather, our brain is causing our pen on paper to draw strokes reflecting our personality traits.

Chapter 2

Brainwriting

Identifying Alcoholics, Drug Addicts, Embezzlers, and Ax Murderers

If you wrote with a pen in your mouth or between your toes, your writing style would be similar to your hand's.

Povser

That busy t has scores of traits in it. Really? You strain in RoswellMexico1947 doubt to believe it. With that unresolved, you (and analysts too) are spurred to the logical next question. *Why* do strokes, only branches growing from the letter trees, reveal separate attributes of our personalities? That is a gorilla of a question, if not the kingkong question. A sensible mind struggles to accept any link between seemingly trivial strokes and specific but grand traits, like generosity and resentment. This breeds some of the qualms rational people have about this subject. It's also the reason many analysts reject the trait-stroke approach for the gestalt, which takes meaning from only the ever-present parts of handwriting, like slant and thickness. These gargantuan parts glut any writing and thus can be weighed for their effect on other aspects of the writing and the traits themselves. For example, the writing could be thin all the way through, or thick, or average width. The gestalt view seems safer and less outrageous, more plausible. Grim acknowledges the trait-stroke view is a challenge even to a tolerant person, as he professes to be. He says he originally tiptoed, then marched past the issue, finally convinced the stroke and

33

trait bond is valid. He swears it didn't take him that long in his training to cement it. Too bad his march to certainty occurred decades after tiptoeing through the strokes.

Some with websites if not clout within graphology spout their views. For years Bart Baggett has had a website that promotes his graphology business. He claims research scientists in "neuro-science" have listed "neuro-muscular movement" activity as "correlated with specific observable personality traits. Each personality trait is represented by a neurological brain pattern. Each neurological brain pattern produces a unique neuro-muscular movement that is the same for every person with that personality trait. When written these tiny movements occur unconsciously. Each written movement or stroke reveals a specific personality trait." Although these pea-soup statements sound compelling, he cites no scientific authority for them. Barnard Collier calls himself a Director of Graphology Consulting Group and Graphotechnology. He is on the website of Graphology Consulting Group associated with celebrated Manhattan analyst and author Sheila Kurtz. There he recalls his speech to the American Psychiatric Association convention a few years ago. It included his views on the basis for the trait-brain link. In this dignified, formal venue he portrayed it as similar to an EEG but by visual examination. The writer is his own brain wave machine and the analyst by his expertise reads the strokes through "biosignal interpretation." Sounds good but no particular authority this time either.

Without hesitation Grim still believes our pen strokes are determined from above—in our brains and are not just haphazard acts. That part unites his fellow analysts, whether gestalt or trait-stroke. Without it they can take their pens and go home. When he has seen thousands of writings and the strokes appear to match what he knows of the individual, that petrifies his faith. *Appearing* to match doesn't prove they *do* match. Grim understands that. For him the proof has been in grabbing a spoon and digging into the pudding. His countless experiences with people and their handwriting have confirmed or rejected his trait-stroke convictions. He is proud that his little lab-on-the-go for testing them has been people pursuing their lives rather than a sterile, artificial experiment. He's not evading science's gray formality. He thinks that gauging people in the real world molds a better crucible. If they're unaware they will be analyzed, the writing will be purer and less muppetted. Each analysis he does is a new experiment testing his subject's value. Of course now and then writings didn't match up. This is his continual reminder that he is sailing in social science, not physical science. You will graze a sandbar occasionally and run upon one rarely but the cruise is still worthwhile. The rest of the writings have verified his stroke and trait beliefs.

Although handwriting analysts are beyond questioning the trait and stroke doctrine, outside opponents continue to question it. They will offer some evidence and pose pesky questions. When some of us make certain strokes we are just being cute or creative or different. Occasionally we copy some style that struck us. How can analysts analyze these? Don't they scuttle their belief that every stroke is unconsciously reflecting our inner selves? Aren't these examples merely willful forays into new forms without deep consequence?

One day we assault an unwary Grim with them. He is sitting down, which we assume he would prefer under the circumstances. Without squirming in his seat or twitching his nose, Grim responds. "There's more to it than you think. We are not simply mimicking something we saw or that we create from the sky above. Even if we expressly recall it, ultimately we didn't adopt it consciously. We copy a style for reasons that come from our unconscious."

"What do you mean?"

"Look, we may *think* we are doing it based on our willful intent but it's really something underneath all that."

"Like what?"

"We adopt fresh strokes to satisfy an underlying need to project our personality. No accidental acts or deliberate, conscious ones," he is convinced.

He says he has some support from on high. "Freud said it even stronger: In handwriting there are no slips of the pen.'"

"What happens to these frolics our strokes seem to take?"

"They stick around. Many of our strokes are now so much a part of us that we no longer think about them. Warm strokes we adopt eventually dry out, cool and join the other strokes planted in our character. Until we make other changes later on."

"Don't we have some say in the matter?"

"We don't. Well, not much anyway. It's the thrust of your personality holding its clipboard and ordering your pen to march. You do what you're told and you like it."

"Can't we resist?"

"You can try but when you write, your mind keys onto the strokes' shape. The task will strain you because you have to concentrate so much. Your substantive thoughts will be ignored. That is not a good scenario. Writing should be automatic so you can think of what you're trying to say. Imagine writing a love letter and all you can think about is, Am I making the strokes the way I want them to look? And you can't and you get frustrated because your amorous message is lost."

"The personality is *that* powerful?"

"You bet. You can ultimately win and make your strokes just how you consciously want them to be. But it's at the expense of attention to your message."

The trait-stroke link stimulates Grim to probe deeper. He says now his interest is to know *why* certain strokes relate to certain traits. Grim's "tentative" opinion, he makes clear, satisfies him only partly. Our health teacher told us we have five senses. When we perceive handwriting we use only two, seeing and touching. Analysts believe that strokes come from patterns, forms, and symbols in our natural surroundings and our life experiences. We make the circles, loops, dots, and lines on paper a particular way because they look and feel good to us. We choose those strokes unconsciously since they have an inner appeal for us. That appeal comes from the personal quality related to it. Reminisce about that crush you had on that girl who sat two rows over in math. She lit a modest fire in you by how she looked and carried herself. Something in your brain told you she is the one for your inner impulses and your outer pursuit. You just had to make that homina-homina phone call and hope to hear, "Why, yes, I'd love to go out with you on Saturday evening." Call them feelings if you must. They could be both conscious and unconscious. If you went to a basketball game at another high school and saw a similar girl sitting in the stands, you might have had a similar instant crush. That would happen again because she had qualities akin to the girl in math class. The crush you felt would equate to the writing stroke. (Or perhaps your asking her out would be more apt. As a writing stroke is tangible, so would it be more tangible.) The inner tastes that produced the crush would equate to the personality trait. The two situations kindled in your brain leading to your action is not just a personal, superficial preference. It's something deeper that isn't easily definable or discoverable. Brain research has isolated some of these "feelings." Now science can explain forgetting our car keys, skipping meals, and bumping into chairs, all human fallout when we are in love. Apparently they are more organic than we realize. Their sources are regions of our brain emitting these impulses that flow to the rest of the body to act upon. Grim thinks the personality traits dispensing strokes have comparable sources that science will identify with more research.

More importantly, strokes seem to correspond logically to what they reveal about a person. Most times they *resemble* the trait they disclose. In fact it's more specific than you might think. Analysts can slice-and-dice the meaning into edible legumes. For instance, a capital letter made with large and ornate lines that are attractive and elegant reveals the "showman." He will act to command your attention and your respect. We are drawn to him by his appeal to our needs. We recognize this throughout nature as in the male bird with his colorful finery luring the female bird. However, if those excessive strokes are ugly or awkward (think of a squid trying to dunk a basketball while being hacked) instead of attractive and elegant, a separate trait results called "ostentatious." He is different from the "showman" since the "showman" draws notice by his good taste, which turns you on, whereas the "ostentatious" person may get your attention but he turns you off. His behavior is a model of bad taste. You will notice him but not respect or adore him. Thus the strokes reflecting showmanship and ostentatiousness are both large and showy. The similarity stops there and they are marked by the good taste versus bad taste look of the stroke furniture. Just as those large strokes are different, so is the conduct of the people displaying them.

"Which famous people would you put into each category," I inquire.

Grim pauses, his eyes looking up and left. He finally tenders three comedic actors, Jerry Lewis, Groucho Marx, and Steve Martin for the showman group. In the ostentatious group he suggests Jim Carrey and Robin Williams but mentions them with uncertainty in his voice.

"Maybe it's a matter of taste in the first place," he wonders. There should be consensus figures for each group. "Some people are just desperate for attention. You could cite Lewis, Williams, and Carrey. But are they so far gone that they turn you off?"

"I think you could argue either way," is my take on it, unrequested. "Carrey and Williams can get edgy yet they seem to fall into mainstream comedy acceptance."

For the record, Grim supports the trait-stroke link between showmanship and ostentatiousness. He also agrees with virtually all the others. A few shake and rattle his convictions without rolling them over. He still believes. Usually the dubious ones lack a symbolic connection to each other. Maybe some people who had the stroke didn't have the trait. Although he doesn't believe all stroke-traits equally, he accepts them because his analysis experience has confirmed them. Where he has a good idea of someone's personality before he has seen their writing, he has found that the strokes relate to the traits with few exceptions.

"Any surprises?"

"Yes, some real surprises have arisen. I would say for a handful of people I knew a long time, the writing didn't seem to match their qualities."

"What do you think accounts for that."

With a weak laugh he replies, "I probably really never knew the person," blaming his faulty insight rather than the doctrine for any disparity. "I know surprises should occur now and then. After all, handwriting analysis is social science and imperfect when applied because its practitioners are human analysts."

The link between strokes and their meanings seems to be rational and consistent. The illustrations tell us the connections aren't arbitrary, but relate to the stroke's contour. Analysts falter explaining the visual tie to the traits in the person's make-up. The writer with large strokes wants to make an impact on his surroundings and prefers not to be tied to a desk. A small writer can concentrate and tends toward modesty and fading into the woodwork. Analysts can't explain why the relationship exists, only that it makes sense and is confirmed constantly. Writing that leans forward reveals the person opening up emotionally and reaching out to others, as an extrovert. Logical and verifiable countless informal times. Since the strokes consistently have had similar meanings everywhere as well, it supports the theory that the graphic symbols we use are universal.

We press Grim on this. "Doesn't this assume our behavior is steady and universal too?"

"Yes, it does," he replies. "When you read the wisdom of Confucius and Aristotle from before Christ you gather that it is."

He thinks it hasn't changed much in those two thousand and so years either. "If you didn't know they [Aristotle and Confucius] were the ones uttering the gems, you would swear they are CNN talking heads."

Grim raises his hand and holds it for an additional point. Everyone seems to draw strokes alike for personality traits they have in common. That doesn't mean we each have similar personalities. Just that when a person displays, for example, a generous nature, his writing will show "generosity" strokes (for the record, wide connections between letters and an extended ending stroke that reaches out with a graceful forward swing.) They seem to illustrate the charitable nature of the writer, like an arm extending to another person as if to give them something. Analysts deem strokes going to the left as pointing toward themselves and the past, another pat logical connection between a stroke and its meaning. Grim often recoils defensively when he has said something like this. He expects the skeptic to roll his eyes and snap, "Yeah, right. When the stroke comes out like a giving hand it means they are generous. Come on. Give me a break." He accepts some suspicion over linking this graphic symbol to the character trait. The cynic views it as only unlikely and mystical, not grounded in reality.

Grim spreads his feet and crosses his arms, partly in jest but more in joust. He says he won't budge on this. "I've given this a lot of thought. What I try to do is watch out for the stroke, as well as others, and when I see the writing of someone I have always considered good-hearted and giving, I try to glance at their writing for confirmation or rejection of this stroke. Someone close to me is flush with these strokes. Although I'm biased, she is one of the most generous people I know."

This is not idle talk. He can show you the specific strokes in her writing that reflect it. When pressed to admit he is referring to his mother, his face is quiet as a tomb.

With that Atlanta Braves handchop he adds, "This generosity link has always confirmed itself to me anyway. On every occasion that I knew someone well and they were generally a good-hearted person, I found their handwriting matched that quality."

"How about the reverse?"

"That did okay too. Those I didn't know and I spied generosity strokes turned out to be generous when I got to know them."

Critics insist on sources and causes for claims analysts avow about their subject. Our hands draw lines here and there on the paper and where that comes from and how it occurs gets you only analysts to point to their brains and stop. Their mouths may then move but only to blab theory. Grim too? Yes.

"Okay, they have a point," Grim grants without sulking. "Yes, I wish I knew the answer to this mystery. "But," he adds, "just because we don't know *why* and *where* doesn't mean *what* isn't happening."

Elise Hancock can sympathize with Grim and his hapless horde of analysts. She has a Harvard Master's Degree and for many years edited the prize-winning *Johns Hopkins Magazine* about medical and related items. She retired in 1996. Obtaining another Master's, she launched a new career as a licensed acupuncturist in Baltimore. About her new profession she relies on to pay her bills she remarked, "I can't imagine how acupuncture works, but it does. I hope to live long enough to hear a good Western explanation, which may not take too long. Biomedicine is getting subtler every day."

It's always enlightening to know why something works for us. It's not critical we know why for handwriting analysis to help us accomplish important results. We could shelve it until we know, but that would squander its rewards. We plod along trying to find out why it works and don't quit just because we haven't found ultimate answers yet. It seems to work and work well. If it turned out to do serious damage to us in the meantime, we might pause. Until that occurs we revel in what it can do and use it.

In the meantime, analysts cite their field evidence about how and why our lines form on the paper. In a few weeks Dianne Kalal was to become a bride. She handwrote a letter to her parents. Four years later under different circumstances she was asked to write the same letter. She was given the words but not the prior letter to see. Why? A short time after the prior letter she was seriously injured in an auto accident. She became a quadriplegic and lost her ability to write with her hands. Somehow she was able to move her bicep. With a device holding a pen strapped to her forearm, she practiced to write again. A glacial struggle, but she persevered and learned to write again. After she wrote the second letter it was compared to the pre-accident writing. The styles were remarkably similar. You swear the later one looks as if it had been written with her hand, not through her bicep.

She and other disabled people have innocently supplied a forceful case for handwriting analysis. When they write with pen in mouth or between toes, their strokes match their hands. Don't make me smack you around about this and be forced to repeat this: No matter which body part replaces it to write, your normal style will re-form. Because your body part isn't lithe yet, it looks crude at first. Eventually you should be able to imitate your hand's patterns without thinking about them. Readers won't even miss your hand's work.

No matter what holds the pen, you write from the impulses emanating from your brain. The pen is merely the instrument used to put the ink on the paper. Simple experiments with individuals writing in the air with smoke or at the end of a folded umbrella confirm it. Many years ago in Germany a farmer, hostile with his neighbor, planted seeds in a calculated manner on his neighbor's land. They grew into offensive words. By identifying the letter forms as his handwriting style, the farmer was convicted of a crime. If you are righthanded, put your left hand up in the air in front of you and start writing your name. Though crude, it will follow your righthanded style. With some unusual strokes you will more easily observe the similarities. A maxim of analysts often spoken is that the source of our writing patterns is within our brain. As a result, handwriting analysis really should be called brainwriting analysis. Dianne Kalal and you confirm it.

Other people have sought to verify this in quaint laboratory settings. Grim's nephew Ryan Grim had heard from his uncle about the handwriting-is-brainwriting theory. On a snowy winter's evening he and a friend were having some beers when Ryan cajoled him into testing the concept for themselves. His nephew knew that alcohol can disturb your motor control and alter your pen strokes. Suds in; duds out. He also knew that, to enable them to write, people with disabled hands will stick a pen in their mouth or between their toes. His uncle had told him that even these people will write as they did with their hands. With each beer instilling a more creative scientific spirit, they sought a different way of writing than using mouths and toes. Ryan suggested they go outdoors in the frigid night for their test. Seizing some nearby tools to write, they knew these "pens" had plenty of "ink" from their quantity of drink. Aware that winter had also laid out a vast parchment for their writing, they unleashed their writing tools and dispensed a cascade of yellow ink.

In due course Ryan reported to his uncle that their experiment confirmed the standard belief. Their style of writing appeared the same as their usual mode with pen in hand. Probing their methodology, Grim asked the lads for proper evidence of their experiment. Regrettably they were less than forthcoming. As to the "pens," they said they would rather not show them. As to the "paper" with the "writing" on it, they said they were no longer able to produce it.

———

When told handwriting uncovers personality some people waver in visualing what happens. Grim has his way of looking at it. "Think of it as a person issuing a report unconsciously but it's not about some other individual. It's about himself. He is saying, 'This is what I am really like based on what I know of myself inside and outside. And I know myself really well.' It is actually a first-hand account, a self-portrait, given to another person to review. That other person is the analyst."

"Do they know what they are saying?" I ask.

"No. The writer gives an account of himself but is unaware what he said about himself."

Still, without insight of psychology's rules, he may become self-aware. For instance, you may not know about jealousy, except as a layman. Yet your writing reveals whether jealousy afflicts your disposition. Essentially your writing appraises you honestly and without bias because most people don't know what handwriting strokes convey. At bottom it may be more accurate than observation by another person since the writer provides the information without knowing what he said. When someone else observes you and reports about your personality, his comments are cursed with the human tenants that you can't see and can never evict—subjectivity, prejudice, and error. Thus handwriting yields a pure, objective assessment of a person. The traditional method of one person witnessing conduct of another is bent through the observer's personal prism that never seems to be cleaned properly.

An unsurpassed virtue of handwriting analysis is its authenticity. Because it avoids your conscious mind, you don't misstate your traits to the public. If you were conscious of the trait in your strokes, you would be tempted to color the trait to make you look good, or to avoid looking bad. With handwriting you tell us your traits unflinchingly and candidly because you have no choice. You don't delight in releasing your hidden self even though you are the messenger of the good and bad news. You spill the beans without knowing what's in the bag.

————

Which of us do analysts seek as targets to analyze? They focus on both the regular people, those doing just fine, and the irregular, people with neuroses, those who are still with us but are battling destructive phantoms. Who is in this latter group? It's you and me and the rest of our human animals, imperfect but still attached to reality. In fact, it includes virtually anyone still with us mentally, no matter how tenuous. For the most part analysts ignore the psychotic's writing. They've slipped from their reality moorings and need professional help to rejoin us. They don't need the customary evaluation to determine their quirks. As members of society with expired cards, we must probe them more deeply. They are sadly beyond the range of your handwriting's meanings. Hence, analysts don't get involved. Hopefully they are already treated by a psychiatrist.

Grim says he can see why his brethren overlook those flying over the cuckoo's nest. Most analysts and lay people would believe that the handwriting of a person with psychosis is likely to look wild, unrestrained, bizarre. At the very least you think it will appear more radical than the rest of us. If the psychotic is detached from reality, you would think he can't conform his writing to the conventional styles of the normal person. You would be wrong, at least according to one survey. Ironically it showed that the strokes of the psychotic surprisingly run close to normal. The reason remains a mystery. Perhaps, it is believed, the psychotics vary in the way they manifest themselves. Then there is the growing evidence of physical causes for some mental illnesses.

Maybe the same for the writing of alcoholics. But it might help to focus on the kind of person who becomes one by tallying the cluster of traits in strokes common to alcoholics. A few analysts researched to see if alcoholics registered common strokes in their writing. None of any significance were found. One survey comparing alcoholics and non-alcoholics when both were sober showed alcoholics with more pressure on the paper and more variation in pressure. Oddly, when they each drank, the effects were opposite for both. Analysts have long hungered for the magic signs in the writing of alcoholics and drug addicts. Since no research has found any of note, their hunger is now famine. When I ask his take on it, Grim, no expert in the field, is willing to say only that "the answer might be more complex than it seems." The causes of each can vary widely from person to person. Alcohol and drug are infamous choices for relief of failing personalities. Why we fall down and need aid to get up and keep going depends on what knocked us to the ground in the first place. Everyone's story is different. You would think the differences are so wide that common patterns in the writing wouldn't emerge. But perhaps not. More surveying would be a wise step.

What about the criminal mind or the criminal personality? Are we going to find common patterns there or are we left with wide differences also?

"I don't know who that person is," says Grim. He expands. "The criminal codes are filled with offenses from petty to heinous. The offenders commit murder, robbery, rape, arson—the ones we deplore the most. Others do car theft, disorderly conduct, malicious mischief, shoplifting and speeding. Surely they each act from different motivations. To ask handwriting to tell us whether any individual will, or might, commit any particular wrongdoing inflates its power."

Human behavior is just too complex to tell with certainty who will do it. Predicting criminal behavior was hard before handwriting analysis appeared even where the person had a long rap sheet. Criminals get married, old, religion, and reformed.

"Aren't there people whose personal make-ups are *programmed* to inflict harm on others, or even themselves," I ask.

"Yeah, but few of them ever act on those impulses. Others shock us with their wicked act. 'He was such a quiet, decent guy, I thought. Wouldn't hurt a flea.'"

"But don't those people, secretive or not, betray a criminal type?"

"Not usually. Yes, we read that about them in crime articles where we are shocked with the perpetrator's identity. However, motivations for any crime or immoral act are often hidden, and sometimes unknowable and, finally, unpredictable. All are problems for the authorities and handwriting analysts."

To provide comfort to those concerned about harm to their loved ones, Grim offers some hope within handwriting. Some studies have revealed stroke patterns for certain kinds of problem people. Where certain strokes continually show up in an analysis for specific wicked conduct, the results give us a person to look for. Grim cites one study that analyzed the writing of 32 convicted embezzlers. They had letters that don't look like the letter they are supposed to be. They seem like some other letter or form. You glance at them and they shout deception. The criminal behavior seems to track them since embezzling is a fraudulent act by someone with access to money in an organization. Although the link is not locksolid, it's enough information to conclude that an employee is more likely to engage in this wrongdoing. If the strokes appear strikingly similar, his prediction is fortified that this person will likely commit similar acts. Businesses can use this kind of profiling in seeking the workplace thief or embezzler. Stroke patterns may reveal an unsavory personality. If so, the employer's analyst deals in probabilities. With human behavior that is the most you can ask for. If two applicants have roughly equal backgrounds but one has writing with the tell-tale signs of the troublemaker, can you blame the employer in rejecting that one? Today businesses spotlight the disgruntled, vengeful worker who is likely to pollute the work environment. These workers know businesses rely on computers. Some of them pursue their grudge against fellow employees or the employer by sabotaging the computers with viruses or other damage. Analysts can help businesses look for these scoundrels, who might apply to work for them. Or they can be called in to help identify existing employees who have already bashed the computer.

With the public's often lurid interest in criminal behavior, Grim regularly hears what he calls "the ultimate shameless question, Can you tell if my boyfriend is a serial killer?" You can easily fill it in with mass murderer or ax murderer. "The Serial Killer Question," Grim calls it. It won't go away and is often offered with a chuckle, a worried look, and a shaky voice. This inquiry seeks a specific kind of diabolical criminal, not a general type. Grim seems to bite his tongue and suppress a roll from his eyes while mustering as much gravity as he can.

"What's the problem?" I ask.

"My colleagues and I don't so much detest the question as for how it demeans our subject and us."

"How do you mean?"

Grim is ready to explain but begs patience. On this one, I am glad to give it.

"No one magical stroke announces that someone is an ax murderer, or a serial killer, or any other narrow stereotype. Since an analyst surveys over a hundred strokes to uncover personality traits, these specific types won't register with one.

"Is it found in a series of strokes?"

"I'm not aware of any study for that. There may be one. But I haven't explored it nor have I run across it in my travels."

"Is it possible, you think?"

"I think so. But you would have to record a lot of writings of known serial killers and take it from those. But the motivations and causes of the killings may come from several directions. Maybe there is no serial killer type. I've heard about the person who kills without a conscience or empathy, things like that. But cataloging them would be a lot of work and patience and some luck getting samples. They would have to be captured killers or those who wrote notes in their handwriting if not caught."

I return to the comment he made about its demeaning effect.

"It just drops us into that laughable topic bin in a macabre situation. When people ask the question, they often do it in hahaha mode. It's degrading. They will follow it with a snide reference to the boyfriend and wonder if he has the strokes to qualify. It implies what we are doing isn't serious."

Grim seems sensitive here. I go for more with, "How about other kinds of profiled people?"

He cites surveys that tried "reverse profiling." Disorders such as anorexia and bulimia and sexual abuse and some others were studied, but not the diabolicals. This profiling takes the writing of, for example, known anorexics, and scans it for common strokes. When a girl is suspected of anorexia, her writing is reviewed to see if she has those same strokes shared by other anorexics. Since many of these girls are in denial to their parents, they can be confronted and given help before it's too late. As with Karen "Close to You" Carpenter, death is a potential outcome.He questions if they will be revealing enough to predict the behavior in other people suspected of being diabolicals. Some of these personality types commit such horrible acts with an empty conscience. He and his colleagues claim their discipline is able to backhoe to the deeper reaches of character. After all, isn't conscience something at or near the surface of our awareness? If so, you would think an analyst can easily discover these types just below that level of moral topsoil. Grim concedes all of this but wonders if the diabolicals are such unique types that their motivations don't appear in the standard strokes analysts use to explain behavior. Hopefully their uniqueness will show up in a much-needed study that remains to be done.

Meantime some analysts are surveying the criminal type for lessons to be learned. Veteran Graphoanalyst Kathy Urbiha from the State of Washington is one who has done it for several years. She has obtained the writing of actual prison convicts, the worst of the worse, seeking the strokes related to traits common to prisoners. Although she has found what she calls "a far greater multiplicity of clues suggesting inner disharmony," she has also seen those in regular people never arrested. We may have clean rap sheets but our personal lives have dirty sheets. Her conclusion is that "criminals do not have handwriting all that different from the grocery clerk that bags your groceries or the barber that cuts your hair." So much for the criminal personality. Or is it, dare we say it?, so much for the value of handwriting analysis? Urbiha and others have also surveyed convicts' writing for signs of dishonesty. She does not find that they "appear with any more regularity than in the general population." How many of us break the law despite otherwise moral lives?

———

Skeptics have a whale of objections to handwriting as a source of personality. They harpoon analysts that it's too unstable, too ornery, and too undisciplined to make secure judgments. As whitecaps break all about, it won't sit down in the boat. Analysts are used to hearing this blubber. One way they counter skeptics is with, yes, more analogies. Our face is a common one. We may exult, pout, or groan even as our basic features stay the same. If you fix on those that move, plenty remain to recognize easily. Our expressions are temporary; when they end our features return to their default appearance. If you try to disguise your writing it's no better than the guy who makes a goofy face trying to conceal his identity. Not very effective because he has too many features to alter. What's left gives him away. Yes, the metaphor is limited because the face has physical features which don't change much except through aging or personal trial or jelly doughnuts.

We are not robots or computers. Yet our manner of writing should look similar each time we write. Not identical but close enough that your friends and family can recognize it as yours. Handwriting is dynamic and changeable from moment to moment. However, just like our face, many of our writing strokes hardly change, they readily say. As your personality evolves it will transform in tandem. Those changes will be reflected in different strokes, maybe even new strokes or strokes deleted. That may occur gradually over years, or at once from trauma. If you are shattered by an adverse incident, maybe a bad car accident, or your girlfriend's pregnancy, your writing can change. If you are inspired by a captivating speaker or are graced with a new boss who spurs you to improve your work habits, your writing can change. As the nets get clipped after a basketball championship, so does handwriting transform itself in step with its owner's life.

To divine meaning from strokes, consistency is less of an issue than you might think. In another area of writing it is a big issue because consistency matters. At the beginning of Grim's class segment about signatures he asks why we use them to identify ourselves. He hints that the answer has two fundamental reasons, both of which must exist or else we couldn't rely on our signatures. He also tells them not to work too hard for the answer. Otherwise they will think right over it. They usually do, rarely even tendering the correct answer without more hints from Grim. He lets them know that we can rely on our signatures since they are uniquely our own and we consistently repeat them. Without these elements, society would shatter. Your lawyer and your banker join to thank you for your devotion to your steadiness. Centuries of legal history will vouch for your signature's importance. In preparing your will or your power of attorney your lawyer hopes you remain faithful to your past stroke patterns. Your bank, which expects certainty in transactions, will have you sign a signature card when you open an account with them. When you sign one of its checks they want you to repeat what you drew on that signature card. We satisfy these authorities by giving them our most personal possession, our signatures. If we didn't keep them individual and consistent, no one could look to them to enforce a contract or take our check. With no dependable signatures, we have uncertainty and breakdown. Some of us make unruly stabs at the paper. If you must stoop to that, at least make them roughly similar each time.

It doesn't even need to be script. Printing is fine. Probably it is better because it is known for being readable.

Sure we can alter our writing styles, either purposely or non-consciously. A few try to devise a new and more creative way of strutting their names. Those who hazard it are on their own. We can't do much to stop them, short of grabbing their hand while it's in action. You can't threaten them. With what? You could write your signature swathed with mammoth balloons and tongue-whipping serpents and get away with it. Of course public curiosity and ridicule would follow. That's your signature because it's your private selection of your public face. No one can tell you what it has to be, not even Miss Pringle from penmanship class. Some of these signatures look like a gargoyle had a one-night stand with a troll. "No law prevents it, but there should be one," snarls Grim. Thankfully only a few of us are this rash. Aside from the criminal forger and the sometime doodler, we don't fiddle with our signatures. Those who fiddle pollute the legal system as well as handwriting analysis, stirring up work for document examiners and of course lawyers. If one day you randomly fashion your signature into the new you, that innocent change of style can create havoc. It's legal but it's asking for trouble for yourself and those you confront in your travels, especially in business transactions and serious personal ones. How about your voting location where they compare your signature to their recorded one? It is one thing to have your individual signature and your own method of writing. You are entitled to that. It's another to avoid using them regularly. When you ramble, you can wreck the engine of social order, which runs on expectations. If you don't maintain your trademark, people will disrespect you as unreliable and flaky. More important, they won't know this person you have devised when you offer only writing they don't recognize or can't read.

———

Many oldsters recall the Palmer Method with wistful fondness. Through his famous style your school compelled you and your classmates to mimic his ideal form using your pencil. Palmer was Augustine N. Palmer whose method of writing commanded the primary grades through most of the twentieth century. Other schools of writing have existed—Zaner-Bloser, Rinehart, D'Nealian, Spencerian, and others.

Some of them are still around. Palmer survives only here and there. Like the other Palmer from golf, Augustine Palmer used to be king. He modernized school handwriting by diverting children from the peacock-and-turkey styles of the nineteenth century, such as Spencerian, to more practical ones. Although the capital letters had a cultivated elegance and the rest some lesser grace, Palmer introduced an overall restraint in the strokes. In place of the florid nineteenth century styles began muscular movement writing. Now the student rested his arm on the desk and barely moved his fingers or wrist. This allowed free and tireless hand action. His sensible strokes emphasized ease, legibility, speed and endurance. Previously, copybook writing deterred students' individual and flexible movement. Because of Palmer, handwriting was liberated, permitting the writer's uniqueness to bloom. Freedom of writing meant that finally young people could meet their budding personalities. With the door open, handwriting analysts marched in knowing that individual styles they crave would be more available. The true individual could better be found. Personality, largely hidden from view in forced handwriting, was out of the closet.

Writing's emancipation has thrust us miles from the school model's musty dungeon. Since an avalanche of different modes of writing have floomped educators, the result has been sobering. Many would see it as a collapse in the discipline of proper writing. For handwriting analysts it has been exhilarating. Students have been free to follow their true nature reflected in the strokes. If there has been any decline in the quality of writing, it is mirroring the individual's character. Unfortunately, something must be amiss with the writer the more he abandons the school model. Where writing developed into scrawl, check for upheaval in this person's life. Don't blame it on the reform in penmanship. It's our Paul Bunyan personalities, who refuse to give up their ax.

Today few of us write close to what we learned. Many haven't given much thought to how they should write or how they want to write. They may knead their signature with a variety of forms, knowing society allows them to play with their dough. Who's going to slap their flour-dusted wrist? They will powder it countless times over their life. Even knowing this, many of us write poorly with a juliachildmess of consequences. We waste strokes. We drape them with inventive but needless garpistles, heedlers, wicknipes, and frivvels, adding only frill. Our hands tire easily and often. We press too hard. We hold the pen as if it will attack us. We divebomb the paper from odd angles, especially our lefthanded friends, seeming to fight a curse. For Grim this is one of graphology's most cogent arguments. If we are trying to reach others, why do we make trouble for ourselves and our readers by taking blue highways? Our journey should be on the smooth interstates. We can't seem to help it. Our personalities are doing our talking—make that our writing. After all, writing is just our talking planted on paper.

Few of us realize the Palmer Method wasn't created primarily to make school children learn some discipline in their writing. It certainly did. But so did those before. Palmer's intent was to make your writing easier and more efficient while still being readable. He hoped to reduce our time as writers and, ultimately, the time of our readers. Thus, when we deviate from Palmer we make it harder for us to write. Actually, as we have found since Palmer, an even more efficient way exists. D'Nealian is its name. Printscript could challenge also. D'Nealian was introduced into the schools in the 1960's as a more simplified cursive. Don Neal invented it to ease the transition from manuscript to cursive writing. Previously, no new handwriting system had been started in America for about a half-century. In brief, it's Italic with letter connections. As you should know, Italic looks slim and flexible and leans forward. It's graceful and modern and runs like Secretariat. In truth it has been around for centuries. If you notice, the word has many letters from a European country. It began in Italy in the 1700's and forms the foundation for modern calligraphy. Structurally it has only strokes necessary to identify each letter. All the excess and the frill are absent.

Printscript is writing drawn as script without linking letters. The letters have stubby strokes that would link up if they need to. If you are a script writer and you try it, you feel the impulse to join each letter. If you've been scripting all your life, switching isn't easy. Check the Palmer capital letters. While mildly flourished, they're polished and appealing. Flourishes only decorate. Like the curtains on your living room windows, you can see the street without them. At least the lavish Palmer strokes are not as gross as the Victorian ones they replaced. In view of Palmer's benefits, we must question our wayward approach. Are we not vacant of mind and bereft of sense? We have chosen a careless, sometimes unreadable, often foolish way to put our thoughts on paper. If you want to know why we have fallen so hard and refuse to get up, ask any handwriting analyst. Within our brain resides a power insisting we reflect our personality through ink impressions on the paper. You may have read this before. Now maybe it will sink in. Though you doubt it, analysts swear by it.

Grim wonders what penmanship schools think of handwriting analysis. Do they believe it warps their sacred methods? Do they acknowledge that students wander from their models once teacher no longer hovers? Grim has discovered a sense of Palmer's view. In an astonishing admission, the director of the A. N. Palmer Company once told Milton Bunker, founder of Graphoanalysis, that they didn't expect children to follow their school models. "We try to help them cultivate a legible style of execution, but after they are out of school, they begin to show their individual personalities, and their writing becomes the picture of the individual writer." Bunker, who gazed at thousands and thousands of writings over his life, was more emphatic and certain. "Not one in ten thousand stuck by what he learned in school," he observed.

Once we have fled from the Palmer grade school setting, what model does our mind see? Some experts believe it isn't the Palmer Method. It's, can you believe it, and are you sitting down?, yes, I'm saying it, our *own* writing style. It's the one most familiar and for the longest time. We barely recall the Palmer strokes. It may be unconscious but we can't help employing are own method on our mental screen up there above our heads or wherever it is. Oddly, the closer you write to the Palmer Method, the pedestal-squating icon we barely remember, the better adjusted you are in society's view, declares handwriting analysis. For those who scoff at our brethren who display conventional writing, you should be envious. Maybe you are. The best way to tell quickly is to see if your writing looks regular, shunning any extreme strokes. In its calm normality it will stand out like that dazzling hot-air balloon above yonder woods.

If your writing qualifies from this, contort your arm and give yourself a pat on the back. You are conformist, traditional, conservative, respectful, comfortable with the status quo, God-fearing, and prudent. You think inside the box. You can't break the confining mold. When you try, people will giggle as you are no more than a sheep in sheep's clothing. You drive through life badgered by a backseat driver, society, barking commands to stay on the narrow, winding road. To meet those norms you have to be stable, reliable and controlled. We all know these people. Some of us *are* these people. Analysts point out that from far away they can spy their writing and instantly know it's theirs. On the other hand, they are also not exciting, adventuresome, creative, adaptable creatures. They are not open to new experiences. An individual with grotesquely drab handwriting will have a personality to match. Studying the writing of conformists helps the doubter to understand analysts' argument that handwriting reveals personality. Should someone mock your writing because it lacks inventive strokes and resembles how you were taught, you might want to say a quick, satisfying thank you for confirming your solid personality. Conventional writing indicates you are doing well as a member of your community. You may be a little too enamored of Lawrence Welk, Walt Disney, and the Reader's Digest, but you're muddling through whatever you do.

———

Grim is proud of the virtues of his handwriting analysis discipline. At the same time it is both serious and fun. It is an aid to understanding yourself and others. It is mentally challenging, and a constant learning experience. You can make money with it, merely amuse yourself, or entertain friends and family. It breaks ice and connects you with people. It involves everyone's favorite subject—themselves. Because of that everyone is drawn to it, unlike other subjects, which can have limited appeal. It commands respect from its singular knack for penetrating the intimate portions of peoples' lives. Remember that caustic remark people spit to yuckify someone's well-being? "I'll expose you for what you really are." That is what handwriting analysis will do. Not to punish or embarrass you, however. It's only to let you know about your inner self. A major source of its strength and uniqueness is that it doesn't lie to you. It lays out the truth about you to the best of its ability. It shows you as you are behind closed doors.

Graphology's stigma comes partly from its being fun to do. To discern your friend's qualities from a quick glance at his writing strokes is appealing. Learning your own features the same way stirs you even more. Laugh as you can as your drawbacks chasten you and your friends enjoy learning them as they silently recoil from their own.

Since it is often done at parties, family gatherings, on boardwalks, at carnivals, from machines for a small fee, by fortune tellers on the side (which is a scam within a scam since few of them have any real knowledge of the subject), doubters will heckle it as bogus. That is what it has had to overcome.

Why does Grim believe it is so compelling? "It latches on to you and won't let you go. Except it's not like an octopus or a python. It's more subtle. It's mesmerizing."

It's easy to understand how people are drawn to it. We all learn to write and we find ourselves slowly drawing strokes that seem to wander farther from what we were taught. We marvel at what our writing has come to and speculate that it must mean something important. You think it can't just be random and devoid of meaning. What do those strokes say about us? Then we move from what it can do for ourselves to what it reveals about others important to us. What can we learn about about our girlfriend, parents, brother and sister and best friend, not to mention our worst enemy or the surly neighbor, or the nasty boss. If we could get inside them, what are all these people really like? Underneath are they really what they seem to be? Some toughies are softies. Some arrogant or egotistical types are self-haters. Some who think they're so smart are only feckless frauds.

To apply handwriting analysis is to become a detective, a social service agency and a traveling psychologist. It can also lead to surprises or confirmation. Suppose we want to know about someone we must deal with in an important area of our lives but we lack deep knowledge of them. Maybe a business rival or a competitor in an organization. Or we must spend time with someone on a trip or in a project or at a conference or meeting. It's not just curiosity; it's potentially saving your peace of mind or a job or a major sale, or a relationship. Or one person you must confront determines success or failure in an event. With prior insights about an individual you can act in your best interests. America and its allies were aiding in winning World War II in Europe with Germany and in the Pacific with Japan after we broke their secret communication codes and they didn't even know it. Handwriting analysis is one of the sincerest and mildest forms of espionage that deftly breaks everyone's secret code to their underlying nature. Those who surrender their writing to an analyst expose a wealth of personal intelligence of private desires and tendencies, despite attempts to remain inscrutable. Although you may want to avoid an intrusion into your character, you act in vain. We stroll about in our daily lives in a perpetual Halloween of deception, obscuring our true selves. When we place strokes on paper we rip off our own mask, betraying our faults to the world but humbly proclaiming our often-untapped virtues.

Confucius

Aristotle

Two of the greatest minds in history, one from Ancient Greece and one from Ancient China thought their nation's handwriting conveyed information about the writer's personality. This is astounding since their separate writings were centuries from modern handwriting script styles, thousands of miles apart, and several centuries before any modern concepts of personality and psychology.

Chapter 3

History

There is a strong case to be made for handwriting analysis. Critics who say, flatly, that there is nothing to it are simply wrong.

1930's Harvard Psychology researchers Allsop and Vernon

Do the names Robert Browning, Julius Caesar, Dr. Albert Schweitzer, Emile Zola, Sir Walter Raleigh, Thomas Mann, Sigmund Freud, William Shakespeare, Albert Einstein, and Elizabeth Barrett Browning mean anything to you?

History Hall of Fame people who believed in graphology

Although mankind has been around for thousands of years, he existed only when history began. We don't know how or when that moment happened. We do know writing was there at the creation. History started when man invented writing to record it. History couldn't have started without it. Don't count the spoken memories of old men to young men as its start. You need something readable and lasting. For ancient man the best form was a hard and durable object, like a rock. In fact, it was. The oldest piece of writing comes from about 5,500 years ago in the Middle-East. You may recall it from your period in public school or Sunday School when smiley faces meant you did something good. It was called Mesopotamia and it was in the Fertile Crescent. You might know some of this today as a country called Iraq. Although we aren't sure what the writing's purpose was, it was on a limestone tablet. Pounded into it are a foot, a hand, a sledge, and maybe numbers. It might be a tax record.

If you're expecting some progress in these ancient times, events only camel-clopped along. For the next marker on writing's passage through the Middle-East you will have to take a running broad jump a few thousand years.

An enterprising nation arose in the area around present-day Lebanon on the Eastern Mediterranean shore. The Phoenicians were superb craftman, traders, sailors, and explorers. This impelled them to record their business and other items. Snipping reeds from waterways, their "scribes" impressed wedge shapes into soft clay tablets and baked them hard in the sun. That worked for a time before they saw the reed's shape was inadequate. The impressions were simplified into symbolic wedges known as cuneiform. Slowly the picture images were refined into logos known as ideographs. They were easier to draw and increased the information conveyed. Now if a circle was drawn it could mean more than the sun. With some special touches and detail it might project light or warmth or maybe a hot day.

Another Middle-East nation with a grand history of progress offered its own version of writing. To the southwest Egypt developed a better surface and a different substance to write on it. They took the papyrus plant and beat it flat, combining the pieces into a rough parchment. Vegetable dye or water mixed with soot or gum became their ink. Using picture symbols called hieroglyphs, they tried improving their pictures with their better paper. Expression was arduous and the numerous images were overwhelming. At last a breakthrough arose when the words were divided into different sounds and parts that we now call syllables. Versatile, they could be cut from one word and pasted in another. By 1300 BC the enterprising Phoenicians and the nearby Canaanites split the syllables further into parts as specific letters, which became the model for the first alphabet. (*Aleph* and *beth*, its first two letters, spell a familiar word today.) You recall those Phoenician letters from your dictionary. Always the first one on the page for each letter, they look drunk and disoriented. To their glorious innovation we owe the Phoenicians a big wet muwah today. We have honored them by creating a child's soup, spelling bees, and a dim TV game show. With a complete alphabet of letters, the Phoenicians showed the Greeks that separate words goosed communicating and recording to new heights. Sailing ships commerce carried the new method of writing west to the Estruscans in Italy, who passed it on to their Roman successors around the birth of Christ.

Meantime in Egypt, writing progress was sultry-desert slow. You know those figures they painted on their walls who always faced sideways? They didn't turn their faces toward us for, hold on to your fez, 3000 years. The primitive cuneiform wedges and the hieroglyphs joined the cultural freeze on friezes. None of them thawed for 3000 years until the first century AD, when they finally copied the Roman advancements.

The earth is a huge planet. Just ask the Man in the Moon and Ferdinand Magellan, and that guy with the circumnavigatin', sleep-in, hot-air balloon. The Middle-East and Europe were not the only areas to advance in writing. All this time far away another culture developed writing in isolation. A nation begun about 3,500 years ago, China sandaled a different path. Despite China's long history, archeologists can trace specific objects of writing only to 14 BC. Remains of animal bones, flat and polished, with engraved pictures are Exhibit A. These were not just one man's carving. They were its national way of writing as they devised 2000 images to represent thoughts and objects. The Chinese language still uses these renowned pictorial characters. Although Chinese characters are images, each word has only one syllable. Hence, it did not need to evolve into particular symbols and letters as Western writing did. Unbelievably, only in the early 1970's did China haul its language into the modern world. To compete and join with other nations, the Communist government compelled sweeping changes, such as easing the mouth-twisting pronunciation and the head–scratching spellings. The inscrutable Chinese now became, how you say, less inscrutable.

A short pause for a worthy cause. Recounting all this handwriting history is not the purpose here. This book is about handwriting analysis and this history is to place handwriting analysis in context. Everyone has at least a blurry recollection of writing from church or school, especially those three foreign words just discussed—papyrus, hieroglyphs, and cuneiform. Even now they survive baked into our language. Yes, we get the word paper from papyrus. And we all know the testy whine of "I can't read your hieroglyphics." Cuneiform is …just odd enough not to forget. But that's all it gives us today, except for another tricky word in a spelling bee or Jeopardy question.

As we approached Christ's birth, the ruling class, scribes, and religious figures hogged writing. Few others were reading and writing anyway. They were too busy chasing their pigs and planting crops.

The writing was not even *hand*writing as we know it. None of the advancements yet resembled the loose, inky, wavy writing of today. Centuries away were small letters, script style and flailing strokes. It was not writing that was flowing and natural and likely to yield personality traits. Special devices were used to write, distant from our current versatile pens and pencils. Usually it appeared in official documents where neatness counted. With this primitive look you would think that handwriting analysis lies centuries away. You would be wrong. Incredibly, it existed not only in Greece but also in China, each place a few centuries before Christ. The evidence comes from a pair of the giants of history. Not only do we celebrate these men today; they were big then and for good reason. They were two of the smartest, most learned and, universally-hailed wisest men of history. Even though their nation's writing's shapes foiled easy analysis, these men were analyzing it. No matter in the picture images of Chinese or the printed-capitals-only Greek, the unique strokes emerged. By their immense personal influence Aristotle and Confucius fostered handwriting analysis simply by indulging in it. With language FredFlintsonian, and psychology centuries from Freud and Adler, their graphology grasp is astonishing. We know little of their efforts but they're worth reviewing to learn their knowledge so long ago.

These days we get one-liners from comedians. In ancient China they were delivered without the humor and with solemn wisdom by a man still honored today named Confucius. As youngsters we heard or read his sayings everywhere. They spawned parodies, often as risqué knock-off jokes. They would begin, "Confucius say" such as "Confucius say, Man who run in front of car get tired." Reading many of his real sayings, he knew what he was talking about. He even created his own Golden Rule, which follows the Bible's, with negatives: "What you do not want for yourself do not do to others." His thoughts bang our gongs today. You swear he is living in the twenty-first century because they apply just as well to us. "Man who have clear conscience often have bad memory." His words were addressed to his fellow Chinese way, way back when, around 500 BC. His beliefs dragon-danced through China with typhoon impact. Chinese governments adopted his principles of moral character as the official philosophy of the state. With timeless power (perceptive thoughts have it) they lasted in Chinese officialdom to the twentieth century. Now they belong to everywhere forever. No doubt you can do the math but it needs to be stated for the record: His precepts survived in China officially for almost *2,400* years. Following his beliefs, his survivors also began a movement called Confucianism. Often wrongly thought to be a religion, it flourished for centuries. Since it had no clergy, no worship of any god, or beliefs on the after-life, it was merely a sensible way of living.

In his intellectual journey he became interested in handwriting analysis. Although little is known specifically, one astute observation he made about handwriting endures. His words were "Beware the man whose writing sways like a reed in the wind." This simple warning with a glued-on simile glistens with value to handwriting analysis. It establishes three important facts. Handwriting analysis is eternal since its inception 2,500 years ago. Second, it's worldwide, especially coming from China, as far as you can go from our old backyards. We dug in them as children and our parents told us if we kept going we would come out in China. (They lied or didn't know better. Our digging *straight down* would bring us to the Indian Ocean southwest of Australia. China *is* on the same longitude as our backyards, however.) Third, it does not simply mean that the Chinese practiced handwriting analysis. That *is* important.   Even more is how the Chinese wrote and still do. In America we arrange our letters into word units that go from left to right. The Chinese use individual characters that can represent a whole word and a related idea. No other culture has that way of writing today. With about ten thousand languages in the world only about 85% even have had written language. Until recently Chinese language read vertically from right to left for about 4,000 years. The Communist leadership has directed a change to the European style of left to right. Whichever way the words run, Chinese characters consist of strokes and American letters have strokes. American or Chinese, each style conveys the same meaning for the same strokes. Consider what's implied. Despite 2,500 years of time and 12,000 miles of distance between him and us, as well as a very different way of writing, and a different culture, the strokes revealed personality for Confucius as they do for us today. Finally, in this Chinaman Confucius is also the earliest evidence of handwriting analysis anywhere.

Also examine the actual content in the statement Confucius made. His warning about a fellow Chinaman's writing is still germane today. That is phenomenal. The Chinese know it as just another of his clever observations. What did Confucius mean with his statement about the writing that swayed? He was using handwriting analysis for a clever analogy to describe a fluctuating, volatile temperament. Specifically he was telling us of a man whose writing slant varies from stroke to stroke. When he walks into the room, you don't know what you're getting. You can't trust his behavior as his moods are too unpredictable. That kind of person is everywhere today. We all know someone who acts this way. Personal characteristics repeat over the centuries. Doesn't this confirm analysts' view that human nature is eternal and universal? Confucius walked among these volatile people 2,500 years ago. That is hardly the surprise. They are still with us. Unbelievably, those same people continue to reveal their glum-to-fun behavior in their *handwriting*. That is the surprise.

Another notable figure boosting handwriting analysis appeared a few centuries later far from China. His name is familiar to those who know great minds from history. He is in the Hall of Fame of cerebral thought. Maybe even the Michael Jordan of philosophy. Around 350 BC in Greece Aristotle was a teacher whose ideas were recorded and still inspire us 23 centuries later. He gained additional prominence for being Plato's instructor. His observations about the significance of handwriting, beyond the content itself, must be noted: "Speech is the expression of ideas or thoughts or desires. Handwriting is the visible form of speech. Just as speech can have inflections of emotions, somewhere in handwriting is an expression of the emotions underlying the writer's thoughts, ideas, or desires." He also published a fundamental truth, now established today, about the individuality of handwriting: "Handwriting is a symbol of speech and speech is a symbol of mental experience. Just as all men do not have the same speech sounds, so do all men not have the same writing."

After the distinguished actions of Confucius and Aristotle, handwriting analysis faced a three-century lull until Christ's birth. Nothing turns up until the Roman Empire grew more powerful. Its leaders snatched this unfamiliar, unproven subject for themselves. Even with handwriting's crude status, the upper classes in early Rome took to handwriting analysis. The notorious Emperor Nero, disgraced for fiddling while Rome burned, reigned from 54 to 68 AD. He studied handwriting analysis and believed in it. Once he declared about a court official, "His writing shows him to be treacherous." He later had the official put to death. The esteemed Julius Caesar also practiced it. In 539 AD the Roman Empire's famous and laudable Justinian Code of laws also recognized that each person's handwriting and signature was individual. In the Middle-East in the years around 70 to 200 AD the ancient Hebrew laws were assembled in a volume known as the Mishnah. This volume pronounced that each person's handwriting was different.

Meantime, from scarcity and cost papyrus was losing its appeal. Replacing it was parchment, a surface more durable and receptive. Probably Greece was its inventor. For its base material animals replaced plants. Skin from goats, sheep and calves became the source for parchment. In the West this lasted until the eleventh century when paper emerged as the permanent writing surface. China merely nodded that whattookyousolong look. It had been using it for over a thousand years. The reed pen, developed in Egypt from plants along the Nile, had a pointed end that dented the papyrus with those famous hieroglyphics. Eventually the reed pen was supplanted around the seventh century by the quill, made from goose and turkey feathers. As the paper smoothed, the pen got pointy, and its ink began seeping. From stiff and stilted printing writing evolved into curves and finally cursive style.

After the first centuries of the Christian Era handwriting analysis has more lost history for several centuries. Chinese interest continued well beyond Confucius with successors, such as Kuo Jo Hsu, an eleventh century artist and philosopher. He remarked, "Handwriting can show whether it comes from a person who is noble-minded or from one who is vulgar." As the Middle Ages crawled along some itinerant analysts ponged from castle to castle, (like their familiar music troubador counterparts), displaying their skills in this still mysterious subject. The only other practice at this time seemed to be among the monks. Finally in seventeenth century Italy a formal publication about the subject was circulated. Doctor-instructor Camillo Baldi compiled a treatise entitled *"A Method to Recognize the Nature and Quality of a Writer from his Letters."* He offered some trenchant observations on the subject. "...somehow [handwriting] reproduces something of its writer's temperament, personality, or character." Handwriting was not natural or contrived, he declared. When someone writes, his features appear for plucking to establish meaning. His insights prophesied what analysts today believe about handwriting, especially a premise questioned documents experts clamp to their souls. Convinced that our writing is unique and controlled from within us, he believed that copying the strokes of others is hard. This led to the next notion that it's not easy to forge writing. In addition, we each write so distinctly that changing our own styles is difficult. Our characteristics seem to be cemented within our strokes and thus not readily changed. As a salutary result, our writing is stable and consistent. Apparently this 1622 volume did not generate a groundswell of interest. It had minimal impact on the lower classes, which is understandable. Aside from the noble class and the clergy, most of the world could not read or write until the end of the Middle Ages.

Thankfully for the world, they did end. As to a downhill ski race from a curling match, the vibrant Renaissance replaced the stagnant Middle Ages. Movable type printing, educational progress, expanded commerce, and advancing science led all classes to learn to read and write. In 1778 a Swiss intellectual Johann Lavater, a poet, educator and religious figure, determined that handwriting "is unique to each of us, and connects to our personalities." By linking our handwriting to our unique ways of expression, he foresaw what we now call "body language" in our voice and our walking styles. He stated the handwriting-to-personality tie in accurate but starchy eighteenth century terms, "The handwriting of a person is congruent with his actual situation and state of mind."

In the early nineteenth century toddler social science was trying to get off its hands and knees. As a discipline within science, psychology was still years away from headline breakthroughs. However, as a layman's exercise handwriting analysis couldn't wait. It initiated some remarkable events in the early portion of the century. Though they didn't occur within a pure scientific setting they deserve some acclaim for their considerable achievements. After languishing for so long in stop-and-go traffic, handwriting analysis finally varoomed its way down society's then unpaved road. Those at the wheel weren't men in white coats but men in white collars. In 1830 France some clergyman scholars formed a study group to look at the writing of their acquaintances and match their common strokes to personality traits. They focused on what they called "fixed signs," the individual elements in letters, such as t-bars, i-dots, and loops on l's and h's. Today Graphoanalysts and other trait advocates call them strokes. Analysts who concentrate on the minute parts inside letters are sometimes called molecular analysts or atomistic analysts. The terms were borrowed from physics and chemistry where scientists have broken down matter into the parts we know as atoms and molecules. It's the same principle for social science. Within letters are elements which become the key focus of the analysis. These scholars constructed a logical and coherent system for analyzing writing.

One of their student members was Jean Hippolyte Michon. Taking command, he founded a society, coined the term "graphology," and had a major role in spreading the technique around Europe. He and his cohorts rolled up their cumbersome sleeves and got their robes dirty. They didn't just take handwriting and guess or intuit the meaning of individual signs, as many existing analysts were doing. Michon studied thousands of writings of familiar people and published a catalog of these signs with guidelines for interpreting them. By the late 1800's graphology had gained a foothold in the universities of Italy, France, and Germany. Today some of these universities require it within their advanced degree programs. Eventually these founding churchmen established about forty aspects in writing they attached to personality. Those aspects survive today as strokes and as larger factors, like slant, all relating to specific features of personality.

With no ideology or school or organization, prior analysts had freewheeled their analyses. They backpedaled from the writing and appraised the sensation that struck them. This formed the "gestalt" view of looking at the forest rather than the trees. "Gestalt" derived from a German doctrine of perceiving items as a whole, as in the common expression, "The whole is greater than the sum of the parts." Today the term is "holistic," expanding the analyst's perspective by eyeing the writing's grander parts, along with its radiating effect. This brought insight into major areas of the individual's personality. Some of these grander aspects in writing are the thickness, the rhythm, the size, and the roundness.

Many amateur analysts in the nineteenth century continued to use this method. Some were leading cultural figures like Edgar Allan Poe, Thomas Gainsborough, and Robert Browning. In truth these men favored a more intuitive approach to their analyzing. Partly that occurred from lacking a history to build on and a reliable guidebook to apply. In contrast to the French experience, they didn't participate in any formal studies. Thus, no serious growth. Typically they tried to trace the writing to get a feel for what it emits. Poe not only did analyses but had them published in periodicals. He used the term "autography" as he was not familiar with the European term of graphology. His autographies were finally published in one book by Don C. Seitz in 1926 (Dial Press, New York). Gainsborough, the British artist of "Blue Boy," would paint portraits of people not present aided by their handwriting next to the canvas. He wanted to capture their aura from the writing to the canvas. Some other culture figures in the early nineteenth century had some surprisingly keen insights about what handwriting reveals. The British novelist Sir Walter Scott of *Ivanhoe* and *Kenilworth* fame had a character in his *Chronicles of the Canongate* (1827) speak these knowing thoughts of a handwriting specimen:

> "I looked at the even, concise, yet tremulous hand in which the manuscript was written…could not help thinking, according to an opinion that I have here seriously maintained, that something of a man's character may be conjectured from his handwriting. That neat, but crowded and constrained, small hand, argued a man of good conscience, well regulated passions, and, to use his own phrase, of an upright walk in life, but it also indicated narrowness of spirit, inveterate prejudice and hinted at some degree of intolerance. The flourished capital letters, do they not forcibly express the pride and sense of importance of the author?"

Michon had a student he couldn't keep down in the monastery. Fixed signs are only part of the study, thought Jules Crepieux-Jamin. The larger elements should also be considered. Combining the gestalt with single markers whittled a more complete likeness of the writer. He refined the analysis by inferring qualities from syndromes or groups of strokes. This greater blend more realistically denoted personality. If the strokes showed generosity, modesty and friendliness, he concluded the person would become your friend for the right reason, not to boost his ego. With his perspective, people as personalities now seemed less black and white and more with grey. Personalities became complex, displaying all the colors of the rainbow and more. He had discovered how we really are as people.

Today analysts will begin their review of a new sample by seeing how it "hits" them or what "vibrations" leap from it. From there they attack the individual strokes while still accounting for the wider aspects. Handwriting analysis evolved to where a capable analyst gazed at not only the forest (gestalt or holistic) but also the trees and their branches (signs or strokes). We can't avoid considering both, most analysts would say. They are staring at a whole piece of writing knowing the inner parts of letters. It's like telling a red-blooded man to look at an attractive woman and admire her beauty but ignore her breasts, waist, and legs. Stroke analysts contend that unless you consider the large and the small aspects of the writing, you have an unfinished picture of the individual. To achieve the full evaluation today a Graphoanalyst considers over a hundred strokes as well as the global aspects of the writing. He describes them as a complex unit from their separate impacts. You would think that this scheme equates to how psychologists determine personality independent of handwriting.

To disregard any approach with vital information about personality is foolish, say Graphoanalysts. On the other hand, gestalists contend, using the individual strokes is pointless since we aren't sure what they mean. Impulsive, poised, intolerant, stubborn, aggressive, timid. These are Graphoanalysis traits. What do they really mean? When you view them up close they dissolve into an amalgam of everything and nothing. Unlike Maria in *The Sound of Music*, they won't fade into a moonbeam in your hand. But can we give them each a bin in our box of human qualities? Perhaps even more important, gestaltists contend we can't be sure if they have *any* particular meaning. They are artificial tools to explain intricate human conduct. We are thus left to pursue only the larger aspects, items we think we can see and touch. Since they appear everywhere, the larger aspects are so prominent (like the writing size, which every letter has) and thus forceful, we should concentrate on only them.

What strokes are important prolongs the great Protestant-Catholic rift plaguing analysts today. The gestaltists and the traitists thrive everywhere but no big handshake will be offered either way very soon. Truth be told, most analysts from either group probably use a mixture of the two. Graphoanalysis says you have to consider both and synthesize your findings into a complete portrait of the individual. When analysts use the phrase handwriting analysis today, they really mean both schools of thought. Some pundits think the divide is actually more between stroke advocates, who incorporate the gestalt aspects of interpretation and, on the other side, intuitive advocates who analyze loosely with a feel for the writing. That is not much of a contest. In numbers and influence traitists dominate today. Besides, many gestaltists will include so many smaller aspects of the writing that they have become both gestalt and trait practitioners. Although gestaltists may deny it, their use of smaller aspects of writing exposes them as closet traitists. This leaves the intuitives as today's black sheep. Each one has their own approach to stroke meanings, seemingly seized from the air above and their butt below. That is their problem. Who knows where they get them? More importantly, their foundation for those beliefs is less rigorous than the traitists or the gestaltists. Outside skeptics flay them for supporting psychic hogwash. Proud analysts concur and mostly shun them. They retard handwriting analysis from more elevated approval and standing. Today the serious insiders would join the skeptics in condemning the intuitives.

———

It's 1879 and you're in Leipzig, Germany. You visit a laboratory but it's not for chemical experiments; it's for psychological ones. It is run by Wilhelm Wundt and he is trying to determine the structure of peoples' minds. If you guess he wears a beard, wire-rims, and is a serious guy, you would be right. Your presence means you attended the birth of Modern Psychology. More imposing guys with beards followed in Germany and nearby, including a guy named Freud, who began listening to patients as they lay on couches babbling whatever invaded their heads. Psychology had been around for centuries infested with minds offering head-shaking views about human conduct. They dispensed their theories from abysmal ignorance, unable to comprehend it as we do today. In old Greece Hippocrates, the Oath Man in medicine, had suggested we are made up of four humors, or fluids, like melancholic (for sad). Descartes, a French philosopher, knew he was here because he was thinking at the time. He should have thought better since he believed our nerves were hollow tubes and "animal spirits" caused impulses to run through them like water in a pipe. No more nonsense. Finally we were starting to get it right or at least working on it. Psychology was trying to get scientific, not just trying to float lead balloons of whimsy about why people do what they do.

As the twentieth century arrived you would think that handwriting analysis was only a Victorian parlor amusement with a dubious image. You can bet your uncomfy corset it was. Yet, as psychology was getting real, handwriting analysis was adding dignified advocates in Germany. They began theorizing about handwriting's suspected partnership with personality. At last, with sober experiments what individuals were only guessing for centuries found some credible footing. In Germany William Preyer, introduced the formal theory that writing related to the physical brain and that essentially handwriting was "brainwriting." The hand and pen operated only as instruments to register the mind's dictates on the paper. Preyer reviewed the writing of people who had lost an arm and their mouth, toes, or some other body part held their pen. Whatever they used, the writing charted the same style as their hands. This University of Berlin psychology professor concluded that our writing came from within our mind. Somewhere in there were impulses directing the body part with the pen to write from the personality's decree. Preyer combined his topic graphology with other kindred sciences—physiology, psychology, and pathology.

A few decades later another German, Wilhelm Klages, saw that a person's mind is reflected in his separate overt actions. He called it "expressive movement." It's found in ordinary things we all do, such as walking, speaking, gesturing, and, most significantly, writing. Today the popular phrase for it is "body language." He also developed the concept that writing has an overall quality to it, a form level some have termed formniveau. (aka formniwo or formnivo), form quality, or form level. Today analysts are more likely to call it rhythm, one of the larger aspects of any writing. A global factor as termed by Graphoanalysis, rhythm reveals how regular the common strokes flow. When an analyst reviews the rhythm he can immediately know how disciplined the individual is. From that they can make broad judgments about the writer's control over his life. (Read more about this in the chapter on doctors' handwriting.)

Klages got some good press in Germany and elsewhere. Though his work advanced graphology, it speed-bumped it in another way. Psychology experts wanted to see controlled experiments to establish these concepts. Klages dismissed experiments as inadequate since he believed handwriting and its attributes are largely intangible. He actively opposed clinical studies, asserting that handwriting should be studied as an independent technique. Regrettably, despite his insight of writing as expressive behavior, his speculative, mystical views hindered graphology's progress as a science.

In England Robert Saudek, a graphologist and a psychologist, believing that Klages was too intuitive, diligently tried to advance his subject through actual experiments. Transplanted from Czechoslovakia and intent on serious lab work in this new science, he wanted to accept only findings validated properly. Because science respected his meticulous methods, he propelled graphology forward, inspiring others to formally examine data too. In the 1920's he pursued a new area he called "graphic maturity." We reach it when we can write without having to think about any letters or their strokes. Writing becomes automatic and more unconscious, thus prompting our true, intimate features.

Introduced by an Austrian named Sigmund Freud, a new field called psychoanalysis stormed into Europe. In Switzerland Professor Max Pulver added handwriting principles to psychoanalysis. Using Freud's theories, like dreams and symbolism, he saw that handwriting could be applied in the same way. The blank sheet of paper is the individual's life space to fill as their inner self commanded. In upper areas of writing were the philosophical and spiritual realms; in lower ones earth and real world matters. Hacking his way through novel thickets, he believed that criminality, as well as sexual and physical problems, could be found in writing strokes. That clashes with what Graphoanalysis now holds as doctrine: Our writing reflects only emotional troubles, not criminal, physical, or sexual ones. Their source may be any of those three but no strokes will disclose which one or any other. A stroke will reveal you are severely self-conscious. *Why* you are is another question. Neither it nor its fellow strokes will speak up about it, though their features may whisper clues. In the companion strokes perhaps some shyness or timidity plagues the writer. Any of these can accompany self-consciousness. They may each worsen the other too. Beyond that, the cause of any is beyond the analyst's skills. Your handwriting is like a lab report except it's not a physical one. It's psychological. You glare at the print-out sheet, the writing, and it reads: "Overly self-conscious." No reason is given. If you want to know, that's between you and your psychologist.

In the early 1900's growth was a mixture of the anonymous dabbler and the giants of psychology. A few books circulated by obscure analysts cataloging peoples' traits and only speculating on their meanings. Others studied the writing of their families, friends, and whatever clientele they could find to tolerate their tenuous skills and standing. In Italy another clergyman, Fra Moretti, studied around 50,000 writing specimens and wrote 23 books. He and other analysts in the world saw the strokes that seem to bear out from their experience and accept or reject them. When they felt confident, they would ordain some new trait-stroke connections. Along with these minor figures the eminent ones also explored this emerging technique. While Sigmund Freud was experimenting with his theories on psychoanalysis, he also explored handwriting analysis. He was convinced there was something to it. After his modest forays into the subject, he posted this noteworthy judgment: "There is no question that men also reveal their character through their handwriting." This clanked against the prevailing view that our writing is mostly random and unfocused. He disagreed; he saw purpose in it. He thought everything we marked down bared something about us. Apparently when he said everything he meant everything. Once he wrote, "[In handwriting] [T]here is no such thing as a slip of the pen." Since his remark we have adopted our own phrase in tribute to Freud, the notorious Freudian Slip. If we take what he meant by his slip, he was proclaiming that every stroke is one of his famous slips. Each accurately exposes what the person really has on their mind. The pen and the paper record each fateful one as an instant but complete personality test.

This bold view received support from another massive figure of science within psychology. Remember those intrusive tests in school known as the Stanford-Binet Tests? Alfred Binet, a French psychologist at the Sorbonne in Paris, developed the IQ Test (along with Theodore Simon). He also surveyed handwriting analysis. After conducting his own experiments, he believed it deserved further study. Calling it "the science of the future," he found a correlation between signs of intelligence in handwriting and his IQ tests. Some graphologists could make the connection at a success rate of 80 percent.

Binet performed only restricted experiments to determine if handwriting analysis was valid as a scientific technique. Freud none. Progress advanced mostly by nameless amateurs and obscure scientific figures trying to be thorough. They sought to do good and appear good also. They borrowed established findings on trait-stroke links and added or subtracted their own from personal surveys. Much of it happened just by doing analysis after analysis. Then and now, each time an analyst reviews someone's writing, especially someone they know, they are performing one more experiment on the validity of handwriting analysis. This created a tantalizing question for the skeptics, the psychology authorities, and the public to consider: How many informal anecdotes would it take to equal one legitimate, overall experiment that they would accept? As it has turned out, not enough of them. With informal and loose controls, their numbers lacked sufficient protocols. Still, doesn't the Sheer Weight Principle apply? One million informal experiments outside the lab should equal one big formal one in the lab.

Nevertheless, through Freud, Binet and others, steady refinements in their methods gave it some modest stature. As the surveying matured in social science, psychology advanced as a card-carrying member. Handwriting analysis itself benefited as better stroke testing yielded better personality insights. Proponents began measuring the results against other psychology tests and techniques and psychiatric reports. Even evaluations by friends, family, teachers, employers and others aided verification.

After the upheaval of World War I, the light Europe had shone on psychology brightened enough to reach America. Handwriting analysis mooched off those vivid beams. Although their achievements were scattered and diverse, some American pioneers bubbled up through the tar pits of obscurity. June Downey, a psychology professor at Midwestern universities, was intrigued by handwriting as expressive movement, Since criteria hadn't been developed, she knew logging movements would be tough. She studied how her family's writing strokes compared with independent judgments of their observed behavior, like gait, gesture, and carriage. In 1919, building on Klages' findings, she published *Graphology and the Psychology of Handwriting*. She concluded that handwriting was another way we express ourselves, like walking and other acts. Another American, Louise Rice, had been a newspaper reporter and the first woman reporter for the *New York World*. She had toiled in Europe, learned about graphology, and imported it to America. She had been one of the first ten pupils in a new course at Columbia University called "Psychology." After a long career as both a magazine and newspaper writer, in 1927 she published *Character Reading from Handwriting*.

Some would call her the Godmother of American Graphology. As a teacher and author on the subject, she founded the American Graphological Society. She insisted on more than high standards for analysts. For years she tried to elevate the subject against doubt. On occasion her efforts troubled the authorities. In the O's of the twentieth century as she applied her skills in handwriting analysis, she was arrested for "fortune telling." Before the case got to the jury, the judge tested her with a page of anonymous writing. Rice handed him a convincing portrait of the mystery person. When he confessed she was accurately describing his own son, he dismissed the charges against her. Using its fraud regulations, in 1908 the U.S. Post Office stiff-armed her mailed handwriting analyses. The charge again was "fortune telling." Not a timid individual, she took a train to Washington, D.C., and somehow buttonholed the Postmaster General himself. Informed and, better yet, persuasive, she convinced him to rescind the action against her. She also shamed him into admitting that handwriting analysis was a valid occupation. He amended the postal regulations to allow delivery of graphology materials. Freed to flex her marketing muscles, she convinced the New York *Daily News* to do a column on graphology. Soon letters piled up her In box, mostly readers seeking analyses of their writing. To keep up with the volume she expanded her work day to 18 hours. When the work overwhelmed her she drafted a group of whiz-kid analysts to help out. They became the core of the first bonafide graphology organization in the United States, The American Graphological Society.

Even with Rice's sledgehammer, the public responded with Dangerfield respect. As a new business and service, it needed a groundswell of interest. She tried the media and Houston lift-off blasted through. From the Nineteen-Teens American periodicals carried articles and features on the topic. Among the staples were *Good Housekeeping, Women's Home Companion, McClure's*, and the *Saturday Evening Post*. Pulp magazines *Real Romance, Motion Picture, and Detective Story Magazine*, known more for loosey-juicy topics, leapt onto the bandwagon. Even the giant newspapers of the day hushed up their reputations, gritted their holier-than-thou teeth, and unlocked their posh mahogany doors to analysts. After Louise Rice planted her foot in the New York *Daily News'* door in 1912, the *New York Sunday Mirror, New York Sunday Daily News*, and others added her column to their pages. They couldn't avoid it. Louise Rice and Sharon Spencer (mentioned elsewhere) had incited a blizzard of letters from New York *Daily News* readers craving an analysis. Then the snow blew far and wide. Woman's clubs, Rotary meetings, sorority gatherings, nightclubs, and radio. All of this through the Twenties, Thirties, and Forties. The new medium TV snatched it in the Fifties.

This first half of the twentieth century was dominated by women analysts. They struggled initially because they were seated in coach class on society's long flight to equality. These women considered their subject serious and legitimate. Needing to megaphone their message, they achieved impressive media splashes. Grassroots events followed in mostly tawdry hometown venues: parties, carnivals, fairs, boardwalks, and machines dispensing instant analyses. The subject was also highjacked by fortune tellers, tarot card readers, psychics, and astrologists as more income for their phony talents. The chainsaw of progress was thus zzhooooing a cultural path to reach the folks in overalls. This was good for the analysts purses but bad for their prestige. The folks in white coats were watching and they bobble-headed with more disbelief.

In the midst of all this pop-cultural growth some dignified uplift arrived in the 1930's with Professors Allport and Vernon at the Harvard Psychological Clinic. With some striking experiments, they studied handwriting as expressive movement. Their results repeated themselves. That was great for the scientific pillar of reliability. As historical benchmarks, reliability and validity gouged a fair mark in the wood with their work. Responding to graphology's uncertain standing, the professors produced a monograph called *Studies in Expressive Movement*. Their lab successes were topped by their hefty-bag, head-spinning declarations to explain them: "[Handwriting] is a crystallized form of gesture, an intricate but accessible prism with many, if not all of the inner consistencies of personality. [It also] provides material that is less artificial than tests and more convenient for analysis; and since it can be studied at leisure, it is superior to facial expression, gesture, and gait which are so fleeting and difficult to record." They followed their lab work with a 1937 psychology textbook, *Pattern and Growth in Personality*, in which they pronounced: "There is a strong case to be made for handwriting analysis. Critics who say, flatly, that there is nothing in graphology are simply wrong." They also found that our behavior has a unity to it. When someone observes us we tend to act several ways they can judge as coming only from us. How we walk and how we write are two of them.

Psychologist Werner Wolff conducted his own tests and re-inforced this in the revered 1948 volume *Diagrams of the Unconscious*. With various clinical collaborators in New York City he established that how we write reflects other shapes in nature. Almost unconsciously, these shapes develop uniquely for each person. For example, someone pleasant and compliant will draw strokes that are soft and curving. On the other hand, someone irascible and starchy will draw strokes that are stiff, edgy and angular. Besides writing, when we make other strokes in doodles, drawings, musical notes, and paintings, they mimic our personal qualities.

Even doodles were assessed. They seem specially attached to us with an independent purity. Although we may draw them in school, we don't learn them in school. Penmanship has a specific history to follow after or depart from. Doodles seem to appear from nowhere. They're inhibited by nothing. We do them mostly in idle moments. They appear when we're on the phone, at a lecture, or in deep thought at a meeting. Usually we're thinking about anything but doodles. You might say their source is thin air. For that source analysts would join their psychology friends to call it unconscious motivation. Admit it, even those ignorant of graphology seem to think they reflect something inside us. Everyone seems to have their own opinion on what each one means.

Creations away from the paper, like sculpture, are individual too, thought Wolff. In a wider but more mature way this similarity appears in our body language in walking, dancing, speaking, gesturing, swimming, and moving our face. Each of our physical acts shows our separate make-ups. Writing is physical. Therefore, how we write will resemble other behavior we do too. That is the crux of body language. Our unique forms of acting give away our personalities. As physical, our writing is just another form of body language. Wolff called writing strokes "diagrams of the unconscious." He showed that writing is not an act of chance nor one of conscious attention.

Wolff had established the unity of every act we take, including our handwriting. Around this time an experiment was conducted with the handwritings of Michelangelo, DaVinci, and Raphael. A group of judges familiar with their work but not their handwriting was asked to match their writing to the individual. They were successful 84 per cent of the time. The Impressionist painter Claude Monet's technique of separated brush strokes resembles handwriting. When he draws his handwriting strokes they fencepost across the page.

Over and over skeptics squawk that handwriting is too random and undisciplined to be measured for each individual. Both the Allport-Vernon partnership and Wolff addressed this issue. At pages 179–180 in *Diagrams* Wolff concluded that "...graphic movements...have an individual pattern which allows the layman to recognize the individual basis in different appearances." In *Studies* at page 246 they reported that "...research studies show handwriting to be a constant over time and stable to a high degree." These results should have convinced skeptics. Do we write exactly the same each time? No, of course not. For the analyses to be accurate we don't need to. Since people write *substantially* the same way each time, their handwriting is reliable and steady enough for analysis. The key is to work with a large sample so that any variations become minor glitches.

Handwriting analysis had taken some small steps for a man but still had some giant leaps to make for mankind to welcome it to social science. Nonetheless, some countries said we ain't waitin' for no validatin'. Since it had the potential to fulfill crucial roles beyond personal insights of friends and family, they wanted to utilize its potential now. To evaluate their army officers in the late 1920's the German military adopted the graphology studies of its psychologists. The University of Leipzig even added it to its psychology curriculum as an accredited subject. Soon other European schools joined the actions, bowing respect for this growing discipline. During World War II France and England each used handwriting analysis to screen soldiers for placement and ability. Handwriting analysis became part of the curriculum at graduate schools of the twelve major West German universities and at many French, Swedish, Swiss and Dutch institutions, including the prestigious Sorbonne in Paris. Germany introduced national licensing whereby a student receiving a degree in clinical psychiatry could include a concentration in graphology.

In view of the establishment's squabble with handwriting analysis, some analysts have probed to find better alternatives. In tandem with the personality focus of handwriting analysis has been the questioned or forensic document area for forgeries and their related items. Outside of that, analysts have pursued only the handwriting and personality link. Progressive thinkers have wanted to go outside personality. One possibility is the link between writing and non–personality aspects of the writer. A person who actually pursued that in earnest is graphologist Alfred Kanfer. Originally from Vienna, Austria, he fled to the U.S. from the onslaught of Hitler in the 1940's. After his sister died of cancer, his graphology training led him to seek clues for cancer in writing. In 1950's New York City he instituted his medical research to determine if cancer and handwriting strokes correlated. After matching cancer patients against their handwriting, he thought he found that a peculiar neuromuscular act degraded their strokes. Somehow a cancer-patient's neuromuscular impulses created minute tell-tale signs in their writing. The evidence was only slight and unclear to the eye. After looking at samples of cancer victims he found that even a magnifying glass wasn't enough. He needed a high-powered microscope. At first he was aided by an organization called the Handwriting Institute. Later he continued with his cancer research at his own facility, the Strang Clinic, which has attained distinction over the years. His research didn't just establish the handwriting–cancer bond. Uncannily, he was able to find evidence of cancer in the writing even *before* it became physically known to the acquirer. Unfortunately Kanfer was not able to explain why the cancer was detectable from handwriting or why it could be detected months or years (yes, years) before. He found only that the physical source for the writing sign was the nerves and muscles breaking down.

Kanfer was not just a curious dabbler in this area. Going back to Vienna over 40 years, he studied 50,000 samples of writing. He was tough on himself as a scientist. Even at the end of his life he fretted that his work was below graphodiagnostic norms. His false positives lingered at around 26%. He thought anything over 2% was unacceptable. Believing he needed better scientific accuracy, he persisted until a month from his death. His error rate had not improved. His death was from cancer. Don't you wonder if his cancer was detected from his handwriting? If so, when? We don't have the answers to these intriguing questions.

One of the goals of handwriting analysis is to be added to the psychology department of a leading university. European institutions have lived with it for years in the psychology curricula in Germany, France, Switzerland, and Holland. In the Middle-East the same with Israel's institutions. In fact, the Israeli government uses it in significant ways. (See a later chapter on this) In the United States it's a different story. Besides the community colleges and school districts with its non-credit slot along side Yoga and Wreath-Making, universities haven't welcomed it. A few decades ago Daniel Anthony, a prominent analyst from New York, convinced The New School for Social Research, a New York City accredited college, to have handwriting analysis added to the course catalog. Another instructor at this progressive urban institution (now The New School) has helped to advance the subject. Dr. Klara Roman, a Hungarian psychologist, urged them to make the handwriting analysis courses part of the curriculum. She succeeded. She also created a circular visual device called the Graphological Psychogram, which showed graphically how our traits cluster within our personality. In the 1960's she also published the *Encyclopedia of the Written Word*, and *Handwriting, Key to Personality*, and *Personality in Handwriting*, which is valued by gestaltists.

Handwriting analysis has no AMA or ABA as doctors and lawyers do. Over the last half century, advances to organize analysts have occurred. Several organizations have arisen, most of them casual groups of analysts with common interests and formal names. They convened to share ideas and promote the subject. They weren't running a particular school for teaching it nor did they have a specific school of thought. Some organizations are actual schools that began when they were called correspondence schools. They carried the stigma of cheap, easy, and not fit for man nor beast. Personnel managers trashed them and society made them butts of education jokes. That is certainly the historical tag for non-handwriting schools without ivy walls. How this applies to handwriting analysis schools depends on the institution. With the rise of education as necessary to a good income, and now a fulfilling life, correspondence schools have steadily improved in their delivery of education. Their new renown has shed much of its grime and gained a measure of respect. The internet explosion has created new kinds of correspondence schools. They've also discarded their shame by having a new name—distance learning or home study.

Every side of education has improved, including handwriting analysis, which remains a balkanized throng of groups and individuals. They haven't combined into one major organization. They have no national leader or parent organization. A few groups like the International Graphoanalysis Society claim some prestige and influence. IGAS is buttressed by its state chapters and a formal national organization, as do a few others. Attempts have been made here and there to get everyone together in an umbrella group. Conclaves have been held, attended by earnest and sensible people and groups. No unity yet. Partly it's that the groups and individuals differ on the method of handwriting evaluation. Trait schoolers battle with gestaltists. Intuitives, with little weight to throw around, try throwing it and keep missing or giving only love-taps. Facing them all at the door of approval is the brawny Bouncer of Science demanding to see some proof of ID. The poor handwriting group pulls out what appears to be a card with evidence of thousands and thousands of anecdotes from private individuals and some partial studies. Not good enough for entry.

Analysts shouldn't be surprised. This has been going on forever. They know what they need to do: Come together in an integrated group, agree on what research should be done, how to accomplish it, and how to pay for it. The International Graphoanalysis Society is a large and revered organization and has been a force in America for over three-quarters of a century. But it is only one of several groups and its trait–stroke doctrine with global factors riding shotgun conflicts with the gestaltists, the largest opposing collection of analysts. Every so often some diligent ecumenical efforts occur. Sheila Lowe of the *Idiot's Guide* had her Vanguard Conference in California that lasted a few years but disbanded recently. She attracted some of the best and brightest analysts. She has connected analysts for years with her acclaimed newsletter called The Vanguard. She also has her ongoing respected chat group online called Vanguard 2. Another online group of many common but dedicated analysts is Writefully. These chat groups draw large members of analysts from all levels of experience, education, and abilities. They share information and insights about graphology and spar civilly about the meanings of handwritings. The International Graphological Colloquium is a network of the most prominent and respected analysts in the world. Begun in 1998, they have blue-ribbon credentials and unsinkable desire. They have a website, publish some tracts, have had conclaves around the world, and plan more. They invite interested people to join them. The American Handwriting Analysis Foundation (AHAF) is also an informal association of interested graphologists that attracts many eminent practitioners and holds an annual conference.

Research to scientifically validate handwriting analysis has occurred over the years. Most of it has occurred in Europe and much of it in the 1930's and 1940's. Since then plenty of sporadic surveying has occurred there and elsewhere, including the United States. However, the studies have been limited and partial. California analyst Sheila Lowe has a bibliography of research that she has posted on her website. IGAS has published bibliographies of much of the research. IGAS had its own research department for many years, which supplemented the years of personal research of its founder, Milton Bunker. (See the separate chapter about him and IGAS) IGAS last updated its bibliography in 1994. In 1981 David Lester, a Ph.D in psychology, integrated a lot of the published research in his engaging, readable book *The Psychological Basis of Handwriting Analysis.* Mark Hopper, who founded his Phoenix, Arizona, company called Handwriting Research Corporation, reports on his website about research they have done since its founding in 1979. He also has information on available research by others. In 1992 the Beyerstein brothers, Barry and Dale, published their own volume to provide the public with the available research and with partisan commentary from advocates and skeptics, supposedly giving everyone the chance to decide between them. *The Write Stuff, Evaluations of Graphology—The Study of Handwriting Analysis (Prometheus Books, 1992)* According to the book, Barry was a psychology professor at a small college in Vancouver, British Columbia and Dale a philosophy professor at a Vancouver community college.

Arizona's Handwriting Research Corporation has issued data on the current state of handwriting analysis. About 2,200 articles, books and other materials have been published. Roughly 5,000 businesses and other groups are believed to use it for employee selection, promotions, and team-building. In the United States 20,000 certified analysts practice their profession. How many operate without any certification is a good but unfortunate question to ask. That answer they don't supply. Nor does anyone else. As for actual organizations that certify analysts, Sheila Lowe's *Idiot's Guide* lists some schools. She also lists some of the formal organizations of analysts. On the web, groups and individual analysts peddle their wares. Many handwriting analysis courses are taught throughout the United States at community colleges, community education schools, adult education schools, many of which are tied to local public schools, and continuing education schools. All appear to be non-credit courses.

A kingtutpyramid of books on the subject has been published. Many of them consist of attempts to spell out a series of trait-stroke connections and some larger global aspects to enable the layperson to do a modicum of analyzing themselves. These How-to books usually have little else of any consequence in them. As to general interest books, only two have tried to provide a good overview about the subject. One is *You Are What You Write* by Huntingdon Hartford in 1973. The other mentioned elsewhere in this volume is Sheila Lowe's *Idiot's Guide*, which is probably the most complete combination of general information and this-stroke-means-that ever written. For those interested in reviewing the wealth of books and materials, a center for them does exist in Greenfield, Massachusetts. There a private individual, Robert Backman, has informally accumulated the largest collection of books and materials about handwriting and handwriting analysis in the United States if not the world. He is curator of the Handwriting Analysis Research Library, where scholars can review but not remove the items. He is now attempting to make the information more accessible. Backman may have the largest collection of handwriting items. Mark Hopper might dispute that. He is head of Handwriting Research Corporation in Arizona and declares that his organization has the "the world's most extensive database and library on graphology."

If you are looking for a Microsoft among the competing schools of thought or the schools themselves, IGAS is arguably the leader, at least in the United States. That is hard to establish since several schools of thought have competed for prominence over the years without resolution. None has risen to serious dominance and acceptance and they each remain independent. But in assessing dominance your criteria are important. Since it began in 1929 IGAS has probably led in total analyst members certified over the years and most total members currently. To demand comparable statistics on this is asking for disappointment. No one has any to speak of and no national clearinghouse for information on the major schools exists. Cautious in its creeds, IGAS shuns revised trait meanings and dogmas without supporting research. Too many of its competitors liberally pronounce trait meanings with jello underpinnings. Also, unlike most others, it has an Ethics Code that member must swear to and follow or else they can be removed from membership and cannot call themselves a Graphoanalyst.

If you think this is worth a chuckle, stifle it for the moment. Since its inception in 1929 members have actually been removed, although none in recent years. It has loosened its once strict reins. Previously, members have been removed for different reasons, some ethics-related. Mostly it's been for heresy, meaning they instructed or at least gave too respectful an ear to outside doctrines. IGAS still takes the subject very seriously in all its activities and it expects its members to also. The Pennsylvania Chapter has discussed plenty of ideas that go beyond what IGAS has established, especially those that remain undetermined. They are tolerant about meanings and expanding them into new areas within the writing strokes. They think that is healthy. If time and research ultimately verify the connection between the new stroke and trait, it should be added to the inventory. IGAS has its approximately one hundred traits found in separate strokes. It also has its global factors, which are important but are not strokes as such. They are major aspects of writing found in every stroke, such as the slant or thickness of the strokes. Not every stroke has been linked to an individual trait. IGAS won't venture into these new strokes until they have been verified by research to be connected to a trait. This demonstrates one more reason for its appeal and should heighten credibility for outsiders in appraising it. Although IGAS is not opposed to open discussion, when it hears a member discuss an unconfirmed thought, it will politely remark that you are talking about something unproven and hope that you will recognize it as such and politely abandon it as principle. If you're going to accept a lot of unscientific guesswork, go ahead and do it. But then don't consider yourself a Graphoanalyst in good standing. Probably nothing will be done actively to pursue you for eviction from the organization, unless you make a show of it and try to publically win over others. It's a cosmic distance from the Inquisition and the strict and vengeful Catholic Church. If a better idea comes along with some research to back it up, IGAS will take a look. New leadership has taken over at IGAS since 2004 and its new President, Gregory Greco, who also owns the organization, appears to have a more liberal view for dealing with members who stray.

Milton Bunker

Milton Bunker founded the International Graphoanalysis Society in 1929 after decades of personal research validating strokes within letters of handwriting. He pursued his study of handwriting only after wondering why he could not conform his handwriting to his teacher's instructions. Ultimately he solved this mystery in a classroom of young women shorthand students.

Chapter 4

Milton Bunker
Dogged Detective, Reluctant Trailblazer

Stumbling across a mystery
ultimately solved by demure schoolgirls

Bunker observed that only a few of his shorthand students faithfully mimicked his strokes. Why would they disobey him? Early 20ᵗʰ Century budding secretaries were not mavericks.

Povser

In grade school Milton N. Bunker had a hunch something was odd about handwriting. As a penmanship student near Colby, Kansas, around the turn of the twentieth century, he dutifully copied his Palmer Method letters. Each time he drew certain strokes the same but improper way. His letters were too wide apart and the last strokes in his words expanded wildly. Since both breached the school forms, his annoyed teacher slashed her disapproval over the offending strokes. The normally obedient Bunker reacted by continuing the strokes, risking more rebukes. He got them. Scratching his head for answers, he was sure he meant no intentional disrespect. Soon he reckoned something was tugging his strokes off course. He couldn't fathom its source. For now he decided he couldn't help it. His discontent lingered unresolved during his brief schooling of only eight years. He quit and educated himself at home. When he finally left home, he pursued a career in the field that stumped him with the eerie whatdunit—handwriting.

Bunker was not heading for handwriting analysis, which in the early nineteen hundreds was seen as parlor amusement. Few practiced it and fewer tried to make money from it. The public was just discovering the new social science of psychology, which had its swarm of detractors. Handwriting analysis was barely scraping American culture. Although Bunker had heard about handwriting analysis, it was far from the front of his young mind. Handwriting itself was everywhere since typewriters and other devices to record people's words were primitive though improving. As his interest was in handwriting itself, he sought to be a great penman, who engrossed documents in beautiful handwriting. Most of the work was crafting government certificates and similar items. They were distinguished by that graceful, refined, elaborate style lost in musty and dusty places today. Bunker knew the documents were important and his employers' standards high. Bunker prided himself in engraving the documents right. As he drafted the ornate letters, he could not match his lines to the idealized style required. His mystery had recurred, arousing the same dread as in school. Again something potent was detouring his hand and he didn't know what. From his penmanship shame and now his penman's anguish came a sobering thought. Something inside us forces our hands on its own stroke path. Unable to shake this notion, he decided its logic was this: School compels a model method of writing. We copied what we saw in our writing books and on the blackboard. When we were instructed to write that way, we merely had to glance at the style and repeat it. How hard can that be? Bunker deduced that it was *not* that easy. Something mysterious, unseen, and undeniably robust was present. What it was continued to jangle his probing mind.

In the meantime, Bunker pursued other careers. He also became a teacher of shorthand, a discipline now virtually obsolete. He well knew grade-school students can vary from the copybook taught. But in the main they follow the school model. Each day high school instructors, especially those of shorthand, glimpse a lot of handwriting. Bunker saw high school students as a better laboratory for his inquiries. Time, maturity, and distance from second grade had transformed their ordered styles. Shorthand instruction demanded explicit strokes. The correct strokes matter, since their shapes represent whole words and more. The symbol strokes of shorthand were not just guidelines. They were precise, sometimes complex, and necessary. A slight difference can change the meaning to another word or words. Bunker himself insisted on the same exacting rules. Against that strictness he was thumped with demure rebellion. Only a few girls mimicked the shorthand strokes faithfully. This stirred memories of *his* vexing insolence with his penmanship teacher and penman employers. His students now disobeyed him and he was baffled again with no culprit in sight. Unintentional acts, he was sure, just as his were. These starch-collared young ladies had no reason to cross him. In the early twentieth century budding secretaries weren't mavericks. Yet he had flouted his teacher; he knew he wasn't a rebel either; neither he nor his students could help it; and he still didn't know why.

Facing these contrary strokes each school day, in time Bunker's shorthand classes ahHAed him to a watershed conclusion. When we write on paper, we all roam in our own way as individuals. A few students did not stray very far, he recognized. Their writing was meticulous, careful and close to copybook. Years of observation now convinced him that students' writing strokes matched their deeds as individuals. Those with precise and cautious strokes generally behaved that way. They followed instructions and tried to do their best. Conversely, those whose strokes wandered were less likely to obey orders and their work ethic slipped. In fact, he found them unconventional and independent. Their rampant writing was tracking their uncaged personalities.

With the comfort of his discovery Bunker was inspired to explore his insights. He had found some other links between the students' writing and their personal qualities. In 1910 he bought his first book on handwriting analysis. Its contents buttressed his conclusions. However, he was disturbed that no scientific studies were cited for the technique. This spurred him to investigate and fill that vacuum. To do it right he knew he would need a stocky ledger book, ample time, and margaretmead-thomasedison patience. After a spell he noted certain strokes in students related to specific attributes. When he saw a pattern develop that tied a stroke to a definite trait, he recorded it. These correlations soon multiplied to a portly catalog of stroke-traits. Since he found that specific traits connected to specific strokes, this confirmed what he had long inferred. Through their separate strokes, students were displaying their unique personalities on paper. When he reflected on his own encounters, he realized his were similar.

He was now primed to take his work to loftier heights. From 1910 to 1928 he tested each sign against each trait and allegedly was satisfied with the link only after confirming it (yes, you will be reading this correctly) at least a thousand times. He claims to have handled around (same with this) a half million samples of writing. Bunker submerged himself in handwriting analysis, never losing interest in the issues he studied. He wasn't trying to bend to science's demands for accepting handwriting analysis. He didn't care. His efforts thrust him toward his private goal—to satisfy himself why he and his students had drawn those wayward strokes under teacher's glare. Whatever else this begat were jimmies on his ice cream.

Bunker had other jobs that aided him in his quest. For a while he was also a magazine writer. Later he became a corresponding editor of a family magazine. People wrote to him about various topics. Since most letters then were handwritten, he had many specimens to evaluate. He refined his method by starting with the writing slant. His purpose remained the same, supplying answers to himself, not convincing the authorities or the public. Despite having discovered why alien strokes had landed in his writing, he was not content. Other questions would invade his bubbly mind. At times the fizz was enough to corkpop him out his door to explore. When he found puzzling strokes, he refused to stay within the writing. In a time before the car took over our lives, he left home and traveled vast distances by bus or train to seek the writers themselves. On occasion the personal visit wasn't enough. He tracked down people who knew the writer and cross-examined them. He then determined if the trait fit the individual.

He was especially upset if one of his trait-stroke bonds didn't match. Sometimes, instead of rejecting his judgment, he decided the trait existed but a sturdier one had overwhelmed it. Bunker discerned that traits are neither born equal nor become equal. That would later become a core belief of his Graphoanalysis. Traits don't just loiter in your personality either. They're doh-see-dohing and sometimes step into each other. A beefy trait dominates a puny one, which strains for notice. Some traits are reinforced by others. A resentful person will be more bitter if he is also heedless and hasty. Some traits curb others. Hence, if he's got an unruffled temperament, that resentment has a choker collar. Bunker knew this interplay was not novel to psychology. But he made sure analysts applied it in their handwriting analysis evaluations.

If you consider Bunker's exploits, you realize he was conducting experiments in handwriting analysis. By what he noted of his students' writing he reached conclusions based on the results of his data. Although he would not really comprehend it until later, his informal surveys had the patina of scientific legitimacy. He documented thousands of samples. He got confirmation of traits from the writer or those who knew him. Most of the writing he reviewed was of awshuckscan'tcomplaindownhome people in their daily affairs. Bunker's samples had an innocence since few knew they were posing for their personality's snap shot. Even more people did not understand the astonishing power of this unfamiliar technique.

The painstaking work, his objective scheme, his thorough work, his sincere approach, and the decades of travel and travail. Throw in his bull's-eye results. He once judged his stroke and trait findings as 95% accurate. These were his legacy. He was an able amateur never trying to go pro. Good scientific work doesn't require dwelling in a laboratory or wearing a white coat. Grant him his tribute now betterlatethannever: His thousands of informal anecdotes should earn the esteem of one grand formal study.

Bunker's eventual conclusions were bred from his early grade school. They also came from the inventor's lucky moment—serendipity. He discovered a major breakthrough by accident. When his strokes roved in grade school, Bunker wasn't looking, yet he couldn't help noticing. For an agonizing time he didn't know what they meant. When they re-appeared in strokes as a penman, then as a shorthand instructor, he bloodhounded the intriguing insights. Time, squinty observation, and bulky notebooks finally shone the klieg light of discovery. He found that strokes disclose traits and that each person's writing is different from their unique personalities. The prolonged mystery had been solved. As in *Murder on the Orient Express*, the villain was identified—it was everyone. But, wait. One more twist. Actually we are all innocent. The guilty one is our locomotive personalities. We are only acting under their benign sway as our pens choochoo across the page.

Bunker established other tenets Graphoanalysts still clutch as gospel. Letters don't matter as much as strokes within the letters, like the t-bar on a t. How long, how thick, how high and how straight it was—each discloses separate personal qualities. No trait is good or bad per se; it's how the person uses it. Although we all have attributes, they are only *potential* ways of acting. We admire a person who is soft and compromising. They live to serve others. They risk being human doormats or pin cushions. They can learn not to be used by others and to serve with limits. They spend their lives saying yes. They can learn it's possible to survive by sometimes saying no.

In 1929 with his years of research accomplished, Bunker launched a school of handwriting analysis now known as the International Graphoanalysis Society (IGAS). Although Bunker did not create handwriting analysis, on its wobbly foundation he built an organization that became the largest and most respected in the world. One of its hallmarks has been a conservative philosophy. It won't make statements about any stroke and its meaning unless satisfied it's correct. It has performed several studies on handwriting analysis, unlike most other organizations, which merely adopt what has been learned before. Some handwriting analysis organizations were unreflective and hopelessly intuitive. They held suspect rules of construing strokes. Where they would derive some of their stroke-trait links was known only but to God and them. These undisciplined groups gouged unsightly potholes on the road to acceptance for handwriting analysis in general and IGAS in particular. Many just embarrassed themselves and other analysts with daft decrees about what a particular stroke means. With its own steady and responsible ways, IGAS has tried diligently to overcome their damage to all analysts.

Proudly, IGAS also has had an Ethics Code, which it has enforced with a strong hand. Occasionally members have been removed for violating its preachings by, for example, permitting non-IGAS ideology at IGAS Chapter meetings. It takes its hard-earned doctrines seriously. Besides its Certification program, IGAS has conducted a Masters Degree program, an annual International Congress, and an Institute for Advanced Study. No other organization dedicated to handwriting analysis has all of those features. It has attained world stature through its undiminished professionalism. Since it was one of the few schools for years and has existed since 1929, it has certified more analysts than any other school in the world.

When Bunker began his studies he wasn't rushing to prove any-thing and wasn't trying to be a trailblazer for handwriting analysis. He developed his Graphoanalysis principles like red wine, fermented from the plodding serenity of years. If you give him his proper due, he was scientific enough for a man trawling in social, not physical, science. Regrettably, Bunker didn't submit his findings to the authorities for scientific justice. Graphoanalysts after Bunker yearning for endorsement from the psychology authorities want to know why. It might have catapulted Graphoanalysis toward approval. An inquiry at IGAS about his documented results leaves you with the dismaying answer. Despite his otherwise careful studies, his research was poorly preserved. Little survives for study, and Bunker wasn't careless. Why his treasured research doesn't rest in a solid file cabinet he explained in a 1955 letter: "Much of this data went down the drain many years ago because I was not setting out to prove something to someone else. I was setting out to get my own individual answers. I got them." You excuse him for discarding his decades of studies. He was frank that he pursued it only when he failed to follow his grade-school handwriting model.

When Bunker first learned of handwriting analysis, it was a faint, derided subject. From his efforts and others' in early twentieth century America, it crept into our culture and our curious minds. In his own way he helped enhance its image to greater acclaim. Many bright but unconvinced people now saw that it wasn't just a subject that *might* have something to it. He showed that there *was* something to it.

This photo of Allan Grim from 1993 was featured on the front page of his local daily newspaper The (Doylestown) Daily Intelligencer. Grim had just completed his IGAS studies. He is demonstrating the individual strokes and their relation to personality traits.

Chapter 5

Pedagogue

A Feast Aspiring to be an Orgy

In his class Grim brings up Einstein, Time's Man of the 20th Century. When asked the most important thing in life, he answered, "Relationships." Gadzooks. Albert, we never knew. "He is even more like us," says Grim. "He knew about handwriting analysis and was a believer." More Gadzooks.

Povser

Anyone who says they don't like it is lying.

Michael Flatley, about his Lord of the Dance step-dancing show, quoted in class by Allan Grim as applying equally to handwriting analysis

He strides into the classroom, plops his box of materials on the teacher's desk and, after removing them from the box, flips it sideways as a crude lectern. He opens his notebook, looks out at the assembled students, and, begins: "My name is Allan Grim. I used to have two professions. Now I have only one. I was an attorney for over thirty years. Now I am retired from that profession. I have been a handwriting analyst for several years and now that is my only profession."

His current occupation a profession? Yes, he means it. Knowing they must wonder how it qualifies, he explains:

Handwriting analysis is legitimate, should be taken seriously, can tell you intimate and important qualities about people. Be careful in applying it because you can do great harm to people who may be struggling with their lives. Its purpose is to acquaint people with their real selves, not expose their weaknesses. Helping people to understand themselves and others makes it a noble service to society. Since it has yet to be completely accepted, you have a duty to represent it well and to help in enhancing its stature.

As Grim speaks their bodies stiffen, lips part, and eyes widen. If the students rejoiced they were in Oz, now they feel they've been duped back into Kansas. Grim reminds them they have signed up for adult education. In his case he calls it their "fantasy college class." No homework, tests, final exam, pop quizzes or rambling-scrambling term papers. Oh, and they can keep their hands down and their mouths shut. It won't cost them since grades aren't given either. Wait a minute. He takes roll but attendance isn't compulsory. He says he must report it to the school. Okay, no report cards and no need to show up either. Big academic deal. What's left? Taking notes. Just like in college, they're up to the student. Still, Grim finger-wags a message:

"Since we have only four weeks and a lot to cover, very little of what I say will be unimportant. We won't have a textbook. So notes will be especially vital. If you want to retain what I will give you, I urge you to take notes. But I won't be checking and since I don't give grades, the information is solely for your benefit. And now the big difference between your college classes and mine[here Grim pauses]—in here you will actually *learn* something."

Sounds (let's get this over early) grim. Some students have signed up for four weeks of fluffernutter fun gawking at everyone else's writing, laughing at their foibles and saluting their talents. The instructor offers some pleasant and harmless insights about each of the writings, and they pour over signatures of Marilyn Monroe and Terrill Owens. Not exactly. Nor bulky lectures of dense concepts either. A few will squirm in their hard seats and ponder if they will sit still for this throwback pedagogue. Everyone recalls their school days when they endured a stern teacher, humorless, uncaring, unforgiving and demanding. If that's their immediate image, the reality is something else. Yes, Grim is serious. But an ogre? No. After a few minutes the students relax seeing he is not an academic terrorist. Grim's cold start thaws into a palpable delight for this peculiar subject. It saturates his instruction. He wants to implant a solid foundation of handwriting analysis with surgery not just endurable but enjoyable. He tries to convey that handwriting is not just roving lines filling up paper. Those strokes are drawn by a heart-pumping human being, whose writing is like no one else's. Within those unique strokes prowls an individual whose personal attributes can be detected by their look. That will take some convincing but the class seems willing to believe it and Grim seems up to making them believe it.

After his opening spiel, Grim hands out some blank sheets of paper and a separate paper with a typed passage. He tells them to copy it in their customary style of writing and add their signature. It seems like a random anecdote. Actually it's a long paragraph containing an abundance of letters and strokes full of meaning to analysts. The students guess Grim will analyze each sample of writing and discuss them in the class. Or maybe even force them all to ask for forgiveness. Why? For ditching what they were taught in grade school? Maybe he will make them resurrect their old school model. Someone brave enough occasionally will ask if he will do just what they're thinking. No analyzing or resurrecting, he declares. A few are actually disappointed. Usually the ones with the self-confidence and few hang-ups. Or maybe just the thickest skin. This will not be the only time he will perplex them with his approach to handwriting analysis.

Before Grim has explained the purpose of the samples, a student blurts outloud, "Do you get our writing so you can tell which one of us is a serial killer?"

"Yeah, and sometimes it's downright scary what you people reveal," he lobs back to them with a smirk, rousing a tense snicker among the students. "No, that's not my purpose," he corrects after an anxious pause, lapsing back into solemnity. "I want an idea of your personalities to help me teach the course."

In addition, he will compare the strokes against what he learns about them during the four weeks. Grim will gauge if his analysis confirms what he learns from observing them. All this sets up one more informal experiment on the accuracy of handwriting analysis.

He sets a time limit of two-and-a-half minutes to finish copying. That's to offset the schemers. Some would take too long and that must be curtailed. If he allows liberal time the crafty students will write carefully and unnaturally to inflate stellar qualities.

Some students will grumble that his short time span stresses them. "Won't that throw off our strokes?"

"It will but not much," he replies. "Not enough to prevent a good sample for analysis."

"Won't copying the passage slow our styles too?" asks another.

"Yeah, it does somewhat," he says. "Again it's not enough to matter." All in all he believes his time limit strikes a balance between false strokes from a slow-down, and rushed strokes from a speed-up.

A few don't finish in the allotted time. Sheepishly they hand in their paper certain they will be flogged for their sin. They won't be. If they don't finish the sample or their strokes speak ill of them, they can still rest easy. Grim will not embarrass anyone in front of their classmates despite their frailties leaping from the paper into the lap of his almighty judgment.

After skimming through the collected samples, he announces, "I guess you will be relieved that, yes, you all deserve to live."

More uneasy chuckles from virgin scholars not knowing his aim. Some are disappointed he won't tell them what he sees in their writing. When a few brash ones clamor for an instant analysis, he explains his reluctance. He must tell the truth. So why is that an issue? Since he has already said he won't embarrass anyone and barely knows them anyway, none will be brave enough to decline a public analysis. If they did decline, they are sure their classmates will see that as hiding drawbacks. Some with beachball egos may say, go ahead, let me have it, eager for a hearty slap on their obliging backs.

"They don't realize how exposed they can be," is his answer. Maybe their proud qualities will emerge but they tend to ignore their faults, which also elbow for attention. "Besides," he adds, "telling them about their writing before they know strokes and traits puts the rickshaw before the chinaman."

At the moment they're too green to appreciate the connections. Although he keeps it from these novices, he observes this plum about analyzing their strokes: "Like sex, it's better if you help. It's even better when you know what you're helping." Anyway, he hopes in time they can analyze their own writing.

The balance of the class he serves a feast aspiring to be an orgy for the students' dazed eyes and ears: anecdotes, humor, maxims, quotes, and famous as well as infamous people. The entrée is handwriting marinated in strokes awaiting linkage to interesting traits. A minute or two won't pass before Grim quotes Hall of Fame thinkers, like Aristotle and Confucius (both advocates of handwriting analysis) and Hall of Infamers, like Michael Flatley, the cocky Irish Step Dancer, who said that anyone who said they didn't like his *Lord of the Dance* program was lying. Grim borrows that line to apply to handwriting analysis, giving Flatley dubious credit for saying it. It seems to go over without arrogance.

Between those are stirring anecdotes, such as the woman doctor who tried a dating service and got 80 letters from guys wanting to date her. Guess where she took the letters? He explains how the bewildered analyst slogged through them to find those worthy to woo her. Or Grim will post on the screen writing of Tim McVeigh, the Oklahoma City bomber. He backslanted his writing, which Grim says is a person who locksdown his feelings. When pressured they kabloom out. Or the writing of Henry Hawksworth, a multiple personality with five personas. Grim shows samples of his writing in each persona. They are different. He even cites the deaf lady Heather Whitestone, but doesn't show her writing. He illustrates her as someone stifled early on. Her doctors had told her she would never get out of the Third Grade. "Obviously she wasn't listening," utters Grim, beaming as he reads from an ad in *Time* with a photo of her hand-signing love to the audience as she did a three-point strut on the runway at Atlantic City as Miss America 1995. She was lucky. She overcame her misfortune. Grim's lesson is that young people's handwriting should be analyzed for their precious qualities. Often cocooned and undiscovered because of clueless parents, teachers, counselors, and doctors, they lie dormant. The writing will release the qualities and allow the child to butterfly.

With his zest for handwriting analysis Grim seems intent on injecting all his wisdom into the students' mushy heads. Not a good idea. He's got only eight hours of class time over four weeks. "The subject has so many interesting aspects. It's hard figuring out which to delete," he regrets. Each session seems like a marathon. No coasting or time-outs, it's a constant jog to the finish line at nine pm. To make sure every jujube of information gets heard, he takes no breaks during the two-hour class time. Grim reports that few have left the room during his fourteen years, except for a rare trip to you-know-where. How many others would have gone but held it in so they wouldn't miss a quip?

As Grim's instruction mounts a full-court press, the students try gallantly to take notes. An adult "continuing education" course is supposed to be a pleasant diversion. Experts say give them only light, chewable fare. Grim seems to be trying to stuff them with those godzilla oatbran muffins. Despite the Indy 500 pace, Grim's Pennsylvanialotterypingpongballsonair mind won't let the content flag.

He exclaims, "I may be boring but handwriting analysis is not."

He is half right. Unlike olde school daze, no one nods off or gazes out the window or checks their watch, or taps their shoes, or pines to be elsewhere. Maybe that's because there's no time. His delivery accentuates his frantic exuberance. Grim tries to keep it slow and deliberate but too often slips. His words will quicken and go choppy, jailbreaking his mouth, knocking each other over on their way to the students' ears. By the end of the first class the students should be exhausted. They don't look it. Grim's zeal for this esoteric subject fills the classroom. Mostly on the jaded side of thirty, they seem energized by a subject they know has been woodpeckered by scorn. Like sex, when they sense he is turned on, they are too.

"It doesn't take much to wow people when you get into this subject," Grim volunteers. "Handwriting is about everyone and by everyone. They are dying to know how it applies to them."

Nevertheless, his verve incites him to emboss his presentation. "I don't assume I can just move my mouth for two hours and go home. I take it seriously and feel a need to add more to the lessons. I'm never sure they're getting what some of the concepts are about and I want to make them comprehend the ideas and feel good about their experience."

Grim enjoys pitching questions and not just nerfballs either. Faces will scrunch and foreheads will furrow. In school you hid from teacher's questions unless you really knew the answer. Here Grim won't startle anyone whose hands are resting. Students are here by choice. What can you tell about a person who is 38 years old and still writes as he did in grade school? What are the chances two people have the same writing style? How would you make your signature forgery-proof? When he gets to a segment on the writing of potential partners he invokes Einstein. Yeah, that Einstein. Why him, a man of physical science, and *Time's* "Man of the 20th Century," when the subject is hooking up? He was asked, "What is the most important thing in life" His answer: "Relationships." Gadzooks, Albert. We never knew.

"He's even more like us than that," says Grim. "He knew about handwriting analysis and was a believer." More Gadzooks.

Grim wants them to think, stretch their minds, and look at handwriting a new way. Most students may be tired, coming off a full day at work. They willingly signed up for this course. If they don't like it, they know they can leave. They seem to want to ask questions but also seem too busy ducking to interrupt Grim's verbal machine gun. At 9 o'clock, after two straight hours of Grim, Barnum and Bailey, he's drained, hoarse, and savors a soft chair to ploomp into. Instead he pulls from his materials a single piece of paper and starts reading. It's a story about a dog and a baby and a prince from thirteenth-century Wales. What is this at this late hour, they all wonder? Grim says it will take only a half-minute, so hold on. It goes something like this: The prince has just returned from the hunt and finds his infant son missing and his crib bathed in blood. Nearby he also finds his dog. Its mouth is bloody too. He grabs his knife and stabs the dog. As it lies dying it yelps and, strangely, another sound comes from beneath the baby's blankets. The dog's cries had awakened his baby still very much alive and now wailing himself. The prince looks around and finally underneath the crib he finds something else. It's a dead wolf. Its throat has been torn out.

The classroom throbs with silence and throat-aching recoil. Grim waits a moment for their unease to settle before resuming. "What you are now feeling is emotion, which is at the base of our personalities. If you don't acknowledge that, then you don't understand personality," he finger-jabs at them.

Emotion resides in two major portions of handwriting, slant and thickness. He will talk about both next week. The prince's tale is also about the volatile person, whose writing he will show them too. He throws out a statistic he heard on Dr. Phil: One of four teen-age girls is in a violent relationship. If they can learn to detect it in the abuser's writing, a girl wanting to date him can be warned. Handwriting analysis helps to prevent bad marriages, or even save lives, Grim declares. Finally, Grim says the class is over and he will see them next week.

No one leaves.

He is done with them but what's this?

"Can you analyze printing?"

"What does it mean when people print?"

"Why do doctors have such bad writing?"

A withering but weatherable counter-attack. Grim isn't surprised and secretly smiles. Since the subjects are the intriguing and the unfamiliar, the offspring is a litter of prying students demanding to be fed answers. Years in the classroom warn him the questions can be endless. Rather than point to the clock, he gladly responds with answers to most of them. Others he defers till later classes when he will cover the topic anyway. At 9:20 pm he calls a halt. Looking letdown but resigned to its end, the students wander from the class. They may feel like they just got off the Tilt-A-Whirl. Still, dhey *vill* be baach.

Does anyone rise up and challenge him and his cherished subject? In Grim's classes don't expect fireworks set off by raging skeptics disguised as students. Students are usually too innocent, polite or intimidated to grill their instructor or his subject. All they want is answers to their questions. Virtually everyone who takes Grim's course believes in handwriting analysis. Or they at least want to believe in it. "It's unlikely they would sign up at all if they were so unconvinced," Grim offers. No one has ever appeared in class and disputed graphology's firmness directly with Grim. So he says. Maybe they wanted to but dropped their weapon after observing his own doubt of its doctrines. Despite his peppers-and-salsa staging, they realize he isn't just a shabby shill for graphology. Grim awaits the day for a serious row in class and wonders why none has ever arrived. Although a few students seemed skeptical in their questions or comments, Grim says they "retreated" once he "educated" them on their point.

How much does Grim give them in four two-hour classes with no textbook? More than IGAS wants them to know. It would prefer that Grim and others teach their seminar called Basic Eights. That superficially swipes different areas of handwriting analysis and provides no basic foundation or background. No one would feel qualified to analyze after taking their eight-week course. IGAS admits that. Its purpose is to give the public some idea how Graphoanalysis operates. The eight-hour course illustrates a few strokes from different areas of Graphoanalysis and explains how they relate to someone's personality. If the individual still is interested in learning about the subject in depth, the next step is their General Course you become certified to practice it. Grim's course is somewhere between the two. To be sure many people have not taken the General Course or have taken another one that just doesn't measure up, according to Grim and others. How good the other courses are varies. That's all Grim can say as he has only passing knowledge of them. From what he has seen, he still prefers IGAS and the contest isn't even close. The one he has examined the most is the one of Erika Karohs from California. She has PhD credentials and a set of impressive documents. They include detailed trait descriptions and suggested ways of presenting handwriting analysis reports. She enlightens on just about every area, even the practical steps in building up your practice. That includes marketing on the internet, contracting for lectures, and getting paid for your services. Her bulky pile of items is well-written, serious, empathetic and realistic. For aspiring and veteran analysts, her ears are always cupped and her hand extended.

———

When he began teaching in 1994 Grim soon faced a pleasant nuisance. Sometimes it started before the class sessions concluded. While teaching at night and working as an attorney by day, Grim would get calls at work from students after the first class, moaning that they can't wait until the next class. He confesses what the topic does to him. "I am as enthusiastic about this topic today as I was when I began studying it many years ago," he boasts to his students in the first class. "People might see me as far gone into it. That's overboard. I'm passionate but not addicted."

We flash that try-again stare. "Okay, I'm a junkie and I refuse to go into rehab," he offers with tongue in cheek. When he says it, though, his tongue seems to clamor to exit his cheek.

Maybe he is serious. If Grim's fascination for it is closer to obsession, his perspective on it seems more balanced. He cautions his students, "Don't take my word for how great and valid it is. Go out and learn it and apply it yourself and you will see it validate itself for you."

That's refreshing to hear from someone clinging to a subject with dubious footing. Grim knows a vocal few of his colleagues would rather he just shut up about his pangs and keep analyzing. "That's too bad. They should get real and accept its limitations." He is courageous to profess how strong he feels about it and to suggest others evaluate it on their own. His candor tallies points with skeptics but won't dissolve their nagging doubt. As long as science hasn't confirmed its empirical soundness, skeptics will blitz it whenever they can.

Grim yearns for his students to be more than just four-and-out handwriting analysts, taking his course, then leaving the subject behind forever. At minimum, he hopes they become amateur analysts by buying and studying the focal graphology books, hopefully those from the International Graphoanalysis Society (IGAS). Many do because they know they can apply their learning to handwriting they see for the rest of their lives. Typically they will use it to help family members evaluate boyfriends and girlfriends, and gain insight on bosses at work and other people they must face on the job or in an outside organization. He considers his course a strong foundation to whatever path they travel. If they take the IGAS course and become certified Graphoanalysts, even better. A portion of his students have gone from his introductory course to the IGAS General Course. He prefers they get certified instead of remaining an amateur. Trying to learn the subject on their own without some formal feedback on their progress makes them dangerous to people they should be helping.

If you mis-interpret a key quality in someone's makeup, you can scar them and send them spiraling with hurt down the wrong path. "It's amazing how seriously people take our comments," Grim observes.

"Well, should they?" I want to know.

"Yes, of course. But we are not psychologists or counselors. We somehow get that kind of respect.

They may not hang on our every word but their ears are turned toward us. And they seem to open up more when they know we have some intimate familiarity with their often private fears and inadequacies."

If they choose to become a full-fledged analyst, anyone from his course will breeze through the General Course, Grim is sure. Why he is so certain after a total of eight hours in his class? At minimum he thinks he gives them a solid foundation on the subject, tries to disabuse them of all the major myths, and instills the underlying principles. At the same time he gives them the personality traits they are all craving to know when they first came into his classroom. Everyone wants to know what this little squiggle or that massive hook means. He tenders them plenty but not all of them, partly because of time. Besides, Grim would rather they found the rest on their own time.

"And no textbook to study and hold on to?" I ask.

"A packed shelf of books stands with all the strokes and their traits in them. Most disappoint in some way," he says without explanation.

They are all important for an analyst to know and understand. They are not important to know completely by the end of his course. A working knowledge of some of them and familiarity with the concepts suffices. A student can buy and read a book with all the strokes in it. As too many loops and lines exist, they won't remember them all. That's okay. They have the book at their side whenever they analyze and that is good enough. In time a practiced analyst will digest and retain all the strokes. Since imperfect memory afflicts even veterans, they will return to the books for help.

We wonder, "Does it happen much?"

"It happens a lot. No analyst needs to be a trivia expert in handwriting. He should know what each trait means and what each stroke looks like."

"For over a hundred traits?"

"Sure. The key is knowing they are there and knowing where to look them up."

He thinks opening his books should be an ohTHAT'Sright NOWIremember review, not a fresh lesson.

Grim worries that his students' learning is shallow and the public is at risk. He concludes his sessions by telling his students, "You are not fully competent to analyze handwriting. Maybe you have reached the equivalent of intern in the medical field. But you are not ready to diagnose a patient, much less treat them, and don't even think about surgery." To operate would be our equivalent of preparing a comprehensive handwriting analysis. Maybe it's inapt. The doctor has some medical experts around him, including nurses and anesthetists for assistance. You have no one besides your books and materials, which doctors also have handy. You can consult with other analysts. Doctors don't have to leave the hospital or maybe their own office. Plenty of help is close

by. Be careful and get your MD, which for us is your CGA, Certified
Graphoanalyst diploma.

After the initial class Grim tries to ensure they will come back
for the next. Not that he needs to. He tries to portray it as lick-
chopping, hand-rubbing irresistible. No, he doesn't say, "Stay tuned
for scenes from our next episode" or "You don't want to miss next week
because…." But close.

He will hurl a stirring anecdote or other enticing item, like telling
them next week, "I'll show you how to find the honest man just by
looking at handwriting." Although this may seem as puffing, he won't
be far off the mark. Grim says what he is really looking for is not so
much the honest man (the Greeks are still searching too) as people of
good character. In his lessons he discusses how integrity can be found
in handwriting. No, it's not simply found in one particular stroke. You
must scan a cluster of them.

I must ask that naive student query we know he's heard many times
before. "Can you tell if someone is lying from their handwriting?"

"You cannot tell from handwriting whether a person will lie or not,"
he readily admits. "Honesty is only part of integrity," he instructs.

This is not surprising. If he said you can, *that* would be surprising.
It would also lower his regard among serious skeptics and their
psychologist counterparts. And well it should. Unfortunately some
other analysts may not be so frank about it. Blithely they will tell you
they can detect if a person is honest.

Grim says that is extreme. "No one can predict honesty in any one
situation."

Since he has said handwriting will reveal the overall character of
the writer, you may think that is remarkable. Grim says, "No. What
analysts do is no different from what you can tell after knowing
someone and observing them over many years"

"What is that supposed to mean?"

"If you've been married for 20 years and as situation comes up
where you ask your spouse a critical question. Is the answer a lie? You
don't know except in a general way that it may be or may not be, based
on your experience with them and the situation itself. You actually
evaluate its truth from your sense of trust with that spouse built up
over years. That's integrity within the marriage. Its foundation is time
plus observation plus interaction."

"How is this captured in handwriting?"

"All the experiences of the past building this writer's character are reflected in the entirety of the strokes. It's a summary report in writing saying 'this is my character.' What's special about handwriting in revealing character is that, although the writer is the one telling you his character, he doesn't lie about it since he doesn't even know what he is telling you about his character. The analyst doesn't have to spend the twenty years with the person like that spouse to get a good idea of the writer's integrity. It's all laid out in the strokes as a kind of profile report where the person who compiled it lived with the writer for years and sat down and wrote up their conclusions about them."

"So what can we tell about the person from their writing?"

"All we can sift from the writing is our best guess on how they will treat their fellow man in general in the workplace, in a marriage, and in the community."

"How good a guess is that?"

"It's probably somewhat better than a weather report."

"As of what day?"

"The day before—using Accu-Weather of course. They used to say weathermen were accurate at about 86%. Today may be better. It depends on how far in advance you're predicting. We are talking human beings here and social science, not physical science. Actually weather is physical science but it demonstrates that a lot of variables can affect weather. Just like our behavior. Give us some slack, please.

Chapter 6

The Loyal Skeptic

Grim speaks his mind about graphology and personality, and then really opens up about his own personality, and finally, lets us know the most important thing in life

Most students seem persuaded of graphology's validity after the first class. Not that they should be. Grim hardly has the watertight answers to the tidal-wave questions that have drenched his subject. Handwriting analysis has far to go before psychology will allow it on its swaying oil rig. Grim makes a good case for it in his opening class. With zealots such as Grim, and wordsmiths like Yogi Berra to lead the way, analysts seek the light at the end of the rainbow. Grim eagerly accepts the role as one of the promoters and defenders of the faith. He fervently lobbies for its due niche among other psychological techniques such as the Rohrschach Inkblot Test, Draw-a-Picture Test, and others.

I am curious but not yellow. So I ask, "Where do you put it among them?"

"No," he corrects. "not *among* them. I think it should be rated *higher* than those so-called established tests." Within psychology they all take their BB shots for their obvious defects. The best known of all, the Rohrschach, has been studied extensively for decades. Around 3000 treatises and studies have appraised it like a savanna full of lions on a wildebeest. Many experts would discard it as only spilled ink needing a hint from Héloise. Personality itself is an elusive notion. Trying to determine it from someone's view of hazy inkblots is futile, goes one of the prime objections. All the psychology tests and techniques seem to stumble along with varied acceptance, surviving by default. Nothing superior has come along. Or, as a dedicated man of science would better phrase it, a technique valid and reliable, the twin mantras of science, must emerge to supplant them. That is a mixed consolation to analysts. They grumble that they shouldn't be singled out for criticism from the other techniques since *they* aren't so great either. On the other hand, they're all in the same boat and it leaks.

Grim and his colleagues abide the disquieting questions because they get them wherever they go. How can you analyze writing that changes all the time? I use a style I took from someone I admired. How can you analyze that? How can you analyze my writing if I print? How can you analyze a signature that's illegible? This subject breeds stalkers who won't yield to politeness. They seem to surface at every occasion, a party, a speech, a casual lunch, or a barroom. Handwriting analysis typically enjoys respect at civic organizations. The analyst is a guest and working for free or a mere honorarium. You don't bite the hand that is feeding you interesting insights about your writing. The subject triggers a rash of questions commonly snarl-free. Truth be told, Grim would like to encounter more doubters and critics. They are the thinkers and analyzers. For 30 years he confronted them often in his law career. "If someone doesn't naturally question it, they haven't spent much time thinking about it. But since we all write, we must ponder things about it silently for years," Grim states.

Grim accepts his IGAS doctrines but with hesitation and question. He claims to re-assess the challenges they present. Many exist and most await definitive answers. On occasion in class he will discuss a stroke and its corresponding trait, then reflect if it bears out in his experience. To be certain he has to know the individuals well. The "generosity" trait, for example, validates every time, he has found. Writers with it always seem to be genuinely decent and good-hearted. He also ponders larger issues. Grim wonders why the "stubborn" stroke equates to its trait of "stubbornness." And how is it that, young or old, East or West, black or white, whoever draws the stroke the same way, it means the same for everyone? Those are a hard swallow for him. The overriding factor is that they work for him and his colleagues.

"Do you accept it all in general?" we demand.

"Well, not blindly. I constantly examine each of the principles, especially the particular trait-stroke ties. I've had my eyes open and all the while I've kept the faith of its legitimacy."

"How convinced are you compared to when you started?"

"The more I study it, the more I'm convinced it's bonafide. That's why I'm still into it, and my conviction strengthens with each encounter."

Countless times Grim has faced the doubters. He exudes a well-earned loyalty for a tenuous subject still struggling with its self-esteem. Skeptics may lambaste the subject, knowing science is on their side. When Grim is present, they're asking for trouble. With thirty years of legal experience and a handwriting analysis background wide and deep, any contest he faces is unfair.

"Most people don't give enough effort, primarily from ignorance," he observes. He understands that and tries to ease up, lapsing into teaching mode rather than dukes-up combat. It's too bad because the ultimate burden of proof about its validity falls on Grim and his fellow advocates. Somehow he seems to make the doubter distrust himself. When people know he is an active skeptic himself, the debate becomes more of a discussion.

"I relish a jab from a doubter. What they do is what I have been doing all along. Make it stand up and take a hit. For me it's still standing."

Somebody wise said nothing great was ever done without enthusiasm. Grim doesn't know if what he does is great but he does confess to his enthusiasm for this arcane topic. This is a catalyst for people to take it seriously, or at least listen to his message. Experts on salesmanship emphasize that an avid spokesman for a product or service can excite minds as much as its quality. Grim has always been energetic. You can also see passion in his support and defense of his subject. When Grim first applied for membership in the Society to begin his studies, they asked him what he deemed his three biggest qualities. He replied: energy, curiosity, and impatience. Students will say it's obvious he revels in it. That stimulates them to appreciate it, you can tell. They also say that his emotion about it makes it easier to accept. Although professing their skepticism, most people seem to think there is something to it.

Grim insists on speaking of its appeal. "Because it uncannily reveals many private qualities, it has an immediate draw to people." Grim sees himself as just a volunteer messenger for it. "It virtually sells itself with its native charm. People want to believe in it."

Since its dubious past demands an image revision, it can use allies like the loyal skeptic Grim. When the spokesmen are informed and fervent about a controversial subject, skeptics seem to allow it a chance for redemption.

———

Grim currently teaches at several adult evening schools. He is lucky since every school district in his locale has these "continuing education" classes. Americans are discovering the quaint concept of learning after formal education. It's not just school districts that are providing the life-long learning. A bonus for Grim has been to teach at three local community colleges. They are becoming monsters of the higher education midway. Cheap and focused on employment skills, they also have entered the non-credit arena with courses that are sometimes more life-style than life-work. Subjects with questionable relevance and credibility have sneaked into the curricula of these non-traditional schools. Astrology, tarot cards, tai chi and the other mystical diversions are now getting a new life on their fishy beliefs. With these inroads into public academia, Grim forecasts a greater future for all these subjects. If the drum rolls long enough for handwriting analysis, Grim is convinced the public will inevitably endorse his subject. This can be boosted by businesses, schools, police and other high-profile groups increasing its use. When an employer hires several workers after thumbs-up ratings from analysts, and the workers confirm their worth by acting as projected, the good word gets out and around. Thus, the public may accept it before science does by effectively helping people and organizations in the everyday world. The public will be ahead of the curve with science lagging behind until the groundswell of support compels colleges to accept it for formal credit. Or, if that isn't good enough because of the proof problem, perhaps the major handwriting analysis groups will finally come together to determine its spot as a scientific technique. Until then analysts will hope they can follow in the recent good fortune of acupuncture and chiropractic. Formerly shunned by the major medical groups, they showed that if an unproven technique actually helps people, it can't be dissed or ignored indefinitely. Those with a need for it will insist on using it. Those who know what it can do will help inject it into the healthcare mainstream. With graphology's use in the real world and now its entry into education, public recognition is forming.

Since Grim uses no textbook, we wonder what graphology books he prefers. He emphasizes that he is a Graphoanalyst and is partial to his school's numerous publications.

In fact he raves about them. "They are serious and sober treatises that never allow themselves to stray from its conservative principles. I respect them for that," he remarks.

For books outside of Graphoanalysis Grim questions more than a few over their stroke readings. They make a few radical assertions that IGAS can't accept. A visit to Amazon.com or Barnes and Noble or Border's will give you no more than a fistful of all books on handwriting analysis. To be sure, shelves of non-IGAS do exist. Many are just old, obsolete, incomplete, and inaccurate. Most begin with some sketchy information about the history of handwriting analysis (much of it pilfered from other equally inadequate books). Typically they follow with a cheerful and breezy introduction about how wonderful it is to learn since it will spill secrets about themselves and others and how it is really scientific and not occult or similar to astrology and they can use it in countless areas, and zappa my cappa and doodle dee doo. Finally, they tell you about the interesting information you will learn and how it will lead you to a new way of looking at yourself and others and your life will never be the same.

The lines, swirls, and curlicues of analyzing will follow with confident talk about slants, size and thickness of letters, the minutiae of strokes in letters along with their meaning in personality. Grim shutters to read the meanings blithely declared in these rickety books thrust upon the unsuspecting public. "Where they get them, I don't know," he shrugs. For advocates like Grim, some of the stroke-trait connections are so silly they topple him from his chair. Maybe that's too much to expect unless he's on the edge of a stool. Try this: If he were dead, he'd be turning over in his grave. He says you can pick almost any one and within a few pages you accost a stroke-meaning absurdity. "You want to dropkick the book to oblivion," he rants. A 1969 book by Reneé Martin, *Your Script Is Showing*, says a short or absent lead-in stroke means the writer is patient. Grim's IGAS says it's the opposite. The person is probably impatient because he wants to get right down to business and will be direct and efficient in his conduct. Thus the lead-in stroke is short or missing. When you draw a slow, long lead-in stroke you tend to take your time. No letter needs a lead-in stroke to be understood. Which do you believe? You make the call. She says a looped t-stem means a person is talkative. IGAS says it means they're hypersensitive. A tent-shaped t shows altruism, she says. Nonsense, says IGAS. It means they are stubborn. He has no idea where she got these meanings.

Grimaces. "Despite an air of authority," he says, "what these appalling books provide instead is pompous garbage."

So solemn, so wrong. He recognizes most of these books are pre-1970's. Since then books have improved, the logical result of experience. The critics listen to both Grim's group and Grim's targets and wish a plague on both their houses. A few of the books are petite, slim, koolwhipped, graphology-in-a-nutshell paperbacks, often displayed in grocery store check-outs or drugstore spin-arounds. Some are just poorly marketed. A few get most of the promoting and the attention. The authors are mostly obscure and offer handwriting analysis as entertaining but helpful to assist you in finding your soul mate or judging a possible friend.

Woe is the naïve but interested buyer. What they don't know will hurt them. Paging through most of the books won't enlighten you or clarify which one to buy. Although Grim uses no textbook in his classes, he brings IGAS volumes to class for his show-and-tell segment, which begins each session. He views them as stately without stuffing, coherent, and accurate. They work well together and most are specialty volumes. They don't overstate their worth. He wants his students to acquire some books partly so they will continue to learn the subject and they will have volumes that cover the entire subject. Actually he covers much more than IGAS wants. It has its own course called Basic Eights, a series of eight one-hour lessons illustrating mostly strokes and some greater aspects of writing called global factors (like slant or writing size).

"The idea is to give the students a sampling of the subject and instill a desire to take the IGAS general course," he remarks. "At the very least, they should purchase any of these books and get a solid idea of Graphoanalysis."

When pressed for a book or two that he can recommend, Grim mentions only two. One is *Between the Lines* by Reed Hayes, a

Graphoanalyst-trained professional analyst from Hawaii. His book is a straightforward, frugal, competent basic primer on the subject. When you skim through it you think it is short on the traits. Not so. Subtly place throughout are all the IGAS strokes and their corresponding traits.

Equally important, it includes the global factors, which Grim insists are a critical part of the analyst's reportoire. "I commend Hayes for featuring them. This contrasts with IGAS, which doesn't give them enough prominence."

Grim thinks these global factors should be found together in its basic textbooks and the students' noses rubbed in them. Instead, they are scattered and not fully explained and emphasized. Hayes no longer promotes himself as a Graphoanalyst, just a handwriting analyst. Grim concurs with Hayes' viewpoints until he deviates from IGAS doctrine over some of the meanings of the lower extenders, like the y, g, j and z loops. Hayes tends to see material world or sexual meanings in the way some are drawn.

One area that outsiders ask Grim about is sex. They want to know if sexual desire or prowess or inadequacy is reflected in writing. Grim says that what Hayes culls from those lower extenders goes beyond what IGAS believes. Grim goes with IGAS, which is no shock.

"Those extenders *may* involve those material and sexual areas. We can't know that specifically enough."

"Where do you see sexual meanings in handwriting," I ask.

"If anywhere it would be in the lower loops."

"Aren't you sure?"

"Trouble is, the lower loop area also contains the social aspects of our conduct," he says and so does IGAS and other schools of thought. "After all, this is the tangible or material part of life, the real world. The upper loops in the l's, b's, h's, and k's are the abstract, immaterial area. Therefore, any peculiar loops below the baseline could amount to social instead of sexual dysfunction."

"Do we know what is going on?"

"The individual may be unfulfilled or unsatisfied, but in what particular way we don't know. We just can't reap enough from the strokes or from the research to distinguish the merely social from the sexual frustration. Of course, they may relate also."

The other favored book is *The Complete Idiot's Guide to Handwriting Analysis* by Sheila Lowe. She is more of a gestaltist, finding meaning primarily in the larger aspects of writing. IGAS and Grim consider the individual strokes inside letters and then combine them with larger aspects to erect the overall personality. Grim lauds her book for being thorough and readable. Before *Strokes*, it's the most complete book he has ever seen on aspects of handwriting analysis outside the strokes themselves. It covers history, schools, theory, analyzing as a career and others. It is for the consumer who presumably knows little about the subject. This is what *Idiot Guides* are for. For the most part he can't quarrel with her meanings in the writing. He just wishes she would join him and his trait-school colleagues to delineate the individual strokes as traits along side the large areas. She emphasizes the large areas, like spacing, slant, margins, rhythm, and thickness. IGAS cites them as global factors that are pre-eminent in force and meaning within Graphoanalysis. Although she claims to be a gestaltist and not a traitist, she homes in on several little strokes and seems to adopt their meanings.

She decries that the traitists do not "reach the soul of the writer." However, she comments in general, "Most agree, however, neither the trait nor the holistic method is best, but when used in combination, provides the most complete picture of the person's disposition." Both trait and holistic elements should be combined as the "best method" to analyze. She is an established professional from California with a stellar reputation. A serious analyst, she finds meanings beyond what IGAS has determined.

For Grim's taste, "She makes too many unsupported judgments on certain personality attributes. Sometimes it's hard to figure out if she is offering a stroke interpretation as her own belief or just to illustrate what some analysts believe."

Even so, he thinks it's a book worth adding to your library of handwriting analysis. It's the best general interest volume on handwriting analysis he has ever read. Her book has been out several years and was revised in 2007 with more interesting handwriting samples and more of them. Her book and Hayes' book are the only books he recommends to his classes, except for any IGAS volume.

He praises some other items she includes. "She deftly brings the meanings down to earth by illustrating how a trait works in actual behavior." That's something he enjoys doing also. "She even demonstrates the trait qualities in handwriting for a person who will make a good analyst."

––––––

Although Grim slathers his class sessions and talks with handwriting strokes and other writing signs, he also ventures sideways into personality itself. Grim's inventory includes performance art with props to make a large point. Some are cheap and close. Enlisting his head and hands, he forms a smiling face. With his hands, he covers his eyes like a Lone-Ranger half-mask, the fingers interlocking as the gleeful eyes disappear. His mouth still smiling and visible, he gravely utters the words, "Handwriting analysis is special because it removes the mask of personality we all wear (here he slowly removes his hands from his hidden eyes revealing furrows around his eyes, nose and on his forehead), and exposes the all to human being underneath." The look jars you. Although the cheerful mouth remains, it still matches the anguish above. Starkly this all shows how the public face often obscures the private torment.

"It's eerie but effective," he remarks. He calls it "removing the mask of personality."

He concocted it early in his teaching when he sought to illustrate the "mask of personality" metaphor for his students. He could have bought a Halloween mask, snapped it on his head, and removed it slowly as he spoke the fateful words. Grim enjoys gripping narratives without store-bought props. Once you see Grim do this one, you can't help an EEeeeeuuww response.

Doctors spend their time on our bodies. Analysts obsess over personalities. Since analysts trumpet that handwriting reveals personality, they must confront it as a concept. Modest reflecting on it confounds you. It's hard to fathom. Yet we speak about it as if we have mastered it. In truth we could spend all day on it. Some people think that personality is what others think of you, and that character is what you really are. Some experts would add a third prong to the fork: what you think of yourself. Grim questions that trinity and thinks it may be so much fleechgubble. How would he put it? With Grim's fondness for the concrete and the colorful, he has tried his own way to capture it. He says he has been forced to ponder it because it is so central to their profession. Somehow you know it's going to be unusual, maybe even wacky.

"How do you define it?" I want to know.

"First, I want to avoid that eye-glazing cant from psychology."

His version wouldn't impress psychology mavens but he says he doesn't care. It's good enough for what he wants his students to know. He views it as the natural consequence of lessons learned through the years dealing with traits and personality in handwriting strokes.

Easy on the noggin and just off the front-porch rocker it begins: "Personality is really just how we see ourselves and, as a result, how we treat others. When you look under the hood it has two components—those that help us connect up with other people and those that pull us away. The more of the first we have, the better we are doing. The more of the second, the worse we are doing."

The nub seems to be that personality measures how a person relates to other people. He concedes some traits don't directly relate to his pop definition. Some may involve good or poor thinking habits, which only indirectly affect our relationships. Most of our qualities of character distill personality to the basic questions of, Do you want to relate to your fellow beings? And, How good are you at it? What things in your make-up help you do it? Which detract from it? His perspective seems more Cheech and Chong than Adler and Jung.

When we follow up to ask him about viewpoints on life, he frowns and shifts his posture. Interesting, as he is used to dealing with people close up. To ask him to step back a few paces seems to leave him reeling with unease.

When pressed he finally opens up with this: "The *only* thing we really have in this world…" He pauses for a moment. "The most *important* thing we have in this world is each other."

"What about the rest?"

"Everything else is there to help us in coming together and remaining together." That viewpoint fits like a tongue in his groovy definition of personality.

How are we doing with what is so important to us?" I continue.

"We could do better. Women are better at it than men. It's not that we don't want to connect up with others. We don't know how to do it effectively. We let our vulnerability, fear of rejection, and loneliness get in the way. We don't want people to know how imperfect we really are."

———

In his first class Grim tells his students that handwriting will reveal a person's anxieties, insecurities, and fears. IGAS identifies thirteen of them, such as self-consciousness, hypersensitivity, and jealousy. Some who are less formal may call these weaknesses, faults, or the late twentieth century term "hang-ups." Try not to use those terms if possible, he advises. Their effect can jostle a writer already reeling from the decimating fear. They tend to be judgmental and hurtful.

"I prefer words like 'imperfections' or 'drawbacks,'" he says. "They don't sting as much."

Since none of us is perfect, he wants them to use these words to show the individual is inadequate. "You will see them in almost everyone's writing. When you do and you must discuss them face to face, be tactful and kind. You are showing the person who they really are. Your purpose is not to point the bony finger of accusation at them for having flaws. You are trying objectively to give the individual an untouched photo of themselves, a sobering peek at how they really are."

That is humbling for anyone but he believes it allows them an honest self-portrait. Whatever the writer's faults, a behavioral counselor can help, if necessary. The favorable qualities can be harvested to apply toward a better life for him—a job, a relationship, an educational or training program, a worthwhile activity or hobby. Once you have that insight, you can plumb the character of your family and friends and accept them with their faults, not condemn them or, worse, reject them. As the esteemed psychologist William James said, the worst hurt we can give someone is rejection.

Actually IGAS stresses that going straight to our inadequacies is misplaced. The qualities in handwriting work according to how we use them. By itself no trait is good or bad, Graphoanalysts chant endlessly. We don't have personal assets or liabilities. We have properties whose function remains to be determined. We have all been softwared to act certain ways. They are just potential kinds of conduct. Whether they will surface in actual behavior will depend on many factors. Some of the rare traits may not appear unless the person is under severe stress.

An analyst may find a writer's slant shows them to be withdrawn emotionally. The person may seem outgoing but is uncertain how people will treat him. In reality he guards his feelings, afraid to open up lest he be hurt. The insecure person may rush to protect his feelings when they are under pressure but otherwise will be forthcoming.

We are complex; we vary immensely. To predict how a person will manifest a trait is hard. As analysts we deal in tendencies and probabilities. For instance, someone with a strong desire for attention might irritate those around him. To deter this, an ego-driven person can channel it into good works that reap notice while helping others. Even someone with jealousy, in whose wake often lies death and destruction, might focus on aggressive but fair-minded competition. You can't ignore the effect of other traits either. Take again that individual with strong desire for attention. If he has cool emotions and a cautious bearing, the combination might be powerful enough to suppress even a robust desire for attention. A jealous person might also be outgoing and generous, both traits that suggest empathy with others. Hence he may feel like working with them, not outdoing them. A person who is stubborn might steel himself in defense of a noble cause. Or he might summon his more edifying brother called courage in a public battle over a worthy principle. Ordinarily stubbornness implies a person refusing to give in, fearful of looking bad even though wrong. Rather than always trying to save face, he can learn to pick his fights. Where a writer's trait might be deemed harmful, the person can choose to do only good deeds. The option to pursue it positively always exists, unless his lot is so intolerable he must act to protect his sense of self.

For Grim self-consciousness is not just another "drawback" trait identified by his school of thought, Graphoanalysis. It led to a defining moment for his devotion to Graphoanalysis as a deserving doctrine of handwriting analysis. In his later studies Grim reached the thirteen traits IGAS identifies as "fears." In the Graphoanalysis curriculum, personality arrives at a major crossroads. The traits seem to just exist, hung on our clothesline to display their cues and their spot in the letters. Suddenly you are faced with thirteen separate traits that can each thrash mayhem on individuals. These traits expose the real problems an individual has in his everyday life. Call him neurotic, a person in need of a small make-over, not a major intervention. Having just one in strength can hobble a person in their hike over life's bumpy trails.

Grim recalls a savvy analyst once remarked that if you have four or more, you won't even leave your home. They can be disabling. Each one except "timidity" can be found in a single stroke, says IGAS. When Grim saw the list he immediately did what any other normally anxious student would do. He cringed, then rushed to see how many he had. Since none of us is perfect, we all possess anxieties or "hang-ups." Gingerly matching himself against the list, he determined the only one he had was "Self-Consciousness." Having only one was encouraging but not necessarily blissful. If the one you have rears up enough its effect can devastate you. He wasn't surprised to see it. Thankfully his writing showed it only moderately. He knew he had reduced its hold on him from his youth but considered it either under control or out of his life. Apparently it wasn't, at least as much as he had thought.

Grim likes to describe traits through showing how a person actually behaves in real life. His fondness for concrete and color illuminates what might otherwise be illusory. He thinks analysts too often assume their listener's understanding of a trait matches theirs. In fact, the listener may have only a vague notion of its meaning. Trying to define a particular hang-up can be tricky. You never know how much psychology they know. Grim will start by defining it but using lay terms if possible. He follows up with an example of how this person, as he phrases it, "handles himself in everyday situations." This rips it from the abstract and allows understanding that clicks with the client.

One trait he can explain well is how "self-conscious" people exist and how they survive and progress. "They get by and then overcome it by penquin-step triumphs of forced public exposure."

He continues. "They shun a group setting, especially one where they must address it." Being mostly a litigation lawyer sent him to many public gatherings inside the courtroom and out. "That was like being pushed in the deep water at a pool and being forced to swim." After all those dousings he ultimately learned to swim. But he did a lot of treading water, thrashing about, and doggie-paddling on his way to the Australian crawl.

He keenly recalls his youth. Oddly, he also recalls no reason to feel that way.

"I had no ridicule, no bullying, or other traumatic event or even a continuing adversity." Nothing to engender its stressful aura.

That's why Grim thinks that much of our personality is inborn. He mentions the common example, the person standing in front of a group, struggling just to have words lurch from his mouth. Spontaneous speech is Code Red for the self-conscious. They need to work with a net. If it's an actual speech, experts advise any speaker to have only an outline of notes, and no reading it. The self-conscious may not read it but notes will be detailed. Most times the notes will be virtually full sentences rather than sketchy thoughts to fashion into steady, articulate remarks.

The audience doesn't look at the self-conscious; they stare. Their private agony follows them everywhere people lurk.

"These people don't handle success well, I know first hand. For example, if they win a competition, they react differently from most, especially the applause-seeking vain. That kind will throw up his hands to the re-assuring sound of clapping and beam for the unrestrained cheer. Not the self-conscious. His hands will instantly cover his scarlet face. He dreads to speak anything at the moment of his success. Any words he speak are halting and fickle. He may blurt, 'I can't believe I just won.' He's often speechless and may say only that. He is shrouded in humility that shuns ego."

Grim anecs another dote: "If he is with some people discussing an issue and he is making a point and he is finished his point, if no one chimes in at once, he rushes to fill the vacuum by prating some more. The self-conscious don't want to be the center of the discussion. Meek is they."

He continues and we wonder why: "Often when they speak they can't help but hear the sound of their voice. They don't like causing a scene. When someone praises them, they can barely accept the compliment."

Though these may derive from Grim's past, he has confirmed with others their shared anguish. Grim is mostly over the misery.

Yet he says he's "not sure you ever completely lose your fear of the water. After all, I just admitted it was in my handwriting. That confirms it still hasn't left the building."

Perhaps it is "in there somewhere" as he points to his head, and by the mass of time and public airing, now he can confine it. But it's still there under layers of success overcoming moments of awkwardness.

To convey how it appears now he re-visits the Nightmare of the Self-Conscious—stage fright.

"I guess for me it's mostly a thing of the past. I don't have that jittery clutch in the throat anymore. Before, speaking to a group meant everyone was staring at me. Now they're just looking at me attentively. You know how they tell you to overcome self-consciousness in front of a group? Imagine each of them is in their underwear. Great. When I tried that it didn't work. I considered myself naked."

As any student would, Grim also checked for the other fear traits in his writing. They can't help it. They know each stroke that reveals each painful anxiety. Whether they think they have any one, they want to be sure they are free of all of them.

Grim wiped his sweaty brow upon finding no others. "Your writing is like a magic machine telling you if you have any on a list of diseases. It's uncanny what it can do but it's scary to check the list too. You want a clean bill of health. This list gives you an emotional status check. The layman can evade the awful truth since he doesn't know the strokes for the trait. An analyst has no choice. He knows all of them and can't help seeing them before his eyes each time he writes. He can only hope they won't appear."

Consider what this means for Grim as a person. Let's say he suspects he may have a physical ailment, like cancer. As a "patient" he trembles to hear bad news from his doctor. With the non-physical traits, when Grim peers at his handwriting he hopes he won't find any among his strokes. He suspects he will because he has been living and confronting them. The revealing stroke equates to symptoms in physical ailments. The ohmygod moment for Grim was confirming in his writing the major fear trait (self-consciousness) he thought he had. Now the lab report had come back and your own blood verified you had cancer. He himself was providing the evidence unwittingly from his own writing. Since the stroke was unconsciously drawn it was being delivered objectively. That's what your blood does for physical maladies. In his education as an analyst, Grim was shocked to learn his trait from a source outside his own private, conscious awareness. This was compelling validation of handwriting analysis, a subject he had cheerfully marched into with finger-crossed faith and head-smacking doubt.

A realistic student will question their entry into this implausible topic. That he had the "self-consciouis" fear trait plunked Grim with minor anguish. Yet he was grateful for its ultimate message. "I had decided I would wait till the end of my studies to render judgment on handwriting analysis." The sober evidence of his self-consciousness was a giant stride in persuading him of his subject's validity. "As I finished my studies, it pumped me up even more as a believer."

———

As part of their training psychiatrists submit to their own psychoanalysis. IGAS hands out its diplomas without requiring its students to analyze their own handwriting. Grim is asked regularly if he has analyzed his own handwriting. Other analysts confirm this same inquiry. Grim is disappointed when he hears it, viewing it as a question that answers itself.

Typically Grim responds with his own question: "When you happen by a mirror do you occasionally pause to check your hair or your clothing or how you look in general?"

Some will deny this lapse into vanity. It's what Grim calls a "squirm question, one nobody wants to hear and instinctively everyone wants to deny."

It's as if you asked them whether they studied in high school or watch TV. They are desperate to conceal it from the judgmental public. That same universal public is composed of individuals with the same universal faults. Conceding honesty, most people will nod and accept what Grim thinks is obvious. When we pass the mirror our obsession with appearance diverts our eyes to update how we look. When an analyst writes, he is spot-checking the state of his character. For analysts human nature impels a quiet, ongoing assessment of their own writing. It will occur in random surges. They may be conscious or unconscious, but they can't help it. Not in detail where they sit down and draw up a comprehensive written report as for a client. After a time repetiton mashes it into their unconscious and it becomes second nature. They stop doing it at some point, he suspects. Perhaps it only starts up again if some new stroke arrives. Instantly they will spy it. Before they make one more move in their now muddled life they will wonder why it invaded their familiar, entrenched strokes. Since they recognize it for a reason, any reflecting should be brief. Their personality's furniture hasn't merely re-arranged itself. That would mean the same pieces are still in the room. Rather, that part of their personality has adjusted; now there's a new sofa in their midst. They must abide it until that part evolves into some other characteristic.

Grim wonders if an analyst can be objective about himself. He sees biases, prejudices, and self-deception slithering into the evaluation. They are the unsavory agents we can't seem to fire, always taking their five per cent or more from our try at impartiality. When analysts see an unwanted stroke announcing a negative trait, it can shake them. Like anyone else, you want to avoid the cruel truth of the new you. Some analysts try blotting them from their minds. By revealing the analysts' weaknesses these interlopers can only be trouble. Just as psychiatrists are forced to go through psychoanalysis, Grim advocates compulsory handwriting self-analysis for his brethren in training. In a thorough test of their objectivity and skills, each trait would have to be justified. Grim is unaware any school requires one. It would be a healthy learning experience, and maybe an eye-opener as well. In part Grim acknowledges that those who avoid them are evading the unpleasant truths about themselves. He imagines that submitting the self-analysis to their instructor would create tension for both. The analyst would try to polish and buff his faults to shine as virtues. Grim thinks the risk is they would march into a battle with someone irritable and defensive—not their instructor—themselves. As a training step perhaps the self-analysis is a bad idea. Each time they write, analysts can't avert their eyes and can't stop their analytical intellect from a silent, secret, instant self-evaluation. Their telling strokes encumber them with enough discomfort. They are just happy if they can keep those snitches from going public.

When Grim is asked if he has analyzed his own writing the person is usually daring enough to follow-up. "When you analyze it, what does it show?" they ask. Usually he informs them he declines comment. If he's feeling frisky he may summon an amusing deflection, maybe a frivolous list of superlative qualities, all made up of course. When pressed about his evasions, he claims he gets bored discussing his personal qualities. He concedes a Wizard-of-Oz defensiveness about his credibility.

He explains: "You can't let them know that you sweat, falter, and sometimes misfire." Even so, he doesn't enjoy talking about himself.

"Yeah," he acknowledges, "I have things to hide just like everyone else."

Insisting he's not uneasy exposing his faults, let him try convincing you with his own words: "I've just grown weary explaining myself over the years." The words stumble from his mouth. Attorney, spring thyself. Done. Analyst, reveal thyself. Pending?

Handwriting analysis faces another obstacle. Call it their "seagull." Some analysts lack solid backgrounds in psychology or its parent with multiple off-spring, social science. Already taken is the more familiar word "albatross" from the Ancient Mariner. It exists as metaphor because graphology lacks complete proof of its legitimacy. The inadequate analysts retard its progress in several ways. More than a few analysts don't even appear credible. Or they offer only weak arguments for graphology's existence. They embarrass themselves and their discipline, especially when they face off against a psychologist. On the other hand, Grim points out, many analysts have keen instincts for personality and its components and conveying that to outsiders. If they start with scanty backgrounds, they devote time to acquiring some substance. Over the years unrefined analysts learn that being earnest and eager will only carry them so far. When shoddy amateurs or certified pros jabber about their subject and betray faulty awareness, Grim flinches. But he won't bury his head in his hands. Every field that aspires to greatness has its blemishes. These types will trouble handwriting analysis, although their damage has declined recently. With most analysts being older rather than younger, college wasn't always in their cards. Today more high school graduates stream into college, which has become the high school of today, Grades 13 through 16. More high schools are offering psychology courses too. If young people want to get anywhere important, graduate school has become essential. Grim informally surveys his classes and is struck by their demographics.

"I'm surprised the number of students that never took a psychology course or even attended college. But their numbers are not overwhelming."

"Will you put a number on them?"

"No, I can't. But I have always been impressed by their knowledge of human behavior collected from life experiences and the panoply of media sources." They have enough to get them by, which gives him tepid consolation. "I'm buoyed by the people with an acute sense for human behavior. I guess if they didn't have it they would stay out of it."

Grim's classes draw mostly women students, which is par for a handwriting analysis course. He believes it arises from two main factors: the topic is about personality, and women enjoy examining and discussing (usually with other women) it more than men. They can better understand people. Students anticipate they may have to open up about themselves and others. Women also see it as a chance to blab about other peoples' conduct and relationships. To the cynic this is an acceptable forum for women to, Can we say it? gossip, their choice medium of exchange. Men are also more reluctant to reveal themselves. They fear their vulnerability. Any fissure in their manhood exposing weakness can shatter them. They lockbox another secret: they actually have emotions. Most men are uneasy talking about them and shudder if they must expose their own to women around them. Women recognize feelings as vital parts of their being. They don't mind liberating the E- and V-word. They acknowledge them and will express them. A woman crying is a common okay vent. A man smolders inside and expels some rage with a vulgar word, a punch on his car horn, or an overhead smash on the court. Or he throttles his wrath in chronic depression until some upsetting event blows the doors off. This is the price he pays to keep his manhood.

Traditionally, most handwriting analysts have been women. Grim believes this fact has kept the subject from heartier growth and acceptance. It is unfortunate, he maintains, but the kind of people in it too often lacked the dynamic salesmanship and missionary zeal to carry the topic to the masses. That wasn't necessarily bad. The more hucksters around, the fewer serious educators and practitioners. Also, the force of credibility might have been stronger if more men had practiced it. Until recent times, if a woman was preaching its scientific worth, she made less of an impact than a man. No doubt that sweeping generality was true for any major movement striving for an impact on our culture. In recent times women have made great strides in all areas, including handwriting analysis.

———

People ask Grim what person in history he would select for his dream analysis. He says he has thought about it. The individual is someone whose writing he longs to see but it's unavailable. Perhaps he wrote but Grim has never seen any of his pieces. Maybe his writing doesn't survive because he didn't write much. Maybe a signature is still around. Many long-gone notable figures have great reputations perpetuated over the centuries. We also have the infamous individuals who remain scoundrels, according to history's fair judgment. Grim is intrigued to discover whether the historical figure's fame (or infamy) matches his handwriting. Handwriting analysis enables special insight into these revered or feared giants. Grim has no hesitation selecting one for his One Great Analysis. Surely, other Analysts would covet his writing. His would be the Holy Grail of Handwriting. It might never have existed. "Did he write on any lasting surface?" Grim wonders. Since analysis rules persist throughout history and over the entire earth, a writing from, say, 2000 years ago could be analyzed if the writing still exists. In fact, speaking of *that* many years ago and Holy Grails, Grim's dream analysis is the writing of Jesus Christ. Would his noble qualities have appeared in his handwriting? Since we are human beings and thus imperfect, we develop insecurities and other shortcomings. How imperfect a man was he? Which inadequacies would he have shown not revealed by the Bible? Or would his character be truly immaculate even in his writing? What noble qualities would radiate in his handwriting? Grim and his cohorts will never know because no record exists of his writing. He wrote in the common notepad of olden times: the sand, the mud, and the dust of the earth on which he walked. Go to the Gospel of John, Chapter 8, Verse 6, where he wrote stooping down and touching his finger to the ground.

The man on the left is Allan K. Grim, Sr., then a lawyer in Pennsylvania. The woman on the right is his wife, Ruth. This photo was taken a few years before he became a Federal Judge. In 1951 he had a handwriting case and discussed it at the family dinner table. Later that year Ruth bought a book on handwriting analysis and took it up as a hobby. She still analyzes today at age 95. The baby in the photo is Allan K. Grim, Jr., who later developed his own interest and knowledge about the subject from his mother.

Chapter 7

One Profession to Another

The Pen is Mightier When Not Bored

Since he wasn't a psychologist, Grim felt uneasy dispensing off-hand opinions on crippling self-esteem or to-the-bone resentment in the writing of often-frail human beings.

Povser

In doing an analysis, [Grim's mother] disarms a person so nimbly, they forget their impulse to excuse themselves to the john.

Povser

Nineteenth century British author Edward Bulwer-Lytton wrote that purple-prose opener, "It was a dark and stormy night." After a century or so delay, an American professor started an annual contest to see who could top it with creative debris. How many know this British author also wrote, "The pen is mightier than the sword."? Grim and his cohorts agree with that. Grim believes his pen is even mightier when not bored. He wants to play all the instruments in the handwriting orchestra. He's an analyzer of handwriting; he's a lecturer, writer, seminarian (not a Bible student; he gives seminars), and consultant to the media and the authorities, like the police and schools. He has been a speaker at the International Congress of his handwriting organization, International Graphoanalysis Society, as well as several term President of its Pennsylvania Chapter. He has accomplished this in a brief whirlwind professional career in handwriting that began only in 1993 at age 52. Yet his path to the formal role as Graphoanalyst was glacial, not abrupt, reaching back to the placid 1950's. It began as a gentle contagion from his mother. In his early teens Grim plucked off the family shelf books on handwriting analysis his mother had bought as a pastime. He scanned them and did some informal, superficial analyses. Here and there he would buy a book he liked for the family collection. The books were few in number, slight in their instruction, and dubious in their sway. One that prompted a chin-scratching hmmmnnn was a volume by M. N. Bunker, founder of a branch of handwriting analysis called Graphoanalysis. Although Grim analyzed mostly as a diversion, occasions arose where deeper insight of people would be a special asset. In the law he handled court cases often with unfamiliar attorneys, clients and witnesses. To obtain their handwriting and unearth their real natures could mean advantages. In court cases attorneys can skirmish with their opponents well before the big war of a trial begins. Pre-trial matters include procedural wrangling, discovery proceedings (where the attorneys can observe the opponent's witnesses and their testimony and other evidence), and negotiations about issues, especially settlement of the claims. He wanted to know how they could be trusted, if they were credible, what their style of acting was, what motivated them, what their weaknesses and strengthens were, and what mental skills they had.

With the information his handwriting analysis gave him, he thought he had at least a modest idea.   Wherever he spied writing he would study it. Actually analysts can't avoid it. Does a stamp collector get a letter and ignore the thing at the top right of the envelope? Is there water in the ocean? Like Superman and his x-ray vision, he felt specially blessed.

He insists on explaining. "It wasn't as though I had some magical power and was able to put something over on people. This technique was freely available to anyone else. I never understood why more people didn't use it. I continued with it because my experience showed that it worked. Everyone else apparently didn't know or care to know that it does work or else they would have learned it and applied it too."

Using it in many situations helped him gain an edge, he is convinced. Even insights about clients. "It was good to know what makes your client tick. You were always aware that they were going to have to deal with the pressure cooker of a court room, the interminable wait to get to court, the ups and downs of litigation, and, most important, the anxiety of testimony in court. You wanted to know if they could handle it and how they would handle it. And you especially wanted to know if they would remain resolute or wilt under cross-examination. You also want to know if they are straight with you and if they would lie on the witness stand."

As the calendar pages flipped over, his interest in handwriting analysis swelled. Friends knowing of his expertise showed him their writing. They tendered others too—boyfriends, bosses, and problem people headed the list. "What do you see in this one," they would ask, sometimes demanding it. The more he learned, the more he applied it. He became devoted to it and finally realized a profound truth: it was too important to be left to a dabbler. He knew practicing law carried momentous responsibility because any mistake can mean a client is out a pile of dollars, jail, or other distress. For the attorney, malpractice, censure, suspension, lawsuit, news article, crushed reputation, lost clientele, scattering friends. Although its effects could be different, handwriting analysis deserved a similar concern and, he thought, some standards to meet. Many casually approached him for instant analyses to learn if they had a sense of humor or sexual prowess. They treated it as a playful diversion and didn't take the findings seriously, at least on the outside. It covers the full range of human behavior. He was playing with people's real lives and often grave problems. Since he wasn't a psychologist, Grim felt uneasy dispensing off-hand opinions on crippling self-esteem or to-the-bone resentment in the writing of frequently frail human beings. He immersed himself further into the subject, probing its history and its scientific footing. Maybe it deserved its centuries of *some* contempt, but not in the late twentieth century. His search disclosed that, whatever befell it before, now it had solid merit.

He also rejoiced for its potential as a worthy service to mankind. Since it discloses intimate insights about all writers, its value for helping people seemed potent. If he was to continue offering its benefits he felt compelled to buttress his abilities with improved credentials. His requests for analyses continued to climb. He was doing analyses free and taking swaths of time, so compensation increasingly sprung to mind.

Why shouldn't he get paid for his efforts? He recalled the words of a prior lawyer of distinction, Abraham Lincoln, who remarked that a lawyer's time and advice were his stock in trade. Grim was furnishing that stock over countless sheets of writing with nary a Lincoln penny or two in his pocket for picking.

Ultimately in 1992 he decided to make the plunge. It wasn't a MartinLutherHolyChristthatlightningalmostgotmeIfImakeit-outofthisIswearI'llbecomeamonk moment. It was the upsurge of interest, concern about his expertise, worry about damage to his handwriting and legal repute, desire for some compensation, and, catyoucannowcomeoutofthebag discontent about the practice of law. Recalling the remarkable Milton Bunker Graphoanalyis book from three decades before, he applied to the International Graphoanalysis Society (IGAS) to take their General Course. Bunker headed that organization since its founding in 1929 until his death in 1961. IGAS projects that its distance learning program should take about 18 months to complete. With a family and a full-time legal practice Grim finished in 15 months. He knew he had a head start since he had been doing it off and on for 40 years. You might think this was a decided advantage. When you have a modest library of books from a variety of analysts who have their own ideas of what the strokes and grand aspects mean, confusion reigns. It wasn't as though he bullet-trained through standing on his head. The accumulated knowledge came from diverse sources, some radically amiss. It wasn't all Graphoanalysis thinking. What snags the student is the last few lessons. They have been studying and taking tests with open books. A walk in the park to their diploma? No. After a while the trees, the bushes and the underbrush thicken and the student is slowed by actual analyzes. Finally they must locate and capture all these disparate traits and tame them into a halycon home for the individual's character. They must resolve how they badger each other and how they vie for attention in the writer's life.

Grim introspects. "It does become harder but you learn to merge these often unruly elements we call traits. You realize they don't just exist. They have roles to play in the writer's life and they determine how he will act."

Grim was now practicing law by day and handwriting analysis by moonlight. When he started as a formal analyst he *knew* one of his two jobs was a profession. As he thought the other was one too, he wanted to pursue it with that level of dedication. At the time his view of the law was crystallizing anew. In the old days many attorneys handled whatever matters came in their office door. Today is the age of specialties where most attorneys handle only a few subjects. Grim had settled into some specialties. Reflecting on his career, however, he had done it all, and often, and enough is enough. After an initial start with a small firm in his bornandraised home county and part-time work as an assistant district attorney, Grim was invited to join a three-person firm with his two cousins and their father. For clients their doors were always open and their practice reached into wide areas. He soon was thrown into a variety of matters, and became, for good or ill, a jack-of-all-trades. As the firm expanded with a steady increase in new attoneys, he downsized into a master-of-some—civil litigation, including divorce and family matters, banking, real estate and debt collection. After many years of high pressure battles in his major area of litigation, which he saw as legalized warfare because people just didn't get along as Rodney King hoped, simmering cynicism boiled up to blatant disgust. Compounded by what he saw as unhealthy in the modern practice of law. Rather than its tradition of genteel professionalism, it was sinking into business mania with the need to hustle for clients, incivility between attorneys, irksome clients scrapping about money, vengeful clients feigning to fight for principles, guilt at charging clients eye-popping fees, and then the need to collect those fees from disgruntled or deadbeat clients.

He expands. "Law can be a noble calling. Some of the best people in society are lawyers. Society depends on them and reveres them. It can also be stimulating, challenging, and satisfying. You can make money in it and gain prestige. These were reasons I entered into it." Except for the respect and prestige, handwriting analysis also has these qualities, he believes.

With each new file opened, his bonding to the law melted as his fondness for handwriting analysis gelled. He was embedded in his second career, sweeping through all its positions as he did in the law. Not just analyzing samples, he tried speaking, teaching, consulting, and writing. Today he is still a jack-of-all-traits. Finally, the descent of law reached the ascent in handwriting analysis. He was ready to leave law and do handwriting analysis full time.

A good final reason for quitting the law was the passage of time. "Thirty years is enough to do anything," he declares. Physician heal thyself; attorney spring thyself. He did. In November 2000 he unhooked his law shingle for his now sole occupation handwriting analysis.

He was happy with his chosen IGAS for his formal education. He thought he did well. Although he finished in 1993 he didn't get to the formal cap-and-gown ceremony for graduates in Chicago, its headquarters, until the next year. During his July 1994 graduation ceremony at the International Congress of IGAS, Grim was handed his diploma for the General Course. After switching his mortarboard's tassel to the left, Grim barely sat down when he had to rise again. IGAS surprised him and another student with graduate scholarships to its Masters Course. According to IGAS, those who earn it have shown a mastery of the General Course, strong likelihood of becoming a superior analyst, and enthusiasm for the subject. Grim left Chicago psyched and primed to hang his new shingle and display his formal skills.

Grim grants the big risk going from an established profession with status and ready compensation to the tenuous realm of handwriting analysis. Being a lawyer created some advantages for entry to his new profession: established credibility, superb launching site, and foot-in-the-door standing. With its ethics code IGAS has a dignified reputation, makes students earn their diplomas, and employs acclaimed instructors for a weighty curriculum. IGAS cites their graduates' role as helping people know themselves and others in different areas of life.

"Having a legal background gave me a benefit over other analysts. It aided with the initial attention and enhanced my appeal," he thought.

Without shame or hesitation Grim calls what he does now a profession. If he hears any sniping about it, he is quick to respond.

"Does it occur often?"

"Yes, it does," he readily admits.

Primarily from its unscientific provenance and its history of derisive whacks from skeptics and other non-believers. When you declare with a straight face that personality and handwriting are connected and you can't readily produce reams of convincing data, eyebrows rise up in disbelief. Snide words come stinging, and sometimes a spitting guffaw can't be suppressed.   He has endured mashed-potatoes-and-gravy meals at groups where he's given speeches and lesser talks hawking the benefits of his subject, seeking its uplift and lowering of those unconvinced eyebrows. He isn't out merely to change the public view, or to garner more respect. Always the missionary stalking the jungles of public ignorance, Grim wants to attract the uninvolved, silent believer and to yank that fence-straddler into his yard.

"Advocates must speak up on its behalf," he insists.

When they first hear about his involvement, some people may chuckle under their breaths. When they see him close up discussing or practicing his craft, their irreverence fades. Grim's background in law buoys his standing. Thirty years in the law allows him initial slack with the public. Attorneys are pegged as rational figures that won't traipse into unfamiliar areas. If they do, the community will recognize their reasons.

"The public had years of prior notice I was involved, especially from knowledge of my mother's practice," he says.

Grim knew his reputation was at risk. "Is it still intact?"

"I think so."

———

For years as a lawyer Grim wore his suit coat and sport coats closed, against the fashion grain. It's gauche for a guy to button up his suit coat, especially his sport coat. It stood out so much that people were stirred to ask why. After enough of them his stock reply was, "If the Good Lord had meant for men to wear their coats open, he wouldn't have put buttons on them." It takes a hardy sense of self to endure the bemused looks *that* caused. Probably he wouldn't have done it if he couldn't handle it. He was able to absorb the looks and the comments. With this comical, quasi-nerd pose, Grim seemed to be out of character.

This curious coupling of the serious with the silly is a contrast he has bundled together all his life. Could it be a reaction to the uptight era and location of his upbringing? Second oldest child of four sons and a daughter of a Federal Judge, he professes to feeling hamstrung by the *noblesse oblige* of his small-town America in the inhibited

Forties and Fifties. You have good standing in the community so, tarnation, act like you warrant it, Grim's insistent conscience would bellow in his ear. Both parents were sober and discreet types. They weren't AmericanGothicpitchforkandhairinabun party-poopers but they weren't back-slapping, drink-up jokesters either. But they leaned heavily toward the former. His father was a judge; his mother, a housewife, was raised in a strict religious home, her father a school superintendent. After teaching elementary school, she became the dutiful housewife and mother. From an idle amusement graphology became an effective device to meet new friends, a pastime with her established friends, and an activity with her (fill in absurd large number here) grand- and great-grandchildren. Although superb for starting relationships, she hardly needed it. With an affectionate, warm amiability she drew everyone into her gracious presence. That has never changed.

How an analyst conveys the writer's personality to him can be as crucial as the news itself. Bad news swoops into the writer's craw while good news expands his head. If you want to see a pro at managing this news, says Grim, watch his mother in action. In doing an analysis, she disarms a person so nimbly, they forget their impulse to excuse themselves to the john. As they stop squirming and start listening, she conveys what may seem as drawbacks as sedately neutral or chest-pounding strengths. Her way with words that should hurt is to remove the stinger and replace it with a honeyed remark. She embodies the analyst's creed to view all traits as potentials for good, and not to scour for failures. She shuns finger-pointing judgments, and emphasizes the positive. Instead of telling someone they are hyper-sensitive, she will tell them, "You try very hard to do the right thing because you want people to appreciate your efforts." Or if she spies an "acquisitive" stroke that suggests greed or materialism she will ask the writer, "Do you like to collect things?" The vain individual gets some help too. She will tell them, "It's important for you to receive a pat on the back."

Her path to analyst emeritus was gradual and uneven. Married at age 24 to attorney Allan K. Grim in 1937, Ruth (Ackerman) Grim started a family as soon as possible then. That means *after* they were married and at least nine months from the wedding. The arrivals came with proficiency every three years between 1938 and 1947. The result was four boys, Allan Jr. arriving second in 1941. A longer pause ended in 1952 with a daughter named Virginia. In 1951 her husband, then a Federal Judge of two years, brought to the dinner table idle conversation on one of his trials where handwriting was an issue. Amazingly articulate today, but physically frail at age 95, she still recalls some of the facts after 57 years. Despite her circumstances, offspring can't keep her from advising them as she pleases, whether they ask or not. Extreme wisdom and experience haven't evolved from time but from being a caring and informed force in the family. She has earned the title of matriarch, allowing her to enter their lives without a knock or an invite. Neither will she spring on her children, however. Politeness and discretion reign.

Fondly she recalls the events of that first brush with handwriting. After the court case she accompanied the Judge to the Mayo Clinic in Rochester, Minnesota, for his medical condition. Needing to fill some time without her then four children (mercifully left home), she visited a book store and spied a book about handwriting analysis. She bought it, was hooked, but the rest was not pure history. She dabbled with it only as a hobby for years before making an attempt to obtain formal certification from the International Graphoanalysis Society (IGAS) in the early 1960's. Unfortunately, the demands of the family with five children, a large house and yard, chronic illness of the Judge and his eventual passing in 1965 took up her time. She also was dealing with the last illnesses of her father and her stepmother. Needing income after the Judge's death, she returned to work as a teacher in 1966 after three decades and her IGAS materials languished under editions of *Look*, *Life* and *Redbook*. Still, her interest in handwriting never flagged and she continued to analyze handwriting as a much-deserved pastime.

Grim's sister, Virginia, eleven years younger, and an audiologist by profession (all the Grims are in professions. Maybe that is why Allan Grim calls handwriting analysis a profession) is a handwriting analyst student in cold pursuit of her sheepskin. At the moment, and for the record, and only the record, she is a few lessons shy of her Certificate. After encouragement from her brother, she has been working on it with IGAS off and on for a few years. She began in earnest and was rolling along but her hectic work and lifestyle has throttled her from completing her studies. She also seems to have a natural gift for it, abetted by her mother and brother's involvement in it. She also became a student of brother Allan in a separate class that she organized by herself to get him to come to the area where she lives. She has also attended Allan's seminars and conducted a few of her own. Between all that she has informally analyzed writings with her fellow family analysts and on her own. Grim thinks she has an easy knack for it.

He has more than a little to add about her. "You admire people because they get around a lot. She is a true rolling stone with nary a speck of moss on her. She is fearless in going places and trying new things and meeting a wide range of people. She has been around the block several times in her action-filled life. She just lacks that piece of paper saying she is officially trained to analyze."

We boldly ask how she would stack up with him.

"If we had the same experience in handwriting analysis, she would be a superior analyst. And I wouldn't be jealous. I've always encouraged her to get involved in it. I hope she will finish and put up her shingle. She has a lot of other irons in the fire. I understand why it has taken her this long to get where she is. I can't wait to see where she goes with it. I just wish I will be here when she does. The way she is going, that is questionable. She is involved in so much, her devotion to handwriting has tailed off."

Meanwhile back at the family homestead, her mother hasn't let her lack of an IGAS certificate keep her from her self-appointed rounds as an amateur analyst. She is the classic party and casual analyst. No matter the occasion, she has never spurned a request. When someone thrusts that memo sheet into her accomplished lap, her eyes brighten and her mouth opens to saddle-up anticipation. These analyses are an ice-breaker for a lady who can break any ice with anyone. Give her a few moments to be around you and the ice melts to flowing water. She has always been approachably warm and genial. Without edge or ego, she hasn't a bad bone in her body.

Her son the analyst is unaware she has any enemies or that she ever offended anyone, "at least anyone that should have been upset." He adds without tongue in cheek, "If they were, they no doubt deserved it."

She hands out advice to her progeny delivered with sense, sensitivity and dignity in a taco of church-going tradition. This sounds a little like sainthood here.

"If the halo fits, wear it. She has earned it," chimes Grim.

Talking about erecting halos would embarrass her. She would promptly reach up, grab it, and fling it to the quoits pit. By the same token, she won't sully her sainthood. It's not that she's obsessed with her image, but God's unseen but powerful hand gives her little choice. He lets free will operate only so far, not that she would stray. When you have been good for nine decades, thankfully for those around her, little can alter that basic goodness.

"Look, I'm not going to tell you she never went through a yellow light in her life," Grim offers. "But darn close. In fact, I just said 'darn' because of her".

She is a person of character, at peace with herself and her Maker. Over and over, her family looks heavenward in gratitude. When we boldly asked if her exalted qualities appear in her handwriting, Grim responds, "What do *you* think?"

Chapter 8

Harleying through the Countryside

Grim giving talks and not knowing the response, dealing with unruly audience members, running lively seminars, and getting in the newspapers

A prime way analysts promote themselves and spread the word is by giving speeches. Grim, who has given many speeches, was invited to speak at the 2002 International Congress of the IGAS. He gave a talk on, would you believe, giving a talk about handwriting analysis. Since his talk he has written a few articles for the Society's Journal of Graphoanalysis on how to become a better analyst. It's easy to find a group that will hear any analyst. Handwriting analysis is a subject that travels so well that analysts are welcome at any organization that needs a speaker. If the subject misses a tie to the group, it will deftly fit its members. Analysts know each of the members cares about their own and their children's skills and qualities as they look to better their lives. There's always the possibility one of them will be interested in pursuing Grim's subject too. Grim has given speeches to diverse groups, finding a way to connect the subject to any group. Besides, when a group realizes the speaker is a handwriting analyst they are usually psyched to have their writing analyzed. Grim will seize the chance also to tell how great handwriting analysis is and why it should be accepted by the public and used by everyone. He doesn't want to miss a chance to toot two horns—his and his topic's. Drafting some converts is a bonus. Grim's approach is to emphasize educating the group over entertaining them. Although he tries to do both, he runs a risk with a civic group audience. You never know how they are going to receive it.

That prospect jolted Grim in his initial speech to a civic organization. Not just because it was his first but because of the group's reaction. The group and setting were typical, a Kiwanis club, which these days is top heavy with old salts, and a backroom of a restaurant with bar. You are on their turf and what unfolds goes way back, farther than they can remember. It's their customs and you tolerate them and that's that. A speaker may be the featured guest and the temporary center of attention, but that's only a formality. Abruptly they will interrupt the speaker with trips to the men's room, dozing off, early leave-taking, impudent call-out comments, grating chatter between seatmates, and questions you swear were hauled from their butts. When the speaker finishes, a slow-motion stampede scatters them to the bar, bathroom, outside to light up, home, or who-knows-where else. Meanwhile, the embarrassed President rises to thank the abandoned guest and hand them a tangible token of their merciless humiliation, like a metal toy truck or a miniature bell.

Grim's experience was unusual, according to one member who accosted him when he finally got to leave. He couldn't believe how Grim was actually treated. The group had a Ladies Night with almost double the usual 15 to 20 attendees. Grim was told to speak 20 to 30 minutes. Grim's bell-ringing zeal clamored for more. Usually he surpasses his suggested time. For these groups, that is asking for trouble. This night he handed out a few extra chicken fingers of handwriting lore he thought everyone should hear, tasty and tender enough for easy chewing and rapid swallowing. His talk exceeded the time. He finished and sat down.

What happened during his anxious first talk opened his innocent eyes. No one left their seats. No one fell asleep or shouted an insolent peep. No one raked him with an impertinent or silly question. No one ambled to the men's or ladies' room, or to the exit for their cars waiting to speed them home. Or for that edge-off smoke or to the bar for the Heinekens. Before the President could rise to ask if anyone had a question for Grim, he was pelted with a flurry: What does it mean when you print? What about doctors' bad handwriting? How can you analyze something that is scribble? Can you alter your writing so it can't be analyzed? People interrupted each other to hurl a question and shoved others with their own observations and questions. Grim already knew his subject was interesting. Just how much to others still needed airing. Expecting boredom for his topic or carping about its claims, instead he found gleeful wonder and unbelievable respect. Since then Grim has found it a common reaction wherever he goes. The topic invigorates these often-subdued civic groups. After listening to a handwriting analysis talk, members approach Grim with descriptions of "really interesting," "fascinating," "intriguing ."

With undue modesty Grim is convinced the group's ardor sprang from the subject's appeal. It excites buzz every place he visits. Although not one of those sure winners like sex, money, or health, in his experience it's close. As Grim sees it, when you square handwriting analysis against the other three, the winner of most enthralling subject is his topic. REALly?

"Yes. I believe so. It involves everyone's favorite subject, themselves, which it deals with directly.

"But isn't health more important?"

"Maybe for the average person. But that usually means physical concerns. With handwriting you get your emotional health, which people seem more intent to hear about."

"Shouldn't physical trump emotional health?"

"It should but it lacks the gusto of the others."

He sees a clinical, grey aura emitting from the physical. Handwriting analysis is new and different, gives feedback on what you are doing right and, more importantly, what ails you. Everyone can relate to that. It's compelling since it broadcasts about what is really on your mind, consciously and unconsciously. If something is plaguing you, it should show up in your writing strokes. Grim points out that any stroke that stands out reveals a trait that has taken over your mind and therefore your actions. Analysts call them "inappropriate" strokes, those that don't seem to belong there. A clown at a funeral. Donald Trump relishes wheeling and dealing and making The Deal. It makes him rub his hands together and flips up the sides of his mouth. It fulfills him like nothing else does, so he says. An extreme stroke and its related trait possess you. No matter how hard you try, the trait won't leave you alone and go play by itself. It is high-maintenance. It's almost like our symptoms of physical pain. As health class told us years ago, having it is our body's signal that something is wrong inside. Same goes for the excessive strokes.

"Only if you know what makes you tick can you determine what is bothering you inside," says Grim. Handwriting strokes remove the clock face and take you into its works. It shows you the source of the ticking, chiming and hand movements, the qualities attesting who you are inside and outside.

The sunny greeting at his Kiwanis talk tanned him with a reassuring glow. How long it would last was the doubting public's choice. Grim had just finished another talk on handwriting analysis at a Rotary Club. A member moseyed up to him as he gathered his remaining materials. Most had been snapped up by the members to take home and look at or show to the wife.

He stopped next to Grim and, without introducing himself or offering any preliminary comments, puked, "Do you really believe all this stuff?"

Grim's standard answer, both immediate and firm, was, "Yes, I do."

When they follow up with the "Why?" query, Grim's stock response, is "Because it works and constantly confirms itself. Once in a while it won't bear out but it's not physical science so some inaccuracies will occur."

When they enquire further Grim is glad to explain. "I wouldn't have given up a 30-year legal career and invested so much time and money and effort in the last decade if I didn't believe in it so strongly. As he goes around and gives speeches and teaches classes on it and conducts seminars and is interviewed by periodicals that feature him in special articles, his certainty has hardened, he claims.

Verbal assaults do come every so often, more likely in informal settings than at speeches. They don't usually cause any psychic damage. Most analysts develop calloused spirits, which tries their resilience. They don't like the tomatoes, rotten or fresh, but they get used to the splats and the dripping. At a speech it often amounts to refined heckling. Unlike a comedy club, analysts learn to turn the other cheek and finesse a response that admits the critic's doubt may be rational. After all, the subject stands on the outside of psychology's citadel pounding on its oaken doors for entry. Analysts won't require a hug but seek at least a hearty handshake when admission occurs. At a talk at a Jaycee dinner one evening Grim declared that he could look at any of their handwritings and instantly create a portrait of their personality.

A woman professional abruptly screeched: "What did he say? Is he serious? Are we going to sit here and listen to this?"

The tension was thick as a frozen bagel. You couldn't cut it with a guillotine. No one said anything. Without pausing, he ignored her and continued speaking. She looked around and found no vocal support. Grim's pronouncement was early in his talk. Once the audience heard his brief for graphology dealt with convincing swagger, her petulance dissolved into curious listening She never said a word again. Grim believes she altered her view after hearing the whole speech. He hopes that any of his talks will broomswat the doubt into the rafters. He has no illusions it'll happen just like that. It helped that her Jaycee cohorts didn't join her in macing him, politely letting him finish. When he moved from the post-talk Q and A session he was treated civilly. No hostile cross-examination. Grim hasn't found anyone else before or after that directly challenged him during his talk or in the aftermath. They may have asked a question implying doubt but they seemed more interested in relieving it than pinning Grim to the mat.

Analysts can well document their professional welts. When they actively and publicly advance their cause, the reaction can be public too. Occasionally more than they seek. When Grim first began as an analyst he contacted local newspapers to let the public know he was available. He sent them a sparse bio article about himself and expected a humble slot somewhere in the back near the Classified Ads. He waited with gloom for their response. They could ignore it or write a polite NoThankYou note, or even a searing Don'tevertrythatagain letter. Maybe tell him to put it in a paying ad and like it. Sometimes they would print it verbatim. In a few instances a reporter called him to tell him they weren't publishing it. Rejection? No, they were doing better than publishing *his* dreary data.

"This is an interesting topic. We're curious about it and wonder what you can do. We'd like to delve into it with you," was typical. They expanded the topic and poured on salsa rather than salt. They came out for photos and asked questions, some soft, some hard.

Grim hoped for dignified respect from the local daily paper in his home county. Before he had become an official Graphoanalyst he had sent a blurb hoping for some kind notice. They didn't print it. They contacted him, asked for more information, and visited his office for photos of him in action. A few days later a staff-written, moderately-long article appeared on the bottom right of the *front* page. His picture was there too, in color. After he got his diploma and was setting up shop, he contacted them again hoping for a bland announcement of his new status and availability. He thought five of his fifteen minutes had been used up. Maybe they would grant him ten more. He wasn't optimistic. He thought he was pushing it. They might say no article but we'll take a paid ad. He heard from the newspaper. Not only were they amenable to an article; they visited his law office, interviewed him, and snapped some photos of him at work with handwriting analysis.

Only the half of it. As part of the visit the interviewer surprised him with a pile of the writing of the local Congressman, a County Judge, a County Commissioner, and the State Representative. Truth's moment for Grim. Powerful public people and little writing to go on. Another uneasy day at the office and it wasn't even his office. Yes, it was his law office, but his other office was in his mind, which means in his home. He didn't know any of the officials personally except the judge, who had also been District Attorney. Fearing he might be pulling the pin on a hand grenade going nowhere, he was reluctant to analyze their writing. His lecture to students and other analysts was always to decline the instant analysis on a small sample of writing. That is what he faced: small samples, no time to reflect. Here each of the writers wasn't just anybody. They were all prominent. Even more reason to beg off and retain your reputation and professional ethics. On the other hand, he pondered every novice's dilemma. You seek publicity for your cause and your budding business. That little marketing voice on your shoulder whines for you to drum up business and demands you go ahead and do them.

He analyzed them all on the spot, expecting only a few to be mentioned in the article. He further hoped it would be buried in the amusement section of the paper on a Thursday morning, brief and unassuming. When Grim picked up his paper the next *Monday morning* on the *top left* portion of the *front* page of the paper was an eye-widening spectacle: each of the officials' writing blazing as call-outs, with select quotes from Grim about their personalities, and, below, a large photo of Grim showing their traits. A long article followed underneath with the interview and fuller descriptions of his analyses of the writings.

"This subject sells itself," Grim comments with undue modesty.

"Please. But this is America," we respond. "You are entitled to your wrong opinion."

It does make its own splash. You can't ignore the person who pushed it into the pool, however. Those who know little about it jump at the chance to learn more about it. When you are a newspaper you want to inform the reader about it too. It sells papers.

"I know," says Grim. "But you don't expect it in the same spot with U.S.S. MAINE SUNK IN HAVANA HARBOR."

Grim survived the reaction from friends and acquaintances, who were mostly delighted with his publicity. The feedback on the analyses was that he got his men. For one of them it might have been in his pride. Apparently the only outcry seemed to be his observation about the County Commissioner.

I ask what the problem was.

"I said something like he was not that great a people person."

"So?"

"He was unimpressed by that judgment, I heard."

Although Grim didn't relish making the observation, his duty is to the truth. Cynics will tap him on the shoulder about truth being relative. Sometimes, as Grim should know, it's a matter of finesse. Probably he could have couched it more tactfully.

"How would you say it now?" we want to know.

"Good question. A man who thinks he is of the people wants to be stated as, how can I put this, a man of the people. I'd have to think about that some more."

"Don't you have to tell the truth?"

"Sure. But maybe I could have focused on another stroke and trait where I found something positive. That is the problem with these instant analyses. No time to think and you look for strokes that stand out."

Although he felt bad about the reaction, discretion stopped him short of uttering what he might have—if the shoe fits, wear it. Grim decided to let bad enough alone. As Grim learned, the instant analysis can backfire. Luckily he hasn't run into the County Commissioner.

Other analysts can suffer a similar fate. Where the analyst finds an undesirable quality, and, without wrapping it in some nicety, flings it at a writer who is present, a moment of truth for the writer can become, how to put this, a moment of truth for the analyst. During an analyst's talk an audience member insisted on showing his handwriting and demanding an impromptu analysis. After a quick glance at the writing the analyst found an obvious trait, one where the strokes stood out, bluntly telling the attendee "You can be argumentative and confrontational." For the next few moments the attendee quarreled with the analyst, denying his shortcomings. The bewildered analyst finally moved to close the dialogue, but the attendee refused to yield on the issue.

The analyst looked at him directly, briefly paused, and declared, "I'm sorry. I must move on. But in the meantime I guess I rest my case."

The audience howled.

A seasoned analyst will not let that happen. Since analysts consider no trait positive or negative per se, they will be prudent with deficient traits of character. Grim suggests the analyst might have uttered something like, "It is very important to you that when you have a viewpoint, it will be heard. You don't take things lying down and you don't shrink from a good verbal skirmish. That is an admirable feature to have when you hold a view dearly or you believe an injustice may have occurred." By and large these misstatements occur during instant analyses, where the analyst's time is short. Afterward he will have much time to go looking for the three Czech excuse-makers, Wuda, Kuda, and Shuda. Try a bar. They regularly show up there, slumped over a beer, their heads swiveling in regret.

––––––––––

Grim does workshops and seminars. For a long time IGAS frowned on these group learning sessions. It believed the only way to teach Graphoanalysis and to make you a competent Graphoanalyst is through its General Course. Sometimes its heavy hand came crashing down on insurgent members. People have been ejected for allowing speakers or sessions about non-Graphoanalysis doctrines. Grim has done seminars and classes for years and has not been threatened or dismissed from the Society. Actually, in recent years it has loosened up. Today Graphoanalysts like to discuss their own school's doctrines but are eager, as necessary, to venture outside to appraise what might be better teachings. Analysts are poised to make a Filene's-Basement dash toward anything that gives them more information about handwriting analysis. Discussing other doctrines is one way toward enlightenment, Grim believes. If we should find something that is sound but contradicts our canons, he thinks IGAS should consider it. If you are a Catholic you are stuck with the fundamental doctrines. It can't grow and evolve after deeper insights. You can't vote on, pick, choose, or change items conferred from way up there to a pontiff way over there. On the other hand, handwriting analysis evolves just like any other social science, discarding ideas if they no longer make sense. Research and new discoveries can lead to revised convictions of imperfect human beings.

Grim began his seminars after his first adult education class in 1994, treating it as a supplement to the class. Some of his students implored him to teach a Handwriting Analysis 102 course. He's never done one. Because of his full schedule they are tough to fit in and, anyway, he prefers they go straight to the General Course at IGAS. His latest seminar runs at a quaint restaurant called the Spinnerstown Hotel, near Quakertown in Southeastern Pennsylvania. It attracts former students and independent analysts. They meet on a week night for two-and-a-half hours in an informal setting. Grim's agenda is usually some show-and-tell from attendees about items they read or heard about on handwriting, handwriting analysis, or psychology, with focus on personality. Grim calls the show-and-tell portion of the evening "Breadsticks," which he started in his classes when he asked students to bring in anything they came across about handwriting. He chose the name Breadsticks from the tiny basket on your table when you dine out. (Melba Toast has been the item of choice for years but Breadsticks have taken over most tables) As you chomp on them awaiting your meal, they silence the hunger gurgling in your tummy. He follows that with advice on being a better analyst, suggestions on enhancing the prestige of their profession, news from the world of handwriting, and a mini-lesson about handwriting analysis.

After this initial agenda the group analyzes samples of writing they bring in. The samples are converted into transparencies for viewing or merely photocopied. The person presenting the sample can lead the discussion and withholds most information about the writer until the members have had their say on what they see in the writing. Primarily it is to keep the analysis pure and untainted. When you know something about the writer your knowledge may color your comment. Sometimes the member knows the writer very well and can tell if the analysis was accurate. Other times he doesn't know him and seeks more insight for personal reasons. He may have begun a new job and wants more information on his new boss. Maybe his mother, now divorced, is dating some guy and it's getting serious. Should she end it or pursue it further? Some samples just display a new and interesting style of writing, perhaps only a few different strokes but quirky or different. For analysts the wilderness of unique writing methods seems endless. Each new sample of man's expressions on paper will be like no other, today or yesterday. It will be unfamiliar and they haven't seen it yet. Handwriting variety is infinite because *we* are infinite in make-up.

Grim presides over one of his seminars, standing behind his familiar cardboard box resting on its side for his notes. On a nearby table is an ancient overhead projector bleating for a Power Point to end its misery. Aside the projector is a heap of transparencies of writings ready for placing on its top. A huge screen stands behind Grim. The lighting of this upstairs room is muted, like a bar room. Dark enough for clear viewing of the writing on the screen but light enough for taking notes. The members are arrayed around him in a squared arch of merged, white-apron tables. Eager for handwriting chunks to learn by and remember, members have pen and pad ready. Grim begins with a few Breadsticks. He shoots on the screen a book cover for *Defining the Wind* by Scot Huler. What does this have to do with handwriting analysis? Before the assembled wonder too much, he explains: This recent book is about a wind scale for nineteenth century sailors called the Beaufort Scale. He comforts their patience as they know he enjoys springing on them alien items, then linking them to graphology by some provocative allusion. The wind scale was devised by a British cartographer, Beaufort, who arranged every few miles-per-hour of wind speed into categories. Each slot depicts the kind of wind-speed (gentle breeze) and states its range of speed (8-12 MPH). That is not the good part, he interjects. Each also has a column showing the usual effect on objects ("Leaves and twigs in constant motion").

"No one can see the wind," says Grim, "and wind speed by itself portrays little to the mind." Beaufort's descriptions neatly create word pictures for each range of wind speed.

When Grim mentions word picture the attendees know his familiar aim. Previously, Grim has told analysts that too often they assume the recipient understands their trait descriptions. They must be creative in their trait descriptions. The wind scale shows that we can describe personality attributes by a clear method. Illustrate how they operate in the real world. Just like the effects of the wind, show the trait's effect on their conduct with other people. For example, someone who is "narrow-minded" you might initially describe as having a closed mind. Instead, say this person already has their mind made up. They really don't want to hear what you have to say. If you give your opinion to them, they will ignore it or look for what's wrong with it.

Grim flings another Breadstick, an article he found in a recent *National Geographic*. A Massachusetts woman doctor has a grotesque malady called hyperagraphia. She has a compulsion to write and it seems her world is her piece of paper. Wherever she goes she carries a pen because she must use it. She is impelled to write anywhere she can. Not only on a piece of paper, she writes on her clothing, her skin, her walls, her shower stall, and whatever else is left. A compulsion is an impulse to constantly repeat an act. She certainly proves it. She has become a boundless graffiti buff, except it's unconscious and she draws only random words, not statements of rage or art as in urban graffiti. The group has heard of disorders like dysgraphia, where a person mixes up the spellings of words or writes letters backward. Hyperagraphia is a new one for everyone there.

Since so many strokes appear in writings of millions of people, analysts appreciate every oyster of knowledge about their subject. They will explore the inlets, bays, and estuaries of writing for some new stroke or an odd form of a familiar one. Some new stroke seems to appear almost every time they review a writing. Most times, however, that new stroke can be pigeonholed into one of their many trait slots. Tonight wind blowing tree branches is quaint, and writing on shower stalls is weird but engrossing. These are only tossed bones gnawed on. When Grim shows them a new stroke or other aspect that they can't seem to classify, it's finally giving them red meat. Drool oozes most for an insight on some stroke they've pondered for years but the meaning eludes them. They know they might feast tonight when Grim begins their favorite segment, the mini-lesson on some aspect of handwriting. He flashes on the screen a sample of a stroke phenomenon where a person will replace small letters with capitals inside a word. It looKs sOmething like thIs, except it's handwritten script. Grammar students know capitals are supposed to appear only in the front of sentences or in front of proper nouns. No question these misplaced capitals are unusual. Grim knows these strokes are so rare that they probably lie untested for validity. He sees research needing a multitude of samples to reap their gist. Laypeople don't notice them because they are so rare. Not so with analysts. From their experience they find items in writing outsiders miss. Where research is lacking, such as with capitals inside words, analysts will deduce meanings from other similar strokes. They fill in the blanks with their parallel theories and that is the best they can do for now. Grim tells the group these odd-spot capitals express defiance and rebellion.

"People who employ them," Grim observes, "go against the grain and you should expect them to be independent in different ways."

Someone barks out, "What are things they will do?"

"They may also utter inappropriate comments and do head-shaking acts."

"Like what?" someone yells out.

"You will say, I can't believe he just did that. Let's say you're biking on a path with him. All of a sudden he will veer off the path into the woods for a bit and then return. You ask him why he did that. He replies, 'I don't know. I just felt like it.'"

Based on his and their knowledge of comparable strokes, the group sounds convinced. No one clamors to differ. Until formal research takes this further, that's as good as they can do.

Grim isn't finished with those misplaced capitals. He introduces a more common variant. Some people will put capital letters in Front of words Within a sentence and The words Aren't even proper nouns.

Grim expounds: "People who do this seek recognition or reward even though they haven't done much to deserve it. They have strong egos that must be gratified because, after all, these are capital letters. Capitals are about your sense of self. By putting their capitals where they don't belong, they are seeking approval though unwarranted."

Again, sounds good to the group because nobody pipes up. This is also the tentative conclusion of the authorities who have assessed them. These too would need further research.

Where any of Grim's group sees a TV show that features an analyst, they are under order to videotape that portion and bring it to the group. After they view it Grim will ask the group to grade the analyst's performance. Did he advance our cause or set it back? How did the host treat him. Respect? Amused? Fawning? Attacking? It's a learning experience for the group. With their subject's coverage limited to short bursts in the media, analysts fret about their image and their rappelle up the craggy slope to mass approval. Typically on TV the analyst is asked to analyze a sample of writing on the spot without a prior look. If they do, the advice older analysts give younger analysts about shunning a quickie analysis goes out the window. They say they just won't be accurate. However, TV presents opportunity over principle. Analysts treasure their media exposure and want to display their expertise and their subject. That they might botch that big chance disappears in their eagerness to impress the public. This evening Grim critiques an interview that Scot Simons of National Public Radio conducted with Mark Hopper of Arizona. Head of Handwriting Research Corporation, Hopper runs probably the largest commercial organization doing handwriting analysis in the world. Grim informs his group that he doesn't have the audio of the interview. They can get it on the NPR website.

"Hopper was given a sample sight unseen," Grim begins. Everyone knows this is not a good start. God knows Grim has railed enough about the instant analysis. Foreboding about the results looms and glooms over the room. Simons told Hopper the writing was done by someone close to Simons. Hopper devoured it like a starving dog, bullet-pointing some qualities he found in the strokes. Almost as a throw-in he mentioned that the person showed some immaturity. PBS has dignified, heady people on the air. Simons is one of them. When Hopper finished his instant analysis, Simons politely disclosed that the handwriting was his own.

One reason television vanquished radio is its visual effects. NPR couldn't flaunt Hopper's humiliation nor Simons' reaction. But you could listen between the words. Vocally a dumbfounded Hopper offered nothing further and neither did a perturbed Simons. Grim cautions the group that this is another lesson on analysts acceding to quickie analyses, especially without verifying the actual writer. He tenders this little M&M: most of the time, where the writer is not identified, the sample will be the person present or someone close.

Hopper is a serious, well-spoken, veteran professional. He probably has told other analysts not to take on instant analyses.

After Simons' disclosure, "The silence was ear-splitting," Grim says.

A pause to let that oxymoron register and Grim resumes. He conceded the writing might have showed immaturity. Accuracy is not the point. Would he have used those words if he had known Simons was the author? What better words might have been chosen? More directly, should Hopper have kept his mouth shut about this feature? More importantly, what if a large sample had reduced the immaturity to only a glitch? As Grim catches their still-stunned looks, he forehandsmashes at them one more M&M: that possible glitch is one BIG reason to forego the instant analysis of a small piece of writing.

After the group volleys comments about Hopper and Simon, Grim glides to another TV item. He cites a lesson he learned from Dr. Phil. Frequently the TV counselor announces that the number one predictor of divorce is when spouses' quarreling deteriorates into name-calling and character assassination. Persistent verbal gusts that destroy the other spouse's self-worth meant divorce was a 95% certainty.

"This is all relevant to analysts,"Grim makes clear. "It's about personality and relationships and analysts do compatibility studies for partners." He follows with, "Where in handwriting are signs that the person is a character assassin?"

The responses are quick and perceptive. Note-takers scribble to keep up. These comments will aid the compatibility analyses. Grim searchlights the room, spotting a few stealthily checking their own writing for evidence. Handwriting analysis is not just about people out there you can help. It is first about the knolls and the dells in your own life. He is sure others are wondering about a friend's writing and their marital discord.

Grim is not always grim. Yielding to the inane this evening, Grim projects on the screen the signature of Britney Spears, which Grim VCRed when an entertainment show featured her impetuous Las Vegas marriage. The writing was from a court petition to annul it after 55 hours. The group discusses her personality and that of her trivia-question husband.

"Does Britney betray any ditzy blondeosity in her writing?" Grim asks. After a herd of engaging comments, a consensus forms that it does. Grim's dignity battles its way back to his senses and he pulls the sample to move on.

Apparently Grim can't help himself with the absurd this evening. From the depth of Spears he sashays only sideways to a question posed to Marilyn Vos Savant, the sage who has a weekly column in *Parade Magazine,* that Sunday supplement hidden in the ad circulars. Supposedly she has the highest IQ of anyone in the WHOLE UNIVERSE, INCLUDING REDMOND, WASHINGTON. She was asked to address the illegible signature of a businessman. She never really answers the question. Her response is to lapse into levity, saying his writing is no worse than hers. Obviously, she hasn't taken the time to check into the topic, Grim observes. She has a dim view of handwriting analysis from prior questions. This time her comments say more about her than about handwriting analysis.

"With the thousands of questions she gets, why does she include one she doesn't even try to answer? She should learn about the subject and try to answer it, or get an expert like us to supply the answer," he growls writeously. "*Parade's* Sunday circulation is up there in the millions with *Reader's Digest.* It's in the top three of U.S. magazine readership," he points out. "With the impact she has on America, her remarks slow our march toward understanding and recognition by society."

Mr. Ramsey,

Listen carefully! We are a group of individuals that represent a small foreign faction. We respect your business but not the country that it serves. At this time we have your daughter in our posession. She is safe and unharmed and if you want her to see 1997, you must follow our instructions to the letter.

You will withdraw $118,000.00 from your account. $100,000 will be in $100 bills and the remaining $18,000 in $20 bills. Make sure that you bring an adequate size attaché to the bank. When you get home you will put the money in a brown paper bag. I will call you between 8 and 10 am tomorrow to instruct you on delivery. The delivery will be exhausting so I advise you to be rested. If we monitor you getting the money early, we might call you early to arrange an earlier delivery of the —

Ransom note of Jon Benét's killer

Mr. Ramsay,

Listen carefully! We are a group of individuals That represent a small foreign faction. We respect your business but not the Country that it serves. At this time we have your daughter in our possession. She is safe and unharmed and if you want her to see 1997, you must follow our instructions to The Letter

You will withdraw one hundred eighteen thousand dollars from your account. One hundred thousand dollars will be in 100 dollar bills and the remaining eighteen thousand dollars in 20 dollar bills. Make Sure That you bring an adequate size Attache to The Bank. When you get home you will put the money in a brown paper bag. I will call you between 8 and 10am. Tomorrow to instruct you on delivery. The delivery will be exhausting so I advise you to be rested. If we monitor you getting the money early, we might call you early to arrange an earlier Delivery of the money and hence a earlier delivery pick up

Handwriting of Patricia Ramsey

The Jon Benét Ramsey ransom note was printed. Patricia Ramsey, Jon Benét's mother, was asked to submit her own printed writing sample to the Boulder police for comparison. Her normal style was script.

Do you think she is the writer of the ransom note?

Chapter 9

Word Stories

Revisiting the Ramsey Ransom Note
Examining a Nasty Anonymous Letter
Identifying an Eco-Terrorist

The Graphology of a Violent Fiancé
Firing an Employee after a Glowing Analysis

The media has consulted Grim for his opinion on cases of widespread public attention. A writing as part of the evidence will prompt a call from a distant reporter. When the Jon Benét Ramsey case broke, Grim braced himself since a major item of the investigation was a ransom note. The Ramsey matter is still only an investigation. No charges have been filed, let alone arrests made, since Christmas 1996 when the little beauty queen at age six was brutally murdered in her Boulder, Colorado, home. That note may be the biggest piece of evidence to convict those responsible for this heinous crime. Some features of the note are significant. It is printed. It is very long for a ransom note, especially one that was probably written at the scene of the crime. At the time the Ramsey family was away from the house but in the Boulder area for a Christmas get-together. You would think any perpetrator would rush to write it or would write it before entering the house. The note was written on a yellow legal tablet from the Ramsey home. Not unusual but potentially damaging to the note's writer is that it is handwritten. Ironically, the note also demands from the Ramseys $118,000.00, the exact amount of a bonus Mr. Ramsey had just earned. To expand the mystery, the note's statements are thecowjumpedoverthemoon bizarre.

No doubt Boulder investigators have explored the handwriting itself to establish two important identities. One is who wrote the words on the paper. They would take the writing style and have a forensic document examiner compare it to chosen suspects' writing. Steve Thomas, a lead detective, had resigned because he thought prosecutors and police were not being aggressive enough. He has said they surveyed the writing of 73 individuals and found no close matches. Except for, are you sitting down?, Mrs. Ramsey. The police didn't say she was a good match. They just said we won't exclude her as the writer. That's a different conclusion but it doesn't help Mrs. Ramsey. By the same token, it doesn't help the DA's case either since it hinders him from obtaining a conviction. The criminal standard requires proof beyond a reasonable doubt. Of course he could introduce other evidence compelling by itself. Yet he must confront the ransom note and it raises some doubt. Maybe she was involved but someone else wrote it. Maybe she wrote it with a clever disguised style. She was known to be agile with both hands. One of her teachers in the Parkersburg, West Virginia, high school she attended in the mid-1970's clearly recalled she could write with both hands. Also a tabloid paper published a photo of Mrs. Ramsey about to enter her car with keys in her left hand. Chet Ubowski, the Colorado Bureau of Investigation's handwriting expert, thought the writer of the note did it with their "off-hand." Detective Thomas wrote a book about the case, *Jon Benét: Inside the Ramsey Murder Investigation.* He says Ubowski believes she wrote it. Personal certainty is Bud Abbott; proving your certainty is Lou Costello.

To see if her writing style coincided with the note, the police asked Mrs. Ramsey to come in and supply writing samples. In case you're now silently pleading self-incrimination for her, you may dismount from your high horse. Under the U.S. Constitution that is not a protected part of your person. You can be compelled to supply your writing, same as submitting your fingerprints, a DNA swab from your cheek, or a hair from your head. Still, the police got her in the door after only intense weeks of squabbling with her attorney over the ground rules. After she had given three samples in three meetings, they invited her for a fourth. In that session the police finally asked her for left-handed samples. If you think in the meantime she got shrewd with her writing, you have a sound point. With even Mortimer Snerd as her attorney and the cops' requests, she figured out to give them writing different from the ransom note. Thus, she probably made up some new strokes to avoid a match between the ransom note and the samples submitted.

This may seem a ploy that could avoid a conviction for murder. However, every devious left hook deserves a roundhouse right. To counter her well-crafted samples to the police, they requested writing done just before the murder. These "innocent" samples included those where she used a printing style, as in the note. Her customary style is cursive. A problem? No. The printing came from a document on which most cursive writers will print—a form with blanks to fill in. An application was found for one of Jon Benét's beauty pageants. It had Mrs. Ramsey's printing on it. We don't know the police's assessment of the writings or their method of obtaining the samples at the station. Did they give her a legal pad? A similar pen? And like that. Of course, as a starter, Grim would have insisted she write spontaneously rather than deliberately.

"I've seen some of her cursive writing and some of her printing. There were similarities between her printing on the form and the ransom note.

"Many?" I ask.

"No. And that is the problem."

However, word has leaked out on another development in her writing. Someone has said that, after seeing the ransom note, Mrs. Ramsey's writing changed in her samples written for the police. One major change was that she made the manuscript a's in her printed samples different from the manuscript a's in the note. (Manuscript means they are printed as if made by a typewriter, or, today, by a word processor) Mortimer Snerd earned his money.

Most of the Boulder police detectives are convinced Mrs. Ramsey did write the note. Since the writings have only a few similarities, they speculate that the writing may be Mrs. Ramsey's but disguised. Employing an "off-hand," (the left for a righthander) is rare. Therefore, at first it will differ from the regular style. Once up to speed the "offhand" will resemble the customary hand's. The initial writing in the ransom note appears somewhat shaky, then firms up to finish.

Aside from the forensics, Grim wonders if the police examined Mrs. Ramsey's normal writing style to ascertain if she were capable of the horrible acts. I ask him, "How about the personality side of this.

What do you see in her normal cursive style? Could she have done it based on her revealed attributes?"

"I've seen Mrs. Ramsey's normal cursive style and nothing jumps out that says she was capable of this act," he says.

He knows forensic analysis was done to match styles between the note and possible suspects. If the police did any handwriting analysis on the personality of the writer of the ransom note, he's not aware of it. He believes it was also done but questions its value if the writing was disguised. Some personality traits will emerge but the analyst would need to speculate how much disguise was used. That wouldn't have been easy. Supposedly if a personality profile analysis was done, the results were compared to the personalities of the suspects to see who was closest.

Grim was contacted about Ramsey but not for the forensic issue whether Mrs. Ramsey wrote the ransom note. Sometime after the murder a national periodical called on him to evaluate if her handwriting showed she would be willing to make a deal. The only writing he based it on was a sample the writer faxed to Grim. It was a short note from Mrs. Ramsey to a friend in her normal cursive style. Grim could only say that the writing in this note showed her to be a reliable, solid, but amenable individual, a peacemaker, and an affable social being. On that basis she would be willing, he surmised. Whether someone will likely do something that critical in their life is not easy to predict, even for their friends of long standing. For an analyst who knows her only through her handwriting and media statements, that is asking much. Grim's opinion was published in the *National Examiner* in an article where a possible deal with Mrs. Ramsey was said to be in the discussion stage. Grim was not amused pondering this part of the matter. He was glad to be asked however. It showed the level of respect graphology has reached at the advent of the twenty-first century.

The Ramsey murder has caused a massive investigation. However, it has never been a court case. Many have been accused, pursued, and excused. No one has been charged. In July 2006 Patricia Ramsey died of ovarian cancer. Have the Boulder police and District Attorney now closed their files?

———

Grim does the personal analyses, the staple of the profession. Although he doesn't pursue it, forensic document examination is one area he will do. The police, the state, the media, hospitals, attorneys and others have contacted him to consult. Typically they will ask him to determine if a writing was actually done by a certain person, such as signatures on wills, checks, and other documents. Insiders call them "questioned documents" or "forensic documents" and the experts who analyze them are called "examiners." Most documents involve only an alleged forgery of a signature. Others could involve a whole note or letter written in longhand, not just a signature. Some cases involve writings termed "poison pen" letters, such as anonymous notes or letters, usually disparaging, threatening or harassing the recipient or someone they know. The Jon Benét Ramsey case with its notorious ransom note, the Anthrax Terrorist case, and other public matters are variations on the "poison pen" article.

One "poison pen" letter Grim analyzed a few years ago he won't forget. Ethically, Grim provides only enough detail for an idea of what happened while also changing some of the facts to protect the client's privacy. A venomous letter was sent to parents about their teen-age daughter. (He won't disclose the venom either) The writer did not identify himself but he handwrote it. The girl's parents retained Grim to identify the writer. They gave him samples of the writing of possible suspects. Fortunately the couple had the writing of several of them since they thought it might be someone they knew. When an analyst has several samples to compare to the subject writing, generally it is easy to match them, especially where the writing contains several lines. After a close comparison of the writings, Grim tendered his clients a report that shocked himself beyond his professional belief and experience. *Four* of the suspected samples were so close to the actual letter that Grim could not rule out *any* of them. All the samples had been written in innocent circumstances. They all were written well prior to the subject letter and under normal circumstances. Where a "poison pen" letter is handwritten, disguise of its forms is always a possibility. Grim saw no reason to believe disguise had occurred with this one. Usually it will look clumsy and unnatural, which apparently Grim can detect with no prior view of the writing. To this day he still cannot fathom this monumental coincidence. Grim's inquiry ended there. He asked the parents to approach the four possible suspects in some tactful way to confront them over authorship of the abominable letter. What their efforts amounted to Grim is unwilling or unable to say. Cases like this are often gimmee putts for analysts. Since they see so many strokes unfamiliar to laymen, several telling signs will betray the writer. Some of the samples were scanty and thus Grim was hamstrung from an adequate appraisal.

"I can't believe what I got stuck with. I had to get a quadruple puzzler that ended only in doubt."

Still, it was a challenge he enjoyed. As a professional curiosity he would relish meeting the four individuals whose writing couldn't be distinguished from the actual letter. Not just to confront the perpetrator. That moment would be for the victim family. Since similar writing equals similar personalities, he wants to see if each of the personalities matched. If they did, that would be four more successful validation experiments for his topic.

It's bad enough someone will communicate a wicked message in any form. When it's in the sender's bare handwriting, red-blooded analysts will salivate with anticipation. They know it leaves the writer open to discovery. Disguise is the work of the secretive individual, he who fears exposing his true identity. Presumably the smarter the person the better the disguise. What methods someone will use to protect his intimacy reveals much about the individual.

"You suspect that whoever writes in his own hand has a submerged desire to be caught," Grim speculates. "If they are trying to remain anonymous, they could do a better job of it."

These days it's not even necessary to write something bad when you can quickly print something from your word processor using common type fonts. "When it's a public writing, the door to discovery would seem to open much wider," he says. "Writing a message on a document in your own hand is not very bright. What's more personal than that? And more distinctive? Every other form would have common features unrelated to the individual messenger. Type it for crying out loud."

The handwritten Ramsey ransom note readily exposes something for the authorities to assess. You would have thought it was a fatal mistake for the writer to handwrite it. Unbelievable to analysts and probably most of the public, the careless writer apparently wasn't careless enough. The murder remains unsolved.

Smart people make few mistakes. Because they are human, smart people are not immune from carelessness. Whether they are careless enough to be caught in some wrongdoing severe enough for prison depends on the circumstances. A few years ago the Phoenix, Arizona, area was in turmoil because someone was burning down new homes built by local rich people. Every few months the person struck, leaving a warning note produced by a word processor. Included also was a handwritten note warning people not to build homes in an area called "desert preserve." Fomenting one of its frenzies, the media furthered the story with a caravan of articles. Wealthy people wanting to build lived in constant alarm that their home was next. Finally, through two sources the case was broken. A video camera caught the cryptic arsonist when he planted a note at a luxury home used as bait. In addition, a friend of the suspect, wearing a wire, got him to admit he was the eco-terrorist. The culprit turned out to be an upstanding, educated former newspaperman and PR man. He pleaded guilty to multiple counts and got 18 years. Asked about his handwritten comments, he confessed he disguised his writing by using his left hand, adopting capital letters in block-print style, and misspelling a few words. He hoped the misspellings would steer the authorities toward a lesser-educated suspect. He revered the "desert preserve" around Phoenix and wanted to keep it pristine. Although he was educated and had a laudable motive, Grim calls his disguise tactics "banal and uncreative." The writing helped to attract attention on him. Still, his friend's stunning betrayal was essential in nailing him. After word-processing the main note he switched to handwriting for the warning note. Was that carelessness, a throwmeinjail wish, or tantalizing gamesmanship?

Smart analysts can careen into trouble with their analyses if they fail to follow some guidelines that organizations like IGAS insist on. Ask prominent analyst Beverly East from Washington, D.C. In her sprightly, informative book *Finding Mr. Write* she adroitly conveys how the way to a man's heart is through his handwriting. Analyze it and see if he is worth pursuing so he can catch you. As a gift for her fiancé, a woman asked East to do a comprehensive report on his writing. Despite finding some marvelous qualities in his writing, East also detected repressed anger and a violent temper. The woman confirmed his good traits but could not agree about the anger and temper.

She called him a "puppy." She expanded: "We have been together five years and he has never raised his voice to me."

The woman wanted East there when she presented the analysis to him. When they surprised him and he had a chance to read the report, his reaction was to throw a table into the air and punch his betrothed in the face, breaking her nose. East had never asked for his consent. Since then East gets the approval of both parties in a couples analysis.

Even with consent an analysis can boomerang where the analyst doesn't witness the writing. On occasion analysts have a sample delivered to them on a virtual silver platter. Typically a business will want a prompt report for a quick hiring decision. The analyst may be getting it second or third hand and must rely on those who hand over the written item. When the analyst can't easily verify the author of the writing, they have a fateful decision to make. Checking no further means the analyst must bear the result. A professional analysis can raise the stakes and the ultimate risks to both handwriting analysis and the analyst. One young analyst was asked to review the writing of an applicant for a position at a trucking company. The applicant delivered his sample from home to the personnel office of the company. The analyst evaluated it and found several superb qualities. Based partly on her report, the applicant was hired. Two days later the company had to fire him. He turned out radically different from what his handwriting suggested. When the personnel manager informed the analyst, she was shocked. She re-visited the writing and her findings and remained puzzled. After investigating (lo and behold was made for this spot), she discovered the sample had been done at home—by the applicant's wife. Apparently he was fearful the report on his writing would expose his deficiencies (a rational fear as the days revealed). Now this chastened analyst will analyze writing done only in her presence. When Grim relates this war story to a class he ends by asking its lesson, hoping he has pulled a clay pigeon for a willing shooter. Most of the time a student will murmur only that we must be careful to verify who wrote a sample. Certainly true in general but missing the clay pigeon he really meant. Usually exclaimed by a perceptive and witty female student, the better shot is, "They should have hired the *wife*."

Charles
Lindbergh

Bruno
Hauptmann

Ransom note allegedly written by Hauptmann

American flying hero Charles Lindbergh was involved in what was called the Trial of the Century in 1934 when his infant son was kidnapped and he received a ransom note demanding money for his return. He had been killed soon after the kidnapping. The German immigrant Bruno Hauptmann was convicted of the crime and elecrocuted in New Jersey. He protested his innocence up to his death. The founder of IGAS, Milton Bunker, said he didn't know who wrote the note but whoever did would have confessed. Why did he say that?

Chapter 10

Science

The Proof Has Been in the Pudding, Not in the Lab

Think of your writing as a print-out prepared from your computer software, your brain, except it is about yourself, not others.

Povser

Handwriting provokes curiosity. We all write and we crave answers to all those questions it arouses. Analysts never seem to be around for our questions. When we finally find one he is waylaid like wailing teeny-boppers on a rock star. Okay, maybe that's a bit strong, even for analysts' most fanciful dreams. But they do get approached with everyone's carpetbag of inquiries saved up for that special day when an analyst appears. Several of the serious and stimulating issues have already been addressed. One remaining is as serious as you can get. Handwriting analysis has The Big Question or the Ultimate Question. It takes different forms. Just how scientific is handwriting analysis? Does handwriting really disclose personality? What studies have been done to prove it's valid? Has handwriting analysis been proven to be true? These are its milder forms. The more blunt and disparaging versions will be, You don't really believe all this, do you? Or, Come on, handwriting analysis isn't scientific, is it?

We try asking it. Here is where Grim probably wishes he smoked. To assemble his thoughts he would need a long draw and a slow exhale on his Camel. With none to reach for, he shifts in his chair and stares across the room.   Many other analysts will turn to stone at the sound of it. Of the rest a few aren't bothered by it. Grim thinks those analysts are naive or in denial. Their certainty shouldn't be so solid. To betray some doubt about it is to be rational.

Finally Grim is through staring and starts up. "A single, comprehensive formal study has never been done," he admits readily, his tone deliberate and measured.

That confession might surprise you. Quickly he adds that much research has occurred over the years, all partial studies. Grim is surprised how much has been done. Every so often he learns of more. Somehow it doesn't get the press it should, primarily because it has been so scattered and so tentative and small in scope. Much has been done elsewhere, largely in Europe, mostly in Germany, which is understandable. That is the native land where psychology was born as an experimental science in the late 1800's. For sure the research hasn't gone deep enough for the psychology establishment. Several studies have shown a positive correlation between graphology findings and those from other methods. Yes, critics will trot out neigh-saying limited studies showing that this nag can't get out of the gate. "They didn't think much of Seabiscuit but he proved them wrong," Grim responds.

Whether handwriting analysis is valid as a measure of personality is the major issue. Under that is a separate issue that must also be addressed. It's the question of personality itself. Analysts don't seemed bothered by it. They accept its existence and sturdy structure. Nevertheless, psychology cynics want to whine about it. Is personality a definable concept? Or are we doomed to reach for it and have it elude us? Just what is it? As with much of psychology, a youthful soft science, experts squabble about the major terms and concepts. Many have their own definitions for personality. In the 1930's Gordon Allport, the distinguished professor from Harvard, (see the chapter on history of handwriting analysis) conducted experiments in "expressive movement," which included handwriting. He delivered 50 definitions for personality through history. After reviewing all of them, he arrived at his own hefty-bag, eye-glazing definition. "Personality is the dynamic organization within the individual of those psychophysical systems that determine his unique adjustments to his environment." Dynamic implies constant, energetic movement. When your   definition has "dynamic" in it, you will be condemned for thinking you can clinch enough to identify it. We are perpetual moving targets, are we not? How can you say what we are?

You can sense Grim's mind pouncing on a metaphor. "Well, so is our face. Surely parts of it all the time, like our mouth, eyes, tongue, nose as it breaths, cheek in smiling and frowning and displaying our other dipsey-doodle emotions. We can describe *these* items."

Some would say that personality is unlike physical science, which can be examined under a microscope, in beakers or with gauges. We can't see it to describe it. Grim says we can. We observe it in how people act. What we see is physical too. As we differ, we aren't robots. That is the tough part. Predicting future behavior is difficult as it involves frequently changeable human beings. Physical science is very predictable. When an individual acts, a multitude of variables can influence what he will do. We work with patterns and probabilities and human judgments and that is the best we can do. To say we just can't nail down personality traits and meanings from people or their handwriting is inaccurate. Outside handwriting analysis we have been describing people's personalities for thousands of years. "He's outgoing, egotistical, witty, temperamental, irritable, and bright." They may be layman's epithets but they have worked for ages. We instinctively know what they mean and we even calibrate them as necessary. We have followed people in their behavior, assigning them traits and other acting patterns. We may not mimic dignified men of science but don't sniff at our efforts. It is the best we can do and it should be good enough for our purposes. Millions of anecdotes from laypeople and experts over the centuries can't simply be rejected as lacking worth and significance. We all make decisions and judgments and take secure steps based on our knowledge of other people from our own perceptions and what others tell us about them. "Watch out. He's slippery but he's otherwise a pleasant guy to be around. He'll talk your ears off and he's a jokester." Okay, we note these elements, understand them as non-experts in human behavior, and act accordingly.

If handwriting analysis is under psychology's banner as a social science, it will never attain the scientific certainty of chemistry or physics. When you held your nose for those two courses it wasn't always in the lab. Although they may have seemed dull and difficult, their physical nature allows for eased measurement and reliable results. No human behavior needs to be evaluated to arrive at their wambamexactlyonegram laws. We know the balloon with helium will rise. We also know these laws aren't always black and white. At 32 degrees Fahrenheit the water in the puddle will freeze. Boom. Sunrise-in-the-morning certainty? Actually no—only at sea level and under normal conditions. Not as certain as you think, but more so than social science. If you know the specific conditions, physical science allows you to comfortably predict the outcome.

The so-called laws in social science seem to fluctuate. Initially those laws are established by scientists who profess to follow scientific techniques. All the same, these human beings are biased, prejudiced, frequently tired and stressed, at times even ignorant, and in rare moments soaked with agendas. Any of these will disturb their objectivity. As human beings their subjectivity can never be completely erased. The rules for chemistry existed centuries before scientists discovered any of them. They also exist whether or not the scientist testing them is a frumious bandersnatch. If his mortar pestles and his bunsens burn, his outcomes repeat. They work for slouches and for geniuses. In psychology those rules come from one group of very human beings making judgments about how they and others, also very human, behave. With that as backdrop they try to predict how they will act. Although studies have confirmed handwriting analysis above chance, the best we can hope for is that its rules are valid and reliable to a high degree of probability.

No system or technique or test or assessment in psychology is perfect, including handwriting analysis. Because psychology is imperfect, detractors regularly attack each of its areas. Psychologists and others have used the Rohrschach Inkblot Test since the 1920's. After piles of studies grading it and decades of relying on it, a 1964 movement tried to shred it. Like the star-spangled youknowwhat, the test still stood and waved, but weakly. Since then its status has actually grown somewhat. Commentators seem to want to retain it. Those who still embrace it aren't feeling its warmth. Apparently the only reason it survives is that nothing better has been devised. The best known figure in psychology is Sigmund Freud. Psychologists now mostly discredit his revolutionary concepts of the early twentieth century. Psychoanalysis and even its non-Freudian notions aren't resting easy on any couch these days. Some critics charge psychoanalysis is an hour on a couch wasted. They claim that most people get better from their sessions, now usually on a snug chair, because they *think* they are better. Some psychoanalysts are making large fees and practicing, oh no, it can't be, look at this, Winthrop, placeboanalysis. With his flip comments over a half century ago, film mogul Samuel Goldwyn (the G in MGM) may now be a sage. He remarked, "Anyone who goes to a psychiatrist should have his head examined."

Critics carp that analysts see personality as a Christmas tree. Its ornaments are all the traits just hanging as they await a call to interaction. "Well, we do," Grim frankly admits. Graphoanalysts champion the trait theory—personality as a series of qualities that combine and influence each other to form a complete structure. Whether a trait lies above or below the surface of our awareness, trait assessment must be precise.

That is one of the critics' points. "How can you analysts glibly award someone a certain trait? It's one thing to find it in his writing. It's another to find it in his personality," they say. When analysts find a trait in the writing they knock over everything foraging for its support in the person himself. Suppose an analyst finds "open-minded" as a trait in your writing. Critics contend you and he will both scour your present and past to confirm that you have it. If you want to find it somewhere, success is likely. You may be open-minded for some things but not others, they say. It is so vague that it can't be culled from conduct. A friend may agree you are but another may disagree. Your Mom will say you definitely are but your Pop will say "Yeah, but..." Regardless, you will consider yourself open-minded. That's a positive quality and you're delighted to say you have it. Grim grants this all makes sense. With Graphoanalysts espousing the trait theory of personality, in the face of other theories of personality, they make judgments about a trait's presence based on evidence from whatever source.

"We can't do any better than that," he declares. "This is social science and we live with it and constantly seek to improve it where justified."

It's easy to nitpick about social science precepts since you can't establish the feet-or-meters proof that physical science can. Knowing someone well and erecting their whole person with readily observable attributes intimidates close friends. Hopefully your knowledge is enough to independently verify the analyst's finding of a specific trait. Consider the possible sources—spouses, parents, children, friends, bosses, co-workers, teachers, counselors, family, psychology tests, personality assessment tests and techniques, questionnaires, and some self-appraisal.

Grim points out that "Pinning down traits is a problem not confined to handwriting analysis." It's a problem for any other psychology professional trying to determine personality. Don't single out analysts for criticism. We accept that it's tricky to know a personality with its separate traits.

"We have made our bed on these issues," Grim insists. "So far we have no problem sleeping in it. If a psychologist says our sheets are soiled, have him check his own bed."

Grim emphasizes that analysts work goes beyond isolating traits. That is important but only a starting point. Analysts also assess the strength of the trait. A person found to be "open-minded" will gain an adverb calibrating it. He will be termed somewhat, moderately, largely, very or some other qualifying word. He also points out that everyone else outside graphology evaluates personality the same way.

"We copy psychology. We just do it in the context of handwriting. Our decisions on traits arise from the writing strokes. But the descriptions of the traits themselves are on loan from psychology."

Even ordinary life, he declares. If we asked your brother how willing you are to accepting other people's opinions and ideas, he will say typically, "He is very open-minded." Or, "He is not very open-minded. Or instead, "He just won't listen to what you have to say." Analysts are specific too. They just happen to take handwriting as the source.

The skeptic questions if handwriting analysis is scientifically valid. Grim says he does too. He has scrutinized it and plumbed its depths. He looks for that daylight of doubt, the parts that just don't add up. A doubter asks where he gets his certainty for this topic. He may ask if Grim has a tangible method of evaluating it to convince the, ah, unconvinced. Grim has what he calls a "practical exercise" that has helped him know he has been "on the right track with the right train for these many years."

He explains: "If you were to give me the handwriting of your old friend from Oregon, someone I have never met, and I were to analyze it and provide you a comprehensive report outlining his personal qualities, and you were to agree the report is substantially accurate, would that do anything to convince you?"

He can't just do the skeptic's writing. He may have gathered too much data about him from meeting him or going behind his back. Grim knows he must do what he calls a "blind" innocent analysis, one where the skeptic will be satisfied Grim doesn't know the individual.

Grim well understands why people feel the need to initiate the Big Question about his subject's validity. The man who stalked and grilled him after a speech at the civic club was one of many analysts will endure. As Gypsy Rose Lee's Momma might say, "If you're gonna flaunt it, you better have it." Even so, he barely tolerates those blunt questions about his topic's legitimacy. If he is petulant, where they stand is from where they sit. He grants natural suspicion, but he's upset about the skeptics' vantage point.

"I believe in the Indian Moccasin principle," as he calls it. Sounds familiar. "Most doubters are not qualified to question handwriting analysis. They don't know enough about what it is, what it reveals, and what it can do."

For a bonafide evaluation, they should first learn Graphoanalysis, then apply it and see if it works. "You don't know what we Indians go through until you have walked a mile in our moccasins," is Grim's Indian drumbeat. Now we know. Although a skeptic may cede Grim's point, until he takes him up on it, he won't know if it's true.

"Wouldn't it take some time for any doubter to learn it and apply it?" I ask.

"Yes, it would." Grim concurs. "But I think it is crucial," from both his and his colleagues' experience. "The best way to verify it is from actual use, the surest test." Grim believes the vast majority of those learning the subject and applying it confirm its legitimacy but hasn't seen any data on it. Some analysts with hefty credentials have gone farther. Doctor A. A. Roback, Psychology Professor at Harvard University, has written 40 books and declares: "Thus far I have not encountered a single individual who, after considerable application of graphology, has rejected it as unscientific."

Grim's faith isn't just about its validity; accuracy counts too. That would seem to relate to the scientific standard of reliability. Your results replicate. His belief is more than cottoncandy conviction. It's from his actual experience. Based on his own survey of countless samples of writing squared against his acquaintance with the person, his matches line up. Not every time, but close. When he doesn't know the person well enough, he'll get help from someone who knows them well. Often that will be confined to the writer himself. If possible he tries to avoid the writer for confirmation or rejection. They are too near the evaluation to be objective.

Some analysts have uttered more steely statements about their own accuracy. "Handwriting has never lied to me," flies from the mouths of a few. Grim chortles at that. "They must be very good, very young, or very lucky analysts. And also about 15% deluded."

His rough proportion of success is about 85%. Other analysts have also suggested numbers in that range. For the 15% that don't seem to match up, Grim confesses he's baffled each time it occurs. "Keep in mind," he says, "we are dealing with over a hundred traits. With so many common traits among many people, you have to draw the line somewhere." He underlines the majority of important traits. When he limits it to them, he estimates an 85% accuracy rate.

"If you are demanding better than 85% certainty, you ask for too much," Grim squawks.

You overlook that any social science discipline is not perfect. Each one has its upturned-nose detractors on one side and its shield-bearing defenders on the other. Even the predominant theories in psychology and other social sciences spend much of their time dancing while critics shoot at their happy feet. Since each social doctrine assesses human conduct, they're all deficient. One set of fallible human beings, prejudiced, biased, inadequate, neurotic, judges other humans hopelessly fallible. Despite applying systems with sensible criteria, those applying them have those same prejudices, and other frailties. A respectable, conscientious person appraising the worth of handwriting analysis will admit their prejudices. They will try valiantly to appraise it objectively. For their part analysts will do what they can to apply the proper standards and shun their flypaper biases. No appraisal of writing will ever be faultless but it can be exceptional and unsurpassed. That should endear it to the elevated mind. Before handwriting is even applied, human conduct is complex and elusive to predict. Handwriting raises the heat for everyone because it's already cursed with poor credibility.

For a moment forget about seeing their handwriting. When you live with someone for decades and you are asked to determine what they will do or say, your predictions can be very wrong. After living with someone for years you evaluate them. The most you can expect is a high probability of accuracy. Much of the error, Grim speculates, is from the observee's systemic veiling of their true nature, feelings and attitudes.

"Bestow the same leeway to us analysts, please," he implores. "Don't expect us to outdo high probability when we compile a handwriting analysis report based on stroke evidence."

"Isn't that rationalizing to save your subject from censure?" we respond. Analysts seem to hide within the folds of psychology's big apron and harbor their excuse to be as right as *they* are only *most* of the time.

"And why not?" Grim volleys. "We get the bad press for our infighting over meanings and for not getting reports accurate all the time. Give us some slack."

"Yeah, but at least psychology has had many validation experiments," we say.

"Still, many of the same problems afflict other disciplines in psychology," he points out. "Some of these critics are psychologists. Haven't those respected giants Freud, Adler, and Jung also suffered through critical barrages? They saw human behavior from their age's perspectives and their science's progress. Should analysts attack *psychologists* because they cannot agree on their ideology? If they all weather similar differences, then give us the benefit also."

"Well, but psychology has had more formal science confirming its theories.

"We know we have to do better in the science of our discipline. But at least concede that our subject is just another one in which rational, fair and honorable people disagree."

"We can do that, but you must get going with the grand validation experiments once and for all."

Actually analysts do agree more than they disagree. In astrology you will find hazy statements that can be applied to many people. An analyst is supposed to identify particular qualities of being. He declares specific elements with quantifiable standards. This is human behavior being measured for presence and intensity by other human beings. Go easy on the measurer. An analyst makes judgments on whether a stroke relates to a trait and how strong it is. That is inevitable with any discipline that observes human behavior. That doesn't mean the analyst can ignore standards outlining what a specific stroke is for a specific trait. The same for how strong the trait is. Conclusions reached should be justified by applying some ascertainable benchmark. If another analyst looks at a piece of writing, his conclusions should be substantially the same as the first analyst. They will hardly ever coincide completely because of human fallibility. When you compare the exact measurements of physical science, singling out handwriting analysis is unfair. Social science principles are never going to approach physical science for absolute certainty. Social science measures human conduct, whereas physical science measures objects and their effects on each other. Physical science is not beset with the subjectivity that social science must endure. No matter who is applying the laws of physical science, the results should be the same. If you combine two hydrogen molecules with one oxygen molecule you will get water no matter if it's Professor Einstein or Professor Frankenstein. With social science you only hope the two scientists come close in evaluating the same specimen of handwriting. If they are both competent experts and apply the same definable standards of interpretation, the results should concur.

Grim has been in handwriting analysis for decades. He insists his enthusiasm and faith have not dimmed. He is as strong an advocate and a practitioner as when he began his formal studies in 1992. In his speeches and his classes he urges people, "Don't take my word on its merits and don't accept me as authority," he dares his students and his audiences. "Go out and learn it as I did and apply it. I'm sure it will prove itself to you." The proof is in the pudding, he is saying. The best way to convince yourself, he advises, is by finding out what it is, how it works, and then put into action. Satisfy yourself by looking at the writing of real people and compare that writing to what you learned. Many astute people have considered its scientific worth. They endorse it in a landslide, he says with an assurance that seems genuine. But he doesn't follow that by handing out sheets of favorable data.

"Where does your certainty come from?"

"My own experiences and dialogues with other analysts and reading of similar experiences of other analysts." He also pleads, "Don't view us as magic or mystical or anything like those unscientific pursuits such as astrology or tarot cards."

It is simply a part of life that can be verified by observation. Most people don't realize the extensive work that has been done, most of it since the early nineteenth century. From a long time observing the writing of thousands and thousands of human beings, handwriting analysis has compiled a loaded barge of figures to sustain its findings. Much of it came from earnest amateur analysts surveying those around them without formal protocols. A lot of the data has been floating around for years seeking a welcoming dock to unload it and an ample warehouse in which to stockpile it. Critics will assert the barge has been laden with garbage and deserves its nomad status, denying it entry anywhere. The amateur results have been buttressed by many partial studies both formal and otherwise that the public doesn't know about.

If you talk to critics, handwriting analysis belongs nowhere except with those pariahs mysticism, hoaxes, and pseudo-science. Advocates respectfully disagree and proclaim it a genuine addition to social science. If it's within that sprawling area and presumably part of psychology, where is its place in psychology? Grim puts it into applied psychology, functioning as part of two methods. It is a projective technique and a personality assessment test or technique. Projective techniques draw out the individual's personality either by an external stimulus, or no stimulus. The most celebrated test with a stimulus is the Rohrschach Inkblot. Ambiguous images seeks to flush out the person's private self in his interpreting the image. These familiar images are ink-blotched, strange, intricate, and symmetrical. By design they can't be easily recognizable objects or the test is not doing its job. Handwriting is different. No image lies in wait to stimulate the writer, who is the test or technique taker. Any drawing out of the inner self is from scratch by writing on a blank sheet of paper. Impulses stem from unconscious and conscious parts of the person's brain reflected on the paper. Whatever traits in there waiting to come out are projected onto the paper merely by the act of writing itself. Any inspiration for what comes out to play on the page is in the mind of the penholder.

Handwriting is the tangible result of your private thoughts and feelings leaving the mind and declaring to the world, "This is who I am as a person. Take me or leave me." Think of your writing as a print-out prepared from your own computer software, your brain, except it is about yourself, not others. Imagine, your writing discloses how you really are inside and outside and you don't even know what you said. The unconscious impulses direct the hand how to maneuver the pen. Another step follows that only an analyst can perform. He decodes those strokes and other elements, like spacing and thickness, into discrete, understandable traits of personality.

Handwriting analysis is unique among personality tests and techniques. The individual doesn't know what he's revealed about himself. He is confessing his rap sheet of sins and misdemeanors without benefit of the clergy's sympathetic ears or the watchful eyes of the police. The others falter because most of what they elicit spills from a conscious answer to a question, comment or statement, or from their interpretation of a picture. People of modest mentality intuit the purposes behind each question. When the question asks you if "You often feel sad," you know it is asking about depression or melancholy or manic-depressive behavior. Although more refined in recent years, these other tests may not do any better at mining our lode of diamonds and veins of coal. An example of a true or false inquiry: "I am more outgoing than shy" has been replaced with "I really enjoy being the center of attention." You can well question if this is an improvement.

Handwriting delivers the traits objectively. Though you may express them by merely scratching out strokes, they are impartial and unbiased. Because you're oblivious to what you reveal of yourself, an innocent purity envelopes your writing. This factor alone gives it an advantage over other personality tests and techniques. Some of them gather their information from other people evaluating the individual. Since other human beings with their biases are making the judgments, that can fall short of objectivity. Many require another person to interpret actions of the test or technique taker. More bias.

Handwriting is also better than an evaluation from others because it reveals the whole person, inside and outside. Many professionals can appraise the outward actions of another person. To burrow into the private portions of their being can be thorny. Even psychologists stumble seeking unconscious traits and motivations. They are confined to tests and techniques and their powers to observe the individual's statements and actions. With handwriting analysis the unconscious portion of traits will appear in the writing. Most psychology tests cover only a portion of the individual. With over a hundred traits, handwriting analysis divulges the full range of personality, including a solid grasp of how the writer thinks and how he manages his emotioins.

The Rohrschach is the best known technique for getting at personality. If you think the competition for handwriting analysis is the Rohrschach and a few others, you would be surprised. In her recent book *Cult of Personality,* Annie Murphy Paul says about 2,500 personality tests have been devised in an industry that does about 400 million dollars of business a year. Although the quantity of tests is phenomenal, the quality is not.

One of the most utilized is the Meyers-Briggs test, which divides people into personality types, such as introvert-extrovert. By requiring answers to questions that place people in slots, the individual is limited to broad, arbitrary categories. Paul cites the statistic that 89 of the top 100 Fortune companies utilize this test to hire and train employees and give them self-knowledge or information for working with fellow employees. A cousin to the Rohrschach, is the widely-used Thematic Apperception Test (TAT). The test taker is handed a series of big cards on which appear people in unidentified situations. For each picture the test taker is asked to provide the story they believe explains the scene. People in the pictures are clearly seen but their circumstances are not. They are so general, however, that you cannot objectively deduce what is going on. The intent is to provide an image and make you create the story from your own inner perspective. Presumably whatever is on your mind, conscious or unconscious, will come spurting out as you fashion your version of life. As another projective technique, this allegedly extracts the real individual by leading you to the source of their troubles. Or at least what is really on their mind. The test giver then interprets the responses to reveal their personality. A more modern projective technique is the Wartegg Test, more widely used in Europe than here. Instead of hazy inkspills it shows a series of familiar lines in various forms, asking the test taker to elaborate on what he sees. Another leading test, not a projective one, is the Minnesota Multi-Phasic Inventory (MMPI), which presents true/false statements. Most of us are familiar with this exam from school. It takes your answers and develops a profile of your personality. It is called a self-reporting inventory since you are providing the information about yourself. This is one of those exams where you should have good insight into what is being asked about you. This differs from handwriting since no question is asked but you still supply multiple answers to the question Who am I? and What are my attributes?

These prominent tests and others bear the heat of critics for not getting to the heart of personality. The intent is to know the true, complete person, which will enable their actions to be reliably forecast. Detractors charge that these tests/techniques don't adequately appraise or predict human behavior. Both the test taker's and the test giver's roles have been pummeled. How can we be sure the test taker's interpretation is correct? How can we allow the test giver so much room to interpret the results? How competent is he? How experienced is he with this test? A few thousand studies of the projective techniques have left them with third degree burns and layers of gauze.

Critical blasts aren't confined to the psychology fraternity. Groups outside psychology condemn these tests and techniques and would curtail their use. Recently the U.S. Equal Employment Opportunity Commission (EEOC) has denounced tests or techniques that don't measure relevant skills for particular jobs. As a consequence, novel tests have stepped forward with thrusts at real-world relevancy. One gaining notice is the Assessment Center Technique. The leading practitioner is Development Dimensions International, a company that creates role-playing for a prospective business executive. The employer provides an applicant with a phone, computer, and tape recorder. The Center gives him a simulated business environment and a series of tasks. A panel of observers evaluates his performance. This method attempts a more direct and realistic appraisal of the individual's job skills and personality. On-the-job behavior will allegedly disclose if those skills and his personality mesh with the position. Although it may be early to grade the Center, Grim welcomes this innovative approach. Yet he questions how real it can be, especially the interaction between employees and between employees and customers. Under the gaze of harsh human judgment and artificial settings, unreal attitudes and demeanor tend to surface.

He wonders if it's merely an audition for a play, or another reality show. "If the set is a stage, are the players not acting for their director and the audience? I guess it's better than the uneasy tension of the interview, where no workplace actions commonly arise."

Intelligence tests can involve handwriting and they haven't escaped censure either. Some people would discard the eternal SAT's as measuring only someone's test-taking skills, or other irrelevant factors. For years minorities have accused its administrator, the Educational Testing Service, of discrimination against them. Grim adds this to his discipline's inventory of benefits. Handwriting analysis doesn't discriminate as you can't tell race or sex or anything else under the sun these days that has demanded protection and gotten it from the law. It also doesn't present you with a worrisome test to take, yet magically yields test results through unbiased evaluation of the handwriting.

"Handwriting is behavior similar to shaking hands," says Grim. Hence, he and others think it should be added to the list of expressive behavior.

Experts have wrestled whether our expressive behavior is consistent. The findings seem to say so. Handwriting is also what we call body language. Putting your finger against your nose may tell us you are lying when you speak. Wrapping that finger around a pen in a hand using pen and paper also conveys information about you. Much information. Since handwriting registers strokes on paper, it should be better than other body language, like walking, gestures, facial movements, and others. They are brief, mostly unrecorded, and disappear. By contrast handwriting is recorded and thereby permanent. In addition, whether it was written years ago or far away or the writer has died, it can be evaluated anytime.

———

Handwriting analysis advances steadily. Limited research has occurred all over the world. The grand validation experiment awaits the money, a coordinated plan for the focus of research, and earnest efforts to accomplish it. In the meantime, handwriting analysis inches forward with alternative methods of partial validation. If you can only see darkness and doom for handwriting analysis, step back a few paces. Astronomy began as astrology. In the long medieval nighttime, alchemy had metal-to-gold practitioners for centuries before chemistry filled them full of lead. Prior to Columbus, geography would've had ships niagarafallsbarreling off the side of the earth. Deemed the center of the universe by the Catholic Church, the recently-round earth lost its place in the sky from an Italian scientist named Galileo. Not only sharp, he was steadfast too as he defied the Church, the establishment at this sixteenth century moment. He was tried for insisting what his empirical heart told him: the earth is not the center of the universe. He was right, of course, and the light of truth finally blazed from the actual center, the sun. In China as a health technique acupuncture pricked Asian skin for centuries. Elsewhere traction for it was only slip'n'slide. Finally in the late twentieth century, medicine stopped slamming the door in its face after being shamed into recognizing its value. No one knows for sure why it works. This is a lesson for handwriting skeptics demanding to know the place in our minds handwriting traits begin. Graphology's corporate parent is psychology, which flourishes after only gradual growth in the early twentieth century. As a social science it is a youth with a long journey ahead to maturity. To unlock our behavior, graphology wants to join psychology for the trip to discovery.

Some skeptics maintain that when you square the results of handwriting against other methods, they split. Stubbornness and selfishness, for example, may be in your writing but it doesn't bear out in an evaluation by the MMP Test, so they say. If this charge is warranted, more research is needed. Over the years, minor surveys have been done with evidence going both ways. Analysts suggest that they don't coincide because handwriting is simply independent of the others. It reaches your attributes so well that it leaves other techniques mumbling to themselves. These other methods yield superficial, questionable, or incorrect findings. Maybe to interpret handwriting a unique set of rules must be followed. Further, the other matching source could be unreliable, such as a defective psychology test. In those tests that ask if the analysis confirmed their personality traits, the individual might not know themselves well. The psychologist or the analyst judging the analysis might be inept.

I want to know, "Aren't these standard excuses by advocates seeking recognition for an unproven concept?"

"By themselves they don't invalidate handwriting analysis. They are just another generic argument against it," Grim replies. "Yes, graphology may not coincide with the findings of some other tests or techniques.

"Why do you think that's so?"

"I would offer the same reasons just outlined. It's one more urgent basis for the comprehensive research to be started and completed once and for all."

Handwriting analysis is imperfect. That doesn't make it worthless. We need to be careful in applying it and continue to test its validity. Meantime we can apply it to aid in solving human problems. Your daughter may have made several bad choices in careers or husbands. What is it within her make-up that leads her to the choices? As we strive for perfection, the most we can hope for in handwriting analysis is high probability in assessing someone's writing. One obvious way we measure the personality of individuals is by observation. That is the best way we have to evaluate a person. You might live with your spouse for twenty years and then be asked to identify their prominent personality traits. Or be asked to predict how they will act in some situation. Your judgments about this may be very good but they will not be perfect. At most they will be highly accurate. Should we ignore your judgments because they lack perfection? In fact, we make informal judgments about people all the time in our daily lives. We do it because we *must* in important areas like picking a spouse, evaluating an employee, or deciding on a partner in a business.

The lack of widespread testing of handwriting analysis has meant that the important professional organizations, like the American Psychological Association, have not accepted it. That doesn't mean it would be rejected by this group. Ultimately it might be confirmed as a valid and reliable technique to measure personality. It hasn't been researched enough to satisfy the scientific community. Some people consider Tiger Woods the greatest golfer of all time. Despite his considerable achievements, experts should withhold that award. For now it is Jack Nicklaus because his tournament record is superior over a greater span.

Grim asks this perspective be applied to his topic. Few people have embraced it to create a groundswell for its growth and approval. "Give it a chance over time and acceptance should come," he says.

Graphoanalysis has grown from a foundation of thousands and thousands of analysts surveying the handwriting of tens and tens of thousands of individuals. The results were often compared to the known personality traits of the person as confirmed by their family, friends, teachers, and professional counselors. This both preceded and followed up on the lifetime studies of handwriting by its founder Milton Bunker, who evaluated the writing of several thousand people during his life. Therefore, traits have been established by a multitude of informal experiments over a few centuries involving real people, not merely by intuitive guesswork as many critics have suggested.

"Yes some misguided analysts veered by assessing traits in their own way. Please don't hold them against the rest of us serious, responsible analysts," pleads Grim.

When the studies are finally achieved, analysts think their subject will establish itself admirably. Until that happens the sensible and logical view is to allow them to prove its worth by actually doing an analysis for you. Most analysts convince public skeptics of their subject's validity and their own competence by showing what they can do. Let's say you have a good friend who moved to Idaho a year ago. Before he moved you spent most of your life with him and think you know him inside and out. He just sent you a letter that you received yesterday. You take the letter to an analyst who swears he has never heard of (let alone knew) your friend. You are convinced he is telling the truth. Your friend confirms that he doesn't recall the analyst either. You ask the analyst to survey the writing and give him a comprehensive report specifying all the traits your friend reveals in his writing. This is what Grim calls a "blind analysis," fresh and untainted . If the analyst happens to know the writer there is always the stain of that knowledge slinking into the analysis. You also ask the analyst to measure how strong those traits are, not just identify them in general. Then you ask him to put all the traits together, show their interaction, and give him a detailed description of his friend's character and personality. The analyst complies. You review the report and agree it substantially outlines in detail your friend as you know him. You even show it to your friend and he concurs with its findings. Maybe his wife or mother reads it and concurs also.

Grim calls this the Pudding Proof. "Until the grand research has been done, is this not a reasonable way to accept the validity of handwriting analysis?" he asks.

In the meantime this is the major mode analysts seek to establish their credibility and competence. Where their work is corroborated from people who actually know the individual writer well, that buttresses the results. You can quibble over what personality is, or what a trait is, or which traits are legitimate and which are illusory, or which traits are too far into that unconscious or whatever you call it. Those are bonafide concerns over which rational minds can differ. For now give the analyst a hearty handshake, if you won't hug him, with recognition of his service to you. He never met your friend and he has told you, a lay person, what you should concede are personality traits *you* accept in evaluating people.

"The proof is in the pudding," says Grim. "You verify the accuracy of the traits found in the writing by handing them to someone who knows the individual well. He confirms them. He also knows no fakery was involved."

Doubters snipe at Grim's beloved subject and he knows they must be tackled. Skeptic Barry Beyerstein, who authored and edited with his brother *The Write Stuff,* attacks handwriting analysis. One target is the trait findings. For example, an analyst terms a person as "stubborn." Beyerstein says there must be at least five million other people in the U.S. who are also stubborn. What does it prove to make that empty declaration?

"That may be so," counters Grim. "Millions of people have common traits. If he is describing an American, *that* only covers around one and two-thirds per cent of the country, since the population is now just above 300 million."

Beyerstein should also understand that a Graphoanalyst takes more than a few seconds to declare a trait. He would be surprised with their spadework and refinement. To begin, the analyst will describe a trait from the strokes of the writing which are part of letters, not the letters themselves. A single letter can have several strokes and can yield other traits by how strokes vary from letter to letter. A skilled analyst doesn't simply seize on a trait and announce it to the recipient of the analysis. He refines it by saying how strong or intense the trait is in the constitution of the writer. On the one hand, the writer may be only occasionally stubborn. On the other, he may be so stubborn that whenever he is shown to be wrong, he will refuse to give in, even where he really knew it. This calibration of the traits separates handwriting analysis from the other subjects it's often compared to, such as astrology. Customarily an astrologer will describe a person or an action so broadly it could apply to many people. That is a sound point and astrology should be disparaged for it. In contrast an analyst takes a trait and specifically defines the writer's actions. Initially an analyst may say someone is stubborn but is quick to add detail on the degree or intensity of the stubbornness. A trait should be described in more than just black and white. The shades of color must glint, not just fill space.

"People are complicated, not stereotypes of qualities," says Grim. "Analysts know this. Beyerstein apparently does not, as he fails to grip the skills of able analysts. I really think his criticism is at slipshod analysts, not Graphoanalysis."

Beyerstein wants to shishkabob the backers of another recently-surging technique—body language. He uses it as an analogy for handwriting's failure in revealing character.

He said: "There are individualities in the way we walk, too. Not many people say that has to do with character."

"He is wrong here too," says Grim.

Body language buffs bloom everywhere today and they believe each gesture discloses *something* about us. People walk straight up and smartly showing sturdy self-confidence. Some walk stooped over and unsteadily, exposing uncertainty and meekandweakness. You don't have to be an expert to know walking's value for personal information. Just ask any urban punk looking for an easy mugging.

"Yes, I know that walking stooped over can be age or disability. But where it's not physical that doesn't detract from its meaning. Either state can be verified easily."

Some critics look at a sample of handwriting and see only strokes that scamper aimlessly. They vary so much that they're hopeless as signs of character. They contend our strokes are too inconsistent to be measured precisely for stroke patterns. Thus, they wonder how an analyst can make judgments about them when the strokes seem so irregular. The strokes hardly ever touch their imaginary baselines, the differences in height of the small letters, the spacing between letters, the height of capital letters, and so on. How can an analyst be objective in looking at strokes made by imperfect often sloppy human beings? In short, how can you gauge something so inexact? What's more, our writing has become more wretched and the trend seems to be toward, how can we put this, even more wretched. To try to glean traits from this casual mix of shapes and forms grows harder each time.

Graphoanalysis, which homes in on strokes within letters, has answers. True, the strokes can vary and do vary each time. However, they fundamentally resemble each other. Over a hundred distinct strokes relate to particular traits. They are similar enough that analysts can harvest meaning from them. We can pick each of the McGuire sisters although they are not clones or identical-looking triplets. Asians can distinguish between Japanese, Chinese and Korean while Americans cannot. That is only because Americans don't have the experience doing it. In the same way, analysts can pick out the strokes by study and practice. Where the strokes vary greatly, the original stroke means what it does but the variation transforms it into a new trait. For example, the height of a t-stem will signify the amount of pride someone feels. When the t-stem gradually grows taller, the pride meaning fades and becomes excessive pride, which creates another trait, namely, vanity. With experience analysts learn to identify each stroke as denoted and the trait it conveys.

"I concede it sounds complex to identify and pin down so many different strokes," Grim says. "The analyst has a judgment call to make on every stroke. Once the analyst practices evaluations, they ultimately gain the knack to inventory traits."

This is no different from what we do in evaluating our fellow human beings. We often must decide whether a friend is very proud or whether he has become vain. We do it by observing his behavior. Handwriting analysis does it by measuring writing strokes.

Our writing is too often slack and undisciplined. Erratic writing toughens the analyst's task. Because analysts know that, they overcome it by requesting large samples of the writing. The more they can evaluate the more accurate the analysis. An analyst looks for stroke patterns. The more common strokes there are, the more accurate the evaluations about each stroke. If the writer draws most of his t-bars near the top of his t-stems, the analyst can better project the writer's view of his ability to achieve success. Humans are often unpredictable. The more consistent a person's strokes are, the more predictable their behavior is. IGAS has even published a guide demonstrating the exact manner of identifying strokes and measuring their trait's intensity.

"If you desire precision, this guide gives it," says Grim.

It shows actual strokes and their calibrated differences in meaning. In only a few instances are lengths or other numerical dimensions mentioned. The segway between many strokes and their related traits distills to a careful judgment of the place to draw the line between them. Just as we do when we sit in judgment of friend and foe.

As mentioned before, when analysts find a trait in a stroke, that's only the beginning. They must be sure it's the specific stroke and not one evolved into another one, which means a new trait. Then they must measure the quality of the stroke to see how strong or weak the trait is. This measuring is done each time other similar strokes appear in the writing. For each calculation, the trait's cement dries as a member of this writer's personality.

Grim says, "This process may seem time-consuming and tedious. It's really not. After a while an analyst can gallop through them."

Familiarity needs to breed competence before contentment. Think of it this way. When you get that handwritten friendly letter in the mail, don't you usually know the sender? When you analyze and you unconsciously combine those common strokes, you are mimicking the same actions from memory as a layman. At the moment you first spied the envelope, did you fix on a single stroke or even a few strokes? No. You saw the writing as an entirety. Gestalt at work. Each person has stroke patterns that allow us to instantly see the whole writing as his.

Every time an analyst reviews handwriting specimen of a familiar person he is conducting another handwriting analysis validity experiment. It may be informal and lack controls and other recognized conditions. It's one more occasion for the analyst to confirm or refute what he knows about the person. Hence, in a small way each time he issues a report an analyst advances handwriting analysis, discarding trait-stroke combinations that don't follow its standards. Those traits that are confirmed solidify those traits, which satisfies the scientific principle of reliability. For the last two centuries analysts have built on the progress of others with their own studies.

Grim wants to ask the scientific establishment, "Doesn't this car-adding freight train of analyses count for something? How many thousands of informal anecdotes does it take to equal one comprehensive scientific survey?"

Grim has always wondered about the trait-stroke connection. It stretches his belief that a simple little stroke, not even a whole letter, and occasionally not even a large part of the letter, carries a single personality trait. It staggers him realizing the stroke can vary because it is drawn by an imperfect sometimes inattentive human being. Beyond wonder, Grim has tumbled into questioning and doubt. In trying to understand and accept it, he's had trouble not only visualizing its powerful truth but also portraying that to the public. Toss in that Grim likes to take situations from unrelated areas and apply them to handwriting analysis. Call him Metaphor Man. He enjoys inventing a clever analogy to illuminate often abstract handwriting principles. Listening to his car radio one day he heard a joke that snapped the On switch for his blender-on-a-bender mind. Soon the joke mixed with his trait-stroke musings. The joke's punchline formed the image he sought to understand and to impart the power of those tiny, unassuming strokes. They may be little like atoms but their power is immense like an atomic bomb. Oddly, the joke was about speaking, not handwriting, and the punchline came from the mouth of a three-year-old boy, not an adult. Grim is not even sure he recalls the joke correctly. No matter, as he believes he has recalled enough for a good laugh while retaining its value for handwriting analysis.

It begins just after a father has tucked his young son in for the night. Or so he thought.

Daddy, can I have a drink of water.

Jason, go to sleep.

[Pause]

Daddy, I want a drink of water.

No, stop asking and go to sleep.

[Pause]

Daddy, I really need a drink of water.

No, Jason, if you don't stop asking for a drink of water, I'm going to come in there and spank you.

[Longer pause]

Daddy, when you come to spank me, would you please bring me that drink of water?

—

The punchline ends a droll sketch. Grim expands on the ultimate meaning of that last sentence for handwriting analysis. It is sixteen words of a simple remark from a three-year old boy. It resonates with early evidence of at least seven great qualities this child has:

1.	Honesty	(He really did want a drink of water)
2.	Persistence	(He refused to take no for an answer)
3.	Courage	(He knew he would be spanked if he spoke up again)
4.	Foresight	(He knew that if he asked for the water again he might get it. His Daddy could bring it with him to the spanking)
5.	Intelligence	(It was brilliant strategy that probably avoided a spanking)
6.	Tact	(First, he said please. Second, he didn't demand the drink. He asked his Daddy to bring it only when he came to spank him)
7.	Sense of Humor	(It might make his Daddy laugh, reduce the tension, and change his attitude toward his son's insolence)

From a moment of a few spoken words in his young life we can learn so much about his potential for leadership and achievement in life. Similarly, when someone *writes* a few words, a handwriting analyst can review the individual strokes and discover important traits of his personality. By combining these strokes and the traits, he can construct the character of this human being. This can be done whether the writer is young or old. That is the massive power of handwriting.

If a few strokes of writing can reveal a lot about anyone, what about only one stroke? The founder of Graphoanalysis thought so. Milton Bunker pointed to a solitary stroke within a single letter having a colossal, geometric, Mrs. O'Leary's fire-starting cow, Helen of Troy's ship-launching face, the Archduke Ferdinand's-World-War-I-starting assassination, the bulldozer-stopping-snail-darter, and Royal-Air-Force's-German-invasion ending, William Blake-universe-in-a-grain-of-sand impact. In 1927 Charles Lindbergh became an American hero when he flew the first airplane across the Atlantic Ocean non-stop and solo. Five years later his infant son was kidnapped from his New Jersey estate and murdered. It was called the Crime of the Century. A German immigrant, Bruno Hauptmann, was convicted of the crimes. He died in the New Jersey electric chair in 1936. His widow spent 62 years that she survived him actively protesting his innocence, including a futile law suit against the State of New Jersey. He was home with her the evening of the kidnapping, she had insisted. Several questioned document examiners testified at the trial. If handwriting analysis had been allowed to give an opinion of his guilt, she might have enjoyed all those years with a live husband. A major piece of evidence was a ransom note. After Hauptmann was convicted and still refused to admit anything, the founder of Graphoanalysis, M. N. Bunker, reviewed the note and said he didn't know who wrote that note.

However, he added, "If Hauptmann wrote the note, he did not commit the crime."

Why did he draw that conclusion? The strokes telling him were open-top o's, which reveal a person who must talk about themselves.

"This writing indicates that if Hauptmann had been guilty he would have talked freely," Bunker declared. "[H]is talkativeness would have led him to say so much that he would have tied the rope around his own neck."

Even after his conviction and appeals had run out and he was on death row, Hauptmann never admitted to anyone that he was guilty of the crimes. In fact, he was firm in denying it. Disturbed by these denials and the circus nature of the media coverage and the trial, the Governor of New Jersey visited Hauptmann in his cell on death row. As Governor he had the power to commute the death sentence and save his life. If Hauptmann had admitted his guilt, the Governor declared, he would have saved him from the electric chair. Hauptmann also refused to admit anything to *him*. A newspaper even offered him $90,000.00 if he would confess. He rejected that too. As he was strapped into the electric chair, he denied his guilt one last time. To the last volt he died admitting nothing.

In recent years various journalists and other sleuths have theorized that Hauptmann was innocent. One believes Charles Lindbergh accidentally killed his child in a strange prank and tried to cover it up with the kidnapping. Apparently he had played some jokes on his wife before. Once he had hidden the baby in a closet and told everyone in the house the baby had been kidnapped. He waited a half hour before admitting the prank. The family nursemaid once stated he had "that little bit of sadism" in him. He didn't limit his cruelty to his family. On a sultry day a fellow pilot took a drink from a glass he thought had refreshing water in it. Lindbergh had filled it with kerosene. As the pilot convulsed with uncontrollable agony, Lindbergh laughed hysterically. The pilot went to the hospital. Another reviewer of the case suggested an aunt had done it. Still another says Hauptmann didn't kidnap the child but took advantage of the hoax to get the ransom money, which was found in a garage behind his home. Some believe Lindbergh's guilt from an alleged cover-up. Incredibly, Lindbergh insisted on leading the investigation and he was never interviewed by the police. Apparently his mammoth hero status allowed him to manipulate events.

Analysts tell everyone that one stroke equates to one personality trait. Analysts also know of the incredible command one trait can have over one person, especially from a "sore thumb" stroke. They are cautious, however, in allowing one stroke-trait to influence their conclusions about any one person. As human beings we are complicated and we have a bounty of other traits to affect our actions. Certain kinds of strokes have outsized influence on personality. One trait that provokes many analysts is pasty writing. Analyst Klara Roman, the transplanted Hungarian psychologist (discussed in the history chapter of this book), supposedly developed the word from the Italian word pasta. The writing has a doughy, swollen quality. Analysts also call it pastose or pastiose writing. Felt-tip and magic-marker pens naturally demonstate it. Distinguished analyst Shirley Spencer did employment screening, among her many other activities, including a popular column in the New York *Daily News* from the 1930's to the 1950's. She had assessed the character of an applicant for a sales position at a lumber company. He had pasty writing, which Spencer describes is like "a wagon wheel impression on the road after going through the mud." It's smudgy and thick, especially with fountain pens where ink escapes when the writer pauses or jerks the pen in his strokes. Analysts say people who write like this physically over-indulge. She advised the company not to hire him. Of course they ignored her and hired him. A short time later he disappeared. About three weeks later they found him holed up and untidy in a hotel with a young lady.

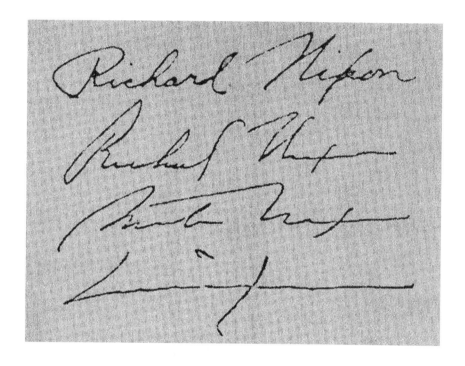

Our personalities can change but usually do only over a long period of time. Traumatic events in our lives can quickly alter our basic make-up, however. Since handwriting tracks your personality, when you are transformed as an individual, your handwriting changes with you. Witness the disintegrating handwriting of Richard Nixon between 1968 and 1974. Changes in signature, from top: 1968, 1969, early 1974 when Watergate plagued his presidency, and late 1974 when he had resigned.

Chapter 11

The Analysis

After Gazing at the Forest,
Focusing on the Trees

Obviously she wasn't listening

**Heading on the magazine piece for the deaf
Miss America 1995 Heather Whitestone,
who overcame doctors' declaring she
never would make it out of third grade**

In the U.S. every twelve seconds an American passes on having their handwriting analyzed. Or is it, twelve Americans every second pass on having it analyzed? That doesn't sound right either. Okay, it's worse but how much we don't really know. Nancy Reagan told young Americans to just say no to drugs. Analysts ask everyone to just say yes to the analysis. How many decide not to have one is like asking how many people didn't kill someone from fear of capital punishment. Graphology wants to know why people pass. Analysts think that people refrain from an analysis for several reasons, all silly of course. They are not sure it's reliable, valid, worthwhile, or cheap enough. Or they're clueless of what it does or they sense the analyst is unskilled. Another reason more often holding them back than it should—What happened in my life, now burned in my memory, stays in my memory. They fear their flawed lives may be reflected in their writing strokes. Of course, say analysts.

If people who passed were more familiar with the analysis, Grim is certain most would step forward with their writing samples. Many are curious but few chose the analysis, Grim finds. Nevertheless, outsiders want to know the analyst's routine in doing his analysis. How does he approach the writing? What does he do first in his evaluation of a writer's personality? How long does it take to do it all? Is it easy or hard?

Analysts are advised not to divulge much of what they go through. If people learn their methods they may buy a handwriting analysis book filled with the strokes and traits, then take the information and try to apply it. This information alone is like reading a medical dictionary, then taking instruments and treating a waiting room full of patients. Alexander Pope was right about the danger of shabby learning. Some will even take the flimsy information about traits and strokes they learn elsewhere and skip the book. Even more dangerous. Grim echoes his subject's alarm. When we press him for some insights, he pauses.

"I'm willing to unwrap our packaging to enlighten the public on something about the analysis. But only so far." He thinks the public will appreciate the analysts' thoroughness and seriousness. After that exposure he wants the public to keep their pens in their pockets until they learn it in depth.

He is adamant about limiting the credentials. "Once you have the sheepskin, as Southwest Airlines might put it, you are free to move about the country and analyze. Until then, I would prefer you have only an idea what we go through."

Grim is glad to discuss what analysts do as the initial steps. Unfortunately, he explains, he has seen two kinds of those steps, ones the analyst should take and ones many analysts actually take. He can tell an unripe analyst by what he does first with a sample of writing. He looks for what Grim calls "sore thumb" strokes. They loom large, often with radiating lines as if a wayward hammer just slammed them. Deviating so far from the school model, anyone with decent eyesight notices them. Their desperate excess announces them. They need not be large. Just radically different from their grade school matrix. Think of a caricature. Some objects are natural caricatures. If you think of Arnold Schwarzenegger, sore thumbs would be his bloated muscles and his blockhead face. Some are obvious: a giraffe and his neck; an elephant and his trunk; and Simon Cowell and his sarcasm. They can be subtle too. The writing may have exceptional roundness, resembling a hutch of dishes. Or tightness between letters suggesting a snow fence or a squished accordion. Neophyte analysts snatch these sore thumbs to discuss for their obvious meaning and easy description.

"Focusing first on the sore thumbs is premature," Grim says. "Wait. They will have their importance and their moment."

What do these abominable showmen strokes say about their creator? By themselves sore thumbs expose what's bothering the writer. Like global factors they are powerful. They affect the rest of the writing and thereby the entire personality, just as a bad auto accident can thrust you into a wheelchair and disrupt your life. Excessive strokes are the person over-responding to his surroundings. Usually they reflect inner torment related to the feature of the stroke's location. The person deals with his pain by overcompensating, leaving the huge strokes as obvious marks.

"People who overdo their reactions often express inappropriate thoughts. That's what is happening with sore thumbs," says Grim. "If it were sound instead of writing, they would be wailing for their troubles to be heard. As lines on paper, they are cries for help. In the old days, an SOS call; today 911."

Although ultimately he must address them, a veteran analyst bypasses sore thumbs. As his first step he backpeddles and gazes at the forest, the overall wilderness of writing. Thus the early vantage point is broad, Grim says. The eyes are on the whole person, who is greater than the parts. Or maybe just different from the parts. Does that sound like a cloudy concept from your distant past when Introductory Psychology was a college class? That gestalt applies here too.

"Working on the big picture is primary," Grim insists. "Take a bird's-eye view of the writing. You want to see what emanates from the lines on paper. Like a heating grate on the city sidewalk, what steams up to your eyes reviewing the passage on the paper? Does this person seem to be doing okay? Does he show peace and contentment? Or does his writing betray stress and tension?"

Other impressions could be coming at you. They all depend on the overall look of the writing. Not just analysts, but everyone does it first when they see someone's writing like a letter or some other item they read. Because we are far from the writing and can't help it, our tendency is to take a mental snapshot and think big. Click. This is really graceful writing, isn't it? Click. Boy, this is some sloppy writing. Click. Man, this person's writing is harsh and aggressive. All typical responses, though we had no intention of appraising the writing's overall look when we first spied it. A novice analyst does this too, but only briefly like you, then quickly jumps to something else. A veteran gives it priority.

Some writing will have no sore thumbs. Hurray for that because this means the strokes appear regular and the writer can cheer his normalcy. That's the good spin. Yet it's likely what we have here, gentlemen, is a person who is, dare we say it, and forgive us our trespasses in doing so, hopelessly inert. Where the writing is ordinary with nary a sore thumb to disturb it, give the individual his due. He's a regular guy and getting by very well, thank you. He's also morbidly dull. Maybe a worker bee in life's garden. That's okay. We can't all be queen. We need drones to do the hard work, not mind it, and keep their mouths shut about it. This blah writing can unsettle the novice looking for sore thumbs. He opens his mouth to speak and the only letters exiting are "a" and "h" or "u' and "m." Their separate combinations spell "ah" and "um," either one the first refuge of the speechless.

At this point can appear the analysts' version of stage fright. Though rare, panic triggers it, usually from an analysts unschooled rawness,. The antidote is experience and many pats on their flabby backs. For the seasoned, it stuns them and tags them with "page fright," as Grim heard it called. Literary writers like Hemingway and Fitzgerald had their own when they took out the blank sheet of paper and they couldn't make their pen flicker or their fingers strike the keys. It's different for a handwriting analyst. At the first sight of a writing sample, a nervous analyst is spooked. Most times it's when he's doing a face-to-face analysis on the spot. Though the audience may be only one, that's enough to rouse his sleepless insecurities. The analyst looks at the writing and what inspires him? OhGodhelpmeIwantmymommy, nothing. He freezes, struggling to address from between dry lips something, anything, about a parchment now mysterious, devoid of import. It usually happens with writing that is conventional and without sore thumb strokes, as in the blah writing. Thus it's somewhat justifiable. This is not fresh dogdoo nor a penetrating cologne. The writing releases nothing to discuss and the analyst gropes for an instant perceptive comment. He grabs dead air. Usually the pause from looking at the writing to speaking about it is only momentary. But it can be enough for an uppercut punch to that analyst's clout. He better compensate for the extra time taken with a flurry of insight. Otherwise his stature freefalls on the spot. Grim informs green analysts it will arrive for almost everyone. To prevent a relapse, do many on-the-spot analyses and deposit canned comments about troublesome writing in your mental bank. Focus on global factors like slant and size, which they typically know very well and are easy to chat about.

The novice's next blunder is the individual strokes, where they will hunt for an adverse trait. Admirable attention, but it's the wrong way to approach it, says Grim. Since we consist of a gaggle of traits honking for notice, centering on one or two strokes up front leaves you miles from your eventual pond. When analysts look at the writing from afar, they should conjure an image of the personality. This sounds like a vague spiritual endeavor, which gets skeptics nagging about graphology's mystical bent. No, the first step isn't an intuitive fancy with no structure or meaning. You are seeking an outline of this individual. If you are interested in an initial impression of the writer, you must look at the general aspects of their writing found mostly in the global factors. That is what a veteran analyst will do.

To review, global factors is an imposing phrase from IGAS for aspects of writing that appear in every stroke. They are crucial in affecting every other portion of the writing, especially the strokes themselves. Yet none is a stroke itself. These factors are the slant, size, thickness, and rhythm of the writing. Include also the balance between the three zones found in the lower loops, the small letters, and the upper loops. Grim says that once you have gauged the global factors and noted any sore thumbs, you have actually erected "the skeleton of the individual", as IGAS calls it. You have an advanced idea who this person really is. What remains are the hundred or so strokes that reveal specific traits.

"These strokes are less important than you might think," he asserts. "They fill in the blanks of this skeleton with the nerves and muscles."

"What makes them so slight?"

"In most instances, the broad conclusions drawn don't change after you've erected the skeleton of the globals. It's amazing how little this assessment ever needs to be altered."

"What about sore thumbs or other strokes that are prominent?"

"Oh, some new specific traits will be found that the skeleton did not give you. More detail evolves too. But you have now finished the brunt of the work."

After the detached first glance at the entire writing, then the review of the five global factors, and then the many traits he finds in the strokes, Grim measures the strength of each trait using a one-to-ten scale. A few other checks follow before he puts it all together. These additional checks are more broad-viewing that pleases gestalt analysts because that's mostly what they do. He checks the speed and tempo of the writing. He checks if the writing is simple, copybook or elaborate. Aside from the global factor of thickness, he also checks the lines for length and straightness versus shortness and curves. People who have many long lines in their writing tend to have more energy and endurance. People who have straighter lines throughout tend to be more inflexible and decisive. Those with many curved lines tend to be more forgiving and pleasant. Spacing is in the checklist too. Is the writer using the page with control and order, or does it betray immaturity with its shoddy appearance? Spacing also involves more specific areas: between the letters, between words, between lines, and top and side margins. These areas reveal how much space the writer wants between himself and different segments of society. Next, every word has a lead-in and a lead-out stroke. Grim will quickly assess them. Some are very long, some short, and some are missing.

"That's as far as I'm going, Grim utters suddenly. "I've given you the meaning of some of these lines, but that's it."

We've reached his self-imposed limit. Some analysts will say Grim has gone too far already. They believe that trying to convey to the public how we analyze is dangerous. Information should be confined to a few superficial points.

'If we want to know more," Grim says, "we can take a course in handwriting analysis or buy one of those books with all the strokes and their meanings."

He meant only to give a rough idea what an analyst goes through in his analysis, not explain the meaning of everything along the way. He does say he will continue but only with a general outline of how the analysis is concluded. Analysts say don't give away the farm about how the analysis is done. It seems as if Grim would obey that command.

Then he gave up the homestead and the barn and now says he wants to stop, except for the final stage.

Here the analyst assembles the traits and their combinations into a coherent and detailed picture of the person. This may appear intimidating, daunting, arduous, yet Grim suggests that the final step can readily be mastered. With some practice and a modicum of writing talent, complete and accurate reports should arrive in due course. Having a working knowledge of psychology and specifically personality helps too. Learning to do analysis reports with all the global factors and the one hundred plus separate traits and then measuring them takes some time. Important, serious tasks have a way of doing that. However, IGAS's training program helps the analyst to synthesize everything. It has a splendid document called the "Green Sheet" (for its color). It contains a list of all the traits IGAS identifies as making up any personality. Each of the traits is shown under a heading, such as "Social Traits," telling their purpose. Students welcome it as it gives meaning and coherence to each element of personality. Otherwise, they might see each trait as floating through the cosmos of our beings with no connection to each other or the person who has them.

It really puts personality traits in perspective and shows they can have a particular role in the personality. For example, "Sarcasm" is a trait listed under "Defenses," where it is in the "Resistance" trait category. Sarcasm is verbal abuse. Its role is to enable the individual to carry on in his brush with society. For this person, however, it's a constant cage fight for survival. It protects this writer in often ugly ways since sarcasm is an immature defense, fending people off by verbal barbs. They may not bug him anymore but they won't cozy up to him either. It reflects meanness, sometimes concealed in humor, sometimes overtly hurled at the victim's self-worth. Therefore, pigeonholing of a trait like sarcasm into familiar categories aids in the report's sense and meaning.

In other ways the Green Sheet provides immense help in doing a report. The traits are even grouped according to their positive or negative impact on the main heading. For example, the Social Traits category has Positive traits that aid the person's social abilities. Some of these are traits like "generous" and "frank." Under the Negative subheading are included "aggressive" and "timid" and others. When the analyst reviews the writing to inventory all the traits, he doesn't merely note whether a trait exists. He looks at all the places it appears and puts in the block next to the trait name a number from 0 to 10 to establish its strength for that individual's personality.

In doing a report an analyst may meet traits that conflict. When merging the traits into a coherent whole, the young analyst must learn how to reconcile these clashes. This is no different from what we might find when we judge someone we have known personally for a long time, like a girlfriend. How do we tell our parents or our friends that she is generous and outgoing but has a defiant streak? The analyst resolves this by weighing the strengths and weaknesses of each trait and deciding how they might influence each other. A man shows that he is open and honest but he also shows he is passionate and weak-willed. An analyst might evaluate this man thus: Might his honesty crumble when his love for a calculating woman is tested? This guy would never make it as a spy, especially before some Mata Hari. He would be an easy mark for her. He might even spill his heart out to her, innocently proclaiming that he is in love with her.

You may be surprised that the IGAS General Course for certification is done through the mail. Formerly correspondence course, now called distance learning or home study, the lessons would seem a cinch. Although the first part is a series of objective exams on the traits and other aspects of Graphoanalysis (open book, obviously), judgment day eventually arrives where the student has to show his analytical skills. This last segment has the instructor assigning them analyses of handwriting. Starting with short ones, they grow longer and more complex until the final exam. Here the student gets to choose the person to analyze. If you think this is ripe for cheating by picking someone you know well, it's not that easy. Your instructor won't let you rely on your personal knowledge to get you through the report. You have to justify each conclusion about the traits and their effect on each other and point to their strokes. Most students select a relative or close friend. Grim selected his sister partly because she is such a fascinating personage and often a rebel to category and partly because that kind of person, typically rare, was a challenge. He knew her strokes were "interesting and different, just like her personality." Students aren't usually shocked at the findings of the familiar person they chose. They're shocked at how close they come to what they know of the individual. Each of these "dissertations" acts as another small confirmation of the validity of handwriting analysis before your eyes, another informal experiment to fling at the cynics and the skeptics and the doubters.

Analysts do not diagnose the problems of the writer. They understand that is for the mental health care professional. Yet most general anxieties appear in the strokes. For example, whether a person is "timid" is revealed in their writing. How serious it is can also be determined. Although the writing may suggest clues about it, the analyst cannot determine why the individual is timid. It tells only that he is and how much he is. Outsiders are amazed how insecurities and other neuroses surface in our writing. No other source in or outside psychology can provide such a quick, deep, and comprehensive insight into our shortcomings. When an analyst looks at a piece of writing, he has before him a spreadsheet of a personality. It may be written in code but that code is one he, and only he, and his fellow analysts, can decipher. No psychiatrist or psychologist can do it without special training in handwriting analysis. If the analyst sees severe problems, he may suggest the writer get help. But he does not provide it. Only a professional in behavioral health care should do the spotting of emotional ailments. A competent analyst knows his role and his limits. If someone is struggling, their writing will display it. Too many times analysts will point out those problems to the writer, who may be blundering through life in a roller derby of troubles. At times when the unsettled person realizes the analyst knows of their emotional upset, they may whimper about it and even ask for help. These unfortunate souls must be treated with delicate compassion. Once he shows proper concern and suggests some further evaluation, the analyst yields to the mental health professional.

In his first class session Grim tells his students that handwriting will reveal a person's insecurities and fears. Some may call these weaknesses, faults, or "hang-ups." Try not to use those terms if possible, he advises. They tend to be judgmental and hurtful to someone already reeling. He prefers words like "imperfections" or "drawbacks," which don't sting as much. Since none of us is perfect we can use that term for anything that tends to show the individual is inadequate.

What Grim says next he delivers in his best Olympian tone: "You will see these imperfections in almost everyone's writing. When you do and you must discuss them in person, be tactful and kind. You are showing the person who they really are. You are not pointing the bony finger of accusation at them for having flaws. More importantly, the qualities you will find function in that person's world according to how they might use them."

You may want to know if a trait is good or bad. Banish that inquiry from your mind. The serious question for each trait should be this—Does it help or hurt the person's ability to succeed in life? Besides waiting to see how the trait plays out, it helps to soften the impact for those who might naturally see a negative trait. Since traits are only predispositions to act a certain way, the resulting conduct can be a surprise. Or the trait may not show up. What matters is not how the person is programmed but how he acts when he goes out into the world. After all, what we do as individuals is substantially a conscious choice. Admittedly we must also recognize the unconscious, subconscious, or non-conscious in motivating us to act. Experts can differ on how much motivation comes from those mysterious steamer chests of our beings.

The founder of IGAS knew a lot about how traits function. With the wisdom of his years of handwriting experience Milton Bunker once wrote: "During the many years I have been analyzing handwriting I have found very few real faults, but I have found a great number of excellent character traits which have been seriously misused."

As a human being none of us is without flaws. If you think you have a fault, you should confront it, not let it cramp you. You might, for instance, consider yourself impulsive. Often you embarrass yourself with abrupt actions you later regretted. You leap into action without deliberation. Instead of obeying that impulse, you can channel that quality by aiding a noble cause. With the enthusiasm and energy that accompany your impulsive nature, you might arouse others to join you in achieving great results. You might use it to pursue a worthy goal. Impulsive people are dominated by their feelings. Sometimes all they need is a push in the right direction. Have them focus on positive actions for which they can get properly excited. If they believe in them, it won't take much. They tend to work harder than less emotional people. They can achieve a lot for good just by the passion they have. This is a temperament you should want on your side. You can take what seems a drawback and convert it into a healthy attribute for the individual and those around them.

––––––

An accurate analysis is vital to person evaluated and vital to the standing of the analyst himself. Grim emphasizes his subject's scientific focus. To enable the analysis to be correct and complete, Grim prods analysts to try to do analyses under what he calls "ideal laboratory conditions." He wants an original sample, not a photocopy, which reduces the quality of the lines, especially their thickness. He would like to see at least a page or two of writing, on unlined paper written in the person's customary style. Attaining that style is often trying. It is a goal to aspire to and is a good measure of the analyst's skills. Grim insists the writing be done spontaneously and unrushed. A sample written in front of the analyst may not be the best for analysis. Under tension the strokes can lose their natural shape. Tics, skipping, wavering, uneven pressure, and other odd strokes can appear as your nerves disrupt your writing.

Certainly it will solve the occasional problem of authorship. Some analysts refuse to do an analysis if they can't watch the writer penning the sample. Conversely, if the writer has been wracked with personal disorder, better that it comes out in the writing. After all, if the purpose of the analysis is to reveal the actual person in current mode, you want those defects readily observable. If his writing shows any cries for help, you want to know the source to suggest any professional counsel he might need. The actual source may be deep within the writer's psyche. If beyond the reach of the analyst's ken, at least the tell-tale strokes emit clues to that source. The professional can take it from there.

When people see an analyst coming a few look for an exit. Sometimes the writer is too fearful of exposing his weaknesses to allow the truth to spring from his writing. He may try artificial changes to his strokes to make himself appear as a better person. It's not typical for people to know what is good and what is bad in writing. Still, the average person seems instinctively to know that certain strokes tend to make them look bad. Well he should since these strokes do have an inherent tinge to them. Somehow laypeople know to delete any extreme stroke, any wild and crazy stroke, any stroke that looks strange, any stroke out of balance, any ugly or excessive stroke, any strange or goofy stroke, any demented stroke, and any stroke that doesn't appear to fit with the others. Go back and read this last sentence. Each of the strokes described form a grand group. Put it this way: If it doesn't look close to what he was taught in grade school, something is probably amiss with this person. That is part of the struggle analysts have with writings they must analyze.

Most people actually know too much about what makes them seem abnormal. As a result, analysts must guard against distortions by people trying to keep from looking bad in the analysis. One major way is to make sure the writer takes a brief time to compose it when he is asked to provide a sample on the spot. Keep the lines flowing so that they have no real chance to think about any devious strokes. It should be natural and unplanned. A reasonable time limit will help while also letting the writer finish without feeling rushed. The key is to prevent the writer from slowing down so much that he can actually think through enough strokes to deviate from his normal style. If the writer is going to look good in the analysis, hopefully it's from the normal writing speed. The ideal setting for a sample is to imagine sitting down at your familiar desk and writing a social letter to a friend on a rainy Sunday afternoon. Knowing a napping child will awake or a spouse will need something soon will hasten you to finish soon. Thus it will be free of stress and distractions but call for deliberate speed to finish. The strokes will scurry unimpeded across your stationery. For ideal conditions to analyze handwriting, that's as close as you can get.

Women aren't afraid to show their emotions. Men are. The subject of emotions is not easy for men or women to fully comprehend. Trying to define them isn't easy either. Without thinking too hard, try it. Your mouth may open readily, but your lips stall in uncertainty. You don't see it as an eye-glazer; it seems simple. But the more you think, the more it becomes one. It takes work to explain it in basic terms. Graphoanalysts will assist you since they know emotions are crucial in the human make-up.

Early on Grim informs his classes that emotions are "at the base of our personalities. If you do not acknowledge this, then you do not fully understand what personality is about," he says, chopping the air like JFK.

Analysts didn't discover the emotions. They just confirm their enormous strength in our personalities. Scottish philosopher David Hume understood this when he wrote that "Reason is a slave to the emotions." Grim piledrives this into students when he conveys the first two of the five global factors. The slant of the writing and the thickness of the writing are blimps among balloons in the world of Graphoanalysis. They aren't just larger in scope but much larger in importance. The globals are part of the gestalt perspective. Many outside gestaltists don't realize that Graphoanalysis looks at both the large aspects, (the blimps) like the thickness of the writing, and the small ones, (the balloons) like the strokes, such as a t-bar on the stem of a letter t. Slant tells us about someone's emotional temperament, Grim points out. When the writing slants rightward that tells us how he is programmed to release his emotions. The farther right the quicker and more frequent his feelings will spurt. Writing that slopes backward shows the person who tends to hide his true feelings. Most of these people need to feel secure that they won't be hurt before their feelings come out. Those whose slant is straight up tend toward poised, cool dispositions. Since these two emotional components are global factors, they exert massive influence on the rest of the personality found in the traits.

"The globals are more than the elephant in the room that you can't ignore. They possess you every waking moment and follow you wherever fate takes you," Grim declares.

Their force can fortify other already unpleasant traits. If someone, for example, shows strong resentment or jealousy in their writing and they also have writing that slopes sharply to the right, their resentment or jealousy will intensify. Their quick feelings insist on it. They want action. By the same token, the emotions can moderate other traits. For a person with vertical slope, any resentment they harbor will be held in check because of the overriding tide of their calmness. Upset over their resentment requires a big charge, in contrast to those with pronounced right slant. People who write straight up slant have a governor on their feelings. By being placid, their ability to react to stresses is more measured. Their emotions are usually under control.

This is all interesting, but this was emotions in action, not emotions defined. Grim admits he has trouble with a definition. After a long pause he pitches one that seems to derive from days prior. Regardless, you know it will be downhome rather than psycho-techno.

He tries this: "Emotion is a physical reaction you have when something stirs you."

"It seems that being stirred means you are having a physical reaction, so it sounds redundant."

"Well, the stirring is coming from outside the person feeling it. Maybe it's something that *will* stir you, although it's momentary."

Maybe that's closer. Otherwise it sounds as inadequate as any other people will offer. Emotions make even wordsmiths stammer. We all have emotions but nobody can define them as a concept or object. As they say about obscenity—"Maybe I can't define it but I know it when I see it." Or like, forgive me, orgasm. You can't properly describe the sensation. You just want to be there when it's happening. As with most attempts at explaining things, when we find we can't, we lapse into analogies, trudge to our rusting warehouse of comparisons, and unpile the scraps of similes and metaphors. Inevitably they pale or just fail, or we nail the Holy Grail. If orgasm is the ultimate physical experience, comparisons fall short. The closest we humans have for orgasm are gazing at fireworks or a July sunset or eating chocolate or hearing you won the lottery, or shooting a hole-in-one on the golf course, or, forgive us, Lord, once again, when our arch enemy goes down hard.

———

Curious outsiders raise the subject of pen strokes and their impression on the paper. Analysts call them "ductus," the width and the darkness of those meandering lines. How hard you press the point on the paper creates the stroke's width. We all know certain kinds of pen points will make different width strokes. In this day of felt-tip and gel pens along side fine-point ball-point pens the ductus has become the duchess in this realm. These unusual pen points can distort the stroke width the writer intends to make. Ideally analysts would prefer people use the old–style fountain pens, better than today's in registering the ink's breadth. Actually, good fountain pens are preferred for other strokes too. They have a lie-detector's knack for recording every nervous tick or careless stray of a writer's pen. Since few people use fountain pens anymore, analysts can only reach Grim's ideal laboratory conditions by letting the person choose their pen and its point. Analysts assume the writer will pick one that reflects how thick they want to make their strokes on the paper. Too often analysts are handed samples done without the writer's choice of pen points. Or the writer picked the least offensive choice. They didn't have a choice. Whatever point is used, the effect may be minimal. A good analyst can gauge the actual pressure the writer sought. They learn to detect the pressure from knowing the pen stroke made and the kind of paper used. For instance, a person who intended to make thick lines had to write with a fine ball-point pen. No thick point was around. His stroke on paper may not be thicker but it will look darker than normal. Where in doubt the analyst can turn the paper over and note the impressions.

You probably think that the thickness of handwriting has some meaning but small influence. Not so, say analysts. A person with thick writing savors the physical part of life. Although the thicker the more sensuous the writer is, it means more than that. The thickness of the writing, sometimes called depth or pressure or width, adds another emotional dimension to the personality. Since it is also a global factor, its effect on character is monumental. Unlike slant, the width of strokes also tells us how deep and lasting our emotions are. Since heavy-line writers savor rich food, dazzling colors, and soaring music, they see life as a smorgasbord of delights. Each experience marks them emotionally more than a light-line writer. Both stressful and pleasurable experiences are well-recalled. Thus they tend to retain grudges, biases, and resentment. On the other hand, the positive and gripping circumstance, such as an inspirational teacher, or a patriotic moment, also burns into their memory.

When we observe someone over time we make judgments about their personality. Those judgments can be colored by several factors. They may not be their usual self. We may meet someone for the first time and they might be feeling sick, or fatigued from a long day at work. Perhaps they are bortsnoggled from losing their job or a girlfriend. We might not know the tremors shaking them. Although they may be only temporary, an analyst is stuck with them in the writing. A crisis may be greeting the analyst and he doesn't know it unless the writer volunteers it. The writer may have just learned he has cancer. If he suspects something, he can be bold enough to ask. Just as the person's fortress might be shelled by events, so does his handwriting reveal it. The greater the shelling the greater the ruin to the writing. If the analyst obtains a sample prior to the trauma's onset, he can compare it for evidence of the trauma's impact. Analysts try to be alert for these factors since they can disfigure an analysis.

Physical changes to the writer are common and can distort the strokes and the resulting analysis. They can affect the writer's personality, such as alcohol or fatigue or fury or grief. Physical illness can make our hands tremble. When we get a nerve disease our hands may quiver. Because of her age and physical decline, your grandmother's once graceful cursive style may slow to an unsteady petterwetch. All these factors can change our normal writing strokes. Some changes will be only fleeting until the cause has passed, like effects of alcohol. Whether the factors are emotional or physical, they corrupt the writing into a faulty analysis.

Other factors can weaken an analysis where the writing itself changes. If a person stands up to write, or if they stand far away from the paper, or while sitting don't lean their other elbow on the table, their normal writing can be jarred. Writing done in someone's own lap, without a hard surface to write on, can scatter widely. The quick note scribbled while the paper is held in the palm of the hand, or against a friend's back, or against a wall probably won't be the scribbler's customary writing. Although these factors will alter the normal style of the writer, they can still be analyzed. The more the factor's damage, the less accurate the analysis.

Some factors began years ago. If you have held your pen an unusual way most of your life, that has probably skewed your drawn lines since you began. How much would depend on how unusual. We really abuse ourselves. Grim is amazed the strange ways many young people hold their pens. Their fingers are so contorted that their lines hobble or crawl across the expanse of paper. Some young people strain to keep their fingers together and around the pen and at such odd angles. Printing seems the only viable method to write. Regrettably that seems to be an epidemic among the young. What writing instruction did they receive? Where did they learn to hold their pen?

"Maybe that is one of the reasons printing rules so much," Grim surmises. "They can't write normally because their hands don't grip the pen snugly. Or their grip is so ungainly they have to grip it tight just to maintain control. The grip should be comfortably relaxed but steady."

The tension created forces the writer to revert to printing as a way of relieving the upset. Grim thinks many print as the default method of evading the dislocations of messy script. He and his fellow analysts believe the untidiness and emotional discontent itself can be prime reasons for printing.

Some factors will mar the sample and hinder but not cripple the analysis. Most have only a modest effect. The kind of paper, the surface underneath, the position of the writer, the kind of instrument, the point of the instrument (as the stroke thickness is important), the grip of the pen, paper size and actual area for writing, lighting, location of the writer (car, bus, train) and others. Unlined paper is very important. How a person uses the space is essential to an analysis. Some of the elements revealed on blank paper are the directions of the words, the margins between the paragraphs and the paper's edge, the size of the letters, the space between lines, and more. Each of these tells something about the writer. Blank paper is essential where a concerned individual wants to appraise the current state of mind of someone close. One marker for pessimism or worse, depression, is writing that tapers on the page. With lined paper the writer may feel compelled to stay on the line despite their emotional state. Where a person writes on lined paper and their sentences still hit the line or slope below it, analysts construe that as despondency. How hard is it to keep your writing on top of a line? They can't do it. This is another salient moment of our Svengali personalities ruling our handwriting. It is only one sign, however.

Government forms, applications, especially with small blanks to write in, are also a problem. The personality organ grinder and its wayward-pen playful monkey don't want to be hemmed in by artificial boundaries. They want freedom to be their playful selves. The small box or blank forces the writer to fit the writing to the space allotted. If that's not their normal size, the global factor of size will be warped accordingly. Large writers want to write large no matter where they are.

Shall we say it again? All global factors are important to an accurate analysis.

When he is handed these distorted samples, the analyst cringes. On occasion he has no choice. They may be the only kind available. Maybe the writer didn't consent to the analysis. Maybe he is a dead relative or historical figure. Many analysts won't analyze without the writer's consent. Sometimes the analysis is so important that the urgency overrules the reduced conditions. A prosecutor comes across a writing of someone who he believes is about to do something wicked. He must act fast for a personality profile. It's important the analyst knows the source of unfavorable conditions. It enables him to adjust his findings.

The analyst strives to analyze writing done only in front of them. The non-witnessed sample can cause harm. If the writing was done away from the analyst, he really doesn't know what the conditions were. If they can, someone will usually be glad to tell the analyst about the circumstances. Maybe they really lack first-hand knowledge or they have motive to lie about it. The practical joker exists in handwriting too. If the analyst can't satisfy himself of bare standards, he has a serious decision to make. The sample done elsewhere, especially where it looks suspicious, creates the analyst's dilemma. If it's not reliable, he may prepare an inaccurate report. This is of course the chief concern, but it can generate side issues of ethics, self-respect and prestige. He should have done it with better proof of desirable conditions. He demeans himself as an analyst, and his standing is soiled if the public learns what happened.

At rare times analysts will encounter a sample of writing so foreign it defies a proper slot. Most of the time the solution is simple. Analysts think any stroke can be easily dropped into one of their trait bins. That's generally true. Some strokes can test that dictum. Typically it has happened when a specimen was written somewhere else. For instance it was done at home, the writer holding the paper against a wall. They delivered it elsewhere to the analyst. Americans would probably just call it a writing glitch. Grim wasn't content with that. He created a name for the phenomenon, borrowing it from the French: *la miette sous le papier*. There are different kinds of glitches, some with strange parents. That often creates the mystery for the analyst and hinders his ability to classify it as one trait. One common example is a sequence of letters with gaps in the strokes. Not printed writing nor writing that occasionally splinters. They are frequent. Consider one where the writer briefly but frequently lifted and then returned his pen to its normal place seesawing across the page. Many people doing it are stressed because they can't contain the pen's scoring, and it skips.

On one occasion a writer delivered from his home to the analyst a sample with these stroke gaps. The analyst was baffled, mainly because the gaps appeared only in a few letters near each other. Since tension and anxiety are typical reasons for skipping, they usually appear throughout the writing. They are often supported by other indicators such as uneven strokes, jerky lines, prickly line points, or jagged i-dots and periods. None of these appeared in this sample, just the few letters cleft by air. Ordinarily analysts don't need to enquire about a stroke. When they must, it's awkward. They strain to avoid it. After pondering his tiny mystery about those gaps, the analyst humbled his way to the writer. The writer paused, equally puzzled why he had them. They weren't normal and he wasn't under stress. After the analyst probed the writing's birthplace, which was the writer's kitchen table, the light of insight flipped on for both writer and analyst. Something was present at this birth, the analyst deduced and discovered. Some cookie crumbs had been left on that table. *La miette sous le papier,* Grim informs all who want to know, is French for "the crumbs under the paper." The now despised *miette* is Grim's term for any outside source that can alter handwriting. He has borrowed it from French analysts with their saying, "Remember the crumb under the paper."

Unique strokes come from unique individuals. Because of marvels like *miettes*, analysts don't know if bizarre strokes stem from a rare individual or the residue of mom's baking. On occasion the analyst has no choice but to analyze and see what happens. The writer of unusual strokes may not be around to explain. He may refuse an analysis no matter what, like the surly boss or your creepy uncle you seek to figure out. Or he could be patently unavailable, such as a deceased relative or renowned person or even an anonymous stalker. Or they might be around but don't bother asking, like the prospective husband or the new neighbor, or your haughty project chairman. If possible an analyst gets the writer's consent to analyze and hopes to witness the writer doing the sample. IGAS has an ethical rule requiring consent but, as you just read, exceptions mount. One exception seems to father another. Some Graphoanalysts get consent if they can but don't agonize without it. Non-Graphoanalysts with no rule sometimes adopt the rule for themselves, typically where they've been scorched by some rip-off. The writer they thought was its author wasn't. For many others, analysts bar no holds. They never saw a sample of writing they didn't want to wrestle.

Since a *miette* can be anything that disturbs a writing, the perpetrator won't have to be dead as a cookie crumb. How could there be a live perpetrator? Grim says he knows how. First he insists on some background. A live *miette* can thrive elsewhere in life, as in Grim's other craze, golf. The equivalent for *miette* in golf is an "outside agency." There is a rule for it covering a ball in flight, or at rest, being moved or re-directed by something not part of the match. Here's an example that actually occurred. In the 1950's Grim's father was golfing when his drive landed on the fairway. MyhanduptoGod, a pig waddled from an adjacent field, gobbled it into his mouth, gnawed it, and waddled back whence he came. That meddlesome pig was an "outside agency" under the Rules of Golf. Usually it happens in a tournament when a fan near a green deflects a wayward shot farther away than its likely spot. With Tiger Woods some fans will purposely stop it to keep it from a dire fate, like out of bounds or in tall trees. The rule tells the golfer where to place this deflected ball. Don't look for a pig as an "outside agency" in handwriting but keep the idea in mind.

A prominent analyst was analyzing samples from a gallery of people. One woman had finished her sample and signed her name. Her first name was Judith and she made the upper part of her J with a large conventional loop. Inexplicably, within that loop was a much smaller squarish loop that dropped into the intersection of the upper loop with the lower loop, also conventional. Every remaining stroke in her sample was conventional. The odd little loop within the upper loop of the J obviously didn't belong there. So different and out of place, this stroke stumped the analyst. She also hadn't seen her do the sample. With no recourse she approached the writer.

Her response: "Oh, that. I had been sitting next to someone else doing her sample when she accidentally bumped my writing arm. I didn't think you would like it if I attempted to re-do it. So I just kept going."

For Grim's father, golf allowed him to throw down a new ball and play it where the pig picked it up. For analysts their rule is harder to apply. If the glitch doesn't fit you must acquit yourself to sense when it's not the writer's style. Approach the writer, confirm it, and remove it from your analysis. If they insist it's really their typical stroke, wrap it up, and take it home as part of the analysis.

———

Grim calls it "our glorious tattoo." You can call it the informal analysis. He has some other names for it. The on-the-spot analysis, curbstone analysis, instant analysis, or bar-room-stool analysis. It occurs any time, any place.

"People consider analysts as masochistic cabdrivers, on duty 24 hours a day even though their meter might be off," says Grim. "The mini is the classic example."

Gatherings among friends and family are typical occasions for these mini-analyses. Grim gets them too, many of them. As it attempts to grow in stature, they are a genuine problem for handwriting analysis. An individual will approach Grim, earnestly thrust a piece of paper in his hand, and beg, request or demand a quick analysis. Usually the writing is only a signature, or a sentence or two, and a signature. The threadbare "A quick brown fox jumps over the lazy dog" is common. As a ready sentence on the shelf of convenience, it's analysts' leading passage. Originally it was created in the late nineteenth century, not for analysts, but as a pangram for typing instruction. It is pithy, featuring all 26 letters of the alphabet and little more. Grim's inventory includes many more, most unfamiliar to the public and all nonsense, like that fox and that dog. They also have at least 26 letters and a few more for minimum grammatical sense. The letters usually need to be shoe-horned into the sentence to sound lucid. For several years Grim has kept a tiny quest under his hat. He longs for a sentence with only the 26 letters in it. Good luck. It's not likely to appear, he is convinced, unless someone cheats by including a formal name with those high-value Scrabble words in it and letters added to complete the alphabet. Until something better comes along he will subsist on quick brown foxes jumping over lazy dogs.

Many of these requests come at a party or other public gathering. When he hears a request for the instant analysis, Grim's customary response is that he would be glad to analyze their writing. However, he explains, he is a professional and it's best he shun a quick, informal analysis. It would not be accurate, as a small sample yields inadequate handwriting strokes. He also has to study it more at an appropriate time. Just like lawyers and doctors, Grim sees his subject as professional and therefore entitled to deference. As with any other professional, his service is performed at a proper time and place and his pocket deserves adequate coin of the realm. For Grim the grievance is not the free analysis or the wrong setting. It's that the request implies he and his subject are unworthy of respect. He covets some valued space up there with doctors and lawyers. Though a pot of gold might await, that desired respect may be far off. Grim is reminded that doctors and lawyers also have their lapels hooked at public gatherings. He says he knows what lawyers face with his own 30 years dispensing after-hours free advice. Since it has followed him into his new profession, he is more sensitive to it. Having been in both he says that people are just less reluctant to approach analysts. Lawyer's expertise gets more respect. Understandable.

Besides, he sees that doctors' and lawyers' off-hour encounters reflect more of the opinion-seeker than anything else. The brazen who corner analysts seem blessed with ignorance and immaturity. "Some of these people can be as annoying as newsprint," says Grim.

He is amazed at the reactions when he must decline the pop-up analysis. They can't seem to believe an analyst can be off-duty. "Somehow we should be glad to give them what they want on the spot, free and accurate," he givemeabreaks.

Making the rounds of analysts is a suggested way to ward off the persistent individual insisting on a quick analysis: When they say to them, "Can I give you my signature to analyze?" some analysts can't help uttering, "Sure. Put it on the bottom right of a check."

Since it is a helping profession, many of his colleagues brook an analysis no matter the venue or the moment. Others, like Grim's analyst mother and analyst sister, welcome them. "They are always on duty," Grim swears.

No one has tried to reach them while they slept, he thinks. But if that occurred they would answer cheerfully and say, "Hold on till I get out of my pj's and this dark bedroom and I'll see what I can do. How soon can you get here?" Or, if they're not feeling that chipper for 3 AM, at least they might advise, "Write two pages and get them to me in the morning."

Meanwhile, back on earth and during the daytime, Grim wouldn't do a full analysis instantly. He will try to give the requester a few Skittles of insight to take home. Not the full jar. After all, the findings won't be analytical or full. He may ask for their questions about the meaning of a particular stroke or about an area of handwriting analysis. Refusing an informal, quick evaluation spritzes an analyst with misfortune.

The person suspects he was spurned because the analyst didn't feel competent to do it. Actually the suspicion wouldn't be off much. With a small sample and little time to reflect, any skilled analyst shouldn't feel confident on its accuracy. He will need at least a page or two of writing and a few hours to go through all one hundred strokes and other aspects (like spacing, margins and slant) before compiling an adequate report. Thus, a sought mini-analysis rewards the analyst with two thumbs down. If he refuses it, he couldn't do it anyway. If he does it, the result will be judged inaccurate.

When his mother and sister (both analysts) are not around Grim tries harder to avoid instant analyses, especially at parties. Doing them invites trouble to his professional repute. Now and then the social pressure becomes unbearable. Temptation seduces him into handwriting sin. If the writer agrees his small insights were correct, he cheers for the knowledge he imparted, the skill of his work, and one more confirmation of his subject. In another way he hates himself in the morning with the guilt of caving in and risking professional calamity. With a small sample Grim knows he will help them only slightly. On the other hand, he may not help at all. He can't help thinking of the doctors' Hippocratic Oath. He might first *do* some harm. He also must recall what he warns his students in the first session: each of us is unique and complex. "A panther and a robin may be more alike than any two human beings," he adds. More reason that instant analyses should be avoided by an analyst, Grim concedes. Uniqueness and complexity don't show themselves in small samples.

Does he have an analogy for outsiders to comprehend the folly of doing them? You know he does. Making broad judgments about someone based on a glance at a small sample of writing is "like having one date and deciding to marry that person as you say good-night." Too many analysts will do them without reluctance," Grim says. "At least I feel guilty when I do any of them."

Analysts are quick in trying to help people and to demonstrate what handwriting analysis can do. Those motives are gallant and understandable. This is the conflict they create for themselves.

Grim sees this practice as a typical impediment in his calling's unsteady march to acceptance. "It's like one of those funeral procession bands in New Orleans. Forward, sideways, backward, forward, and so on to the cemetery eventually."

That final embrace his topic seeks from the establishment is vital to Grim. Doing instant analyses will postpone it, he maintains. It's that important.

Grim insists on another analogy. To his classes and to neophyte analysts Grim nailguns, "The curbstone analysis is like asking Roger Ebert to review a film after showing him only the preview." Sheila Lowe, who wrote *The Complete Idiot's Guide to Handwriting Analysis*, says it's like asking someone to describe their face and showing them just their nose.

The mini-analysis is a particular problem for Grim's students. He knows what they will face when their expertise leaks out. In the first class Grim splashes over their innocent heads a chilly statement: "Like it or not, you are branded for life. Your family and friends or co-workers won't care how little you claim to know of graphology. When people find out you are into it, your life will forever change, especially around holidays. You will be prodded, if not harassed, by them until you deliver. How to handle the pressure for an analysis will reveal how serious you are and how much you care for ethics." Typically the requester wants it done on the spot and wants to offer only a hasty, tiny sample of writing. Even before Grim's classes are done, students have tales of bruises to their tender growth over this issue. He tries to serve it to them with ladles of sufficient gravity: No one can accurately analyze writing with only a small sample. If you must analyze on the spot, you must get more than a signature. Few analysts can avoid the demand. So you must devise ways to handle it. A signature has in it mostly public image rather than the true self. Analyzing with only the signature risks grave inaccuracies. Adding a frayed sentence like "These are the times that try men's souls" only reduces the result to a less-serious inaccuracy. If you find a negative major trait and you turn out to be wrong, you have devastated the writer even more. Focusing on the positive ones minimizes further psychic injury for those burdened by hurt. More importantly, you're risking the future of your good name. Focus on the positive qualities in the writing and only those that really stand out. He calls them the "sore thumbs" of the writing. They are not necessarily large and showy strokes, like a dazzling assortment of capital letters (a drama queen). They could be anything that is overdone, such as excessive roundness (someone who is very accepting).

Grim suggests another way to deflect the instant analysis. It won't avoid it but may boost the accuracy. Try asking the insistent person what they really want to know about themselves. It focuses the analysis and draws the person and the analyst together in a modest bond. For the analyst who has looked at the writing and has seen no salient quality, it will give him a ready subject to talk about. Analysts will glimpse a writing and their immediate reaction is there is nothing to work with. It's the unfortunate hallmark of much conventional writing. You can mutter a washline of platitudes about how he is a regular guy who does what society asks of him, won't raise a fuss, attends church most of the time, keeps his lawn mowed, and you can *ad* to the *nauseam*.

Grim explains, "Yes, there are boring people and guess what their writing looks like? Yes, there is even boring writing. It will look regular and nothing will stand out. It blahs you to death."

But give these people their due, Grim pleads. "For a world that seems to be heading Hellward, they are the duct tape retarding its downward slide. They provide the moral ballast and the conduct that civilize the rest of the world. We need them. They are the citizens that should sit on a jury. They treat their neighbors with decency and they raise their kids right. They just don't make exciting analyses. They should be comforted by the analysis because it shows they are to be respected and admired. Many people can't keep their life together and their actions decline into the immature or the irresponsible. They need to be hog-tied and dragged squealing into adulthood. If you have the conformist writing, celebrate it. They could be worse and suffering for it."

In fact, that is how analysts often present the analysis to them. Tell them they should be proud; they are doing fine. They don't have the major problems many people do.

After hearing them explain someone's traits, critics sometimes treat analysts with a crass guffaw. When an analyst utters simple, direct, but seemingly implausible descriptions, their contempt wants to roll around on the floor holding its belly. Take a typical statement about a single stroke of writing. After a glance at the stroke, an analyst will say, for instance, "This person sleeps well at night." Critics say this is absurd. The analyst can't be certain about predicting specific behavior.

By suggesting what happens when he turns in for the night, his guess is reckless. Grim tries to explain calmly that the critic is over-reacting to the statement and missing its purpose. In describing his sturdy character, the analyst is using a literary device akin to the synecdoche, where an object represents a greater item. Examples: He has been hitting the bottle. Tehran is threatening to develop nuclear weapons. He went under the knife for back surgery. It's a figure of speech. He is merely illustrating an example of the consequence of someone who has sturdy character. He is not asserting that all people of good character never lose sleep. He is also not saying this individual never loses sleep. Every school child is familiar with the statement about George Washington: "He could never tell a lie." Realistically we acknowledge that he probably did lie here and there. Yet it provides a familiar, understandable example of how we portray a person. In this instance Washington had stellar integrity. No one is perfect—not even those with splendid integrity. As to our statement, Can we know how they will sleep on any one evening? Not with great certainty. Yet we forecast how they will act generally based on how they've acted in the past. We of course don't know if we'll be right. But we will be accurate in general. All else being equal, someone who has good character should sleep well at night because they know they have acted morally. No guilt, stress, second-guessing, and other squirmy effects at bedtime if you've done wrong. Yes, people can act morally but still feel bad because they might have cost themselves or their group money or a victory or an advantage.

When the moral choice is made according to the person's decent virtues, they should fall asleep in peace. "At least that's the popular belief I see in it," says Grim.

Analysts recognize that people also have *degrees* of sturdy character. You might even amend the sleep statement where the person is of the highest integrity.

Say this: "When he goes to bed at night he nods off instantly with no disquiet, won't be stirred by a nearby dog barking, and a burglar could break glass and enter his home and run amok. When he awakens in the morning his mind is clear and he is fresh and ready to do what is right by his fellow man without second thought."

Maybe a bit of hyperbole but it's a spunky, coffee-shop way of explaining who these people are. Don't read too much into it. As a literary device we use it for simple clarity and creativity, illustrating how people with strong moral fiber live their lives.

Most of us recall taking English in high school or college where the instructor stressed we should develop our themes and essays with concrete images. They urged us to draw word pictures that the reader could easily muster in his mind. Grim never thought much of himself as a writer or speaker despite years of dutiful action in the legal trenches doing briefs, summations, motions, pleadings, and oral arguments. When he began analyzing he realized that he would have to do both face-to-face and written commentary on his discoveries. The analyst's trait meaning may be different from the client's. To guarantee the trait is understood and echoes in the client's memory, he thought he needed better ways of conveying traits. IGAS and others have published books on describing traits but Grim thinks they are largely inadequate on making the meanings lucid and imaginative. Some analysts like veteran Shirley Schoenrock from Colorado are brilliant at "bringing the traits to life," as she expresses it. Grim concentrated on creating word images that got rapt attention and nodding ohyeah grasp. Occasionally he described the trait in the abstract but followed with a picture showing how it operates in the daily world.

Grim has taken many of the traits, borrowed from other analysts, and created his own ways of presenting them. Two important ones that are polar opposites are extroverts and introverts—what they do and how they're different from each other. To a large degree they can be found in the slant of the writing. His cement mixer produces some real-world concrete for pouring into clients' laps: "At work extroverts keep their office door open, and prefer to communicate by talking directly to their colleagues. They are drawn to the water cooler. People who slant to the left keep their door closed and use e-mail or notes to convey their information. At home they erect No Trespassing signs or No Soliciting signs. People who are outgoing put their name on their mailbox, live near the road, and drop a Welcome mat. They treasure their cell phones. They keep them on. When their phone rings their energy jumps and they twinkle, 'Ah, a person to hook up with; someone wants me; and someone to spend time with.' They enjoy reaching out to you and me. Backslanters put only their house number on the mailbox, buy a house off the road, and have cell phones only if necessary. When their phone rings their mouths droop and they shutter, 'Oh, no!' A knock on their door sends them in retreat."

"Why? Listen to the off-hand comment of PGA professional golfer Fred Couples with a backslanter mentality: 'I don't like to answer the phone when I'm home because someone might be on the other end of the line.'" He is known as being reserved and retiring.

"While forward slanters relish bonding with people, the backslanter's impulse is to pull away," says Grim. When asked why, he refers me to their psychologist.

That's a dodge from the man with many opinions on psychological matters, who reminds me he is not a psychologist. He knows being a handwriting analyst gives a lot of sheer weight to his experience of dealing with people and having to understand them. When pressed he offers how "pop psychology" would view backslanters. It's also how he might describe them in class.

"Typically they are reluctant to open up as they are afraid of being hurt by others. It makes them vulnerable. When a man appears weak, he is not a man. He loses his macho-ness. That destroys his sense of value to the world."

––––––––

Analysts are asked occasionally to look at the writing of, say, an infamous historical figure. After a brief glance at the writing, they glibly recite all his horrendous qualities. That kind of analysis troubles Grim. Although an honest swindle, he thinks it's unprofessional.

"I want the analyst first to evaluate the writing *without* knowing the person's familiar traits. If his evaluation is similar to their known traits, good for his competence," he declares.

When you already know their overall nature, it is unfair merely to confirm what is already very public. Let the analyst do it "blindly" and see if the found qualities coincide with the known ones. To do it right Grim believes the identity of the famous person should be concealed until the analysis is completed. The possibility of bias is too strong. An expert analyzed Donald Trump's writing and one quality he found was that he was "acquisitive," the analysts formal adjective for someone who craves money or property. Grim hasn't seen the particular sample analyzed but wonders, if the analyst had not known he was doing

Trump's writing, would he have found that trait? Interestingly, Grim has had the reverse "blind" circumstance with Trump. Grim had seen only Trump's signature (which is strangely unique. Geniuses or one of a kind people who do great things tend to have distinctive signatures, if not writing styles) But he had not seen the rest of his writing. One trait Grim had admired about him was his visionary outlook epitomized by his skyscrapers and other colossal projects. Finally he was finally able to see a sample of Trump's writing.

His eyes focused on how Trump crossed his t-bars on his t-stems. "A visionary will place them at the top and they should look solid," says Grim. When he confirmed that Trump did just that, Grim silently rejoiced. Analysts cherish these moments.

Grim likes to portray handwriting as the DNA of your personality or the fingerprint of your personality. The metaphors stop at one important point: Fingerprints and DNA don't change, but your personality does. When it does, the strokes change too. Sometimes the changes are dramatic. A prominent example from the political arena is the signature of Richard Nixon. He has four samples of it, from the years 1968, 1969, early 1974, late 1974. The two from the Watergate-plagued 1974 period are striking, as they show a descent from the vibrant of 1968-1969 to the moribund in early and late 1974. Grim points out that middle strokes reveal your everyday social activity. How is the person doing when he gets up in the morning and goes out and about doing his customary activities?

"His middle area looked like a virtual straight line with no readable letters," observes Grim. To Nixon the Presidency was his whole being. Since his actions destroyed it, he was disintegrating as an individual."

The long straight stroke suggested a medical EKG that had flat-lined. In effect, as a functioning member in society, Nixon had died.

Grim sidesteps from Nixon to the next logical inquiry. If personality can change over years, and the writing does too, what about over a few days? Or even more interesting, in a few hours? Will the writing change that quickly too? Is it possible that entrenched strokes going back to childhood can radically change if the personality does too? Grim tells of an extraordinary incident that covers those few hours. One evening when his wife was out a man kept a diary of his thoughts. He suspected she was being unfaithful. As the hours passed and she did not return home, his diary entries worsened from very legible and controlled to beleaguered scrawl. He had fallen into a jealous rage. His last entry declared, "When you get home…" and the writing drops off. Later that evening she returned home. He beat her to death. Not the end of the story. His suffering was deep. When his fury dissolved and he realized his actions, he committed suicide.

Emotional trauma affects behavior and the stronger the trauma the greater the results to the psyche. If the person feeling this trauma is writing, it will shadow the trauma's intensity. Grim has no other samples of his writing. If he had stayed alive and returned to his sober, controlled temperament, his scrawled writing also would have returned to its normal structured mode.

Grim takes the direct correlation between how you act and how you write and applies it further. The multiple-personalities disorder is a phenomenon splayed over the media in books and movies. In view of the handwriting-personality bond, it raises stimulating curiosity. What happens when this kind of person writes during his moments within each personality? Henry Hawksworth wrote a book called *The Five of Me* about his odyssey with five personalities. Grim has samples of his writing when Hawksworth acts inside each of the five personalities. Each sample is noticeably different from the others.

People in altered states have been asked to write to see the effects on their customary manner of writing. Some have been hypnotized and asked to assume another character. While in that character they were asked to write. If they became an emperor they wrote with all the pomp and majesty of a ruler. If asked to be a child, they wrote with the unskilled effort of an infant.

We learn to write script style around second grade, slowly evolving into our unique ways of writing. Grim thinks some of us show signs of it right away. He believes much can be learned from children's writing. The closer they are to penmanship class the closer their style will reflect their learning. The pull of a child's evolving uniqueness seeks recognition in his writing. The stronger and the more unconventional the child's personality, the more the writing should reflect it. Grim bemoans children that might have enjoyed better lives if their singular writing had been analyzed early on. Singular individuals pen singular writing strokes. One instance where it should have mattered is the captivating story of Miss America 1996, Heather Whitestone. She became deaf at 18 months from an infection. Her doctors told her she would never make it out of third grade. Fortunately, she overcame their gloomy forecast. Although she never had an analysis, Grim is sure that if she had one then, those above her would have seen her splendid qualities. Instead, she struggled for years before conquering, not just her disability, but also the appalling authority figures who misperceived her talents.

It happens all the time in school, at home, at work, Grim laments. With dormant abilities or interests, many young people spend their formative years stifled. In their way stand unfeeling teachers, clueless parents, inept guidance counselors, and snooty psychologists armed with often unreliable tests. Any of them might have helped these unrecognized youth realize their gifts and enable them to flourish. Even without the obstacle of dense adults, the youth's own naive self-knowledge may cramp them. "If I had only known my true talents when I was young…," they might say with a fade-off sigh. Heather Whitestone was fortunate crawling upward through the cracks and ultimately gaining reward. In the year of her reign she was featured in a full-page ad in *Time*. The heading cleverly captured her success in overcoming her lost hearing and her witless doctors. Its triumphant words resounded: "Obviously she wasn't listening."

———

A flag droops, craving to flutter from a fresh breeze. An analyst has his erotic moments too. Grim awaits the bliss from chancing upon a friend's writing he's never seen. Maybe he has seen their signature and a few words but nothing more. It may not reach the joy of a stamp collector finding the rare issue, but may equal the archeologist after months digging in ancient ruins. He finally discovers incredible artifacts, perhaps some that revise major conclusions about the culture. Another rush for Grim is coming across the writing of the celebrity or famous historical figure. Not the signature, which is much image-creation and often available, but the actual style of that noted person. The singular event surrenders their inner self all at one time, enabling the analyst to confirm or reject his suspicions about this now-exposed person. The analyst can rip open the opaque wrapping on their public persona and behold a gleaming icon of the real being. Will we still admire them after this depth of insight? They used to ask what the hidden Johnny Carson is really like. Grim has never seen his writing or his signature. It would probably be a revelation, he is convinced. Despite his comedic and other public talents, Grim thinks he would show some significant inner qualities clashing with his public face.

In fact, analysts have the stamp collector's equivalent of the rare find. Now and then an analyst will examine a piece of writing and find a stroke or strokes so different, so bizarre, so rare, so unique, so unusual, or so individually creative that he rushes to make a good copy of it. Grim is amazed how many of those strokes he has seen over the years.

"You would think that there is nothing new under the sun and every stroke of writing looks similar to others in some way. But human beings are sometimes so special that déjà vu can't be applied," he remarks. "Find me a really different style of writing and you have found a really rare individual." He even has a phrase for this marvel. "Déjà nu."

Another form enlivens Grim differently. When he discovers writing that resembles another one he already knows well, the thrill begins. Since handwriting follows personality, he reasons, people with similar styles must have similar personalities. To see if it bears out he dashes to compare them. No two writing styles will be the same, he knows. That's beyond man and nature's scope. A multitude of *similar* strokes might connect a sketch of kindred personalities. That's as much as analysts can hope for. Similar personalities should have similar writing styles if handwriting analysis means what it says.

What's been Grim's experience? Has he found the similar writing styles of two strangers to have like personalities, only in general, of course?

"Yes, I have," he responds. Although he is the judge and jury for these comparisons, he wants to add a comment. "These have all been confirming moments for handwriting analysis," Grim revels.

Chapter 12

Member in Good Standing
National Guilt-by-Association

Is handwriting unique among individuals?
**Justice Department study
conducted under pressure of the
status of law**

*A thoughtful person might consider
a partnership between an analyst and
a psychologist a marriage made in
heaven. These weddings are not
happening.*

Povser

Handwriting analysis needs a finishing school. Not one of those that make you walk balancing a book on your head. One that will get its doctrines straight once and for all and complete the research to satisfy the authorities that it deserves acclaim. For now handwriting analysis is a still-evolving field aiming for the hearts and minds of the authorities. God knows it's had a lot of evolving to do. Like so much of social science, it developed from different civilizations and languished for centuries with little notable work to refine its doctrines or nudge it toward the Big Hug from those who matter in psychology. Real breakthroughs in human conduct occurred in the nineteenth century. Now in the early twenty-first century graphology's grand research remains short and stagnant. No one has taken the lead to complete the grueling work left to verify the meaning of the several strokes, slantings, and spacings.

You're now removing your thinking cap to scratch your head and ask, "Why would I waste my time with a group that wants you to accept them but won't get on the same page with each other." That would be a natural but hasty response. Conflict is not a problem only to handwriting analysis. Name a discipline within social science without detractors, sharp viewpoints, revisionists, lunatic fringes, and conservative and liberal segments. This is especially so in psychology, a relatively young science and a social science. Within its concepts many have an opinion but few have a justifiably strong grip on truth.

Psychology's real birth is fixed at sometime in the late nineteenth century in Germany. Medical science, a physical science rather than a social science, was taking only baby steps at the time. A century before, King George III was making war on us Americans. He began acting strangely during his later years. You would think the king of the most powerful nation in the world would get the best medical attention. Among the now laughable treatments he received was blood-letting. We got it right with that war for our freedom and that idea called democracy but we wrongly also bled our moribund Founding Father George Washington, hastening his death.

"Now it's unfair for critics to disparage handwriting analysis for having sharp internal differences. Graphoanalysis relates over one hundred different strokes to specific traits," Grim volunteers.

Granted trait-school proponents quarrel over what some of them mean but many they agree on. The greater divide exists between the trait-schoolers and the gestaltists. Traitists look at individual strokes and letters. Gestaltists say that approach is too specific and unproven. You must step back and look at the larger features and view the writing as a whole. Some of those elements are the slant, size, thickness and rhythm of the writing. Grim's organization, IGAS, uses both perspectives. First, look at broader aspects of the writing, like the size and the slant, ascertain the particular strokes and their matching traits, then combine them for a thorough judgment on the writer's personality. It fuses both methods while allowing more weight to stronger elements.

"That's not always easy but the only way to make it complete and correct," Grim insists.

If you think the steps are too steep for anyone to attain a personality as just described, consider what occurs in your daily life. Handwriting analysis is not alone in merging information about the individual's make-up. We all do it when we evaluate a friend or acquaintance, employee, or other person. The difference is that we do it by a combination of observation, dialogue, rumor and reputation. We don't customarily dissect it. As Nike told us, we just do it. In conscious and unconscious ways we combine what we have become used to. When we first meet someone we do it on the spot and call it our first impression. That is revised constantly and updated to the moment in our helterskeltermorethanfoodandshelter lives. Whatever its value, that's how we view and determine the personalities of people in our lives. Handwriting is different. When you approach handwriting, the parts in the person's constitution are pre-determined for you by the person's own strokes. No fuss, no muss, no having to cuss and leave the divining to us. No having to go to different sources. No having to wait months or years to make judgments on their worth. Our strokes just sit there posing in their finery, or their spareness, waiting for their close-up from an analyst. They declare unfiltered and unabashed that this is how the writer is as a person. Thus the handwriting approach of IGAS and the separate one we all use to discern personality take the vital information from different sources but construct it into the complex Angkor Wat of personality.

Grim clutches tightly his handwriting dogmas. When pressed about his doubts, he doesn't bristle, but he does shift in his now uneasy chair. Handwriting analysis is worthy to be embraced, capable of defending, and serious and important enough for promoting to the masses. All the same, he confesses to misgivings. He wonders if they should be probed more seriously before the subject goes further in its plea for acceptance. The areas of doubt haven't slowed the growth it has earned. Perhaps they have kept it from going further. Grim thinks they have been overlooked by both friend and foe, the adherents and the skeptics.

"I don't insist on answers for them, only some thoughtful theorizing, and I'll resolve them for myself," he wants me to know.

Since they haven't been addressed by any research that he has seen, social scientists will have to resolve them sometime with dignified experiments. First, he wants to know the locus in our minds for the individual traits of personality. He knows brain research thus far hasn't shown us what we want to see. Yet the recent advances in other findings about our brains vault him closer to real hope that we will soon pinpoint those traits. Brain research produces astounding advances every few months. Every article about recent progress on the brain seems to trumpet that science has learned more in the last few decades than in the entire history of the brain. Much of this stems from the check-this-out technology that records colored images of areas of the brain and their activity. This is a major issue for Grim. Unfortunately, what is "soon" is the inscrutable loon. Will it be by noon, in a blue moon, next June, or will it never sing its plaintive tune?

Some of the other areas to probe are—What is a trait? Are the traits we have identified truly traits? Are there more we should identify? Where does one trait end and another one begin? Graphoanalysis has it names for these separate traits. Some are clearly independent. Some seem to have close ties: will power, persistence, determination, initiative, and aggressiveness. Do you know what these mean? Do you know where to draw the line on their definitions? Here are also seven separate traits identified in IGAS's gallery of over one hundred traits: sarcastic, evasive, loyal, cautious, stingy, secretive, domineering. Should any of these seven be removed? Here are seven qualities not part of this gallery: conscientious, tough-minded, docile, agitated, suspicious, adventurous, restless, arrogant, and fun-loving. Should any of these be added to its gallery? The IGAS traits listed each can be found in one stroke. In fairness to IGAS it also lists additional traits that are a combination of traits, such as poised, sympathetic, timid, and ambitious. These it calls "evaluated" traits since they are made up of a squad of traits found in individual strokes. These individual ones are called "basic" traits.

None of these issues are the sickle-cell anemia for handwriting analysis. From its inception psychology also has grappled with these questions. In trying to comprehend the workings of personality, studies have searched this absorbing arena. The reports from them seem to be arrant guesswork, however. Definitive answers are elusive butterflies. Nothing is captured that can't escape to flutter away. Some other issues closer to his subject animate Grim much more.

Why does a particular stroke relate to a particular trait? Since we all write differently, why does every common stroke we write convert to the same trait? How is it possible that similar strokes made by people over multi-cultured, multi-language, multi-ethnic world and back into history have the same meaning? Do other cultures and their writing have their own traits and strokes? Why does a particular stroke mean what it does? Where does that come from? Is this an argument that human nature is universal? These are all central questions handwriting analysis should address. It has yet to fully answer any of them. Some people have tried guesses and some have merely accepted them without question or studied interest. Others have idly wondered about them but haven't let them hinder their work. Many of these people are analysts.

This bothers Grim, who says, "I feel inadequate even pondering any of them."

Grim needs more convincing by the supposed broad reach of his subject. Analysts have been told and accept that stroke meanings are widespread and historical. Wherever you go in the world they are the same. However far back in history you go they were the same then too.

"You really can't blame a skeptic if they swivel their scowling head several times for this notion," Grim admits.

"A sensible person will consider words like 'preposterous' and 'unbelievable,' won't they?" I ask.

"Yes, I know. Tentatively I accept it and it bears out from my own limited experience."

But he would like to see some substantial evidence of it. You do have to allow for cultural and ethnic variations, even today. All of the examples seem to be famous figures, which is understandable. At least we have some historical record of their actions to square against their handwriting strokes.

A few more unresolved issues have ignited in Grim's churning, burning, discerning, mad-about-learning mind. Do individual strokes really disclose individual traits? Or is that a futile hope? Aren't traits, as egregiously-light scraps of human behavior, too rabid to be captured, penned up, and tamed as beasts of personality? Are we therefore limited to only expansive portions of handwriting for meaning about personality, such as slant, thickness, rhythm and size?

"After all," he observes, "they permeate every writing and bless us with the salve of greater certainty."

Grim has never heard any cogent answers to any of these questions. No, it's worse. He has heard or read little speculation or even casual discussion of them.

Before these big-sky-country questions, Grim and his colleagues have borne the ultimate question. Does handwriting reveal personality? Whether it does seems past question to most analysts, including the benign doubter Grim. Analysts have that seemingly self-evident premise handed them from the start. Grim has always accepted it. What secures it for other analysts he doesn't know. For him his rationale is comfortably logical and uncomplicated. Handwriting yields personality from our handwriting experience in school and its aftermath. In grade school we all learn the same essential way of writing, the Palmer Method or something close to it. Soon we all evolve into individual styles, often not close to what we were taught. The farther time takes us from Palmer the more our styles differ from Palmer. Among ourselves we differ also. The only reasonable conclusion we form our unique styles is that we are expressing our individual personalities. Doubters will say it is random or intentional, or at least they say it isn't our unconscious mind triggering those strokes equating to personal qualities.

"Well, then what is it?" Grim growls.

A. N. Palmer, the master penman, acknowledged each person had personal styles that would emerge in due course. Still, he said it arose as simply a mechanical procedure unlinked to our minds. It "could reveal nothing more significant than the utterly arbitrary habits of muscular movement stored in the unconscious." Other skeptics have granted its uniqueness. This would include questioned document examiners. Grim thinks that by necessity they would have to accept handwriting as particular to each individual. Otherwise, how could they say they are distinguishing a genuine writing from a specious one? Among many critics and skeptics they acquiesce in its uniqueness but justify it as "physiological idiosyncrasy" and nothing more. We write our certain ways only because our muscles, nerves and bones are different from everyone else's. When we throw a baseball or swing the 5-iron, we generate our own styles since we are each bodily different. Our markings on paper are just following orders. But they're not coming from up in there; they're coming from down here close to that pen.

Grim's outrage over these skeptics is already swollen. Now it wants to burst.

"We write differently for no special reason, as if it's simply the result of God's guiding our hands?" Grim booms. "If it's just physical, how do you account for all the odd, wild and frantic extra strokes some people make? Or how about a simple stroke like an extra long t-bar on the letter t? Are you going to tell me this is only physical?"

Whether the strokes seem creative, or whether they appear different from anyone else's, there's an underlying basis, say Grim and his fellow analysts. They acknowledge that saying everyone's writing is unique doesn't prove it's from our personalities. The next step is critical to make the faithful leap to personality as the logical source. Analysts find that each person who has a certain stroke related to a certain personal trait *has* that trait. People with common strokes thus have the common traits. Everyone is different. Nevertheless, people who are, say, "defiant" have the stroke representing defiance. The indecisive have the indecisive stroke. Grim believes this fact eliminates the argument that our writing is random or physical or any other non-personality source.

"It's worth saying it again and another way to not miss the point," says Grim. "Not only does handwriting reveal our separate personalities. People with certain traits in their make-up share the strokes that identify those traits. Those who don't have those strokes don't have those traits." The logic is central to convincing people of the legitimacy of his subject. After that, the key is matching traits to strokes and establishing their validity.

Analysts are sure everyone's handwriting is distinctive. Probably most non-analysts concur with that too. A few years ago a very important organization outside handwriting analysis seemed to question that. At least they were forced into it, they thought, and they tested it in a very scientific forum to see if it was true. It began with a decision by the United States Supreme Court in the 1993 case *Daubert v. Merrill Dow Chemicals*. The Court ruled that where expert opinion evidence is submitted, the court must itself determine if it meets scientific standards before allowing an expert to testify. This decision lit an uproar for the legal community, especially prosecutors. Much of expert testimony previously allowed in courts for years was now in doubt because it lacked scientific studies on which to base it. In the old days evidence requirements for expert testimony were less stringent. A big reason was that in the old days money wasn't available for research and social science itself wasn't researching. It was just a toddler. Many acquired their expertise by years of study and application. For years since then experts have been getting away with their expertise because it had been allowed by prior courts. The Court in *Daubert* slung this bootstrapped expert testimony into question. Some areas of expertise lacking serious scientific studies were fingerprinting, questioned documents, and handwriting analysis. (More on this later) Because fingerprinting and questioned documents, which are often forgery cases, were in jeopardy, the alarmed U.S. Department of Justice began its own scientific studies. Its research and development arm is the National Institute of Justice. One study it was asked to do was, can you believe it? this question: *Is handwriting unique among individuals?* Although analysts are sure of it, some skeptics are not and they aren't just dolts. Grim learned about the study only after its results in 2003.

He couldn't believe it had to be researched. "It was like going back to re-invent the pen and inkwell for handwriting disciplines," he quips. The study's conclusion was that, yes, each of our writing styles is unique.

That result was re-assuring to handwriting people like Grim, mentally wiping their foreheads in relief. The study was conducted by determining if one person's writing could be detected from a pile of writings. To test the hypothesis free of human judgment, a computer program was used. It could scan the strokes and square them against samples in the pile. The results more than rammed the doubters off their barstools. It heaved them through the swinging doors into the pulsating street of reality. The computer was 98% accurate in matching the individual writing to its counterpart. When a human analyst went through the stack of writings, he could find it 100% of the time. Of course handwriting people knew this all the time and wondered why the holler and need for test-tubes-and-beakers research. The sample the machine and the human being reviewed was two pages of writing. The testers tried an even tougher side experiment. For a sample to review and match they cut the two pages to only *one word*. Not a problem. The machine was able to correctly select its match 84% of the time.

Despite the analysts' quarrel over stroke readings, psychology also has its intramural tiffs. Because handwriting analysis has not studied writing as thoroughly as science demands, its own frays concern its advocates. The dubious public views the conflict as a fractured image.

"When you get together on what parts of writing are important and what those lines all mean, let us know," the public scoffs. "Meantime we are going to ignore you as a serious technique for determining personality."

This stroke-meanings issue goes back a long way. It's more than heady analysts armed with sheaths of accomplished research differing over interpretation. Regrettably for its standing, too many graphologists have reached these meanings by intuition, guesswork, or some other meager outlook, setting back Graphology's standing and lengthening its time till approval.

Grim believes a consensus exists among handwriting analysts about what most of the strokes mean. This consensus is stronger for the gestalt portions of writing. This is important since analysts give them more weight than strokes. Within the trait community the contest is over the more obscure strokes, which disillusions eager neophytes and delights sour skeptics. Obscure strokes scatter far from the school model. They also tend to be rarer strokes and thus minor traits. As they are so infrequent, they defy easy recognition. IGAS has a few. A backward lower loop as on a g, revealing a person who has been rejected. A downward curved t-bar meaning self-control is at work. Stunted downstrokes on upper loops, as on an l, reflecting frustration in following through with great ideas. It takes a village of peoples' writing to verify a trait finding. When only a few in the village have a specific stroke, you need some more villages. Translation: get more writing. The farther the stroke strays the more likely the person is seriously flawed, analysts contend. Where those problems lie specifically creates most of the conflict. Grim prefers that all of his colleagues just kumbaya and agree on the stroke meanings. That they don't concerns him but doesn't deflate his helium-filled spirit.

"Conflict infects behavioral science," he asserts, "and meeting of the expert minds is often scarce. Many areas within psychology linger as constant battlefields."

Since handwriting analysis must prove itself further, it endures the bloodletting. Some are more than skirmishes. Without the convincing proof of stroke meanings, the public should understand why they split on meanings. This discord will persist until analysts reach their critical mass of money, goals, methods, and authorities to research it.

The image of handwriting analysis has impeded its progress. When an analyst seeks to make inroads with public institutions like colleges, he doesn't know how he will be received. One college asked Grim to come to their school to present his topic. The official e-mailed him that she had the event all set up and "it would be a hit with the audience." She would have a series of tables where members could sit and provide paper and pens where they could each write out samples and analyze for themselves. This kind of response fires Grim's cracker. After some teeth-grinding he replied that he preferred a different approach. He was offering an academic discussion of what he considers a serious topic. From her disappointed response Grim could tell she was taken aback. What he wanted to add, solemnly and firmly was that a university should be a forum for assorted ideas. Give it a chance to be heard. If it doesn't strike a chord or seem plausible to the students, so be it.

"I was not coming to provide party entertainment two steps up from Carrot Top, who somehow appears too often on college campuses."

"What were you coming to convey?"

"I wanted to give a general talk about the subject with illustrations of what it is and what it does." After this pointed message, the official suddenly became unavailable and the contract he had prepared for the occasion languished unsigned. To this day Grim doesn't know whether she pulled the plug on him, or her committee that selects the cultural event vetoed Grim's appearance when the anticipated mirth disappeared.

Handwriting analysis has an abundance of skeptics. Grim sees the vocal ones as science-minded types with little compassion or patience for unproven beliefs. That's understandable. He thinks most of them would unfold their pretzeled arms and perk up their ears if they understood what it is and how it is done. He doesn't shy from the intellectual challenge of trying to alter a skeptic's viewpoint. On the other hand, he doesn't rub his hands together and go look for a rumble. Gaining a new supporter from chronic suspicions is a small victory and one to celebrate. They do occur.

"I've found some of the most abrasive skeptics become fervent analysts once they are broken," he observes.

Not native to handwriting analysis, the phenomenon can be explained by the adage no one is more religious than a convert. Adds Grim, "Especially a recent one."

He thinks his subject is important for what it is and what it can do for humanity. Yes, it doggie-paddles near the deep end of plausibility, risking submersion and drowning. The public rightly has its natural doubts about it. Unpracticed analysts before him have suffered ribbing and contempt. When they first realize Grim is an advocate, many smart people have trouble handling it. Because they know he is also a lawyer, they hesitate. With his decades in the law and additional years as an analyst, he has earned some respect. In person few people will attempt to flout him. When he begins speaking about his subject, most people defer their instinct to mock him or his topic. He may not sedate them but they listen. A few collapse into a crushing dread that they may have to give him a sample. "Will he expose me for the loser I really am," Grim supposes many are thinking. Mark Twain once said that deep down most men don't really think much of themselves. Grim claims he is not seeking if this is true about anyone he meets. He is only trying to identify who the person really is and hope they embrace the insight. If it stings their pride, work on raising their spirits.

Countless times where someone just learned of his expertise and is engaged with him about the subject, they remark, "I will have to give you a sample of my writing sometime." An eye-roller for Grim, he can't recall the last time a person said that and later tendered a sample. "When I hear that word 'sometime,' I take it to mean 'when the cows come home.'"

Grim sees it as a nervous reaction to the subtle intimidation he and his subject generate. When they are with an analyst who seems serious, isn't a dummy, won't apologize, exudes some authority, doesn't giggle, has no crystal ball and no turban on his head, most people are silly putty in his hands. If they are brave enough to try wielding a critical sword at him, he won't recoil from the moment. Most thrusts at him come with toys'r'us blades, not Damascus steel. People "know not whereof they speak" about the subject, he declares. That means the little learning they have doesn't make them dangerous enough for a serious discussion, let alone a convincing retort at Grim. Some analysts welcome silence on their subject's worth or legitimacy. They want to do an analysis, hear some praise and pocket some money, not answer why an analysis may be garbage unfit for a can. Grim doesn't mind a spat even if it tumbles into a verbal brawl. Once a lawyer, always a lawyer. He misses his legal scuffles.

Grim knows that analysts have a lot to answer for. The public holds most of the cards but plays them poorly. Whether he's verbally jousting with the curious or the critical, he usually gives direct, rational and non-evasive answers. Admittedly, he doesn't have all of them but he seems to know what the answers should be.

I want to test this so I try: "Where exactly in our brain do the handwriting strokes come from?" Promptly he answers, "We don't know. They seem likely to come from the cerebral cortex." Then he will add, without yielding an inch more of uncertainty, "This doesn't make the strokes and traits invalid. They work well for us. Science just needs to find the answer. With the pace of brain research it appears to be on its way."

His answer may be forthright but it's not fulfilling for analysts or outsiders. It's not the answer he wants to give either. He wants to pinpoint the locus in the brain. If the outsider wants to believe, it doesn't grace them with the certainty sought. Nevertheless, answers like that seem to neutralize most people for the time being.

Grim is a valiant goalkeeper for his handwriting topic. He knows he has to wear as much padding as he can stand. He's taken enough critical doomps, thwacks, clanks, and blops to send him to the bench. He says he can take it. In fact he is not satisfied to play defense; he wants to score points too.

One way to maximize his efforts, he believes, is to go to the top and take on, yes, professional psychologists. "They need to go behind the analysts' woodshed for some educating," he squeals.

Whoa, Nellybelle. Grim is coming up to speed. They better have a huge shed and a sturdy rod. Few psychologists have more than a slim insight into handwriting analysis. They have an even slimmer yen to learn it in depth. It can't possibly be taken seriously, they deride, spending no more time discussing it than their good name can tolerate. If somehow an analyst can dialogue with one, the psychologist will lighthousebeacon their eyes around to verify no one is looking. They will lose status if seen consorting with these mobster analysts. A psychologist will consider taking a course or learning further about handwriting analysis only through the mail or traveling to another region where no one knows them. If you can grab their lapel to get them to listen, they will shotput their deadweight demand for scientific proof at you.

"It's their first refuge," Grim grumbles. "Just because you're nearby, these skunks lift their tails."

Analysts may hold their noses but those skunks have their point. They know the burden of proof is on the analysts. Until they see the research, psychologists don't want to get near it, or at least be seen with it. Studying psychology in school, they kept their distance too. Besides, their academic duties didn't allow time for this "nonsense." No sound incentive arose for them to learn it. They were just learning the rudiments of psychology, which was burden enough for their young and pure minds.

"With more time would they have looked into anyway?" I ask.

"I doubt it. Certainly not in the depth necessary to understand it."

Today Grim is convinced the story is much different. They actually live in fear of it. Just as the Puritans worried they might get pleasure from doing something, Grim is sure psychologists secretly concede it may have some legitimacy.

"It's the 'sneaking suspicion' phenomenon," Grim calls it. "Maybe there really is something to this idea that won't go away and seems to be getting closer, they must be thinking."

The crux of their historical snubbery is their public image. They can't be seen as giving it a clothespin hug or even a stepladder hug. This would damage their credibility with the public and especially their peers. "But not destroy it," Grim is certain. "And anyway it should not. If only they knew its worth."

A few years ago a psychologist was at Grim's Pennsylvania Chapter of IGAS to consider becoming part of the organization. After a tolerable first meeting she was curious enough to call the headquarters of IGAS. She asked the official directly where the research was for establishing the validity of Graphoanalysis. She was told it effectively went along with IGAS founder Milton Bunker when he died in 1961. With that the psychologist refused to join IGAS or consider its course. Grim tried to get her to re-consider and reserve judgment until educating herself more completely about it. She wouldn't and hasn't been back. It is hard for IGAS to satisfy some skeptics about the research.

"If they only understood what research Bunker did over decades and what he did with it, psychologists and others might change their minds," Grim says. (Read more about what this means in the chapter on Bunker) "Of course they should also learn the subject and try it and then make up their minds."

A thoughtful person might consider a partnership between an analyst and a psychologist a marriage made in heaven. These weddings are not happening. Analysts who want to consult for psychologists or supplement their work find only rejection. Grim believes his colleagues would help them gain better insight of their patients. In this instance, guilt-by-association is not the only obstacle. Analysts are slighted as coarse rivals who would steal their business while threatening their image of scientific purity. Besides, the pie is just not big enough for all. If analysts are willing to provide referrals, that would be an incentive for breaking the arctic ice between them. Psychologists prolong the gap by their ignorance of graphology's benefits. Those blazing insecurities analysts can find in the neurotic's writing will ease the psychologist's diagnosis. If that is not enough, as a supplement analysts can help to confirm or reject their diagnosis.

Like the U.S. and Cuba, the two have stared and barely tolerated each other for years, according to Grim. "It's a shame for analysts that psychologists haven't partnered with us. But when they finally realize how effective a technique it is, woe to analysts. Psychologists will try to corral it for themselves."

If you doubt that, ask hypnotists. Recently psychologists have discovered the value of hypnosis, another technique for helping people. Gone are those images of evil-eyed men, dark of hair, vile of intention, slick of mien, enticing naïve maidens into their power. Hypnosis is now mainstream. Psychologists usurp the hypnotist's dominion as they gradually learn hypnosis, the better to treat their clients with their adopted skill.

———

We know now computers and their software can do everything. We've all seen the explosion in word processing type fonts over the last two decades. We've had electronic signatures for decades. Signatures by computer and the rest of our writing have progressed to new fonts created to simulate the writer's actual style. One that is gaining users is by Signature Software of Hood River, Oregon, where the person's whole writing style has become its own computer font. Politicians and sports stars and even doctors, lawyers, and realtors want them. If they can convince the reader it's their own writing, they will seem more caring and personal. These all involve matching the type font to their personal styles.

In view of computer's agility, you are now wondering if computers have entered the realm of handwriting analysis to generate an electronic analysis. The work of analyzing demands intellectual efforts. Is it possible to create software that will actually analyze handwriting for personality traits? For a few years the prominent West Coast analyst Sheila Lowe has been selling her *Sheila Lowe Handwriting Analyzer*. At first it seemed a daunting project even to develop. After her skepticism of its probable accuracy, the software experts finally convinced her. If she could separately identify all the variables in the many trait-strokes and other elements, like margins and slanting, the program could be achieved. It *was* a daunting project, she found. Working with a major software company, she accomplished it.   Their final product is not all high-tech. Initially a human being reviews the writing and inputs each of the traits and other elements. Since our attributes can gyrate in their strengths within the person and from person to person, the human catalogs the intensity of each trait. Once those are inputted, the computer takes over. It produces a complete report integrating all the items. It has some refinements too. You can check out a person's fitness for work positions and determine compatibility of partners, as in a business or a marriage. In her book *The Complete Idiot's Guide to Handwriting Analysis* Lowe discusses it and reports that it has done well.

Lowe has not cornered the market for software analyses. Mark Hopper, President of Handwriting Research Corporation in Arizona, has built probably the biggest handwriting analysis enterprise in the world since its founding in 1983. He declares that they have developed what he calls a Computerized Handwriting Analysis Profiling System (CHAPS). Put together over fifteen years and at the cost of two million dollars, it was featured on "ABC News with Peter Jennings," where it was called "uncannily accurate." Apparently with his computer he has persuaded the psychology establishment to give some respect to handwriting analysis. His organization declares that the American Psychological Association has been willing to say that there may be something to it. At the annual APA meeting a study was presented that found, with computer assistance, handwriting analysis can be a reliable tool for determining honesty, emotional stability, substance abuse risk and judgment.

As a cultural artifact handwriting analysis is narrow of reach, obscure of understanding, and defiant of category. If you do grasp it and go to its proper shelf, you crumple with hesitation. Grim was asked to participate in a Career Day at his old college. As part of the data form each attendee had to classify his occupation. Traditional ones were printed on the form. As no category seemed close, Grim struggled with his. "Medical" field was in the vicinity, was the closest one, but didn't work for him. Luckily the form had a blank for "Other" in which Grim tried to explain by writing "Social Service profession–Personality Assessment." Maybe too long, an eye-glazer and unclear, he thought. He was right. Where to put it has always been a problem, at least for the serious analyst, who sometimes feels he has taken on a pitiable waif. The nay-sayers would gladly toss it into the smelly dumpster with fortune telling and astrology, both hard to cubbyhole.

The authorities haven't been much help either. The administrators of bookstores and libraries have wavered to find it a proper shelf. If you wander around Borders or Barnes and Noble you will look hard before finding it. The current location in Barnes and Noble is the "Psychology" or "Self-Improvement" section. If you turn this book over, the back reads that it's a "Self-Help" book. In Borders it's on the shelf in, would you believe, "Metaphysics." A recent visit to a shelf found the few books in the "Other Divination" section next to palmistry books. Other stores had it in "New Age" and "Philosophy." A few years back your Uncle Sam began tipping his big, gaudy hat toward the subject. The Library of Congress re-classified Handwriting Analysis (apparently termed "Analytic Graphology") in 1980 from "Occult" status to "Applied Psychology," or "Individual Psychology." In 1991 the United States Department of Labor removed it from "Amusements and Entertainment" and slotted it in "Miscellaneous Professionals, Technical, and Managerial Occupations" under the name "Graphologist."

Course catalogs for adult schools have their own anguish. From "Self-Improvement" to "Literary" headings, they will feature it under the hulking Army icon "General Interest," the confusing "Special Interest," the vague catch-all "Miscellaneous," the salad bar "Potpourri," or the thankless pit "Other." Thank God they didn't start a new one, like "Don't Know," or "Your Call." The Temple University Continuing Education catalog has numerous courses to choose from. It breaks them up into several headings. Only Arts, Literature, and Language had any connection. Not even close. The only heading left to consider is the default one, Special Programs. Thanks to computers, where would we be without "default"? In the nineteenth century Phillip Nolan was sent adrift from the United States for a good reason. He denounced us in a moment of fury and deserved to become The Man without a Country. With no anger or flippancy, Grim decries that handwriting analysis is the "subject without a shelf and the course without a catalog."

———

For any other area of expertise, handwriting analysis is only as good as its analysts. Grim wishes more were qualified to do full-blown analyses. This is a large obstacle on its road to progress with the authorities. No state has formal state or local certification for handwriting analysis. California has a certification for handwriting analysis to be taught in one of its graduate or specialty schools. Fortune-telling's history has been notorious as sizeable amounts of money have been paid for specious services, mostly predicting the destiny of the forlorn. Grim from Pennsylvania says his state has a criminal statute against fortune-telling, although it is rarely enforced unless someone gripes of being cheated. Those usually come where "some sap handed over cash and got what they deserved." Fortune-tellers seem rife as gas stations and always seem to have large signs hyping their expertise in other areas too. Put some thick quotes around that word ""expertise."" If you have the money, no doubt they will have the "expertise" in handwriting analysis too. For analysts these fortune-tellers deposit more yuck on his topic's rootch up the slimy pole of cultural recognition.

Despite the quality of the practitioners, unhappy clients exist in any profession. Complaints about analysts have been only here and there, primarily in job hiring. Those who may have lost out on a position where handwriting was involved looked for a scapegoat. No analyst has ever been successfully sued, as far as Grim knows. Since handwriting analysis hasn't attained the acclaim or use of other psychology doctrines, psychology hasn't tried to ban it or license it. Since it remains unrecognized, they don't want to regulate it. They might if they saw it creating havoc throughout the land. So far no harm, no foul worth punishing. If regulation appeared, it likely would arise from disgruntled people claiming they were hoodwinked. They would have contacted the Better Business Bureau or the county consumer affairs department or a state or county medical society, or a licensing board. Since more businesses utilize handwriting analysis, the probable person to run to these agencies is an unsuccessful applicant blaming graphology for missing a job spot. Grim sees no reason for grievance since it has worked well for companies utilizing it to screen for new employees. Apparently none of the public agencies has reached the tipping point of complaints where legislators sought to enact protective legislation with administrative oversight. That is generally true although rumbling has occurred in a few states. Around 1990 some legislators in Rhode Island and Oregon tried to ban it as an employment step. They were rebuffed. After federal law banned polygraphs in employment hiring Oregon tried outlawing it a few times. In Rhode Island the proposed ban for graphology was defeated largely by the efforts of a Ph D and graphologist, Marc Seifer, who testified before their legislative committee. An important point he made, among others, was that graphology is a personality assessment test that brings out the individual's personality similar to the Meyers-Briggs and MMPI. If you ban graphology, other personality tests should go too. Otherwise no laws have been enacted against it.

Lie detector tests, abolished for employee screening, survive for limited purposes in government and other positions where security is critical. If so, why do you always hear about them in the media? They do prosper in criminal cases and TV shows and other contexts. In those the individual has voluntarily taken the test. In court cases prosecutors use them selectively, often where they don't have good evidence, such as word against word and not much else to go on. They may ask someone who claims they did or didn't commit a criminal act to take one voluntarily. No one is required to submit. However, a prosecutor can decide to file charges if they don't take it. Lie detector tests (polygraphs, more properly), every informed mind knows today, have limited value. Competent criminal and other attorneys will counsel clients against taking them as they are unreliable for getting at the truth. They measure physical reactions to questions, which vary from person to person as they react to pointed questions. They also need further study just like handwriting analysis. You have read about clients with lawyers submitting to a lie detector test. Those circumstances occured only after the client first took their own private test. Presumably, since they passed the private one, their lawyer and the client felt confident enough to subject them to the public one. A typical instance is the client is close to criminal charges in a questionable case and the prosecutor must decide on charging him. If the client passes, the prosecutor is less likely to pursue the case against him.

———

Grim used to be a lawyer. Tradition placed him and his cohorts in a league of professionals. When young ones start out they are shocked to realize one great truth. Since people in professions are paid money like everyone else, they have to establish where the money will come from and how to get it to come. Starting out, most don't think much about it. They vaguely assume that because they are exalted members of society, people will call on them in droves and money will swan dive into their bank account. Soon their elders deliver the shock that their profession is also a business. New professionals may have seen themselves as mighty oaks as they graduated from their esteemed schools. Now they are reduced to acorns. They will need a lot of sunshine, water, and those trunk rings to become prominent in business. To get there they also realize they can't just dig in with their roots. They must leave their comfy offices and dirty their hands by hustling clients for business. The neophyte analyst would rather hire a salesman to generate those welcome fees. He realizes he can't afford one. The one he does hire lacks experience in his field. That's because the salesman is himself. Glancing around at the other professions, he shudders knowing he has begun the race several paces behind them. Medicine and law have enjoyed rank for centuries. Analysts know their place on the ladder of prestige is a few rungs down. But they hope their day is coming.

Conceding a gap exists, analyst Grim is aroused to bangzoomalicetothemoon his subject into the rarefied air of the distinguished professions. He plugs handwriting analysis as a profession that should be included within psychology and mental health. Its lofty purpose is to help individuals to understand themselves and others through their handwriting. By conveying that knowledge, the analyst enables the writer to make better decisions about their lives. To become a competent analyst takes diligent training and education. Inevitably it also requires them to understand personality. On top of that is the ethics code of IGAS, which should help. Whether these factors raise handwriting analysis to a respected profession is arguable. At least an impartial observer can find that it is a calling that tries to help people in various ways. That surely makes it a service business. The hard part is calling it a profession when it hasn't yet attained the scientific credibility it seeks. Grim wants you to fix on the word "yet."

Grim thinks a prime drawback for his subject's flourishing is its practitioners. Most analysts could improve their marketing skills. When they learn the basics, they fall short on the follow through. The kind of person attracted to it has lacked the don'ttakenoforananswer, don'ttakerejectionpersonally, knockonalotofdoors approach businesses need to launch and prosper. They have been more charming, tactful, affable, caring sorts rather than aggressive and driven. That can be appealing and won't be a turn-off. For better or worse the field has been dominated by women, who themselves have too often treated it lightly. Most analysts begin their practices later in life when they have been in a job for a while and decide to pursue their secret dream to analyze writing. Thus they have the experience of years to acquire the wisdom and tactful way they aid their clients. Analysts see themselves as providing a genuine service to mankind and a professional one at that. When you must contact people for business, it's hard to portray a caring attitude as you approach them. That is the bane of any service business. As sole proprietors analysts must tread in a wary world that wants to scoot from their advancing footsteps. Shy ones need not apply and usually don't, especially when you are solely charged with developing your practice. Although most are outgoing by necessity, if not nature, and eagerly seek out the client, a polite timidity runs through many analysts. The subject requires that you open their long, heavy public curtain and let them know what lies behind. Once you have probed deep enough you want them to understand their intimate selves and assist in bettering their lot. That's not easy for the genteel or the meek. Yet an aggressive stance in this caring and obliging profession repels many potential clients. Those who can finesse the balance between the two succeed admirably. Could we not say that about many other service professions?

Most analysts grow their practices by speaking and teaching. Adult education has arrived in most areas, usually run by school districts or community colleges. Getting the course listed in the school catalog alone is superb marketing. It's a free ad for an analyst regardless if anyone signs up for his course. Giving talks parachutes them into schools, colleges, libraries, as well as civic, social, charitable and business groups, like chambers of commerce and conventions. A droll diversion and free vacation tempts some analysts to entertain and inform passengers on cruises. Ads or even yellow-page listings are not that common. They don't seem to garner business. However, with the proper targeting, an ad is effective. Connecticut analyst Irene Lambert has been promoting her genealogy practice for years with ads in the genealogy journals. She provides insights into ancestors' character for their curious descendants. California analyst Sheila Lowe has herself in legal and bar association periodicals for her twin graphology and questioned documents enterprises.

For analysts in general word-of-mouth is probably the next best method for attracting work. It's a natural ripple from teaching and speaking. Of course for the word to get around some reason must exist for the word to make the trip. Many analysts find the word slow getting out. Grim has found that a line to the media, especially newspapers and magazines, often results in good publicity. Sending a blurb about your handwriting business to the news outlets has been a success for most analysts. With a factory-installed curiosity factor, people want to know about it. Everyone writes and wonders what their brand of writing shows about their good and bad points, particularly those they think are hidden from public inspection. A segment of analysts shun them but others will do analyzing for high school after-prom events. As marketing they capture a wide audience of the future consumers and clients of the community. If the analyst does enough of them over the years he has cultivated a wide swath in that locale. The wave of the present for businesses, including handwriting analysis, is the internet. Whereas teaching and speaking will bring in income, the internet has outlay to create and host a website and maintain it. Today the possibilities for reaping profits from this investment are promising for any entrepreneur. Analysts are just beginning to get their business toes wet with this growing, world-wide opportunity. As a business tool, especially for timid analysts, it should result in recouping of expenses and achieving long-term success.

Any business sells something, either products or services. Yes, believe it or not, handwriting analysis is a business. What does it sell? Grim's answer is to cite companies like Kodak, which sells a product, not a service. That product is not film but something you can't hold in your hand. It sells memories, or at least advertises them. Of course its purpose is not as wispy as you might think. Those memories are in the form of photographs, easily held in hand. Sometimes what a company believes it sells can be comical. Harley-Davidson sells motorcycles. Right? Not according to its marketing spokesman. They sell the ability of a 43-year-old accountant to dress up in leather and cruise through a small town and force the residents to flee in fear into their homes. Both Kodak and Harley promote captivating images. You swear they each sell tangible items. When you ask Grim what handwriting analysis sells, you can tell he's thought about it. Unlike Kodak and Harley, his business doesn't sell a product. It sells a service. We weren't prepared for the length of his answer. And written down forgodsakes as he goes and pulls out a metaphoric list of joyful benefits. He lists self-knowledge; right choices; peace of mind; a lighthouse alerting your journey to trouble; disaster avoidance; a sound investment by saving on money, heartache, stress, and time; deep insight of yourself or others; removing the public mask; inspecting under your hood; taking apart the watch to see what makes it tick; a physical exam for your psychic being; and a flashlight for personal soul-searching.

Most analysts otherwise mean well and practice commendable ethics. The ones with the shallow backgrounds create special problems for other analysts. They give opinions off-the-wall, especially about the meanings of strokes. They take their cues from books written by analysts who got their cues from prior analysts. Thus the source of their wisdom is often suspect. Frequently they compound it by unprofessional acts and unscientific approaches. One way this happens is how they speak and write. Books, blurbs, and articles often refer to handwriting analysis' ability to "reveal secrets" and "solve mysteries" about your personality. Grim is willing to grant some license to use these descriptions as gonzo marketing or puffing. They may get the public's interest aroused but the subject's image is unburnished. He especially recoils when he hears a fellow analyst utter words suggesting mysticism and other non-scientific pursuits his subject has been linked with for centuries. Some of these words are spiritual, reality, energy, ego, mystical, harmony, material, and philosophical. Astrologists and psychics and other New Ageists dapple their comments with them. Too many analysts do also, and that bothers Grim. It's not wrong to use them. They are important terms to understand personality, which was one of the chapters in your Psychology 101 textbook. Whether the public wants to acknowledge it or not, handwriting analysis is about personality. Grim devoutly wants the public to accept his subject as another serious area under the psychology banner.

Using these words requires you to elaborate, which many analysts don't do. It's partly because many don't really know what they mean. Also they assume too much in the listener or reader, who is commonly repulsed by them. They are words from our education heavy with significance, we are sure, and vague with meaning, and usually beyond our meager mentality. To properly understand them in academia was to require hard and deep thinking, not something high school gave us. Grim tries to avoid them and mostly succeeds. A few he finds unavoidable, like ego, in discussing personality. When he must discuss it, he breaks it up into edible images. They may not be downhome but the public is more apt to get the idea.

———

One of Grim's sidelines is treading on words he calls "eye-glazers." That's his phrase for words that lumber along with obscure meanings that upset the average person. He also wants people to understand handwriting analysis, a trying enough exercise without further mental strain. He is bothered having to use eye-glazers from psychology. He wonders where we go wrong in our grueling march toward life's wisdom. From the warmbathwaterfreshdiapercleanpjs solace of bedtime stories, to exciting moments of learning to read, and then the increasing and final dread of school learning, especially reading. The monsters in our path were those strange, dense words, often longer than words we already knew. As we hobbled through high school we ran into these thingamabobs we couldn't get our hands on and could not see. They thudded against our fragile minds giving us instant headaches and a stupor allayed when we escaped to lunch, a study period or phys ed. When we focused our minds on this situation, a vague disquiet seeped into our unripened brains. It started when the books lengthened, the printing downsized, pictures disappeared. The reading got duller, the subjects harder, and the homework longer. The words we couldn't avoid hang as heavy sides of beef on meat hooks in our memories: theory, morality, philosophy, dichotomy, algebra, logarithm, hypothesis, rhetoric, semantics, ecology, ethics, ego, ideals, causation, values, entropy and metaphysics are a few too many. You can count most isms and ologies too. Some of them we tasted and spit out earlier in church with its own Hell-on-Earth eye-glazers: Grace, Sin, Resurrection, Communion, Resurrection, Purgatory, Redemption, Ecumenical, and those yeahbutourbiblesaysthis church names, like Episcopal, Baptist, Evangelical, and Presbyterian. These highbrow words disturb us because we reflect on them so seldom in traditional education. We read them or hear them but we never really absorb them. We stumble our way through our educational brush and we can't avoid them. They velcro their burrs on our pants or prick us with a wait-a-minute bush. When we take liberal arts courses the burrs and prickers proliferate. Eventually we leave school for the real world and wonder if we ever grasped any of them. We give ourselves a gentle pat on our back for learning of them. One day we learn that a person is educated who knows what he doesn't know. That's us.

Grim recognizes that, to be taken seriously, handwriting analysis must tackle eye-glazers. After all, the topic is about personality and that is part of psychology. So they live with it and accept that it targets the typical person with his emotional scars and bruises. He may be struggling with life but he is not psychotic (another eye-glazer) or nuts (Ah, not an eye-glazer but something we all know very well. It might even include psychotic.) The term "neuroses" seems close to what analysts find in the writing. If you ask psychologists, the extremes are personality disorders. Grim won't label his afflictions as neuroses or disorders. He is not anti-jargon. He is just pro-clarity, especially where the one babbling about handwriting analysis could be an analyst with little education and the recipient a client with even less. Instead, Grim uses terms like imperfections, drawbacks, and the folksy current ones "hang-ups" and "carrying baggage." He thinks these are adequate for a clear enough picture about people who are troubled but are unlikely to need a building that locks from the inside.

Unless those eyeglazers are brought down to earth, he believes, the public will dump offending analysts in with those other targets of skeptical scorn: psychics, mediums, tarot card readers, fortune tellers, phrenologists, ESP, astrologists, mystics, magicians, parapsychologists, witches, sheep entrails readers, palm readers, and numerologists.

Grim frets over the guilt-by-association stigma that blemishes handwriting analysis. The current irony is that society has retrieved some of these topics from the trash can and checks them anew. He senses a spurt of interest and advocacy of a few of these non-scientific subjects. Many more people have tried to reach departed loved ones through mediums. *Medium* and *The Ghost Whisperer* have been television shows. Astrology and psychic readings have flourished in recent years. Their practitioners regularly appear as seemingly credible guests on TV talk shows. Witches sit before cameras soberly describing their, um, um, craft. Hynotists and magicians like David Copperfield have upgraded their images by appearing on TV, in Las Vegas and other very public arenas. You can even include UFO's and those Asian notions like Feng Shui and Yoga and Tai Chi and others. Despite the populist advances in these areas, science continues to debunk them. Grim concurs in censuring them, although he keeps an open mind on re-casting their images if their skills are validated. He accepts the same sauce for his goose and their gander. Grim recognizes anecdotes seeming to support the phenomena. Many people want to believe in these still unproven areas. As a consequence their status has surged, which revives the threadbare adage of a rising tide lifting all boats. If you consider psychics and numerologists, they are the boats benefiting by the rising tide. Guilt-by-association can work both ways. Besides the progress it has made toward society's approval, handwriting analysis has also profited by the favorable treatment the other subjects have enjoyed.

When the psychic's boat rises, whether he likes it or not, the analyst's boat rises too. "Still, I'd rather not be seen in the *same* boat with them," adds Grim.

On the ladder of acceptance by the establishment, where is graphology? Grim rungs it a few below where acupuncture, hypnosis, chiropractic, conservatism and country music are now. About a generation ago they were disrespected, trashed, not cool. Today they are largely accepted by the establishment. The time is arriving for handwriting analysis. It needs the overall boost from formal scientific research to propel it into tolerant recognition by the psychology authorities. The position of the American Psychological Association on handwriting analysis is significant. It doesn't embrace it as a genuine technique to be used in business or elsewhere. By the same token, it declines to formally oppose it.

Shown above is circus entrepreneur P. T. Barnum. Your Aunt Fanny, sheep entrails, clouds, halos, and Barnum all provide arguments against the validity of handwriting analysis. How so?

Chapter 13

Status

The Search for Acceptance

Pareidolia, sympathetic magic,
barnum effect, cognitive dissonance,
halo effect, and sheep entrails
Several arguments cited by
skeptics against handwriting analysis

It works.
One reason from handwriting
analysts in support of it.

Since psychology is a young social science with doctrines pioneered by human beings, questions stalk it everywhere. In physical science researchers can easily confirm data through constant experiments. Thus reliability is high. As a social science psychology cannot match this precision. Even mediocre skeptics can swipe at it and get away with it. Handwriting analysis aspires to membership in the social science fraternity of psychology. Grim tenders it to psychology as both a projective technique and a personality assessment test or technique. Much of the critics' slingshotting stems from what they call "psychological effects." These effects distort what analysts perceive, trapping them and the public into believing they have a sound method for reaching personality. Critics say analysts unwittingly prompt these effects when they probe for a trait and announce it as found. When you dissect their actions, say the critics, their findings are faulty. There are several effects.

A common one is the Barnum Effect, named for the circus entrepreneur P. T. Barnum, who had some entertainment for everybody. If the analyst announces a trait that seems to fit the individual, the writer is more likely to accept it. He is more likely to confirm it when the analyst attaches some mildly negative qualities. When they are appeased with some flattery about their positive features, the writer regards the analysis as more accurate. Since the analyst conveys the trait so broadly and loosely, everyone gets something. The descriptions cross the line from significant to trivial and drop any stuff of meaning. Water that should have been a chunk of ice becomes mist.

Do the statements really give you personal differences?

The analyst might say, "Your writing shows that you get easily upset."

"Everyone gets riled about something, and some things really set us off," a skeptic would reply.

The statement may be correct for that person but it is meaningless. It doesn't tell you anything specific enough to separate them from others. Psychologists have a phrase for it—the Aunt Fanny Effect, where the traits are accepted even though they offer little about the person.

The analyst might say, "You tend to be a pleasant person."

The scornful detractor will say, "Yes, and so is my Aunt Fanny. So what?"

Professor Barry Beyerstein of British Columbia is a consultant and executive council member of the Committee for the Scientific Investigation of the Paranormal and a vocal critic of handwriting analysis for its empirical failings. He asserts that "you tend to be pleasant" is so illusory it can be applied to several million people. The statement's purpose isn't to make the listener feel good. It's to make him perceive the statement is correct by using a very common quality. Thus, more hot air from an analyst and little insight into the writer's personality.

"If you suggest that handwriting analysis paints personal attributes with too large a brush, you do not understand it," Grim fumes.

At least the IGAS version. To say, for instance, that a person is "stubborn" is inadequate. You must also ascertain how stubborn he is and convey that refinement in your analysis. There are plenty of traits that are common even among millions of people. If he is describing, say, six million Americans, that only covers around three per cent of the country since we now number over 300 million. Can we not find a stubborn person among every 33 people? Beyerstein should also understand that a Graphoanalyst takes more than a few seconds to declare a trait. A Graphoanalyst will not only identify a particular trait but then quantify its strength in the person's make-up. A trait should be described in more than just black and white. The shades of color must glint, not just fill space. People are complicated, not stereotypes of qualities The calculation is precise as a measure of human attributes.

Graphoanalysts use the scale of one to ten (that society seems to adopt for anything these days) as a quick, clear, and convenient way of calibrating evaluation. Thus each trait is both isolated specifically and gauged for intensity. If, for example, an analyst described someone only as "generous," he has a point. A Graphoanalyst is more particular. He qualifies how generous he is, such as modestly so (4 or 5), or very charitable (8 or 9), or some other variation. In fact, if the generosity is found to an extreme, it actually segways into another trait—"extravagant." Analysts are not glad to see this one. It amounts to fulsome generosity. Although it is admirable to be very giving, an extravagant individual has a desire to give but doesn't know how to control it. They overdo it, often to their detriment. They will not only give you the shirt off their back but that farm they live on too. That is descriptive hyperbole but you get the idea. IGAS has plenty of others too. "Self-confident" can become cocky. "Steadfast" can become stubborn. Any trait can be placed on a continuum. When any trait (generosity) is stretched out one way (extravagance) or the opposite way (stinginess) it loses its identity to a separate trait. That gives the traits some precision, which should overcome Beyerstein's criticism.

Graphoanalysis is not unique in calibrating traits. Nor is any other handwriting analysis group. In the same way we evaluate familiar people in everyday life. You may not recognize it but reflect a moment and you will probably find yourself acknowledging it. We do it all the time in our private lives in conscious and unconscious weighing of our fellow man. When you silently judge your co-worker as abrasive, if pressed, you could easily respond that "on a scale of one to ten he is definitely an eight.

Beyerstein should also know that after collecting the separate traits, the analyst has more to correlate for a full report. Once he has gathered the traits, reviewed the global aspects, and assigned quantities, he assesses how they interact and then sketches a complete likeness of the person. Some traits will temper others, chiefly traits deemed stronger and thus dominant. If a person is irritable but has a strong sense of tact or even sense of humor, either of these senses will curtail his irritability. All of these qualities appear in writing strokes. Some people may be volatile emotionally. Yet if they also have great dignity and pride, they can usually rein in those strong feelings. Hence, stronger traits will infect if not govern that person's life more than others.

Some traits are powerful in another way. They will intensify other traits. Resentment gripping someone will tighten if they also have strong emotions or a bad temper. Knowing these intricacies can help a business selecting an employee or a woman choosing her life partner. We may pause knowing a person is very emotional before hiring him or marrying him. However, knowing that he has controls in his personality, we can view him as a complex being, not dynamite waiting for a blasting cap. After all, none of us is that simple in our qualities. Knowing which qualities rule, though, is essential. With a sure swagger stick, handwriting reviews the writer's trait troops and identifies both the reckless and the feckless.

These psychological effects existed before handwriting analysis, and other areas of psychology are not immune from them. When you open your newspaper and read your horoscope, you might fall into the middle of an effect. Astrology has its often vague and general statements about your fate today and hereafter. Since its inception these effects have pestered it. Psychologists will declare many more. Virtually all have thrived for centuries and can be applied to any other human endeavor where the advocate is attempting to convince the listener his subject is valid. Some relate to the so-called expert themselves. The Halo Effect is another common device for the skeptic's quiver. If the expert seems authoritative, whatever he mutters will awe the listener, who will worship his remarks. A commanding presence, dignified, professional clothes, an impressive setting, amiability, sympathetic concern, technical verbiage, a subject with a history, and a sonorous voice aping that guy on *Star Trek*. Each helps erect a credible impression. When the analyst can beam on your mental screen an imposing image, each favorable trait resonates with the listener.

Perception is a typhoon for analysts, according to critics. Grim's answer is that "Perception gets its own chapter in your Psych 101 book. It blows hard in any area of our lives. We should always be aware of its power. Yes, even with analysts. But not only with analysts. It can influence belief for any dubious subject. It's not confined to handwriting analysis as a potential problem. Be careful what you hear from *anyone* who emits an aura of authority."

Grim lies in wait for a critic thrashing his beloved subject. He readily admits that when he hears bad words he wants to pursue the speaker beyond the grievance. He wants to know who's talking. He counters with his own supporters, many who are historical heavyweights. He can gloat as he dishes out the names, many leading thinkers of their times. Make that of *all* times. Aside from formal scientific validation, he wants to know what better personal endorsements it can have. And he doesn't have to pay for them. He believes graphology's status among the highbrows is matchless. The other discredited subjects, such as astrology, tarot cards, and fortune telling, can't cite more than a few worthy names. Yes, a few people of note harbor delusions for these subjects that Grim rejects. Contrast them with graphology's advocates—Confucius, Aristotle, Einstein, Freud, Binet, and others. The critics shoot back that even the brightest minds aren't immune from faulty perception and false notions. Psychology has support from this phenomenon, they say.

None of us can escape a native blight, not even those mental giants. We're all stuck with human nature, say skeptics, which impels us to ascribe meaning to handwriting. We find it in our strokes from our deep need to want our lives to make sense. We long to generate order from chaos, and we see purpose from only chance. Critics see nothing worthy beyond strokes' limited duty to express our thoughts on paper. At least that is the view of some psychologists and others, like skeptic Barry Beyerstein. This inner impulse for meaning is a primal vein coursing through human existence. Hence, handwriting analysis is one of its forlorn hopes wishing for what isn't there and never was.

Beyerstein edited a whole treatise with his brother to consolidate the leading arguments for and against handwriting analysis. In *The Write Stuff* he takes a chapter to convey this counter-theory of sense from nonsense. He plucks from psychology an ancient theory explaining the analysts' delusions. Handwriting analysis evolved from "sympathetic magic," he contends. In this genesis we insist our writing styles must have some rational meaning. Once we get by our elementary school forms, we all go our separate ways. This can't be by chance, says our inner voice. We want the words to look good and feel good to us as they are exhibited to the world. Instead, when we glance at our writing we are agitated from beholding lines that seem lost in a blizzard of white paper. We appease this by giving our strokes significance, which restores our inner calm. Granted, the rest of our bixolated world is tough to endure. If we can have our handwriting make sense, life has one less mystery and is more bearable. To this we add a maxim Christians utter a lot—A reason exists for everything. We just have to find the right one each time. With this logic draped in hope, we find handwriting's deeper role in our lives. Giving our strokes reasons to exist lifts us up and reduces our frustration over not understanding our world.

When your inner self longs for meaning in your writing, it blunders into a mental trap, says Beyerstein. It has an eye-glazing name, "pareidolia." Recall your summer afternoons of youth when you lay on your back, gazed up at clouds, and imagined a bear or an alligator floating along the sky. Likewise, graphology took our writing strokes and created symbolic relationships between them. The bear and the alligator became the pareidolia, the results of our wanderings. Skeptics rip astrology for borrowing it to convert the night-sky constellations into the Signs of the Zodiac. Religious people who believe in the Hand of God know he intervened when their child is saved from a horrible death in a car accident where the other people in the car are killed. Now their child will no doubt become President of the United States. In these minds fate is large. For them pre-ordained or God-as-Edgar Bergen is luck or happenstance for others. Psychologists established pareidolia to explain events that may seem special but, upon further review, signify nothing. As one more deluded group, analysts lassoed pareidolia to explain our handwriting. But Lucy, there eez no 'splainin' to do. To give our often flailing, undisciplined, stark, oscillating strokes import will give us peace of mind. But it's cut from a piece of rind, which no one should want. It belongs in the trash with other absurd ideas.

Now handwriting analysts must weather the spinning nor'easter from skeptics that their stroke-trait ties reflect only their wishful thoughts. Pareidolia and sympathetic magic identify why and how we maintain handwriting analysis in our lives, fending off the distress of chaos. Take, for example, those tall upper loops, as in l's or h's. Analysts have determined that this shows a spiritual or idealistic person since they are strokes far above the baseline (usually invisible unless the writing is on lined paper) on which letters rest. The baseline functions as the earth's surface, representing reality. It is where all conventional strokes begin their journey. It is where all conventional strokes ultimately should seek to return. Since the upper loops of the h and l stand way above the baseline, they are considered in the outer domain of life (think stratosphere), away from everyday concerns. Unfortunately, say the skeptics, the metaphor arose from our natural tendency to make items that look alike to be related even with no attachment. Our creativity lures us into symbolic relationships between the strokes and the world outside the paper. Uniting the two items fulfills a human need for the world to make more sense than it has. With its symbols Freudian Psychology says occasionally a cigar is just a cigar. In handwriting, say skeptics, a tall upper loop is nothing more than a tall upper loop. What's more, unlike a cigar, that loop will always remain only a loop.

Doubters understand the natural appeal of the handwriting link between strokes, mere lines on paper, and traits, actual qualities of people. Their quarrel is with the next step. Analysts want to cha cha cha when they should be content standing still. It's irrational to make that link formal as it lacks the ring of truth, not to mention the bling of proof.

"We are accused of having imagination. That's one we will gladly plead guilty to," Grim affirms. "This is also the imagination of the skeptics doing what they do. This is America. Their views have the right to be heard but not the right to be accepted. They also have the right to be wrong."

He's heard these arguments before. Prior to our modern ideas of science, human beings had to start from somewhere in making our lives meaningful. "Our predecessors in China and Rome and elsewhere created these symbolic worlds from ignorance and innocence without the benefit of a body of serious knowledge on personality and the rest of psychology. Now we are stuck with the taint of centuries from our topic's illegitimate birth."

"But they seem valid and forceful points," I counter.

"Beyerstein's points are generic and old," Grim adds. "He has pulled them from the freezer and microwaved them to serve on modern handwriting analysis."

The Barnum Effect and the Aunt Fanny Effect, pareidolia, and sympathetic magic have been applied to other psychology areas. They go way back in stomping on unusual ideas striving for credibility. In past times lucid minds pursuing sober scientific notions didn't have much to go on, especially in social science. Learned minds didn't really understand man's behavior in the modern sense until the nineteenth century. It has come a long way, most of the great progress occurring in the last century and a half. It also has a long way to go. Handwriting today shouldn't be saddled with the stumble through darkness of prior minds in their efforts to understand their world.

From experiments relating all the body's expressive movements, we now know they're all integrated. As our bodies go this way or that, those actions speak about our individuality. They are readily observable merely by watching the person doing them. As to handwriting, it's observing the results imprinted on paper. For skeptics to explain handwriting analysis as an invention from our need for comfort is just primitive and simplistic.

"We deserve better from the critics. If they are going to throw tomatoes at us, they should be more rotten than what we're getting," Grim rails. Thankfully he promptly supplements that. "They need a more cogent argument. Don't stick us with the old notions when we've come this far. We at least know of the foundations of their criticism. We didn't have much science to build on. Now we do and the critics today talk the same trash."

Grim's indignation seems to be billowing. Still we are brave enough to ask about specifics, like the so-called spiritual people with tall upper loops. That seems like a valid point on something they are using today.

"How do analysts justify things like this? Isn't this just their active imaginations? I ask.

"The difference today is that we don't just churn out doctrine and expect people to live with it or lump it. We have verified the trait by evaluating the writing of people with the tall upper loop strokes.

They all appear to be spiritual or deep thinking individuals. That's not guessing and hoping. That's hypothesizing and then validating. We are proud that our scientific lab is not men in white coats, in some septic room with bright lights. We use the real world where people write everyday as they go about their lives."

One perspective favoring analysts is pragmatic. Despite their often smirking doubts, these skeptics begrudge that handwriting analysis seems to work. All right, make that *some* skeptics. This gives it a patina of appeal. Sadly that concession doesn't live long enough for analysts to cheer. It soon dies a merciless death by the skeptics' own hands. They will say, "This does not prove it is valid and to be taken seriously."

Grim gets up and seems to want to shoulder something drastic, maybe a flamethrower. A verbal one of course. Instead, he pauses to gather himself and sits down again. Finally he says, "If they would also add it's a good start and doesn't disprove it either, we believers might tolerate them more."

Handwriting analysis faces other squalls over its origins. From psychology Beyerstein has deployed a theory that freshman read about in their psychology textbooks. It's called "cognitive dissonance," another obscure eye-glazer that unsettles Grim. Where a person has two clashing ideas, he sooths the resulting discomfort by choosing one over the other. He can deny one exists or modify his viewpoint about either. Other options can occur. The conflict could involve an attitude versus a behavior. A smoker knows about lung cancer so he feels tension. To relieve it he tells himself that they haven't proved smoking causes lung cancer or that he doesn't smoke that much. Since handwriting analysis has not been fully accepted and a person may believe in it and become an analyst, the person must confront his dilemma. Or a person may believe in it and request an analysis but knows of its shabby reputation. The neophyte analyst feels anxious about its repute and needs to quell the feeling. After all, he says to himself, if I'm going to pursue this, the concept should make sense and enjoy some legitimacy. They create reasons to oppose the critics and their own uncertainty. Beyerstein postulates the situation where someone allows his writing to be analyzed and the report has some findings the writer believes are wrong. Nevertheless, to ease the "dissonance" between believing in handwriting analysis and the inaccurate findings, he accepts the report overall.

Grim snaps: "This principle can occur everywhere, inside and outside handwriting analysis, and no doubt does. Besides, a report may be largely correct and in a few areas incorrect. Or the writer lacks the insight to recognize his own features."

Grim says he can stand the heat of a good fight with a critic. For some, though, their poor standing incites him to get out of the kitchen. They don't know handwriting analysis and deserve no respect. When a person babbles and has a wide audience, Grim can be provoked to go after him. In the fall of 2000 one of these critics surfaced and fired a volley directly at Grim. During the presidential campaign for the 2000 Election Grim was asked by Dickinson College, his Alma Mater, to analyze the writings of Al Gore and George Bush. His dual reports appeared in the alumni magazine. In the next issue was a letter from one alumnus reacting to Grim's article. Identified only as a 1948 graduate, he wrote: "I was dismayed to see the piece on graphology in the Dickinson Magazine. Handwriting analysis may have some validity when confined to uses such as comparison of samples in cases of forgery but to claim that personal characteristics of an individual can be deduced from handwriting is pseudo science at its worst. What's next—phrenology, astrology, and sheep entrails?"

Grim could barely keep his pen in his inkwell. His bloody legal battles of thirty years and his instinct to shield handwriting analysis demanded he respond. Although he thought it was a "sucker punch," he did not.

"This is what we're up against. After reading his letter, thousands of my fellow Dickinsonians probably think I'm an idiot. If some didn't have an opinion or knew little about handwriting analysis before, now they are swayed to disbelieve. When someone uses phrases like sheep entrails to compare to handwriting analysis, that's one of those hysterical comparisons you hear these days. If you liked Hitler you'll love Bush. I can't respect someone who speaks in those terms. They're usually so over-the-top in their perspective that answering them gives them undeserved heft. Who knows what his expertise is? I don't know how many actually read my piece. It was not a legal brief for handwriting analysis. It was a detailed, sober profile of the two candidates with the handwriting featured. Hopefully it was at least enlightening if not convincing to most readers. The letter damaged us since it planted the thoughts into many heads."

"Did you respond"?

"The letter really deserved a rebuttal. But composing a short one would have been inadequate to counter the poor image the writer created. To counter this kind of tripe would have taken a lot of words. I also felt it would have spurred him to fire back. It might have worsened into a street-fight between dueling alumni. Probably the rest of alumni would have enjoyed opening their magazine. But the result might have been a lot of heat rather than much light."

It's bad enough the ordinary ignorant hit on handwriting analysis. Grim is especially annoyed when someone with credentials blasts his subject and he knows their firing blanks. As the public thinks the bullets are real, handwriting analysis is still wounded. One he cites is a newspaper article quoting Joseph Horn, a University of Texas-Austin professor of psychology. Since the article was syndicated it got national attention. He dismisses handwriting analysis as "no better than what you get with a 900 number to a mystic to see what your love life holds for you." To Grim that's unfair by itself since it chucks analysts on the same slag heap with those other discredited subjects. As a scientist Dr. Horn insists on evidence. Bad enough to there for analysts. What he says next is where Grim thinks Horn gets goofy.

Nettled by handwriting's claim that its uniqueness relates to personality, Horn declares, "The most unique things we have are our fingerprints, and that doesn't tell us anything about a person's personality."

With this Grim has had it up to here. He takes aim and pulls the trigger.

"Those swirls on our fingers are physical and there at birth. The swirls we craft with ink on paper are physical too. We are stuck with the fingerprints God stamped on our hands before we were born. In contrast, our handwriting comes from the impulses within our minds. These impulses are non-physical and changeable."

Actually their specific make-up is still a puzzle. We do know they somehow get from our brain to our hands where we obey them as we write on paper. We can't see them at birth and we can't produce them until we begin writing. It's true the impulses get to the hand by physical transmitters and that the hand, the pen, and the strokes on paper are all physical. However, the strokes there stem only from the mind telling the fingers on the pen how to draw them. Other parts of our bodies we consider unique to ourselves, such as our ears, hairline, and lips are also physical and present at our births. They are not formed from within the mind nor do they change because of it, except for aging and other natural effects. They don't reveal personality either.

"To compare the individual nature of, say, our nose to our writing is absurd," Grim seethes. Since they were on a national news service, America has read Horn's words. "Since he is an academic and supposedly an expert, and the coverage is nationwide, our image suffers a cyclone of destruction everywhere. The aftermath hurts like more rain and wind."

Since the comments went unanswered, they remain in the misled public's mind, joining their other graphology biases. Horn's opinion says more about him than about handwriting analysis. Of course the public doesn't know that. Grim didn't learn of his statements until long after they were published.

He is left now saying, "The problem with credentials is that it grants a forum to people like Horn. Credentials don't give you a sound position. That has to be tested in the pressure cooker of ideas."

Grim is unhappy with some people outside of the U.S. too. Dr. Rowan Bayne is a psychologist with the British Psychological Society. He thinks handwriting analysis should be ranked with astrology. He calls it "useless...absolutely hopeless." At the 2005 World Economic Summit in Davos, Switzerland, he had just tested some graphologists and was revolted with their performance. He claims that before the summit he was amenable to it. Now he would give it "zero validity" for revealing character. The test was somewhat deceptive. Some British analysts were given the writing of what they were told was Prime Minister Tony Blair. They were casual notes at a conference. They were the writing of Bill Gates from Microsoft. The graphologists offered some opinions that even Grim calls "eccentric and questionable."

Grim begins, "He is entitled to express his opinion in England and the United States. He is wrong in both places."

What really detonates him is Bayne's comment, "It's very seductive because at a very crude level someone who is neat and well behaved tends to have neat handwriting." Grim is thrilled he admits graphology can reveal someone neat and well-behaved. Doesn't it possibly also mean that someone with sloppy handwriting be considered unkempt in habits and needs more discipline? Couldn't you then extend this logic to other attributes reflected in the writing?

"Why must the initial concession stop there? Can't it be extended to other forms once an analysis of each is made?" Grim asks with his teeth bared. Grim is upset enough about what he calls "the putrid analysis" of Gates/Blair's writing. "Fee, fie, foe, fum, I smell the blood of some lousy English analysts, who have tarnished our image," he grouses. He especially objects to Bayne's "blunderbuss" barrage at the subject itself and all analysts. And the peas-in-a-pod, ohnonotagain, image link to astrology.

A secure analyst can tolerate the public skepticism for his subject. He can respect the informed skeptic who shows he acutely understands the issues. Another type should know better but betray they don't. They show their ignorance of handwriting analysis and humiliate themselves to those who know the subject. When that person has a pedestal-type status, a certified brilliant mind, and a national soapbox, the threat to handwriting analysis can be staggering. Marilyn Vos Savant, says the Guinness Book of World Records, has the highest IQ ever recorded. Consider her comments in *Parade* Magazine of August 5, 1990, in response to a reader's question: "Do you feel that handwriting reveals personality and/or other characteristics?" Her answer was this:

> "Not to the extent that it would tell us anything we don't already know about ourselves. For example, a particular sort of slanting may be characteristic of left-handedness, and excessive ornamentation may be common among the young. (I once knew a girl named Linda who dotted the I in her name with a tiny heart. However, she was thirteen years old at the time and I'll bet she has grown out of the habit now, three decades later. At least, I hope so. When our handwriting departs from the way in which we were instructed, it simply may be due to such factors as eyesight or motor control or chance—or even whether we give a darn about it—in addition to the fact that every teacher handles the subject somewhat differently. Still, I think it's fun to have my handwriting analyzed the way it's fun to see if the person at the circus can guess, my age or my weight. I enjoy seeing if he or she can tell what I already know."

Grim wonders who graded the answers when she took the IQ test. "This ignorant, wayward non-answer further shows the greasy wall we try to scale for recognition by those who matter." Again his face pell-mells into a gallery of screwball looks. After a moment it reverts to serious and controlled, and he resumes. "I suppose I may be long gone when we reach respectability, thanks to comments like this. Unless we do it while I'm still alive, I don't want to be cremated when I die." As we try to digest this and guess where it's going, and before we can fathom it, he continues: "When somebody does something asinine like Vos Savant, I want to be able to roll over in my grave." Until Grim's topic gets the salute he is looking for, he won't rest in peace.

Sometimes analysts don't know the direction of flak. When they're vigilant against outsiders, they're vulnerable to friendly graphology fire. Trait school advocates impugn their gestalt counterparts and vice versa. That's always occurred and generally has been civil. Once in a while they dispense some misinformation about each other, maybe a serious distortion. This is no different from politics or other areas of competing creeds in our culture. Since handwriting analysis has yet to attain cultural magnitude, an internal skirmish can seem uncouth and petty, like a schoolyard brawl. No one important will know or care and it's over before the back-to-class bell. When the scuffle occurs in the national spotlight, the impact is magnified, as Professor Horn, brainy Vos Savant, and the ranting Dickinson alumni showed. In this setting analysts will care if they want to defend and uplift their fragile image. When insiders attack each other publically, handwriting analysis reels backward. California analyst Andrea McNichol is not a Graphoanalyst, but she is a handwriting analyst. A few years ago she spoke some words Grim can only describe as "inexplicable." She has published a coffee-table book called *Handwriting Analysis, Putting It to Work for You*. Grim gives her credit for trying to educate the public with it. She has been an instructor of handwriting analysis at several community colleges and other institutions for many years and has some major business clients. Although he acknowledges her elevated stature, up close she's less than meets an objective, perceptive, reflective eye. The book's tone is light and informal. It lobs to the masses hollow, plastic blocks and colored rubber balls of handwriting analysis. She has developed a following in her state of California and her book has sold well throughout the country. In a handwriting analysis article in the national science magazine *Psychology*

Today, McNichol was asked why handwriting analysis hadn't gained better approval in America.

Her answer: "Primarily it's because, about sixty years ago, this country was introduced to a simplistic offshoot of graphology called Graphoanalysis. This method maintains that sweeping physical and psychological diagnoses can be made on a simple examination of our individual letter shapes."

"IGAS thanks her for recognizing its influence, although I disagree it's negative. She got the approximate years right since Graphoanalysis was formally begun as a school and a doctrine," says Grim "The rest," he grumbles, "is ignobly wrong. Graphoanalysis is not simplistic and the examination itself is not simple. A Graphoanalyst makes a thorough and detailed evaluation of over a hundred separate traits along with broad factors, such as slant and spacing. Then he merges the strokes and the broad factors into a comprehensive picture of the individual by integrating how they engage one another."

Grim appears to spit blood. McNichol was wrong on two other points as well. One lesson analysts learn is to know their limits when doing an analysis. Once they have found the traits and other aspects of the client's make-up, correlate them and make up a coherent report. Then get out of the way and let the professional psychologist or better take over. Anxieties do surface in the writing, Grim admits. Afflictions such as jealousy, self-consciousness, resentment, and hypersensitivity can be identified, including their strength. When they do and they are severe, an analyst may be tempted to play psychologist and diagnose what's ailing the writer and why. Although clues can appear in the rest of the writing, analysts don't know why the person has the emotional maladies. When the analyst uncovers them he informs the person tactfully. All he's doing is letting him know about his true self, good or bad. None of us is perfect and some of our insecurities can mortify us. When the person learns about them, he determines if he wants to get help.

"If that is a 'psychological diagnosis' then so be it. She seems to be implying something deeper. I wonder what *she* sees in handwriting. Probably close to what Graphoanalysts can find," Grim speculates.

She's also wrong on the focus of the examination. To glean personality meaning, analysts focus on the strokes within letters, not the overall letter shapes. To the public, which doesn't know any better, this type of description sullies not just Graphoanalysis but graphology in general. Coming from within its establishment, her statements deepen the damage to the discipline. From the inside Grim sees her remarks as "foolishly naïve." Her facts are way off and could have been verified easily.

Grim is not finished with McNichol. The *pissed de résistance* for him was her bald declaration that Graphoanalysis attempts to reveal *physical* ailments. That is not so and he has no idea where that came from. True, the broad factors (global factors, as IGAS calls them) are "sweeping" but that is also what Gestalt analysts do. Graphoanalysis applies both gestalt and trait doctrines and merges the findings into an extensive report, recognizing that individuals are intricate and distinctive.

Fortunately for Graphoanalysis at the time, McNichol's comments didn't go unanswered. The President of the International Graphoanalysis Society fired back at her with a letter, which *Psychology Today* published in the next issue. Finally some damage control was up and running for Grim's organization.

McNichol typifies much of the problem with critics inside or outside the field. Too many non-Graphoanalyst analysts (commonly known as graphologists to Graphoanalysts) don't know enough about IGAS and Graphoanalysis to expound on it. Those outside handwriting analysis have less knowledge and less credibility. As for psychologists, Grim thinks they should hold their fire until they've learned the subject.

Grim prowls around like a boxer with a roving ring in search of an opponent. That is, one who takes a punch at his subject. One Grim would like to pound but hasn't said anything contrary lately is Albert Osborn. Any bout between Grim and Osborn wouldn't be fair anyway. Osborn died in 1946. He is arguably the most eminent authority on the handwriting area called questioned documents. Experts in this field are called questioned document examiners. Their prime role is to determine how genuine a writing is. *Questioned Documents* is the title of Osborn's weighty and rambling tome of over one thousand silver-fish pages originally published in 1910 and updated in 1929, with later printings. He covers all segments of detecting forgeries. Most in this field testify as experts in court whether a signature was fake or real. This has been the most lucrative area within handwritingdom. Wills, checks, promissory notes, contracts, and other legal documents make up most of the cases. Anonymous letters and notes are part of it. Most of the anonymous items consist of ransom notes and "poison pen" letters, items written slandering or threatening others.

Why does Grim want to beat a dead force? Osborn's book was the first exhaustive treatise on the subject. It still circulates and instructs questioned documents students. When Osborn compiled his book in the early 1900's he inserted an entire chapter on graphology. Osborn was not a graphologist and proud of it. He seemed to use extra energy to thrash graphology, citing its unscientific basis. Grim allows for Osborn's living in a time when graphology lacked empirical grounding and too many analysts mumbled nonsense. Surprisingly, after swiping at graphology, in the same book he praises graphology's value, and not reluctantly. Terming it "one of those pseudo-sciences" here and "occult" there and "intuitive" over there, suddenly he concedes it's helpful in anonymous letters and will contests where the writing might reveal the writer's mental state. He claims he has read much on graphology and respects its notable figures. Osborn believes that too many outside factors distort handwriting for it to divulge personality. He says this is its "fundamental defect." Alas, he doesn't mention what they are. Because of his well-earned stature, his brief against graphology should be taken seriously. However, his comments are temperate and only singe graphology's tender nerves, according to Grim. Conceding his point, Grim has his own list of factors that affect a sample of writing. They don't make it impossible to analyze—just more difficult. Those factors are also described elsewhere in this book. Examples are the kind of pen used, the mental state of the writer (stressed, tired, medicated, depressed, euphoric), surface written on, and more. Grim also explains how to confront those factors.

In his book Osborn discusses claims some analysts have made about the personal and physical qualities handwriting can reveal. It can tell of disturbances in the bowels, diseases of the stomach, love of young animals, and male or female sterility. Grim winces when he reads them and joins Osborn in disgracing these individuals. All these are from the early Wild-West handwriting period from the late 1800's to the early 1900's. We can't erase it and it didn't end there.

"Critics citing that abominable period today are unfair," Grim charges. "That is a portion of the period Osborn lived and he was only addressing his experience. If science had any part in them, very little of what these quacks uttered could be seriously justified.

In reading Osborn's view that graphology reeks, Grim is astonished by what he says next. As Osborn admitted, its reeking does not include what it shows of the writer's mental state. Curiously, he mentions *more* ways it doesn't reek. It can show if someone is neat, untidy, fussy, attentive to detail, forceful, weak, educated, cultured, illiterate, efficient, incompetent, passionately accurate, and if he is a bungler. Counting the large exception where the mental state of the writer is crucial, that is thirteen times it doesn't reek.

"If Osborn admits to its showing incompetence, shouldn't it thereby reflect competence too?" Grim wonders. The same for the other twelve qualities. Wouldn't their opposites be revealed just as readily? If you count those opposites we are now up to twenty-six qualities where Osborn says graphology doesn't reek. By now, from all of Osborn's admissions, graphology is actually smelling fragrant.

"Is he opposed to graphology or not?" I now want to enquire.

"If I can glean a few more qualities from him, I think Osborn might be termed a dedicated handwriting analyst."

In fact, without a fine-tooth comb Grim found some more. Osborn concedes handwriting can tell in part when you were born, your nationality, your sex, your occupation, and if you're artistic or manually dextrous. Some of these are not distinct personal qualities, Osborn and Grim would concur. Osborn would say a few are culled from non-personality features of the writing. Wherever they appear in any writing, they convey personal information about us, Grim makes clear. That is the important point to the successors of Osborn. These personal qualities shore up the case for the enlightening power of handwriting. Osborn shouldn't have stopped with his list of personal elements found in handwriting.

"If he had thought more about the stroke-to-trait links, I'm convinced he would have seen most of *them* also," Grim observes.

Although Osborn said he knew much about graphology, he panned it without ever learning it and applying it. Osborn was never that fair-minded outsider giving Grim and his fellow Indians their due. He never trudged those sacred miles in the analyst's moccasins. Learn it, apply it, and see if it works before attempting to criticize it.

If Grim can coax some extra personality traits in handwriting out of Osborn, can he wrest anything from Barry Beyerstein? Grim says he thinks so. Beyerstein has conceded a few attributes handwriting might reveal about a writer. Although not yielding an inch to the subject's validity, he has suggested that cultured people might write with a cultivated style, and stingy people might fill up the entire page with writing to save paper. He no doubt considers these throw-away concessions. Grim thinks Beyerstein may be too gracious and not realize it. He wants to use his charity against him.

He poses, "Why does Beyerstein stop there? If he ponders other ways people mark up their paper, would other qualities arise from them? Would he go the opposite way and say generous people would leave a lot of space around the text? Do uncultured people write in an uncultivated way? What about tiny writing? Would he say the person is modest or unassuming or better at concentrating? How about someone with large and wild capitals? Would he admit they might be attention-seeking or egotistical? How about someone with very rigid writing. Would he admit they are uptight or too mechanical in their actions? How about writing that is very erratic and chaotic? Is this person undisciplined or unstable?"

The list could go on. Shouldn't Beyerstein? Grim contends Beyerstein can't have it both ways. Either handwriting displays your personality or it doesn't? "Beyerstein should state just what it is handwriting reveals. Is it random and insignificant or not? Apparently he says it's not completely random. It may have purpose. Where does he draw the line?"

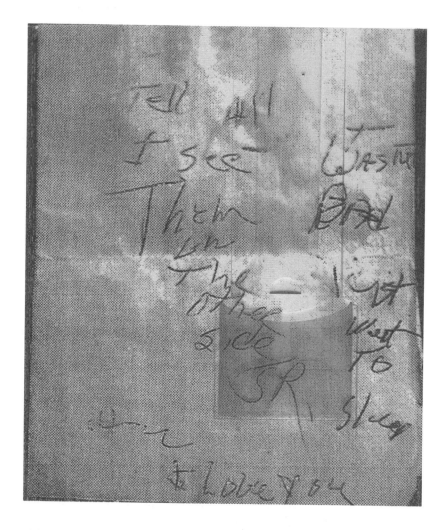

This is the handwritten note of a Pennsylvania coal miner after his mine collapsed and he and his fellow workers knew they were doomed to die. Is this not an example of how handwriting will always survive?

Chapter 14

Handwriting and Penmanship

Will they both fade to white?

Bill Crossman is a philosophy and English professor at Vista Community College in Berkley, California. He thinks that by mid-century written language will hardly be used. "We're simply replacing old technology with newer technology." He has written a book about the future. Talking computers (Voice in, voice out, VIVOS, he names them) will be perfected and become "the last nail in the coffin of written language…" Eventually handwriting will be "an extracurricular activity, sort of like kids joining the chess club."

We're used to signing our names for credit card and other transactions where our identity is confirmed by our signature. It's become so commonplace that when we sign our names, many clerks won't even compare them to the card. How many clerks turn your card over to compare the two signatures? Or we sign in such diddlybop, apathetic ways that our effort doesn't resemble our card signature anyway. Everyone zips through their signatures except for those who probably never did anything zippity-split. We're standing over a counter or table or writing in our lap or some other awkward position. All of these circumstances can beswaggle our customary signature. Presumably that one we wrote when we opened the account was carefully done. Ha. Not so. Many people even obliterate that one. With the speed of life now 186,000 miles per second, good handwriting, especially our signatures, tumbles down our list of priorities.

Other advances shove handwriting further downhill. Verifying our identity by signatures steadily slips away. Climbing upward are photo ID's, your mother's maiden name, pin numbers, passwords, fingerprints and iris patterns in your eyes. Cynics that declare the eventual demise of handwriting will dump these in the lap of analysts. It seems to have put analysts back on their heels. It's true that some advances appear to have hastened handwriting's end: computers, personal digital assistants, e-mail, voice mail, voice pads, text messaging, and other devices. Without our lifting a pen, they all record information that we need to send or retain. What information will we need hereafter that these machines can't record for us? Will we soon be down to the grocery list, To-Do lists, vacation post card, thank-you note, personal notes, and maybe the short PS? Some grocery lists or more general To-Do lists are already in hand-held devices. Thus, as Yogi Berra might have said if he thought about it, obsolete things aren't what they used to be.

Handwriting instruction in schools has declined over the years. It has lost its former elevated place in the grade school curriculum. For a large segment of schools, handwriting's worth has been demoted to minor status. The rules for printing and cursive have been relaxed, with scattered exceptions. Nationally the school pattern is a mix of penmanship approaches. Many private and parochial schools still believe it's important to education. Wherever it is taught, writing will begin with printing, mostly in first grade, sometimes in kindergarten. Eventually students learn to connect the letters through script, also known as cursive, writing. Some educators see handwriting fading away like the typewriter, a vestige with little purpose from our pre-electronic past. The need for handwriting's use is disappearing, they maintain. There's no reason to teach it or keep it around. Besides, those grueling penmanship drills are the foe of our rote-hating, ro-tating, seat-squirming, foot-tapping, eye-twitching, joystick-thumbing, mouse-clicking kids of today.

An irony is that graphology has helped in the decline. Teachers and administrators have heard the message that our personalities intervene when we write. Accepting its truth and trumpeting children's differences, they have fostered individuality. The rueful result is bias against a mold for students to follow. Down with rigid, mind-sapping methods. Up with liberated, creative children. No matter the causes, we're all paying and where the bottom lies is for the blurry future.

Susan Bowen of the International Pen Association thinks the "true culprits" for any decline aren't computers but "colleges of education, public school curriculum directors and administrators who dismiss handwriting as an archaic nicety that is no longer relevant. Many schools have abandoned organized handwriting instruction... for standardized test preparation, computer training, and, ironically, more reading and language instruction." By its neglect penmanship has become inconsistent and unpredictable. Students don't even know how to hold the pen correctly. When they try to write they can't visualize the letters. Since they haven't practiced writing them, it retards their progress in reading, note-taking, and composition. Giving value to handwriting instruction is important as it's "the core of excellence in education." Values like rigor, precision, and neatness are ignored. They are standards of excellence. Handwriting isn't just a separate skill. It provides a foundation for effectively communicating ideas on paper. If you learn to play golf without the proper grip, it impairs every swing you take with each club. Where students can't write properly they are bogged down in mechanics, rendering their ideas incoherent and their compositions feeble and stunted. With the schools' indifference, students don't get the discipline of practice to reach fluency. Writing should be automatic, enabling the student to focus on their words' destination, not the mode of travel. In the past few years a renewed interest in handwriting has occurred in grade schools. Bowen sees an expanding trend that fosters penmanship as "the pathway to mental growth and academic success."

Family psychologist John Rosemond thinks few schools teach handwriting because it involves drill. It is tedious and boring and makes children dislike learning. He thinks that if it's restored, students will acquire better skills and improve chances for later success. Teachers don't insist students form the letters properly, then later tolerate shoddy writing. When it becomes dreadful they're upset. They should be upset sooner. Experts believe it is probably a slim hope to correct faulty penmanship after fourth grade. Good practice should begin with learning to grip the pencil right, keep the words on the lines, maintain proper spacing, and form the letters correctly. These will yield readable, fluent strokes. In education an open secret is that boys' writing is less proficient than girls' as they approach high school. A recent study found that eleventh grade boys are three years behind girls. There appears to be no special concern or steps to close that gap. It's bad for boys and girls. A 1993 survey of teachers showed that 70 per cent of students had inadequate writing skills. No inky-stinky wonder. Only 36 per cent of their teachers had penmanship training.

This second-class status for handwriting will have harmful consequences. Many schools in America lack an overall plan and system for handwriting instruction. Ultimately, children won't achieve well in this zoomboomdoomtomb world. As adults their poor handwriting will barnacle them everywhere they sail, increasing their swells to overcome. Several studies of handwriting and school students found that where the content was similar, the students with better handwriting got higher grades on papers. If you think someone toting deplorable writing won't be harshly judged later on, here is your dunce cap. There is your corner. Sit on that hard stool. An unkempt, immature style of writing faces a series of troubles. Consider a common situation. A job applicant with poor handwriting is matched against others with solid writing and their other qualities are roughly equal. Who will get the job? Despite slight knowledge of handwriting's meaning, companies assessing applicants will notice their unkempt writing and be repulsed. Intuition will tell them it's not a good sign, even with people who think nothing of handwriting analysis. They may think careless writing equals careless mind and they will be right, analysts confirm. Where handwriting analysis is already part of their hiring steps, they will know for sure. Although it depends how it looks, handwriting with the strokes askew, amiss, and asunder tells of a person blighted by the un's and ir's in front of their description: unsteady, irresponsible, uncertain, and, sometimes in tornado writing, unhinged. They are struggling with the demands of life.

"If they don't want to risk this kind of worker, don't hire them where it shows in their writing," says Grim. "Some analysts will relish saying 'Don't say we didn't warn you.' That's not what they should say. But it will be true."

Whereas analysts denounce the lowered standards, they thrill the results for their profession. Where a school has not emphasized proper writing, children are unchained to mold their own styles on paper. An unintended result is truer individual qualities springing from their letters. Children's personal qualities will be unleashed to strut their talents much earlier. In crude form the writings of youth aren't displayed as widely and as deeply as adults' are. Yet their handwriting will reflect them. This liberated writing will yield more traits than the writing of those taught Palmer and the other methods. Children taught proper handwriting progress in their own steps. You would think that the imperious sway of that writing teacher travels far from Second Grade. Not so. Some begin their individuality a year or so after Palmer has left the building. Like Elvis he is not forgotten. For a decent interval students bowed deeply to his unavoidable letters lining the space above the chalkboard. Inevitably, as the students sprout, their memories dim. They giggle recalling teacher's stern looks, her fearsome pointer, and their smacked wrists. However, where she no longer hovers over their shoulders, students thrash about with their peculiar lines and curves remote from the classroom model. Analysts know that since children will forge their independent strokes, we can detect what's on their minds. Wait till they're teen-agers and you'll catch a more radical change leaving school patterns lost in chalk dust. Now the more mature person rears up, asserting his new sovereignty. The truth about this youngster has evolved with new clarity.

"Believe it," says Grim, "that the child and the school are the better for it."

As long as it's readable, the odd style now in charge peels off a Polaroid of his personality. If you save the writing as for a scrapbook, you will have preserved a memorable photo of his coltish but developing character. Just by putting his strokes on paper the young writer snapped his own picture. Although he didn't realize he held a camera, the picture was clear and unposed. If you keep the writing and glue it in a scrapbook, you'll have a superb likeness of his personality at that moment in his early years.

"What do you think will survive technology?" I ask Grim.

He pauses more than a few seconds to compose a list. "Suppose a person grew up with no handwriting instruction and suddenly needs to handwrite something important. He's at a public meeting and wants to jot some notes for expressing his views. He visits someone to make a pitch for his organization and wants to make several points. He's in a hurry and needs to scrawl directions to someone's house or a meeting place. Are there not countless other times information is critical in recorded form and the readily available method is handwriting it?"

He adds some items that he needs to explain. Frequently in dire situations we need to communicate immediately. In this era of the cell phone, it doesn't work in every location, some won't be around to pick up, and others will be without battery power. The only option may be the note scrawled for a rescue or other desperate action. Consider that a written note might save your life but you don't know how to write it. Or you threw out all your pens and pencils as unnecessary. Do you want the same plight for your children and grandchildren? Twelve miners died in a mine collapse in Pennsylvania in late 2005. They left a poignant note aware of their imminent death. Just before perishing, fishermen in *The Perfect Storm* left their note in a corked bottle, the classic sea manner. It's good they knew how to write and had pencils or pens. What would their loved ones have paid to ensure their last thoughts in this world were conveyed to them? Did they suffer? What did they talk about? How did they die? What entered their minds?

Grim sees these "special circumstances" as lasting. They may not always be urgent as life or death but require immediate contact. Paper and pen or pencil may be the only available items for the task. Grim wants to relate a fitting incident in a public parking lot. A man returned to his car to find its hood and fender smashed. On the dashboard he found a piece of folded paper. Written in a neat, feminine hand, a note read: "I have just run into your car. There are people watching me. They think I am writing down my name and address. They are wrong."

On a brief roll, Grim wants to offer another. Years ago someone parked carelessly on a city street. How careless he found out from a note under his windshield wiper. It read, "Thanks for taking two parking spaces, you stupid, inconsiderate bastard. I had to park two blocks away." Grim is sure these windshield notes will survive like the cockroach. For this last one and many other situations the fuel is anger and anger wants to vent. IMMEDIATELY. Where the angry one can't effectively do it with his mouth, what will be available? Civilization's go-to guys, pen and pencil and civilization's everyday recorder and salvation—scratch paper.

Many people stand around lamenting handwriting's move to the recycle bin of oblivion. Thank God it's taking more than a click of a mouse. There's time to act but you really have to search for its saviors. One of those has been distinguished word maven William Safire. After spending two years at Syracuse University in 1951–1952, he took a hiatus and sought other education, became a White House speechwriter, and a recognized expert on the English language. He has a regular column on language in *The New York Times* and has written several books on language. He returned to finish in 1978 and was invited as his own Commencement's speaker. He bemoaned that we are talking more and writing less. We do it because it takes longer to think and write. As a consequence our thinking has become more superficial. His solution for us is to demand our leaders begin crafting words with meaning and uplift.

If you think handwriting is headed for obscurity, check with American high schools. They have something to tell their elementary schools about downsizing penmanship: Don't. 45 states have their own standards for testing high school students. Most of their exams require some handwriting. In recent years at least ten million students have taken these exams. Where will these high school students get their handwriting instruction if grade school won't teach it? Moreover, students wanting to get into college now have their own judgment day after avoiding good penmanship their whole young lives. The high schooler's worst nightmare has become worster. No, they haven't added a grammar section. Ask about this at the Educational Testing Service, the administrator of the SAT's, located in Princeton, New Jersey. A new section requires students to handwrite. It's not to discern how well they form their strokes, although that is a partial concern. They must actually discuss a topic logically, coherently, and rationally, the Three Headless Horsemen of Highbrow that menace students into thinking more than a nano-second. Rather than the look of their writing, students will have to focus on content by composing an essay. As you recall from school blue books, they will need to bring their shovels, disguised as pens. No typewriter, word processor, or other device—just their barenaked hands holding a pen. For those with sloppy handwriting the slimes will be a-changin'. Since the section has a 25-minute deadline, they will be rushed to finish their thoughtful answers. This will mean a downpour hit the wallow. The students will squeal and the test graders won't know the doodoo from the corn cobs in all that mud. Many of these piglets admit they write little; their handwriting is barely readable; and that they now print "so people can understand me." The SAT may spark a revolution in student's handwriting from chicken scratch to, Lord, take me NOW, readable writing.

The brief experience with the handwritten portion of the SAT augurs well for decent handwriting. Those with script writing did slightly better than those who printed. A scary statistic is that only 15 per cent of the test takers wrote in cursive. The rest printed. Poor handwriting stifles the student's intellectual growth as well. Flawed penmanship leads to writing that isn't complex or long enough.

Although he doubts handwriting will disappear from school instruction, Grim does not despair. He thinks the need for penmanship may be overstated. No doubt everyone can at least mimic the letters they have seen when learning to read in school. Seeing script in print or elsewhere is less common. If computers are making writing obsolete, at least people are seeing printed words when they read and type out words on their computer. Doesn't that help the users to recognize and properly write the letters? If you can read, doesn't it mean you can write? You should have no problem doing some printing. It won't have to be cursive. If you want to create script, connect the letters with strokes as bridges. We can't always be near our computers or our cell phones. Times will occur where we have no choice but to write in longhand. Youngsters will someday say they don't write because they didn't learn it and don't write now. Surely they can write out all the letters of the alphabet by recalling them from signs, notes, documents, computers, books, periodicals, mail, and ample other sources. Just what is it you are looking at when you use your computer and other alternative devices and you tap out words? Every day occasions will exist to prop up your dormant handwriting and keep it alive and working.

Grim thinks that early penmanship can function as a form of graphotherapy. Many children come to school in emotional turmoil, often from a family in dire descent. If these children have no model to follow they will craft their own stroke schemes, thus extending their emotional defects. As their life is chaotic and unrestrained, so is their writing left to fend for itself. When they must mimic an ordered style, it can bring discipline to their life. It's akin to the military's corrective grip on boys out of high school paddling with one oar and no rudder with their lives ahead of them. By default they go into the service. They come out more mature and responsible with brighter futures.

If you think handwriting will go the way of the dodo typewriter, consider these items. Some handwritten documents do survive if not thrive. How about applications, and forms? We apply for credit, for jobs or we need to satisfy some government agency or some other bureaucracy. Surveys indicate 90% of job applications are filled in handwritten. School work is roughly 95% with those young hands. This comes from Richard Northrup of Zaner-Bloser, publisher of one of the major handwriting texts for schools. Certain kinds of information would seem perpetually written down. Items you want to note instantly for future reference. Messages you want to relay immediately. Both need pen and paper, whether a napkin on your table or scratch paper nearby. How about received phone and other messages at work, class note-taking, answers to test questions, especially essay questions, memos to self, special occasion cards after a death or memorable event, and confidential personal messages? "I think you're neat." "I can't go. My Mom would kill me." "Coffee after the meeting?" "Dora has a crush on you." "You're fly is open." Laptop computers have unfolded their screens in classrooms to fill the note-taking and other roles. Special occasion personal notes are still a social duty and only your personal imprint will do. We've actually come a long way, citizens and taxpayers. Years ago public debate arose over whether personal letters or notes should be delivered by the Post Office. Allowing your Uncle Sam to deliver them was seen as too impersonal. That must have been when your best girl lived only a few muddy blocks away.

Despite the alleged decline in handwriting, another event might be slowing it. Gel pens and other new creations have aroused sales of pens. Many people, even youngsters, have welcomed the gel pen's agility with its quick and smooth lines on paper. From a half century ago when writing was king, fountain pens have enjoyed a Restoration, abetted by improved technology. The prices can vary from the low hundreds to several thousand dollars. They are better made, glide easier, and leak less. Most important, they lay down a better line of ink. Even with ball-point, felt-tip, and gel pens, and others, the classic fountain pen has engraved its own niche. *Le fountaine* has become the ambassador and secretary of state for those devoted to a personal statement. Formerly the Titanic of the pen world, these pens glitter with lost tradition and polished charm. Even the makers' names inspire refinement and class: Esterbrook, Parker, Conway Stewart, Shaeffer, Waterman, Mount Blanc. When you see words in fountain pen ink, you do more than read them. You savor them and even revere them. You always esteemed their gymnastics on paper. Now delight at their style, flair, texture, and dimension. Turned on an angle, their sensuous lines assumed poses a ball-point pen wouldn't dare dream.

After a time from the advances in other pens, their urbane luster faded. By the 1950's pens became cheaper and more efficient, which the masses gobbled up. Maybe they gave us lines with potholes, lasted a week, and leaked ink, but ballpoint pens became as American as the Louisville Slugger. Today they have escaped their wayward childhood and approach the fountain pen's breeding. But they don't match it. Those who seek the finest strokes on paper bestow the fountain pen the awe it deserves. A reputable analyst will own one and urge his clients use it for their sample. The fountain pen's nib is special for handwriting analysis. Its sensitivity registers each little misstep of our strokes romping across the page. We know we are not perfect. Fountain pens smartly record the seismograph image of those imperfections. Handwriting analysis enters the room to make the diagnosis. In truth this instrument improves our character's MRI by deftly straightening some of those jagged, errant lines. You feel like that guy who avoided the huge doctor bill by having the radiologist touch-up his x-rays. That illustrious fountain pen gives us a cosmetic makeover we should seek and maybe don't deserve. But we'll take it.

Etiquette begs your pardon to speak about the greatly exaggerated reports of handwriting's death. Today polite rules still dictate that you handwrite personal messages about important matters. Where we have waned is in composing the message. If we've become lazy or inconsiderate, we don't take the time. We are caught up in the whirlwind of activity in our modern lives of stress and speed. Like the old Greyhound commercial, we leave the driving to the bus company. With personal notes the company is Hallmark and the actual driver is a nameless employee. We send a greeting card printed with a pleasing sentiment. This continues to appall etiquette's Miss Manners, who scolds us: Don't give up and say you don't know what to write. Don't you care about the recipient of your affection or concern? How you impart the message measures your sincerity. Do it with an item you create and handwrite. Some of us compound the faux pas at Christmas. We not only have the cards printed but we also print our names, or, should we say, our signatures. Maybe that's the height of arrogant, heartless indifference. And don't ask for partial credit for sending something in the first place. Miss Manners views it as beyond the utter phoniness. To shun the printed word and present the penned word elevates it to a statement of stirred feelings by the sender to the sendee.

She has written, "Etiquette is willing to supply the message. It's the sight of paper and writing that supplies the emotion."

Birthdays, holidays, graduations, intimate messages from someone close and wanting to remain so. Miss Manners believes that "serious" kinds of letters or notes will endure handwritten. Only a cold, uncaring person could type a condolence letter. Love letters and Dear John letters should survive in writing. Thank-you and apology notes are more effective in your personal style. If you do form them by word-processor, Miss Manners will shake her Sarah Bernhardt loose with disapproval. Actually if she hears about businesses like That's Gratitude, a Baltimore company, there will be a whole lotta shakin' goin' on. They produce personalized, handwritten letters, says its founder, so genuine that young couples "can take credit for having written them."

With e-mails now common, the issue of thank-you messages would surely follow. Miss Manners has heard the question about satisfying the thank-you via e-mail. Let's say you were invited to a friend's house for dinner. You had a wonderful evening and you came home and checked your e-mails. As you were on the computer and you felt good about the evening, you decided to tap out a thank you e-mail to your hosts. Will that suffice? Promptness good; method bad.

The hosts "spent time and attention on you. E-mail is a wonderful convenience for casual messages and memos, but you still owe your hosts a letter of thanks." Don't even think about typing the letter. Stop shaking your head and get out the good stationery or a blank note card and your best pen.

We are not done with written notes. Some notes are rarely sent, should be sent and should be handwritten. Marsha Egan, a leadership coach from Reading, Pennsylvania, took a column in a business journal to detail them. Congratulations on a job well done; best wishes for a promotion; good luck on a new venture; appreciation for extra effort; pride in a child's accomplishment; recognition for your spouse's support; and kind words to a friend. Since they are so rare, she believes handwritten notes mean more today, as e-mail and voice mail dominate our exchanges. Above all, they show you care.

She expresses it this way: "Handwritten notes are gifts. People really appreciate and enjoy them. The biggest challenge is to get to it. Just remember that every handwritten note you send will help you energize those around you, and maybe even make their day."

Grim thinks "an overtheriverandthroughthewoods outlook" draws Americans together, spurred by the specter of terrorism, endless foreign wars and a domestic one awaiting the next enemy attack. Instinctively we also want to rebel against the invasion of technology. The old, detached traditions Halloween, Thanksgiving, and Christmas have exploded, linking up as a constant maudlin spectacle between September and January.

The edifice of civil decorum survives today, but coarsens with each kablam from society's wrecking ball. That busy ball never calls in sick and won't take a coffee break. Meanwhile, trying to reinforce our culture's frail walls is the handwritten letter. Miss Manners underscores that a handwritten letter shows you are sincere. Okay, it doesn't certify it but it does prove you wrote the letter. Okay, maybe it doesn't either but at least you were familiar with the content. Okay, maybe you weren't but you signed it. Okay, maybe it was an electronic pen and you didn't see it or sign it. But you have good people working for you, right? Yes, it is also duly noted that you may have copied that message or were told what to write. The idea is still there somewhere. You just need more time to find it. It's not as though It Came from Outer Space; it came from you. Woody Allen said that a lot of success in life is just showing up. Somebody else wise said it's really the thought that counts. Much of etiquette is an attentive try at appearing honest and caring toward others. Just as we can't gauge how sincere someone's religion is, we can't gauge how sincere is their empathy. We may know the sender's past. We rely on their present deeds. Unless we have some special insight, determining motives is futile. Some people will come to our funerals to make sure we're dead. We judge acts of courtesy by earnest appearances.

As the husband commented to his wife when he came home from work and she kissed him indifferently—"Couldn't you at least do that as if you mean it?" We settle for the right motions because we cannot know the right emotions.

It's time for all of us to come out of the closet. We need to confess we have a thing for envelopes. What? Not just any of them, but ones laced with handwriting. Our whole lives we have had a secret crush on that handwriting. It doesn't matter whose it is. It helps, though, if we already care for the sender, particularly a loved one. Will we ever lose that feeling of personal connection to someone else from their writing? In your pile of mail your eager eyes spy the letter from a *person*. Go ahead and try to deny it—the mail exciting us the most is the handwritten envelope with the handwritten letter. Upon sight our impatient fingernails want us to forget that tawdry letter opener and dig under the flap. After you slit the envelope, your pupils expand and your lubdubbing heart quickens as you eagerly remove and unfold the paper with the pen ink of personal contact. Savoring the personal letter or card stimulates us in a way we might keep from a psychiatrist. The bills and those wretched commercial items, now underneath our mail pile, will wait. So will the envelope with a check we usually grab and kiss and let rip a shrill, dog-chasing wooohoooo.

We see the sender's handwriting and now hold their paper of choice. If it's from a guy it may be a shabby sheet from a tablet or a memo pad, rough edges at the top. Anything more impressive is too, how shall we put this, girly. Getting a guy to send a personal letter is not easy. Just be glad he sends one at all. As for his handwriting, we don't read it; we decipher it. Girls do much better than that. It's one way we can tell them from guys without undressing them. From a lady you get paper worthy of being called stationery. And the writing will be graceful and readable.

Unabashedly we favor handwritten mail. Just as men's eyes fix on attractive girls, we rush to handwritten envelopes first. A typed letter for a business come-on may be a second away from the wastebasket. If you open it and begin to read it, you will drop to a handwritten P.S. Even if you skip or skim the typed letter, you are lured to it. When the return address is omitted from the handwritten envelope, you are zapped with expectation. Every Christmas Grim scuffles with his wife over their Christmas card envelopes. He pushes to omit their return address so the receiver finds out it's from them only after opening it. She worries about the envelope not being returned if the address is bad. For the record, they both personally sign the cards. She fills out the envelopes and gives them to him to sign. She has won the fray in recent years by having the return address on the envelope when he gets them to sign.

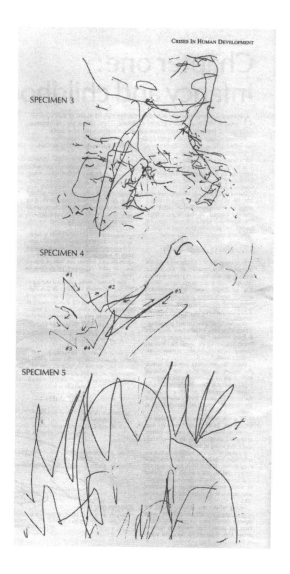

SPECIMEN 3

SPECIMEN 4

SPECIMEN 5

This is a page from the treatise Crises in Human Development by the International Graphoanalysis Society. It shows how the handwriting of pre-school children can be analyzed to a degree. Specimen 3 is from a two-year-old child asserting itself with annoyance and impatience. Specimen 4 shows a restless and energetic child with a need to explore. She is distracted easily but has good mental potential. Specimen 5 reveals a child with keen comprehension but with a short attention span and scattered interests.

Chapter 15

Personal Uses

Helping Yourself and Helping Others

Give me the handwriting of a woman, and I will give you her character.
Shakespeare

A woman doctor using a dating service came to an analyst with 80 letters received from men wanting to date her. She dumped them into his lap, saying, "I've had one bad marriage. I don't want to have two. Separate the wheat from the chaff."

Povser

In th'early pahwt of the 20th Cen'ry in the South Geohge Wawshington Cawveh had a thang for paynuts. People mocked him for wasting his time trying to find so many uses for them. He prevailed, finding over 300, including the staple of American youth and The Last Supper for mice—peanut butter.

Like Carver, the public scoffs at analysts too. It wants to know, "What on earth is an analysis good for?" At times it's more cynical. Someone will ask, "Why would I want to have my handwriting analyzed?"

That baffles analysts. Some people distrust its use and the analyst's skills. It shames analysts to concede again that people don't understand handwriting analysis. This drops analysts to feeling lower than a peanut. Everyone knows you can at least shell it, flip it into your mouth and chomp away.

The question also confounds Grim but he recovers and says he welcomes the chance to field it. Like a nimble shortstop, he throws back his own questions.

"Are you satisfied where your life is? Are you in a rut personally or professionally? Do you really know who you are as a person? Don't you want to live your life more effectively and happily? Would you like to know what is holding you back from being a complete person? An analysis will put you face to face with yourself and on track to resolve these epic personal issues: Who am I, really? If I have my writing analyzed, will I recognize the individual described?"

Like Carver and his peanut, analysts are happy to say they have found many uses for their subject. They are primed to inform you what the initial focus should be. That would be you. Isn't your first duty to take personal care of you? An analysis will acquaint you with your actual self, bypassing the public self you display around people. That self can fool them and from constant use even fool you. Frequently after a while you start accepting the public you as the real you. When an analyst reveals your essential nature, what follows? He should treat you with care and sympathy. He does not try to repair you or judge you. If you are lost and searching for direction in your life, he will you point you in the right direction. Dr. Phil uses the term your "authentic self" to describe the real you and your true desires. This is what your handwriting reveals. What is really important to you? What are you interested in? What gets you energized in your life? Maybe something you never allowed yourself to try. All your life the secret of your raw, unpainted nature is right under your nose. You didn't need to lie on a couch in a psychoanalyst's office or submit to a battery of tests from a psychologist. All you needed is for someone to decode the meaning of those handwriting strokes. They reveal your strengths, talents, drawbacks, fears, emotions, desire for success, integrity and social skills. All the time they were chained within you aching for freedom, and you ignored them or were unaware of them.

Many people worry an analyst will expose their defects or at least try to uncover their weaknesses. They avoid pursuing an analysis, publicly voicing skepticism about it but secretly fearing its hurtful truths. It's amazing the number of sullen skeptics who, when they realize an analyst might call their bluff and offer a free personal analysis, turn and walk away. They can't escape that private sense it amounts to something.

To confess they believe it has merit is to risk censure from those they respect. Other people are reluctant to have the analysis. They see it as an undue spotlight on their problems and a demeaning raid on their privacy. They are intimidated that a technique exists to open the curtain on their basic character. They shouldn't tremble. Eventually they grasp the purpose of the analysis is not to expose insecurities. It is not to wag a finger at you for being imperfect. The analyst may discover unpleasant personality features that could discourage your dreams or impair your more mundane desires. Although unfortunate, analysts say those exposures would help you. The analysis can also highlight your capabilities. With these insights you can now do what's best for yourself. If you don't know really know yourself, how can you accomplish that?

An analysis can guide you toward more than a decent job but one for your disposition and your talents. Are you satisfied that your work makes the best use of your skills? Should you pursue some other line of work? Businesses must realize that each employee's fitness for their position is not just their MBA or a bachelor's degree in computer engineering. Work skills are a combination of factors, not just a special expertise. Businesses are now recognizing the importance of the worker's personality in their value to the organization. Consider the book *The War for Talent* by Ed Michaels, Helen Jones-Jones and Beth Axelrod, which admirably demonstrates that talent in the workplace is not IQ or GPA or sheepskins from institutions. It means special qualities, such as a strategic mind, managing ability, emotional maturity, people and verbal skills, inspirational talent, commercial instincts, functional skills, and delivered results.

Milton N. Bunker, the founder of Graphoanalysis, once wrote, "A person has few actual weaknesses but very often excellent traits of character badly used. Assets become liabilities." Since none of us is perfect and thus we have weaknesses, analysts give you a better way to approach them. No trait should be considered a weakness by itself. The question they ask is not—Do you have faults and what are they? The better question is—Does a single trait help or hinder you to carry on your life and attain what is best for you? Let's say an analysis shows a person has an "aggressive" nature. That sounds negative, a weakness of some kind. It can turn other people off. It doesn't have to. An aggressive person seeks to plow ahead and get things done. If you are looking for someone to run a project fraught with obstacles, the aggressive individual can be your one to get it done. They tend to gloss over criticism or sniping or pessimism. If the job requires dealing with many types of people, this person can bulldoze through them and avoid their hindrances. He might be gruff but it may take that to achieve success in the undertaking. Therefore, in this person's case, to be aggressive can be what's needed for success.

What handwriting analysis gives you was crystallized in a stirring Commencement address given by a prominent American recently deceased. Not referring to handwriting analysis, still his remarks illuminate its role in anyone's life.

Chief Justice William Rehnquist reflected: "Students should look back at their educational institution and feel that their horizons have been expanded through knowledge exposure to the marketplace of ideas." He used the shopping mall, not the kind where goods are bought with money, but where items such as worldly success, love of music, a strong backhand, close relationships with family, a few good friends and countless other things are for sale. The commodity that you purchase them with is not money but your time.

Although he didn't know his wisdom applies equally to handwriting analysis, he would have applauded its role in opening up the personality. Until we know ourselves we cannot possibly discover the essentials of life. Think how wasteful you exist without knowing yourself.

He concluded with these words: "The most priceless asset that can be accumulated in the course of any life is time well spent."

Rehnquist was chronically ill with throat cancer but held on to his seat on the Court. Who could blame him for this quality time? He refused to sit around waiting for the end. He did all he could to carry on as normally as possible. Analysts live by his words because they try to use their training and expertise to help people know themselves and the people with whom they must live or work or deal. With this knowledge they can seize better control of their lives and act effectively.

If handwriting can be mined for information to help you, it can also help others close to you. Your children can utilize it, especially those struggling to understand who they are and where they should go with their education, career, relationships, and activities. You might even discover some emotional throb that has invaded their being.

Their handwriting yields special insight into themselves for selecting, not just the right job, but the right one for their personality. Surveys reveal that the biggest hurdle to job success isn't the employee's poor skills and training. It's that his personality doesn't fit the daily tasks.

Often what is troubling young people is hidden under protective layers of pride, self-consciousness, and hypersensitivity. This creates social camouflage of toe-in-the-sand shyness, strained grins, and bitten lips. Skills or special interests, often unexpressed, may desire recognition. What a tragedy for those plodding through life with stymied hopes. A dominating parent or a clueless parent or an indifferent parent, or an absent parent, have been barriers to youth's potential. If they had the benefit of handwriting analysis to help them and their parents to see their native abilities bloom, crushed lives could become cherished experiences.

One group of analysts was approached by a couple whose son had been playing Little League baseball. As with many kids, he had been funneled into it by his father, who had played ball himself. At age 11 the boy seemed to have only a tepid interest in playing. Timid and unexpressive, he struggled to voice his real desires.

"Does our son's writing give any clues what he might be interested in?" they asked.

In his writing the members found a sensitive young man, who was especially interested in cultural and artistic activities. Revealing to his mother and disappointing to his father.

Ruefully they acknowledged what they shuttered to hear. "We hoped he would like sports as his father did when he was young," his mother remarked.

Even though his own muffled words couldn't say it, their son's writing was unafraid to express his true zeal. With new insight into their son's intimate thoughts, they were now better informed to channel their son toward his true interests. Handwriting speaks from the heart and the soul without apprehension. It says what is really on the person's mind and in their longings. With often hidden dreams obscured by dominating insecurities, young people are singular subjects for handwriting analysis.

Most children begin handwriting studies in first or second grade. For some they have already used a pencil or pen. They played with crayons or magic markers or something similar that writes on a surface.

Their world has been their chalkboard. We have all suffered our walls, driveways, and sidewalks to the innocent graffiti of children trying to express themselves. Since handwriting analysis claims that writing comes from within the mind, do pre-school children have these impulses? Of course, says Grim. What happens with those naked impulses before they are palmerized in school? If their parents haven't started them early with writing or reading, will their scribbling show any personality traits?

"Yes, we can learn something this early about our children," declares Grim. "In fact, since the school style hasn't corrupted them, the writing may be more revealing of their true qualities."

The casual scrawls of children dart about untamed. Because their writing is still primitive, it will display only hints about them, such as their temperament, or their mental abilities. Once penmanship is far behind them their writing will be untied to evolve into its personal uniqueness. Remarkably some of this early scribbling may foretell later refined attributes. For some parents whatever strokes their child scratches on the sidewalk will verify their opinion of his character. To others a surprise. With their crude jottings showing their children's inner workings, they can handle them as needed. Better to know the fleeting disquiet of now than the constant regret of later.

This telegraphing of insights through writing stroke dashes may save you from a lasting alarm bell over what child God hath wrought for you. Consider a child who writes with robust straight lines and angles, resembling lightning. Those zigzags express a child that has energy and vigor . His impulse is to pursue his cravings. He is easily goaded and his attention will be riveted. He can be a terror. When does he want what his little heart desires? That would probably be, I mean it is likely to be, in fact you can bet on it—RIGHT NOW! He is a power mower chewing up the yard, forget the bag and mowing in rows. You will need to be tough to control this potent force. His persistent drive will challenge your parenting skills.

Where the lines are jagged strokes or brutal jabs, be ready for an irritable child. Maybe he's just in a foul mood. On the other hand, it may mean a settled disposition, not a brief spell. Check his writing at different times. If you are seeing the same disturbing lines when he is well-fed, well-rested, and relaxed, then may God bless you. Since they may be few, cherish each moment he is pleasant.

Other more hopeful children do exist and you will see it in their driveway jottings. If the child draws pleasing, rounded strokes looking like sweeping clouds, you may have an agreeable temperament to raise. Like mashed potatoes in your hands, their feelings obey your wishes. When you discipline them, leave the yardstick in the closet. They are soft-hearted and giving. To please you is foremost. To upset you is to disturb themselves. Armed with this knowledge, you can ease your child's discipline on their tender souls.

———

Parents today have a critical need to know their teen-agers. Frequently these often-lost young people maintain secret lives, displaying a different self to their family, friends and teachers. Every so often CNN breaks in with a scene of students leaving a school because a student had a gun. Now with bug-eyed awareness of the problem, authorities have budnipped several of these potential incidents in the planning stages. The community involved wipes its sweat-filled brow, crosses itself, knocks on wood, and swivels its head side to side trying to avoid nightmare thoughts of whatcouldhavebeen. A few years ago in Columbine, Colorado, what could happen did, infamously. With a classmate, Dylan Klebold killed twelve fellow students and a teacher. By all accounts he came from parents who were loving and involved. Yet he deceived them about who he was. Children, especially boys, stoically hide their weaknesses and their dark secrets. Males are not the only sex hiding teen-age problems. Anorexia and bulimia increasingly afflict girls, who often conceal them from their parents and others. Now another insidious often hidden problem. A survey estimates that in young boy-girl relationships, one out of four girls has an abusive, violent boyfriend. If you are shocked, it shows how secret it is. These tendencies can appear in handwriting. An analyst can expose controlling, possessive tendencies in boys and the enabling tolerance in girls.

With these serious concerns, it's not all bleak with young people. More positively, handwriting analysis can unearth their talents and skills and delights. Often they are dormant, Münching a silent scream for recognition. Unknown potential can surface and the young person can learn to rappel the craggy wall of success with it.

"What should be the purpose of an analysis in a job or living-style circumstance," I want to know.

"It should be to determine if it makes the best use of their abilities and inclinations," says Grim.

"What should be the focus?"

"Activities they really are interested in or those they are especially good at."

TV's Dr. Phil says that life is a series of choices. Most of the choices we make are based on fear, rather than from our true wishes and desires. We feel pressure to please our parents or other people we respect. Or don't want to disappoint. The ability to know yourself and your core motivations can guide you to a realistic future of fulfillment. The young person's handwriting will disclose much of their promise. With the insight it gives, parents can assist them in reducing any fear. Young people can approach their decisions with positive attitudes related to their abilities, not the agendas and biases of their parents and other authority figures.

In addition, a young person's writing can guide them into activities outside of work or school. Maybe their specific qualities lie just below the shell of their awareness. Many young people can't even stumble upon their private desires or their potential skills. Whether the pursuits are intellectual, cultural, artistic, mechanical, or others, your son may have no insight into what Dr. Phil calls his "authentic self." Young men especially falter from laziness or apathy. They avoid pondering deep thoughts of their calling or their destiny. Immaturity and fear reign, dooming them to unrelieved regret. Many boys disdain inner reflection, where they must do serious thinking about who they really are and what motivates them. When they don't invest the time, they grow up without confronting adulthood, which insists on accountability and self-control. Their fate is not inevitable. The cost of avoiding introspection might be a disappointed life without achievement and fitting compensation.

"Most people think they really know themselves," says Grim. "Many do not, particularly young boys and girls, who lack the good judgment of experience."

Typically their understanding is superficial and just radically wrong. What do they know of psychology and in particular personality? Too often they live in the present and their interests are material objects and mundane pursuits. Stylish clothing, sassy cars, putrid language, pulsating music, mind-twisting drugs and booze, time-killing mall walks, mindless loitering, and undisciplined sex. Ask them their future plans and they tell you they're going to the shore this weekend. They lack the ability or desire to look long range or to step back a few paces and predict consequences. Their narrow vision and often reckless behavior can't foresee the painful results. Speeding and DUI's beget tickets, fines and costs, lost license, increased car insurance, stripped car privileges, property damage, disabling injury, shaken lives, and even the concussion of death. With a comprehensive analysis of their handwriting, parents can assess what their child has in their make-up to cope with these forces, avoid their dire outcomes, and realize their real desires and abilities.

———

Grim promotes handwriting analysis as a smart investment. As an attorney for over three decades, Grim handled a landfill of divorces. To his potential handwriting clients serious with a partner, he joked of the choices he offered.

"You can pay me a modest sum now for an analysis. Or you can pay me an absurd sum later for a divorce." He was laughing on the outside, vying (for work) on the inside.

In recent years divorce has become an epidemic even for couples who have lived together prior to marriage. With the internet, video-dating services, personal ads, and other ways to meet partners, more effective methods replace many traditional options. Although their importance has dwindled, the bar room hook-up and your church as social facilitator both remain. People are looking for love, or just companionship, through special services using more technology. The client background information is getting deeper and more accurate. Much of it is basic and verifiable, like their birthplace and their work and their education. Background checks for other information, like criminal history, marriage and divorce are vital too. Although improved, these services have their flaws. After the data of raw personal information and public records, the rest of what people really want to know is suspect. They are not getting a reliably true picture of the individual himself. Two people connecting through these methods are strangers. How little they really know of each other haunts both of them. Today our easy mobility has linked us to people from anywhere and nowhere. Some of these people who want to meet you are grotesquely unlike what you read on your computer screen. You don't know if your fate will be a heart-warming story or a heart-breaking tragedy. People using the services want the true, detailed story about the person they might some day marry. What are they really like as a person? Applicants don't want to rely on the computer data to make the decision to meet this unknown personage.

Enter handwriting analysis to relieve their caution. It gives the client a complete and unbiased outline of the individual's actual personality. Handwriting analysis has helped many people seeking serious relationships and possibly marriage. Whether it's you wanting to proceed with a permanent relationship or whether it's you wanting to see your son with the right person for him, handwriting analysis delivers the lowdown about that blind date from the internet.

Analysts have always done what they call "compatibility studies." A client will bring the analyst writing of a prospective life partner to see if this other person would make a good companion or spouse. A complete study will also include the client showing his own writing to the analyst. When the analyst has done his work, he reports to the client what he has found about each partner. His purpose is not to recommend if they should get married. He supplies the personal qualities of both and discusses how they might clash or complement. Whether they should marry is not his call. He lets them decide the ultimate question.

One analyst had a memorable episode with a client using a dating service. She was a divorced-and-looking doctor with little time or fondness for demeaning steps like prowling at bars to find her next soul mate. She had tried a dating service and was overwhelmed with 80 letters from men. Hoping to avoid being a "Sugar Mommy" or otherwise exploited, she brought the letters to the analyst.

Dumping them in his lap, she cracked, "Okay, I've had one bad marriage. I don't want to have two. Separate the wheat from the chaff. No dullards, no penny-pinchers, and no wolves."

He reviewed the letters and trimmed the pile to thirty.

She returned. She wasn't done. "Okay, now pull out the insincere, the cold, and the selfish."

He thinned that herd to ten. From that final list she dated a few and met an engineer, who she found to be cultured, reliable, secure, and sexually healthy. They married and so far so good. Because she had handwritten letters, she was able to know the intimate, real qualities about the men before she met them. As a supplement to the dating service, the handwriting analyst gave her the additional information she really needed.

Handwriting analysis won't ensure you'll find your soul mate. It should drastically increase the odds however. It will do even better to decrease the odds of finding a guy with whom you go necking on a lonely road and find out he's actually Hook Man. As to the doctor, the benefits are clear. She avoided the heartache and stress of a failed relationship. She saved irretrievable time with the wrong man. Ultimately she will hope to escape the mattresspiggybankcheckingsavings401(k)IRAmomdadformerbestfriend-draining legal fees for a new divorce, along with that stress and hassle. Most important, aside from the public records, all the data she got from the dating service and the men themselves was untrustworthy and incomplete. The most reliable source was the engineer's handwriting.

With more women working outside the home, day care has become a major issue. People are better informed on everything through education, the internet and other media. We seek higher standards of living for ourselves and our children. As they demand more for their children, families scrutinize child care arrangements. For many, raising the perfect child has come close to a mania. When your child's mother works and can't be home with the child during the day, that child will spend extensive time with someone else, primarily in day care. Parents want to know their children are spending their several hours away from mommy and daddy with people that are competent, reliable and trustworthy. Handwriting analysis can assist in evaluating not only the head of the day care center but the employees. After all they will be spending several hours a week with the child. Parents can obtain the handwriting of these day care people and make sounder decisions on their fitness to step into your shoes to do what's right for your child. Getting the handwriting of as many of these people increases your chances of selecting a competent center and knowing its employees. There are also nannies and au pairs who will spend even more time with children. Then there is the occasional baby-sitter. Each one of these can be evaluated more completely by analyses of their handwriting.

Couples without children have found new options in the laboratory and outside with willing persons. Surrogate mothers now carry someone else's child from implanted sperm. Egg donors promise couples a new baby with their body in a nine-month rental and decent compensation. Whether it's the man's sperm or the woman's eggs, couples need more than to know the donors are attractive and healthy. They need the most hidden aspect of this whole person. It may be the most important too. What is this person like mentally and emotionally? Do they really have enough credible information to know if they want that person's genes to provide them with a child they will call their own? With their handwriting they can obtain that full, dependable report on their actual attributes as a person, not the pleasantries of an interview or the uncertainty of character reputation. When they have the analysis done before making the big decision, their unease declines and comfort rises.

In personal circumstances we all need to retain outside business people for work around our homes or for our consumer or business needs. Attorneys, landscapers, tax preparers, accountants, plumbers, electricians, building contractors, engineers, doctors, and others. It's important to establish a level of trust and reliability with these people, often strangers. Some of them will actually spend time in our homes and we may not be around to watch them every minute they are there. We need to know if they will be honest and if they are responsible, hard-working people. A handwriting analysis profile delivers a clearer and more thorough picture of people we depend on to provide valuable goods and services for us and our family. It's a great investment as a supplement to the reputation and other information we rely on to select these important people entering our lives and our homes. The effects of getting a dishonest or incompetent one can wreck our orderly lives.

Chapter 16

Business Uses

The Best Hiring Step They'll Ever Have

Personality is the single most important factor in job success — not education, not experience, not age, gender, race.

Results of a 16-year study of 350,000 employees on the most important factor for job success

Handwriting analysis is about personality.
Allan Grim

Tom Payette is a hard-nosed car dealer in Louisville, Kentucky, selling Buicks, Jaguars, and Suzukis. As with many dealerships, the sales force has a high turnover rate. An analyst approached him about applying graphology to reduce it by helping him select salespeople. When she initially made her pitch, he snubbed her. Trying again, the analyst got into his office by asking to analyze his writing. He agreed. When he admitted she accurately described his personality traits, he still held out. About a year later she tried again. When she analyzed his writing this time she found personality changes. Conceding they had occurred, he was convinced to retain her. She evaluated several applicants and gave her input. He took it for his hiring decisions. His attrition dropped significantly to 36%, about half the industry average. Now he exclaims, "I would never be without it." He likes that it discloses the "undesirable qualities" that he terms "obstacles to success."

With its abundant font of information about the writer's personal features, handwriting analysis meets several kinds of needs. People want to know about the variety of individuals they will confront personally or professionally. Its versatility is not new. In the public and commercial world its growth *is* new. Where many organizations apply it, largely for help in selecting employees, they are reluctant to admit they do. The stigma of bunk grips the subject, although it eases with each group deploying it successfully. A business using it worries about a blemish to its reputation. It may be only like a butterfly tattoo on their ankle, but some will see it as a snarling serpent on the company's neck.

If the business prospers, however, the public and its competitors wonder, "What does this company know that we don't know?"

Analysts answer, "Us. And they're smart as a business to know us and our helpful subject."

No hard statistics exist for the actual use of handwriting analysis in business and related fields. Some pundits speculate its wider use began in the mid-1960's. Today a rough estimate is that maybe 10,000 businesses have used it. Without sources Handwriting Research Corporation puts the number that currently use it at around 5,000. Some of the bigger corporations are Ford, GE, Mutual of Omaha, Firestone, USX, Honeywell, Verizon, Westinghouse, Xerox, Boyden International, a senior executive headhunting firm with offices in 15 cities and 26 countries. And even the CIA. Gauging usage is difficult because it is believed many more companies may use it but won't admit they do. Compared to Europe we have not progressed very far. Most estimates say about 85% of the companies in Western Europe use it, mainly for selecting executives. That number seems high to American pundits. In Israel the estimate is about 90 to 95%. Perhaps more current, Handwriting Research Corporation confines its estimate of use to 80% of the large corporations in France and Switzerland. European nations have added it to their college psychology departments in Germany, France, Switzerland, and Holland. In the Middle-East, Israel has it.

France and Germany have formal institutes to qualify experts in the field. For some reason France adores it going back to those Catholic surveyors in the early nineteenth century. Besides French, is there something the French know that we don't? Analysts want to scram when they realize that France adores goose livers, snails, and Jerry Lewis.

Tom Payette was the boss at his car dealership. In the workplace a major hurdle analysts usually encounter is the human resources officer that would retain them. It's not just discomfort about the subject. Grim thinks that HR's are cautious by trade and lack authority. Taking on an analyst is a bold move. Others in the organization, such as the CEO or the President, might be the only official that effectively can do it. By contrast with the HR, those at the top will take risks with suspect options. They will biggamehunt for ways to improve efficiency and lower expenses, increasing bottom lines. Where the HR person has authority, allows the analyst in, and the venture fails, he can fear losing his job. More directly, they worry that analysts will seize control of the hiring and marginalize their role in the company.

A major reason to include graphology in business hiring is its centering on personality. Corporations are slowly recognizing what they knew all along but have to be business-slapped to understand. The entire person comes to work everyday, not just someone with a specific skill. Businesses have been focusing on a worker's job skills in the office, plant, factory, store, warehouse, and workyard. They should've realized a giant flopping whale in each place, and it is called PERSONALITY. Granted, for an executive, job skills inevitably have included personality. What employers have missed is the central role of that element of skills. Unless they use this whale, they will face chronic trouble in hiring, maintaining and terminating workers. With the bottom line the prime factor, more businesses grasp that handwriting analysis makes good business sense.

Why is handwriting analysis suited for helping to pick employees? Don't make me say it again. Because it is about the Great White Whale personality. Oh, sorry if we poked our fingers into your sternum. Handwriting reveals personality. Did we say that before too? Good. In a 16-year study conducted by psychologist Herb Greenburg, President of Marketing Research and Survey Corporation, the question was asked: "What is the most important factor in job success?" After reviewing 350,000 employees at more than 7,000 companies, the study determined that: "Personality is the single most important factor in job success — not education, not experience, not age, gender, race." Greenburg's study found no differences in job success among men or women, young or old, black or white, high school dropouts or college trained, experienced or inexperienced workers. All the traditional job criteria mismatched the employee. Fitting workers to their jobs by personality gave the company what it really needed. When Greenburg surveyed the workforces in various countries, he concluded that "Eighty percent of noncommunist bloc workers are misemployed." Employee turnover, a persistent issue for most businesses, was evaluated in light of this survey. The key to reducing turnover was to ensure employers placed the individual with the personal qualities in the job that harmonizes with them.

Handwriting analysis has another role to play in the workplace. Every worker has his ups and downs on the job. Even people who have been generally good workers, like dogs, have their days. Sadly, sometimes it is weeks. Where a new hire starts showing problems in adjusting to the job or getting along with fellow workers, the impetus is toward firing him. Instead of that extreme step, the company can utilize handwriting analysis for insight into what may be temporary behavior. A declining marriage, emotional unrest, a physical ailment, a stormy teen-ager, or an ill parent. Check if his handwriting confirms his admirable qualities. If so, the company can work on keeping him by recognizing and overcoming the temporary situation. If he has been succeeding there, the writing may tell his acts were justified and he deserves better. For the good of both parties, he might thus earn another chance to remain where he belongs.

Handwriting analysis is not just a stellar idea for businesses. They have a special need for it. Although they may hire an employee with desirable work skills, he shows up saddled with human frailties that can impact the business. To face this handwriting analysis assists an employer to gather intimate knowledge about each new employee. It begins with helping the employer select the right employee *before* he is hired. This is preferable to helping them understand a current employee causing turmoil on the job. It begins with the worldtradecenter piles of resumés desirable employers today have on their formerly visible desks. These businesses need a proficient method to reduce the stack. First get rid of the cactus and toxic personalities. Next dump those who just won't fit their position. Then determine the applicants who don't match attributes the business seeks. Choosing the negatives is easier and reduces the pile faster. After this distill your search to those with personal qualities friendly to both the company and the job.

Handwriting analysis can assist any organization to pick the right employees. Some businesses have really welcomed it from their special concerns. Because of the particular skills, salespeople come and go in businesses. Many try it but don't realize their inadequate skills. The employer may not realize them either until after they have hired them and find out they are failing as salespeople. Picking poor sales people and tolerating them for too long is the disheartening experience for many businesses. Handwriting analysis has stepped forward to help. Insurance companies have a crush on it, particularly to select sales people. Equitable Life, Mutual Benefit Life, Continental Assurance and Manufacturer's Life draw on it. Here's the experience of Robert Wenzloff, personnel manager of Equitable Life in Saint Louis. They used analyst Daniel Anthony of the New School in New York City.

Wenzloff remarked: "Dan Anthony is tops. I've hired a few men that he's rejected, though, and almost invariably they didn't work out. He's 80 to 90 percent correct in his evaluations. We hire 25 people each year and we interview 20 for every one hired—so we want to be right. We use our test and him—and his results are superior. Of all the things we've used, Anthony is the best."

More stark data shows the urgency for handwriting analysis in business hiring. According to Peter Drucker, the business guru (*The Seven Habits of Highly Successful Businesspeople*), "One third or more of all hiring decisions are outright failures and in no other areas would we tolerate such dismal performance." The business stakes are enormous, more so in a smaller enterprise. Too many companies don't realize the fall-out from lax employment screening. When the employer ignores a useful way of hiring the right people, like using handwriting analysis, turnover badgers them. The consequences can be disastrous. Here are some for hiring the wrong person:

1. Time lost in the recruiting process for the replaced employee

2. Time required to recruit and hire the replacement

3.   Time the old employee was not productive

4.   Lost opportunity of the wrong person

5.   Cost, time and hassle of possible legal claims, such as wrongful discharge, discrimination, disabilities or other employment claim, and unemployment compensation issues, with possible increased insurance costs

6.   Impact of morale problems

7.   Loss of business the employee caused

8.   Additional stress to you and the employees who had to tolerate them

9.   Decline in the reputation of the business

Handwriting analysis provides a superb report on the inner structure and outer tendencies of a potential employee. One significant person it exposes is the volatile worker. Surveys and headlines tell us they can be major trouble. The most prevalent motivation for workplace violence is personality conflicts. It's 62%, well ahead of the other factors. In second place at only 27% is workplace stress, with added impact from marital problems. The latter may affect the former. The unpleasant result from the hostility against the boss or co-worker or the faceless company itself can be internal sabotage. With computers necessary, they increase the hostile worker's ability to harass his employer, or disrupt or destroy a colleague's work. Companies report upsurged computer viruses and other vengeful acts from employees on and off the computer.

Also 50% of people hired for a particular position do not last six months in that position. Some just don't fit and know it and they quit. Others will linger and the business eventually realizes the mistake and they fire them or shift them elsewhere in-house. Either way the job becomes vacant and the business must spend time re-filling it.

To understand how essential handwriting analysis is to business hiring, consider the traditional criteria for selecting new employees:

1.   Education and training

2.   Experience

3.	Resumé, Biography

4.	Interview

5.	Recommendations

6.	Psychology tests

The last four are necessary but in the early twenty-first century are they still reliable? A study on resumés by Avert, Inc., a firm that specializes in background checks, contacted 2.6 million job applicants. They found that 44% of all resumés contain lies. The Society of Human Resources Management surveyed personnel directors of businesses and they reported that 90% of resumés contained material misstatements. 24% of them make materially false statements about the candidate's credentials. Another study mentioned in *The Week* Magazine put the percentage at 40%. Where truth suffered most was in their education and their job duties. Pinnochio, say it ain't so. A lot of lying by applicants and unfortunately a lot of relying by employers. If the employer wants a complete, unaltered picture of the applicant, their handwriting will supply it. Granted this is the personality and character portion of the candidate's entire package. However, it is the central one, as it helps to overcome the lies in the resumé.

The interview also flourishes and remains necessary. You want the individual face-to-face. You want to observe his demeanor, how he answers your questions, what he asks you about the position or the company, how he looks and what he wears, and how he handles himself. Maybe have him perform a work task on the spot. Though important and essential, the interview has lost its sheen. Since it's an integral part of hiring today, everyone has read the articles and books on how to act at the interview. Applicants rehearse and preen to make themselves look good. It almost makes the HR guy want to hand him an Oscar if not a company handbook. When he stares across the table hoping for insight he may learn something. It's not the everyday worker sitting there. Regrettably, he sees an amateur, maybe even a professional, actor feigning to be a model employee. As we behave in church or at a funeral, the person submitting to the interview is not himself, the one who will be performing along side co-workers. Despite their drawbacks, interviews will always be essential. Their value ebbs as people learn to play the role of applicant aspiring to become the employee. Should we now call the interview an audition?

Aside from the acting, the interview can muddy the company's impression of the applicant. Under the pressure and artificial tone of the interview many people falter. Some good people give a bad interview. Others may just be having bad days. Maybe they were up caring for a fussy baby, or they are sick but didn't want to cancel the interview. Maybe they couldn't sleep because of the interview. With several other candidates seeking the same position, weak first impressions can ruin the applicant's chances of being hired. The result is the business may miss out on a solid worker.

Against the flaws of interviews is the strength of handwriting. Analysts swear by it, certain it can outdo the interview. In a blind, impartial way it will show the everyday employee, the actual one who will come to work and do his job when the boss or human resources person is not around. In addition, since handwriting can be done from afar, a business can receive a profile on distant applicants without having to fly them in or make them drive long distances. The handwriting evaluation may be enough to forego the interview and reject the applicant. That is an extreme step, a layperson might say. Where the employer must decide from several resumés, he has a sensible way of paring them. Handwriting makes a superb pre-interview tool also. In advance the employer can weigh the applicant's strengths and weaknesses and assess a troublesome foible. Thus, the interviewer will be well-prepared for the interview and armed with pointed questions.

The interview is not the only hiring device that has plunged in value. Executives grumble they can't rely on what the prior employer might say about their prospective employee. Customarily the last employers will offer little information, typically basic facts, even when specific lines of inquiry are sought. Anything adverse that needs telling never gets conveyed to the new employer. Among prior employers mum has been the word for years and for sound business reasons. Blame the decline in recommendations on the company lawyer. A disgruntled ex-worker looks for another job among tough opportunities. We have a sue-happy society where employment laws increasinglyfavortheemployee.Executivesarereluctanttosayanything unfavorable about their horribleworthlesshostilelazygripingthieving prior employee.

If workers sought job changes merely for more compensation, recommendations might do better. Better wages are not the leading reason people go elsewhere to work. Most people leave from problems with their boss. Even workers that stay aren't praising them. 70% of workers said they have a "toxic boss," according to a Monster.com poll.

Organizational consultant Ken Siegel thinks corporate America's "ranting bosses" don't comprehend how people view them, even when their conduct costs them. "People don't quit companies. They quit people," he said. A century ago oil baron John D. Rockefeller knew the importance of hiring employees with social skills. He remarked that "The ability to deal with people is as purchasable a commodity as sugar or coffee. And I will pay more for that ability than any other under the sun."

Most of the time some hostility lingers toward the previous workplace. Face it, most people will leave one job usually because they are unhappy there, not just sensing a better opportunity elsewhere. When he applies at his new place, the upset worker doesn't want to hear badmouthing about his work habits or personality. He is in limbo for an income and sensitive over his reputation, two critical items to anyone. Where a business uses handwriting analysis, the "recommendation" it gives the new employer is honest, complete, and, most important, the actual story about the person under consideration. Handwriting doesn't worry about lawsuits or reputations or attitudes. It just gives the ikea scoop about the person that will inhabit the workplace.

Hiring step number 6 has also lost whatever importance it had. Psychology tests or techniques are less widespread as the other steps. A *Washington Post* article said that about 70% of major corporations have entry and mid-level applicants take personality tests. However, even their meager use has run into sawhorses, like your sometimes flinty, meddling Uncle Sam. From poor experience with in business use, the Federal Equal Employment Opportunity Commission has stepped forward. Declaring most of the tests unreliable for business use, it believes they should be eliminated. The tests don't adequately measure the particular qualifications for most positions. For a long time employers haven't enjoyed them either. They take a lot of time; they can be costly; they are tedious for everyone; they are often intrusive; they might discriminate against certain protected groups of people (which especially bothers the EEOC too); and they hardly ever seem that helpful.

A few years ago federal legislation was enacted banning lie detector tests from the workplace. The general view was that they were unfair and inherently unreliable too. Known more formally as polygraph machines, they measure only the test subject's physical symptoms responding to a series of questions. What the person is really thinking and whether they are actually truthful in the answers don't register anywhere on the machine. That's because they can't be measured. The new law allows the machines to continue their futility for high security and governmental positions. Over the years, few companies had actually used lie detectors in employee hiring or actions against employees accused of wrongdoing, the two most frequent occasions for them. Analysts welcomed the lie detector ban. The effect made businesses scout for other effective methods to evaluate employees. Several turned to handwriting analysis.

Now that resumés, recommendations, interviews, and psychology tests have been trashed, what should be done with the Hefty bag? Eliminate them from the hiring steps? No, not at all. Continue their roles in hiring steps but be wary of their limitations. Certainly the defective portions should be improved. Resumés with misstatements will always be a problem, and cross-checking will have to be increased. Interviews and recommendations remain critical steps and should continue. Lastly, those *other* psychology tests and techniques could be removed once and for all and replaced by, need we say it, handwriting analysis. Otherwise, handwriting analysis should *supplement* all the hiring steps.

We know that graphology works for the car dealer in Louisville, Kentucky. How about anywhere else? Does it work at all or even moderately well?"

Sharon Stockham, Senior Vice-President of Human Resources at Exchange Bank in Rosa, California, eagerly supports it. Her institution has 425 employees and has used handwriting analysis since 1991. She "lives and dies" by it. Limiting the use to picking only bank officers and above, she finds it "invaluable," and "the wave of the future."

Stockham goes even further with results, taking the traits she wants to explore and submitting them to a consultant. Their task is to dig deeper with background and reference checks, such as calling prior employers and asking specifics about their noteworthy good and bad qualities. At the end she shows the applicant their profile and asks for feedback. The "approval rating" for her reports has been in the 90 to 95 % range.

At the Fike Corporation, an industrial products manufacturer in Blue Springs, Missouri, with 325 employees all applicants give a handwriting sample. If they appear to be good candidates, an analyst scrutinizes them further and helps guide the interview. A few years ago Fike began adapting handwriting to their hiring practices when they employed their current HR manager, Hal Cross. He supplied a sample of his writing and when the analysis was shown to him he was amazed how much it revealed about him. In his experience he has been "pleased" and rates the profiles as "high." He likes how handwriting analysis has kept them from mismatching applicants with their jobs. He also admits to its humbling him. On many occasions he found the analysis showed a problem person. Despite their hesitation they hired the person. Each time as forecast the problem erupted in the work environment.

The big tax company H & R Block has been using it for years. In the Midwest it has a phalanx of 135 offices managed by William Smith. Turnover in their offices had been about 25%. He began using prominent Louisville graphologist Iris Hatfield.

"Now the only turnover is if someone dies, retires or moves away. If my judgment goes one way and Iris goes another, I go with her."

Michael Henke is market sales manager of Humana Care Plus, a subsidiary of Humana Inc. He first thought it was "witchcraft" but has become "a believer." He sees it a cost-effective way to pick salespeople. It is as accurate as the psychological assessment tools he was using that cost much more than an analyst's fees. Northwestern Life Insurance Company of Milwaukee has a Tampa, Florida branch. They regularly consult with Phoenix graphologist Frank Budd about sales applicants. James Hough, Vice-President of the Tampa branch claims Budd's accuracy rate as "more than 95%."

Even though he believes graphology belongs in job-screening, Grim foresees its growth provoking applicants to devise clever ways to counter it. The interview has always been an important step in hiring. Recent years have generated a rich stockpile of guidance on how to prepare for it and how to act while doing it. "I think we will see more books and articles about handwriting and its countermeasures.

Applicants will learn what strokes in their handwriting will improve the impression they make," he imagines. Apparently this has already happened in countries like France, where for years the analysis has been a significant hiring step to evaluate executives.

Taking the strokes related to traits employers desire, some enterprising persons have snatched the strokes of superior qualities and added them to their own writing. Just for as long as necessary, of course. Grim calls this "padding their personality resumé." Although he believes employers can't eliminate this kind of scourge, he offers ways to minimize it. One is insisting on impromptu samples. This means requiring them to be done swiftly, although not hurriedly, and without pauses. Allowing time to think means time to scheme. That must be curtailed. While swiftness is important, hurriedness would be unfair too. Where the applicant wants to trot he is made to gallop. The writing isn't genuine, vital to an accurate analysis. Another step is to demand the sample be done in front of the employer. Additionally, asking for writings from different times will assure genuine samples. The key is to verify they were written before the hiring steps began. Presumably this was before the applicant was aware their writing was going to be examined.

"Even those samples could be faked," says Grim. "The employer should demand only writings, like a letter or notes, they wrote that others have."

These are all countermoves to an applicant's treachery. Time will tell how the gamesmanship unfolds. In the meantime, employers and the analysts they retain must remain cautious for each sample obtained. Where doubt exists on any of the samples, they will have to probe further or request a new sample.

Once the applicant survives all the hiring steps, including handwriting analysis, the analyst should not leave the building. Another mounting problem for businesses is theft. Not the petty kind of paper clips or staples. It's more intangible but serious nonetheless: the theft of business secrets. Many new companies have prized intricate secrets that need protection from competitors. The inside job has become a serious problem for corporations, especially with elaborate electronic equipment. Handwriting analysis can be applied to determine the internal culprit. The analyst requests the writing of possible suspects and profiles their now exposed personalities. When a loss or breakdown occurs, the employer takes the writing of the possible suspects and works backward by using the stroke-pattern profile of prior business secret thieves. Common stroke patterns of known thieves are used to find the current one. With the writing of in-house suspects, the employer can limit the investigation to those fitting the profile. Inside a large corporation this method can be effective, whether the focus is an employee as suspect or an applicant for a position. Using the applicant's writing to judge likely misconduct prevents it from occurring and avoids the need to catch them after the misdeed. At bottom an organization will pause before hiring a person doubtful from their handwriting. If there are other qualified candidates, rejecting this one is easy.

As a psychology technique handwriting analysis profiling will be imperfect in locating the business secrets bandit. It won't catch everyone else hired who might steal from or cheat the employer either. The best hope is high probability of success. In social science that is doing well. We never know if someone we hire will steal from us despite a rap sheet of embezzlement convictions. No one can predict the future, not even, yes, handwriting analysts. That doesn't mean we don't try or that we can't be effective at all. It just means we can't be right all the time. That happens only in physical science. Don't expect your analyst to be a Nostradamus. But not trying would be giving up and we can't do that either. For sound business and other reasons we try to predict the future for a panoply of situations. We just learn to do it with our eyes uncrossed and fingers crossed. How we do it is the only way we can. With human beings we weigh the likelihood of future conduct based on the best forecaster of the future. It's known as past experience. That is our best way of predicting behavior to come. By applying handwriting analysis we take a snapshot of all the strokes, which are that person's entire experience accumulated to the moment he wrote them. From that review we calculate the probability that he will act in general in certain ways that are different from other people. These all add up to his personality's framework constructed with traits. Whether we admit it or not, we try to predict what he will do in the future. If we are honest we concede we may be wrong. But we do it and hope for modest accuracy.

Grim adds, "Our consolation is that this is not unique to our subject of handwriting analysis. Fortune tellers do it all the time.

Bogus as their crystal balls, they are of course laughable frauds. We are not lauding them for doing what analysts do, only citing their practice of forecasting our fates."

Analysts don't foretell what will happen to us; they make a good guess what we will do hereafter. If you think they are alone in doing this, please circle the block a few more times. Others in psychology outside handwriting forecast all the time. We also do it in our daily lives. When we date someone and contemplate marrying them, we predict, based on our experience with them and conversing with others about them, how they will act with us over the long haul of wedded existence, otherwise known as the rest of our lives. If that prediction satisfies us that we want to spend our lives with them, we go ahead and marry them, if they will have us. Handwriting analysis forecasts the writer's personal attributes reflected in the strokes.

In his classes Grim shows how handwriting analysis has stepped in to help businesses pick employees. This is the most visible area of analysts' services. It's also where they can make the most money. With a large business client it can be a steady stream of income. Companies with chronic turnover are ripe for analysts. One aspect Grim illustrates is a single trait's power to affect a worker's ability to do his job. Or more deadly, not do his job. To make sure the student and he mesh in understanding what a particular trait means, Grim portrays how a person with a trait conducts themselves with other people. For example, in expounding on business use of handwriting analysis, he echoes what any thriving business believes—It is essential to hire the right salespeople. Without them whatever the employer produces goes nowhere. One important trait Grim mentions for a successful salesperson is persistence. These individuals won't easily give in to rejection. That's good. Even if a person suggests they don't want to buy the product or service, he continues his pitch. He won't take no for an answer and if the customer rejects it completely, he won't take it personally. That explains how a persistent salesperson acts with his prospects. Grim cites a survey about why most salespeople failed (either let go or quit). They had an abundance of one particular trait—persistence. Ironically, their problem was that they were *too* persistent. In their sales approach they got their foot in the door and wouldn't take it out. Refusing to take no for an answer, they turned off too many customers. Thus, no sale. Handwriting discloses "persistence" as a separate trait. It's found in what are called tie strokes, such as a t-bar where the ending strokes wraps back around the t-stem and after forming a loop returns across the t-stem to sweep ahead as the final stroke into the next letter. Since a stroke is a stroke wherever analysts find it, the stroke also appears prominently in lower loops of the y, g, j, and q and the second upright of the capital H. Where it appears many times it is a strong trait. For practical confirmation the analyst can also check the writer's shoes for a mangled front and his feet for missing toes.

This is a scene of Henry Fonda and his other eleven jurors in the 1957 film *Twelve Angry Men*. One of the emerging practical uses for handwriting analysis is helping lawyers select jurors for their cases. If an analyst can find the firm hold-out juror, the defendant can avoid a conviction in a criminal case even where the evidence is strong against him.

Chapter 17

Other Uses

Going after terrorists
Helping adopted children
Picking the Henry Fonda juror
Analyzing 2 AM at a post-prom party
Graffiti—the handwriting is too often on the wall

The concept of graphotherapy is enticing. Imagine ridding yourself of unwanted drawbacks just by altering your handwriting.

Years ago a young mother left her newborn baby girl on the steps of a church. She disappeared never to be heard from again. With the child she left a brown paper bag on which she had written, "Please take care of my baby. I can't. I'm sorry to do this." The baby was taken in and adopted. Years passed and the infant, now a mature young lady of 18, yearned to learn something about her real mother. How could she realize this wish? Fortunately the bag was kept. She took it to a handwriting analyst. Despite the limited writing, he was able to compile a rough portrait of her mother's personality. She was a sad and lonely individual, but sensitive, impressionable, generous and sensual. Also she was someone difficult to understand, an outsider, one who had trouble adapting. Without handwriting analysis this young woman never would have known anything about her actual mother.

Israel has been fighting for its life ever since its founding as a nation in 1948. It has fought two major wars with Arab neighbors in 1967 and 1973. Other times its Arab neighbors have assaulted it in different ways. Internally it has been under constant threat and actual violence from Palestinians and other Arabs like Hamas, Fatah, and Hezbollah with their guerilla warfare, indiscriminate rockets, and suicide bombers. Since the nation and its people are always at risk they have sought the most advanced security methods and technology. Their sophisticated measures have become the envy of many nations. In the 1980's the Israeli Secret Defense Service, Mossad, planned an assassination attack on the PLO Military Chief Abu Jihad Wazir. Their careful preparation for the operation was critical for what was a stealthy night-time operation. The raid on his house was carried out flawlessly. One evening when he was home asleep with his family they killed him. As part of their planning, Mossad used psychological profiling of him and other PLO leaders. They did not underestimate Wazir. Five years before the raid they had determined that he was a perfectionist of high intellect with a precise and analytical mind. They knew he was a dangerous foe. Where did they learn these superb qualities? Aside from espionage, they chiefly relied on a method of profiling unfamiliar to most people. It is called handwriting analysis.

———

Analysts have always done parlors and parties. Some analysts refuse to do them, claiming they demean themselves and their sacred subject in its climb to prestige. Some analysts defend them as a way to promote themselves, to show what handwriting analysis can do, and to pocket that extra money for the mortgage. A growing activity for analysts is the post-prom party. It has been around a long time, developed partly to ensure students don't do what they *really* would like to do—be away from the house, avoid their parents, stay out late, drink, smoke, carouse, lust, and speed around in a packed car of shrieking friends. On a special evening when they're all dressed up with only one place to go they want to prolong the ecstasy by having another place to go and still be together. Inside the school or facility where they spend the evening keeps them safe and parents off edge.

For the analyst the hours could be better. Until they do one, their only activity after midnight is walking in the moonlight with Patsy Cline. In their dreams. They go to bed early in the evening and set their alarm. It's a grueling gig but you do it, they say. The money is good but the work is intense, the hour late, and the music skull-piercing. Many are greeted by an endless breadline of students seeking quick analyses. The experience can be rewarding to student and analyst. Carl Belfiori, a long-time analyst and HR man from Michigan, was asked to do one but said no—until they upped the ante.

"The money was too good," he remarked. "I had done it before but the kids all want an analysis. When you look at their writing, they're all printing and they have that large middle zone and the rounded lettering. You have to reach for originality."

This time he approached the students by trying to help them with career choices. If college is coming up, he projects a curriculum for a major. Helene Keller, an accomplished analyst from Harrisburg, Pennsylvania, recalls enriching times.

"Kids really love the analyses, especially when I can show them what I see as their talents and their future plans," she reveals. In the same way she perceives developing interests they might have in new areas. "You can even get an idea of the quality of the particular school's teaching," she adds.

Respected Michigan analyst Ruth Holmes enjoys the dialogue with the students. She measures her comments carefully, aware they respect her observations of their skills and aptitudes. She regrets the modest time she has to learn about each of them, and tries to leave them with buoyant messages. "I wish there were more time to list all the potential I see in this writing. Maybe you will send me a postcard from time to time, so I can follow your success in the years ahead," is a common remark of hers. "Thank you for the privilege of getting to know you through your writing. You have so many excellent aptitudes just waiting to be made into skills," is another. Grim admires Holmes' empathy, tact and eloquence. Her insights inspire students to improved feelings for themselves and their future.

Grim says a case could be made that the post-prom party *enhances* the status of handwriting analysis. Consider it smart marketing. The subject can use some. If the analyst does capably, the students, tomorrow's leaders and consumers, carry a positive memory into their community and their travels. They discover the subject is not just schmutzlachen. Still, he is troubled by the instant analyses of small samples, which can produce wild inaccuracies. He is bothered by the cotton-candy, giggly mood, which can rouse disrespect. It's important for the analyst to exude stately know-how.

Grim, the prim, predictable, post-prom-party pooper, has never done one. "When I retired as an attorney I got rid of my alarm clock," he smirks. "Frankly, I've just never pursued them as another way of making money or spreading the word about me or our topic. I should do it for the experience and to see what I can do for the kids."

In law, marketing techniques for graphologists and attorneys with jury cases have found each other and they are bonding for mutual benefit. The stakes can be enormous. In many civil cases multi-million dollar verdicts and high-profile-image harm to individuals and corporations have become common. In criminal cases major offenses like murder and the white collar ones, many from business scandals, can jail defendants for a long time. An offspring of this union of law and marketing is jury screening or jury evaluation. One pre-trial method is shadow juries developed by Plaintiff's attorneys in civil cases and defense attorneys in criminal cases. These faux groups provide an independent review on the strength of their case. Reminds you of the old theater try-out in New Haven and tweaking the twaddies before the Broadway premiere.

Other steps to increase the client's chances of getting his or getting off now include a partnership with handwriting analysis. When was the tipping point for analysts to aid in jury selection? Probably in the 1970's it developed when attorneys with rich clients at great risk looking for any edge realized the subject may have merit. Since it draws out the individual's personality, they saw it as another avenue for finding favorable jurors. Attorneys have always evaluated the personality quirks of jurors. They asked them questions and watched their demeanor and their vocal answers. Now they have added the benefits of handwriting. In voir dire procedure before trial, each of the attorneys questions jury pool members to learn more about them. The official purpose of voir dire is to find impartial jurors for the case. That's what the blindfolded lady with the scales wants. It's not what the client wants. In seeking jurors, attorneys have always sought individuals who would be most partial to their case and client. If a potential juror is a severe judgmental type, wouldn't the accused seek to eliminate him from sitting at his criminal trial? If you are seeking big bucks because somebody clobbered your car and you claim major pain and permanent injuries, wouldn't you prefer a generous and sympathetic juror? If you can choose that person from the jury pool you have a great advantage. Jury verdicts in civil or criminal cases aren't simple democratic majority vote. State and Federal jurisdictions vary but most criminal verdicts must be unanimous. Rules on civil verdicts run from unanimous to ten out of twelve, or even five out of six. One or two jurors can affect the entire outcome of a case.

When citizens are called to jury duty they fill out data forms in their own hand. The attorneys pounce on these forms for quick analyses by their handwriting experts. Though the writing sample and the time to scrutinize it are usually limited, many clients see it as a worthwhile investment. The potential outcome is so important that they will spend the money to improve their chances. The advantage sought is especially powerful in the serious criminal case. If you find the steadfast juror, he can hold out for your client and prevent a conviction, despite the verdict of eleven to one for conviction. Think Henry Fonda and *Twelve Angry Men* at the outset of the film. Also, some dominant individuals in that often stuffy and windowless room can hector weaker ones to change their view of the case.

In criminal cases you can't eke out a win. You must win in a blow-out or lose in one, 12-0, either way. The key is finding the resolute people in the jury pool. They are the defendant's ticket to possible freedom or only temporary time in prison. Many are called but only twelve are chosen, with some alternates in case of illness or other excuses. A single hold-out juror in a criminal case (Henry Fonda again) doesn't acquit the defendant. If the juror won't change his vote, the judge will call a mistrial. At least he wasn't convicted. A second trial will follow sometime later. Maybe a witness will die, or change his story. The prosecutor may see the case differently and a tolerable plea agreement reached. At least a trial concluded shows the defendant and his lawyer how one slice of the public viewed his case. It forecasts his possible fate in the re-trial. Consider it a Preview of Coming Distractions.

Just how well jury screening works is the big maumoo question. Since the writing samples are brief, the speedy analysis can be lacking and even wrong. The citizens are writing on a government form. Typically it will have annoyingly small blanks to write in. Jurors may print to be understood when their normal style is cursive. Tougher to analyze. Also, this handwriting scheme is not just for victim plaintiffs. As the goose you may have been cooked by permanent injuries and want your handwriting expert to find sympathetic persons in that jury pool. These evaluations allow sauce for the gander defendant too. That mammoth corporation you sued has rights and suitcases of money to spend too. It may try to thwart your million-dollar claim against it with its own handwriting expert. With so much jeopardy, big-dollar, big-principle, or big mahoff cases often distill into an epic Ali-against-Frazier match. Accident re-construction engineers create their own computer images of how vehicles collided with each other. With handwriting and jury selection these days, a *pre*-trial battle can also rage between rival handwriting experts. Regrettably, how they each are faring is a secret. They do their work privately with their client and the lawyers before trial and, like a boxing match, no public score is kept. Even the prosecutor in that big white-collar crime case can retain an analyst. Nothing prevents it except the frugal public glaring at what it might see as a wasteful expense. Looking at their handwriting to divine jurors' personal qualities? No way, says the doubting public, to analysts' chagrin. Yes, way, analysts plead.

Grim hasn't done any jury screening. As an ex-attorney it would be a natural fit. He insists he has no interest in going back to one more courtroom.

"I was stuck in many court rooms for thirty years and now seeing them all over TV are enough, thanks." Although he hasn't pursued them, he wouldn't reject this work either.

"How do you think you would do?"

"Probably a moderate difference in most cases. How effective would depend on the writing sample size and the time to analyze it."

Even if the client can afford it and big dollars are involved, he's not spurred enough to do it. It takes focus and fast action, both attributes that ring familiar to him from law. Since retirement he wants unfocused and slow.

Meantime capitalism motivates other analysts to do what Grim hasn't. Some have been doing it for years. Alice Weiser from Houston, Texas, has been an analyst since 1976. Her national renown comes from handwriting analysis and questioned documents. In helping attorneys pick juries Weiser includes body language in her evaluations. She even recommends the attorney obtain the writing of the judge and opposing counsel. Every mite of information helps, she emphasizes. With her additional practice in employment screening, she has developed a fascinating new area, helping parents understand their children. When a mother came to her worried she couldn't communicate with her son, she reviewed the writing of both mother and son. Finding that her son was a "reserved introvert" and mother an "emotional expressive," she directed them to counseling.

Grim advises budding analysts not to be so laserbeamed on the writing that they forget jurors are live beings on display. This is the age of courtroom analysts and some probe into other juror behavior. Body language is crucial to Weiser and her ilk. They have a broad view of what that is. Just because their expertise is handwriting, (*how* they write), they shouldn't ignore the juror's content (*what* they write). Note the background information on those juror forms. Their jobs, their names, their addresses. Each datum tells something of the person. You can also spot jurors' overt body language. How they walk; how they dress; how they relate to other jurors; how they answer the attorneys' questions. Some other items may be tiny but revealing hints of who they are. Style of clothes and hair, tattoos, forehead creases, tidiness, make-up, piercings. To overlook anything they do is foolish. It's free and there for the gawking. As that eminent New Jersey philosopher Yogi Berra said, "You can observe a lot just by watching." Everything you do, have, are, and say reveals something. You just have to digest its significance.

"I think," says Grim, "too many analysts inside and outside the courtroom miss the other parts of the whole person. These parts all speak, sometimes loudly, sometimes softly. Be alert for all of them."

Finding the good juror is laudable, says Grim, but it may be misplaced. "Ack-cent-chewate the *negative*. Ee-lim-ih-nate the positive," he warbles. Before handwriting invaded the courtroom, most attorneys sought only to *exclude* the wrong juror. This made jury selection easier and more realistic. Jury consultants have changed that approach little.

Grim concurs with this. "Trying to determine the one great juror for your cause," Grim says, "is probably an elusive search and a waste of time. It is tough enough finding and dismissing the wrong juror."

If they can capture a favorable one too, so much the better. Maurine Moore, from Cheyenne, Wyoming, has been a jury handwriting consultant since 1973. She helps lawyers look for people "who are able to understand a case." That means they go defensive by seeking the person "who can goof up a case."

Since criminal cases require unanimous verdicts, one person can affect the outcome by hanging the jury. In a barrel it's simpler to spot bad apples than the good ones. Besides, rational attorneys can spar over what makes a good juror. Often the good one is barely different from the average, bland type. Lawyers tend to get cynical about their approach. Go for the juror who won't destroy your case rather than the juror who will secure you a victory. After all, jurors are supposed to be a cross-section of the community. Call it being realistic but attorneys know well the motley group they must select from to get to a "jury of his peers." Many jurors just don't want to be there. When most jurors are called to duty their first instinct is to avoid it. When they are picked, bad ones will defy the trial judge's instructions, spout absurd views, ignore the evidence, and flaunt impacted biases. To balance it out, attorneys have certain challenges they can use to excuse a juror for cause, like bias. They also have a set amount of "peremptory" challenges for which no reason need be given. Attorneys' time with each potential juror is short. With a handwriting and personality expert by their side, their judgments about which jurors to accept can only help. Since the only harm is to his client's wallet, Grim thinks it's a good investment.

Not every court case involves a jury. Although parties have the right to jury trials in large civil and criminal cases, they can also give up that right, letting a judge determine the facts and the verdict. Some civil cases don't allow for a jury but the need for handwriting expertise still exists. Grim has taken on analyses in these non-jury criminal and civil matters. Some involved personality and some questioned documents, where the typical issue is whether a sample of writing is genuine. Although they could have, none went to court. Because most of his cases require that his clients remain private and the facts confidential, Grim will not discuss details. Okay, not *everything* needs to be hidden. Grim will only reluctantly say what he can about them. Some of the matters involved a forged will, forged signature on the front of a check, a forged signature of a wife by her husband on a promissory note, a shocking note from an unknown writer to a client vilifying his daughter, a harassing note by a teaching assistant about a college professor, forged signatures of several people on an election petition, review of an historical figure in a church to determine possible motivation in positions he took (no, not Martin Luther), and the writing of a now dead husband to detect suspected secrets.

———

For centuries graffiti has been around on bathroom walls and other places the public appears. In the last decades of the twentieth century it has contributed to urban blight. With the development of spray paint and mushy pens and the decline in respect for most everything, vandals have exploited this optional way expressing what's on their disturbed minds. Some may be cryptic but messages are scattered on walls, bridges, playgrounds, and anywhere else we can't avoid seeing them. The formerly urban phenomenon is now our universal scar. High schools and colleges have felt their paint as well. The fed-up police have cracked down on what is a crime (malicious mischief, for starters) and what is venting or artistic expression, or brutish acts, for the writer.

One way to solve these crimes against property and our quest for a clean and beautiful world is to identify the writer through forensic analysis of the writing styles. The authorities need some writing to compare. If there are suspects in mind they provide a sample of writing. If they don't have the suspects' writing they can go back to the local schools and teachers who may have samples of their work.

"If schools did it right," Grim declares, "they would have in each student's file a copy of their handwriting for future reference."

Who knows if one of those wall writings is a threat to blow up the school? Or an anonymous cry for help scrawled on a merry-go-round? In any of these situations analysts stand by to help. They might even do what Grim calls the "reverse identification." Look at the graffiti and evaluate it for the personality traits and consider who in the community might match that profile. Analyzing the writing could lead to the culprit.

As casual observers note, much of the graffiti suggests an eerily similar but hideous style. From vast distances apart and both urban and surburban locales, the same person seems to be the author of many of them. The disturbing, large, printed, capital-strewn, squarish, loopy, back-slanted, claw-like, hard-to-read, inward-stroking method appears wherever you look from your car window. Grim thinks it is mostly "lazy personal xeroxing, voices of a shared rage, or shouts of campers who are not happy." As Grim says, handwriting is handwriting wherever and however it marks itself on our landscape. The intimate fibulations of the writer are encoded within it. His distinctive mode of writing opens up his private thoughts without the needle of a truth serum. In graffiti Grim sees the common denominator of youth seeking a public airing of their internal inferno. Yes, they are upset about something. What a surprise. This is just another vehicle that has been allowed to disgrace our public areas because they can. Disaffected youth. Take a large number and get in a long line. Your indignation has many friends. And what does that give the authorities that they didn't expect? More suspects than non-suspects if we consider only the young. Does anyone doubt these markings are mostly by angry young men? In *Casablanca* rounding up the usual suspects knee-jerked as the initial response to wrongdoing. With graffiti, since the suspects are a large group, the police have their donut-dusted hands full in linking any of the writings to any one person.

Some of the markings are not just nameless wailings to be read and heard. Gangs marking territory, conveying their dark messages, and providing gang news comprise some of the urban drivel. Occasionally it's just personal ID's, wannabees ripping off tags from the internet, or trainees for gang membership.

Okay, some of what blots the walls is not writing. It's an attempt at art from an unsatisfied but imaginative soul craving a gallery for his inspi-and-aspirations. In her fifth grade class years ago Grim's mother had a student who eventually graduated from Kutztown High and moved to New York City. There he defaced subways and other public areas with his painted drawings of pudgy, featureless stick men and other bald items. His style was unmistakably simple, direct, but always with a broad message. He progressed from outside to inside the buildings as a legitimate artist and a celebrated cult figure until his death at age 30. Keith Haring's drawing art was a major force in the urban art scene and today appears on an array of marketed objects. His trademark image was a radiant baby. Since his death his quarter-hour fame (he was a pal of Andy Warhol) expands as his unadorned work survives to command enormous prices. In California he had done a massive wall mural for a social agency. Recently it decided to move to a larger facility and had the mural appraised for sale to help pay for the new location. The value came in at somewhere between one and two million dollars.

———

Since handwriting is supposed to disclose intimate aspects of your personality, you can imagine where it will be applied next. Researchers survey new areas where it might aid in relieving social ills. They are taking its stroke-patterns to combat troubles not prevalent until recent decades. One of these is sexual abuse, a sensitive affliction old in origin but modern in exposure and discussion. Many of the victims are reluctant to disclose their problem. Others have repressed their trauma and may not recall the incidents. To an extent graphology can burrow under the social behavior and draw out unexpressed behavior from the past. Researchers are testing if any evidence of abuse will appear as specific strokes in the victim's handwriting. Those strokes would be the result of the victim's emotional reaction to the abuse. By taking the writing of *known* abuse victims and looking for strokes common to each victim, they hope to document strokes only these victims possess. With this insight they review the writing of someone they suspect has been abused to find those exhibited strokes. In truth you wouldn't need to suspect any abuse. You could take anyone's writing and look for the strokes, like freckles on the face. If the strokes somehow exist, those close to the victim can approach them gingerly. Hopefully the person will open up about it and receive the care and treatment they need. With research in early stages, Grim has seen some of the results, including some suggested strokes. He declines to reveal those strokes in this delicate area of handwriting and behavior. One concern is that the strokes could indicate *any* trauma the victim has felt and repressed. However, the help is for unrepressed victims too. It is also for physical and emotional abuse victims, not just sexual abuse victims. Since they often deny what they know is true, they can be confronted as necessary. Whatever the cause, any abuse victim with the strokes seems to be a candidate for serious therapy. These studies need more time and work. If they pan out as valid actions to take, this will be one more valuable contribution handwriting analysis can offer to society.

Too bad psychology hasn't bonded with handwriting analysis. If psychologists dropped their suspicion of it, the two could combine to survey and investigate people for a range of ills. Handwriting analysis, for example, might also help in situations where false memory is a critical factor. Much has been written about the knotty situation where a person appears to recall abuse yet the authorities doubt it ever occurred. Handwriting analysis might help to protect the person falsely accused. It might also be used to help resolve the question of child molestation by focusing on stroke patterns of those who are suspects or were actually charged with the offense. Another serious need for it can be justified in disorders such as anorexia and bulimia, where the victims often deny they have it. Some of these victims could be helped before it is too late. They are often in denial and won't readily admit their problem. Some studies have been done of common stroke patterns of those with compulsive eating disorders. Thus handwriting might be used in new areas both to identify and protect victims of many social ailments. At the same time it might separately identify the guilty or exonerate innocent-but-accused individuals of child or other abuse.

———

In pursuing new areas to apply, handwriting analysis has always been intrigued by the trait-stroke association. Skeptics laugh that any exists. Analysts adore it and herald its possibilities. People change their personalities constantly, at times consciously, but most times unconsciously. Maybe the better last word is unintentionally. They don't usually think about it. Events and pressures batter it to and fro. How you wind up acting is your personality, dynamic but ready to sit for its painted portrait. When behavior changes, analysts say, handwriting follows wherever it goes, like a rock star groupie. It simply reflects the state of the individual's personality at the time, changes and all. This shadow relationship has stirred analysts to envision its implications. What if the trait-stroke tie is reversed? We know people alter their strokes all the time. For whatever motive, they are purposely trying to re-set to a new writing style. It may be intentional and they may think they prefer the new look. Few know the meaning of the stroke they deleted or the one they added or the one they just modified. When an analyst suggests the stroke and trait be reversed, his purpose is deeper. Given that a stroke equals a trait, if a person takes one of his strokes and twists it into another trait, will his personality change to mirror that new trait? Usually their aim is pointed. They want to eliminate a bad-quality trait by switching to a stroke connected to a good-quality stroke. Will this result erase the bad behavior the bad stroke reveals? Taking this trait-stroke link between handwriting and personality and reversing it is called graphotherapy. The first time you hear the idea your sip of coffee might instantly snort through your nose. Implausible, yes. To impatient silver-platter skeptics it seems another reason to kick graphology again while it's trying to get up.

To illustrate how graphotherapy works, they even have a simple experiment to try. Take unlined paper. Write any sentence across the top in your normal style and size. Below that sentence write the same sentence again but slightly smaller. Continue writing the same sentence underneath the last one, each time making the sentence smaller. As your writing shrinks your concentration will improve. That is a trait of a person who writes much smaller than average size. The tinier your writing the better your focus on tasks. You will also find yourself getting more intense and stressed. Your personality is being temporarily altered. You have just experienced graphotherapy in action. Stop writing and go back to what you were doing. Soon your personality will drift back to its customary self. Unless you decide to adopt that tiny writing you just finished. If you do, you will have better focus from then on, as good concentration will be part of your personality. That's the theory anyway.

Whether you snort or kick or concentrate well, you may be surprised that analysts began to study it a century ago. Dr. Edgar Bérillon, a French psychologist and expert on diseases of the mind, took the first formal steps outlined in a 1908 report He called it graphic psychotherapy. Two decades later French scientists did some experiments with encouraging results. They worked mostly with alcoholics and children (changing their bad habits). Between 1929 and 1931 Dr. Pierre Janet, a psychology professor at Le College de France worked with Dr. Charles Henry, head of the Laboratory of Sensations at the famous Sorbonne in Paris. In 1931 a pupil of Janet's, Dr. Pierre Renard, a distinguished professor of medicine and psychology, succeeded him and expanded the work, eventually publishing a book on graphotherapy in 1948.

Later efforts of University of Paris psychologist Raymond Trillat were featured in a 1956 *Time* article. Over ten years he had tried and apparently succeeded in helping children overcome emotional problems with graphotherapy exercises. Working with 600 children, he claimed a success rate for about 500. He directed each child to write specific strokes, once in the morning and once in the evening. Though not claiming he changed personalities, he thought his methods were one way to dissolve emotional barriers. This would help their personalities to open up. The success of these French pioneers in graphotherapy was advanced by native Frenchman and naturalized American Paul de

Sainte Colombe. He had been a consultant–assistant in the experiments of Janet and Renard. He was compelled to continue in America only because he wasn't in Paris in 1940 when Hitler took his home city. He was in Hollywood working on a film he had written. He stayed until after the war. After degrees in law, philosophy, and literature at the University of Paris, he studied both graphology and graphotherapy. Applying the therapy techniques countless times for men, women and children, he vastly improved their troubled lives. In 1966 he published a distinguished book, *Grapho-Therapeutics*, his term for stroke exercises by those needing a personality revision. A 1970 *Time* article featured Colombe's accomplishments. It quoted psychologist George Melzer at the Santa Clara (California) Mental Health Center. He declared that Colombe's graphotherapy had produced "astonishing results."

During the European adventures, Americans weren't oblivious to graphotherapy. One who experimented with the technique in the early twentieth century is the founder of Graphoanalysis, Milton Bunker. He enlisted many people to try his version called "30-days-and-30-sentences." He had the participant write thirty sentences every day for thirty days. A few initial results were disappointing. In one testing he aimed for listless people with sprawling, shapeless writing to replace it with sharp-pointed upper wedges as in the top of an m or an n. Their existing strokes had betrayed a sluggish, unfocused person. These wedged strokes show a person who is mentally active. With fifty participants, ten dropped out after just days, complaining of headaches. Some had trouble sleeping and others claimed nausea. For the rest the results were remarkable. Bunker surmised that the irritated groups were mirroring their feeble temperaments and lacked the resolve to change. They would need extensive, long–term work.

Bunker discovered graphotherapy can batter psyches and nervous systems. He grasped its emotional damage potential. Unless the analyst has professional training, he cautioned, graphotherapy should be conducted only with a professional counselor. Even for hopeful candidates of graphotherapy, Bunker doubted progress would be easy. He projected months, not days or weeks, for substantive change.

Hiking into this wilderness with a skimpy guidebook, Bunker tried different strokes, mostly ones reflecting soft minor traits. Despite the potential harm he saw from altering the powerful trait strokes, he still wanted to reform deeper parts of the personality. In one experiment he had the participants draw the "self-reliance" stroke found in the strong underlining of a person's signature. People drawing this stroke are confident they can succeed on their own. Combining this stroke with a solid t-bar stroke (a sign of strong "will power") at least an inch long (a long bar shows "enthusiasm"), yielded commendable personality changes. In the midst of this his prior views were affirmed. Our traits are many; no trait stands alone; and trait effects vary on each other. Centuries ago John Donne said it about the whole man. Milton Bunker said it about each trait. Neither is an island. Each impinges on others and counts on others. Bunker understood that other traits might suppress the individual's self-reliance and will power and radically reduce their impact. At times that happened. Since traits can influence each other, Bunker also discerned that you can't change too much too soon. He had allowed an eager writer to alter four radical strokes and watched him curdle emotionally and physically. That hard-way lesson seared him.

Another experiment with the slant and the size of writing compounded the impact. Size and slant are not strokes per se but global factors, which have massive strength. They appear in every stroke and control every stroke they inhabit. After efforts with those two went awry, he declared that no one should try to change the slant or the size of their letters. He shouldn't have been surprised since he developed them as major concepts in his own doctrine of Graphoanalysis. He *thought* they were powerful. Now he confirmed how much. We each have a way we slant our letters. We each have a size for our letters. Their distinctive meanings for us are engrained in our constitutions, maybe originating at birth. If we try modifying either one, we risk grave harm to the writer. Let them naturally evolve one way or the other.

He carried over his concern for these two factors to the American education system. He worried that school teachers routinely force students to alter not only their size and slant but also other areas of the writing. As he had found out himself, handwriting strokes aren't just flung on paper to express thoughts. They also function to reveal personal qualities of the writer. When schoolchildren were thrust into new writing strokes, collisions with Mother Nature were inevitable. From his experience Bunker knew a close kinship existed between any person's writing and their personality. When that tears it will need repairs.

Graphotherapy has steamed ahead several miles. The voyage continues with the destination beyond the waves. Grim sees the concept as stimulating for the mind but dubious in practice. Some effective results may be due to independent causes. The placebo effect is a familiar phenomenon from psychology. We all know about sugar pills and the like making people better for reasons experts can only speculate.

"I think that when a person adjusts his strokes and his personality changes, he has convinced himself this technique has worked," Grim supposes. "Or his personality change is from the force of motivation."

He tenders this example. If a person changed their writing, which showed "stinginess," to strokes that relate to "generosity," he became more giving because he willed himself to act that way. It may be conscious or unconscious. His generosity may not be from the amazing force of his strokes but the routine force of his will.

Grim frets that people with acute troubles will seek relief by graphotherapy. "If they need it, why not? It's not illegal." In our culture of quick fixes Grim fears people who need serious help will merely tinker with their strokes hoping for the extreme makeover of their pathetic personalities. These people would need their noses rubbed into its uncertainty and its futility. It simply may not work for them. When you explore it you must question its logic. Our so-called negative qualities don't arise from neutral sources. Their source is often deep insecurities. Trying to reverse undesirable traits with a simple pen-stroke may no longer be far-fetched, but it's not near-fetched either. Despite its century of existence, it's too early to tell. To try graphotherapy may be to prolong your troubles, or even worsen them. You don't disgorge cemented problems so easily. If you do, they may re-appear as part of some other trait, like squashing the bulge in a balloon and its popping out somewhere else. TV's Doctor Phil frequently discusses our bad habits, like the obsessive-compulsive disorders and the addictions. When you get rid of one bad habit, it won't really disappear. It's replaced by another bad habit. The habit itself is a symptom through certain repeated behavior. You may eliminate the behavior, such as overeating or gambling, but the urge still tests your will power. The urge is your body and mind telling you to relieve the hurt or fear you are feeling, like the emptiness of your life.

Grim offers this analogy to demonstrate what might be graphotherapy's fatal flaw. He would also apply it to any social addiction, like gambling or shopping. If you go out in the sun and are burned, you may go inside to escape it. However, the sun does not disappear from the sky. You have a temporary respite from further damage. Besides, the burned skin remains, awaiting more damage when you go out again. You can slather on tanning lotion and go out. The sun still shines. You can open an umbrella (parasol) to keep off the rays. The sun still shines. Wait for a rainy day. When the clouds part the sun will re-appear. It was up there all that time anyway. Until you can make the sun disappear, you won't really resolve your hurt. The sun is the cause of your troubles. The sunburn is its effect. The lotion and the umbrella are the overeating and the gambling. Changing one stroke (lotion) to another (umbrella) won't eliminate the source of your problems (the sun).

"Why do we have bad habits in the first place?" I must enquire of Grim.

"Psychologists say serious emotional troubles come from an overriding need not being met. When that occurs, the individual compensates for the hurt or frustration by behavior that gives him relief."

Sounds like Doctor Phil talking. He calls it "our reward" or "a pay-off." It lasts only as long as the comforting acts. Though addictive, we do them only at weak moments, which seem to persist without end. These afflictions don't come unannounced. But when we feel their impact our unconscious devises some tolerable solution. You can bet it will be something that feels good for the moments we do it. The woman who pouts from not getting emotional warmth from her husband may become a compulsive shopper. She will get a momentary high as she hits the mall. Taking the credit card from her won't eliminate the distress that makes her want to shop. Changing a handwriting stroke that reveals distress to one related to a positive quality shouldn't get rid of the distress for that person either. The causal distress (cold husband) remains even though the effect (shopping) is removed. It is only replaced by some other effect (for example, overeating takes over for shopping). As relief in battling a serious disorder, graphotherapy may hear your emotional complaints but it won't treat them and make you well again.

"Writing is an effect not a cause. Writing will show we have an ill, but changing the writing won't purge the source of the ill," Grim is convinced. "I'm less concerned about the mild traits. Since they may not derive from deap-seated ills, graphotherapy might make a difference."

The concept of graphotherapy is enticing. Imagine, ridding yourself of personal drawbacks just by altering your handwriting. If it works, the possibilities are staggering. It seems unbelievable. In any event, like handwriting analysis itself, don't dismiss graphotherapy out of hand. More experiments need to be done. Let the testing continue with scientific procedures and let the results provide the objective message. Given the hurdles handwriting analysis has faced, what's been accomplished in graphotherapy in the last century has been more promising than analysts could have hoped.

PERSONALITIES

Sign In, Please

With National Handwriting Day celebrated this month,
we asked an expert to analyze some local luminaries' scripts

John Hancock may be the only American whose legacy is directly tied to his signature, but experts claim anyone's handwriting can offer a look into who he or she really is. So with National Handwriting Day on January 23rd, we asked Michelle Dresbold, author of *Sex, Lies and Handwriting*, to evaluate eight signatures from our city elite. After she read between the lines (and the loops), the handwriting was on the wall. —*Frank Visco*

1. John Street Dresbold says Hizzoner's unreadable scribble signals he's "very secretive." The cross in his name indicates that he's both religious and "self-sabotaging, because of the way it cuts back through the signature." His thick writing marks him as a powerful man, and the point at the tail of his signature means "You shouldn't get in his way when he wants something."

2. Ryan Howard Howard's thick handwriting points to a "very sensual side, filled with great passion and strong physicality," Dresbold says. So although the cross in his name implies our fave Phillie (a bachelor) is very religious, "He's also probably good in bed."

3. Amy Gutmann Gutmann's signature is indicative of what one might expect from someone running Penn, according to Dresbold. The high and long "T" crossing means Gutmann "sets extremely high goals"; the "star" in her first name hints at "persistence," while the big "G" telegraphs "a mother-hen type."

4. M. Night Shyamalan Dresbold describes the filmmaker's signature as "very bizarre." He "fits nowhere but in his own world," she says. While labeling his writing "pretty," she says the check mark at the bottom of his "M" indicates he "may be angry or aggressive, and that he sometimes thinks about death."

5. Michael A. Nutter Nutter's signature was the hardest for Dresbold to decipher, she says. "He's not an easy person to know." Like his predecessor, she finds Nutter "somewhat secretive," but also "strong in that

he won't be pushed around or walked on." The angles in his writing indicate that he's "a good decision-maker who weighs all the facts." However, the slash above his "t" implies he's also impatient."

6. El Wingador Dresbold says the break in the top of his "L" indicates our wing-eating fiend "has issues with anxiety" (our guess: impending heart disease), while the emphasis on the lower zone implies he's concerned with an aspect of the body (our guess: his waistline). The distorted "G" indicates he "may have a distorted body image," but the signature thickness indicates he's "driven by sensual pleasure."

7. Lynne Abraham There's "quite a bit of tension" in the D.A.'s script, Dresbold says. The slant toward the right shows she's emotional, while the flame strokes at the top of her letters, especially her "H," label her "a sharp thinker who may be close-minded to the ideas of others." Smushed-together letters imply "some confusion in her life"; the downward slant of the "E" shows her to be "a fatalist, someone who thinks about things going bad."

8. Neil Stein Dresbold says the disconnect between the capitalized printing of his first name and the cursive of his last indicates the restaurateur is "unpredictable." His penchant to make his "S" look like a figure eight implies he's "good at explaining things," but the lack of space between words classifies him as a man "who doesn't stop to pause and reflect." His bold and full signature points to "a sensual love of food and drink" while also shouting, "Here I am. Notice me."

This is a short article from the January 2008 issue of *Philadelphia Magazine* displaying the signatures of several notable people from the area. Note that, except for the last one, each signature is virtually unreadable.

Chapter 18

The Illegible Signature

me write pretty one day

A signature always reveals a man's character—and sometimes his name.
Evan Esar, Humorist

Eccentric and spiteful little flourishes darting about in various ways, as it attempts to somersault and destroy the entire word from which they sprung. Some letters slope one way, and some another. Some are halted, maimed, and crippled, and all are blind.

Description of the writing of 19th Century British social critic and philosopher Thomas Carlyle

We who can handwrite have signatures. Some are similar to the rest of our writing. Some you wouldn't recognize from the rest. Some are larger and some are smaller. Some signatures are so ferociously rumpled that a stranger couldn't tell who the individual is. That's odd if you consider your signature's purpose is to let people know who you are. Why would anyone draw their signature so you can't read it? Some signatures are very creative, pasting on curlicues and doodads, even where the rest of their lines are trim and combed. Some signatures don't even include all the letters of the names. Why would they omit any letters? And why some letters and not others? Sadly, many writers just grip it and zip it. Or grip it and skip it.

Other variants seem infinite, many strange and many unique. On the paper a few signatures appear as unassuming blips beneath menacing letters. The more blips the harder to read. Some signatures are amorphous, unintelligible ziphers, or virtual afterthoughts, or out-the-door nonchalance, or wasted time. Some are Mayan warriors, goosed squid, drunken Mummers, tidal waves, a radiator, clothes in a washer, swashbuckling pirates, Shaker furniture, whirling tumbleweed, a stepped-on Slinky, or a rugby scrum.

We don't write anything more often than our signatures. Why we take the writing of our name, enpretzelate it or beat it senseless without mercy, or drop it in a blender, then guiltless serve it to the world as our social ID is another puzzlement for the King of Siam. After this album of individual styles, skeptics still say handwriting has no connection to personality? *That* is the real puzzlement.

Among signature styles the public asks Grim most about is the illegible signature. Probably it applies to other analysts too. Grim finds it the most perplexing. Since every signature is different, what they mean depends on their individual form. Graphology's rule describes your signature as your trademark, your logo, your image to the world. It is your personality's mask, not the real person. Your true nature lurks elsewhere in the rest of your strokes. Since it's your most public writing, your signature is the best occasion to parade your float.

Grim questions the encased belief of the signature-as-public-image. Your signature is what you want to project about yourself, analysts chant as if repeating an ancient truism. At the moment he leans toward the view it reflects the writer's genuine self. He hedges, "Or at least most of it." Saying the signature is mostly the true you launches Grim against that bulwark of graphology authority.

"Why is your signature the real you, not the pretend you?" I ask.

Grim replies, "I suspect that it is really 'the devil made him do it, or the guy can't help it.'"

Those brain impulses are strong. They want expression through the pen on the paper, insisting the writer's personality be allowed public airing. If mayhem erupts and forces a sloppy duo of names asking for acceptance as your identity, it's because it had its way. Stop snickering and start listening to Grim's rationale.

"If signatures are mostly image-making, why would a person compose one that is scrawl and mostly unreadable? What does that say about you for others to admire? That you are a confused wreck as an individual?"

Although each illegible signature is different, emotional bedlam is a broad idea of what it means *outside* of signatures. The person can't keep his car on the road. He is unstable and can't make things happen successfully. His life is in turmoil and confusion. If the primary purpose of writing is to communicate, and the specific function of a signature is to identify the writer, an unreadable signature fails miserably.

With meager conscious thought and away from the frown of our elementary teachers, we fashion our signatures into a comfortable, appealing design. That remains our signature until some shattering event or a patient advancement in our character develops. One day in passing we may see a style of writing that appeals to us or stirs us to reflect. We may borrow it for a shake-down cruise but it may remain as a stowaway. A hard one to throw overboard. Don't call that stealing or even failure to return; it's how we all create our behavior styles. We copy from others, sometimes so creatively we think we're beyond any copyright infringement. At times we are so innocently inventive that we think *we* created the mold. New patterns are born. A few of us slip toward ruin with a signature known but to God. If you consider this a conscious act, you are saying the writer intentionally, knowingly built a signature only they can read. Who would do that? If you are one who does, ponder this and get out your hanky: Since analysts promote your signature as personal logo, presumably you want to be seen most favorably by society's cruel arbiters. You want us to view you as fabulous and admirable. Yet, if your signature implodes or explodes, the message we get is that you have collapsed into a rubble of insecurities, struggling as a person. You need a clean-up crew and a make-over. Maybe you are trying to prevent us knowing the real you lest we spy a besieged soul. Hence, the mask of your signature is an attempt to remain inscrutable. If so, why isn't the *mask* a series of pleasant, harmonious, conventional and readable strokes that inspire a warm, engaging reaction from its reader? Isn't that what you desire?

Take your own signature. How readable is it? If it is hard to read, ask the creative graphic artist who designed it if you can have your money back. Don't you want to sue? Isn't this poor PR person guilty of malpractice? Save your money. Skip the office visit to the lawyer for your rash lawsuit. Go find a mirror and stare into it. That is the sorry artist you hired. You did it yourself for yourself. Didn't you have your best interests at heart? Why did you do such a shoddy job of telling the world how great you are? You don't really know, do you?

Grim thinks he knows the answer and he expects analysts to support his reasoning. Your stormy emotional structure is asserting itself by the gyrations it makes you put on paper, that's why. Your signature may be what you want to hand out as calling card to the world to make you look good. However, for those who have lapsed into the unreadable signature, the powerful weight of their imperfections overwhelms their good intentions. The result is tumultuous marks on the parchment. It's illegible because your personality is a mighty wind believing it is best in show, demanding for your consideration that you manifest it in your writing strokes. If they are illegible so be it as you are a person in a struggle with both himself and his surroundings.

Grim wants to elaborate on his sources for this appalling state of signatures. "Some signatures resemble a pile of wire coat hangers allowed alone for ten minutes. They think they can have sex with each other, forgetting that they're only coat hangers. They try anyway and they're so hard up it takes forever to dislodge them. When we finally do, it seems we're left with a room full of Calder's mobiles awaiting wires to hang from. What motivates someone to obliterate their signature into a tangled mess as they prepare to identify themselves?"

That was an interesting way of looking at it. He won't sit still. He piles it on with this: "Does anyone go to those meetings where everyone slaps on a name tag intending to write something after 'HELLO, MY NAME IS…' and fill in 'I'd Rather Not Say Because I Have Issues.'? It's nice to meet you too. Okay, we usually don't write our signatures on these sticky tags. But we do want strangers to know us. So we print our names on them. Can't we be diligent as this with our signatures at other times? Isn't that the reason you sign on the dotted or solid lines in dignified situations, like contracts, checks, applications, and others not so dignified. Apparently not."

Maiming only one name in our signature is another story. Grim thinks other motives exist for why some people mangle either the first or last names. Often they act from disgust at the name itself. A few people actually take their ending stroke and retain it for a bitter return slash across the offensive word. On rare occasions both names get it. A few of us are thinking of leaving life's party early, not having the fun we heard it is. It's a self-destructive act. Some people detest their last name because it sounds like they are talking with their mouth full or a decent long name spelled backwards. When they introduce themselves and their name to a stranger, the double whammy rears its perpetual head: They are asked to spell their name, then pronounce it again. The curse of the long and unintelligible name. Yes, some are even short and unintelligible. Many of those names come-a from-a de olda country, many in Eastern Europe and Russia. Granted, plenty of other nations never got around to their senses on names that could be said in under five seconds. Women can cure their klutzy last names by marrying a man with a passable last name. Unless she lucks out, a long, heavy price to pay. Or the person is shamed by the unsurpassed oddness of their first name foisted on them by whatweretheythinking parents. "Naming your child Moonbeam Zappa or Apple Paltrow is a form of child abuse," Grim declares. "Time merely converts it to adult abuse before it will become elder abuse."

Grim's father had a black man in his court named Emancipation Proclamation Busby. "All this did was shackle him some more," he shrugs.

Grim wants to withdraw some more from his memory bank of pathetic appellations. "I knew a girl in my hometown, last name of White, first name Snow," Grim mentions.

"Awwww," we must say.

"No—awful," Grim must say.

With last names other namania presides. Some individuals are okay with their last name but they can't stand their family. What do they do? Slash it with covering strokes. Or it's a woman's signature and she's had it with her husband. She slashes her last name. He should be aware of this. It's a warning she may someday do the same to him with a deadlier item.

Those acts of signature violence are marked with symbolism. Grim is amazed the number of people who avenge their signature names. Regrettably these signature conflicts are displayed in public view. You have three options to escape your pilgrimpillory exposure. Live with the disarray of your signature, resolve your inner problems, or reform your signature into something presentable. Until you clear up your personal woes, it will be a colossal battle to keep the signature attractive. The Doctor Frankenstein within our mind is our personality ruling our hands without pity or compunction. The result is our handwriting monster. If we don't recognize this happens, we don't comprehend personality's possession of our handwriting. We can overcome those forces of our character but it won't be easy. Usually we concentrate on content when we write. To create hopeful strokes you will have to do it every moment you write. Not an easy task if you also care about what you're saying. Good luck. You know that expression "Don't mess with Mother Nature."? It will be subtle and you won't see her but she will be handwrestling you and she is no pushover. She's been around much longer than you. As she makes you cry uncle, nearby stands your smug personality holding her shawl and cap, urging her on.

Grim, the expired lawyer, insists on practicing beyond his sell-by date. Outside of court for sure. He scours for more evidence that will mute the skeptics' gloom over graphology's legitimacy. He thinks signatures can be a prime exhibit to cheer them up and maybe win them over. Some people write fast signatures to "get it over with" or some other casual, unreflective reason. Many claim they sign their name so often that they adopted a speedier method. As the pro golfer John Daly says, "Just grip it and rip it." How you rip it is the issue. Many of those fleet signatures, lacking proper cultivation, grow unsightly weeds, those extra strokes that add nothing to readability and celebrate ugliness. Usually the signature also becomes harder to read.

Grim looks to growl. "Adding these strokes doesn't get their task done quicker; it prolongs it. If they intend to be efficient and get it done, it's self-defeating. Those superfluous lines should be lopped off."

As before, Grim explains this is "unconscious intent" on the march. These writers aren't doing it willfully; they're in a hurry and pretty is secondary. From within their mind their personal vigor is in charge. Otherwise, why would they do it? Grim thinks they rarely dwell on these extra strokes. Possibly they don't realize how wasteful they are. Mostly it's apathetic ignorance. Yes, each time they want to be done with making their signature. They have other more important activities to rush through. If they thought about it more, they would remove the unneeded strokes. Inexplicably, they leave the trimmer on the shelf. The strokes remain because they are not as innocuous as they might seem. Extra strokes are laden with insights to personality. Unnecessary for readability, but they contain traits. It's one more piece of evidence that handwriting expresses personality. Whether the strokes come out as extra ones or unreadable ones, our mind dictates the strokes we draw.

Shouldn't the writer want to remove extra strokes? Since few do, they must be indifferent to their duty to be efficient. When you press these people, they may admit their signature is an unruly mob of warring, wasteful strokes. Then they do nothing about it. They allow their unconscious to have its way. This is the secret but undeniable power of personality. Otherwise, why wouldn't the writer take a moment and correct his wayward signature once and for all?

Scribbling the signature generates fall-out when done without thoughtful care. How about intentionally? Would anyone intentionally scribble it? Why would they do that? In Grim's thirty years of law he saw countless signatures on checks, wills, contracts, and assorted documents. Frequently he would see men (women rarely did it) with signatures composed of simple lines forming undecipherable, often incomplete letters. It was impossible to read the actual name. He asked several why they wrote their name like that. Many said that's how they've always been doing it. Some justified it as trying to prevent a forgery of their signature. Grim's usual response was private disbelief. He wanted to tell them they were actually making forgery more likely. Occasionally he had to speak up although he was in the middle of business and even though it was none of his business.

When he brought it up, they wanted to know why their effort was senseless. So do I.

"When you produce a scrawled signature on purpose, you crafted lines with no particular regularity. No one knows what they're expected to look like, maybe even the writer himself. Hence, it's easy to mimic them because no one can tell if you're close."

Grim's solution for forgery-proofing surprises most people. "You can't make it immune from forgery but you can greatly minimize the risk," Grim volunteers. Now take it from his own words: "Draw your signature with clear letters, smoothly drawn without hesitation, and add some complicated flourishes. It's important you write the whole signature spontaneously. Remember, you are changing your signature to an unnatural style. Therefore, if you write slowly your strokes will seem mannered and phony. They may waver and betray nervousness. Your hand will try reverting to its former style."

Again he reminds us your personality is a strong force that insists on recognition in your writing. When you refuse to accommodate it, be prepared for resistance. Forgers have trouble with strokes that are made quickly and unaffectedly. When they carefully try to copy your style, their guilty nerves jerk the pen off line. If you give them flourishes to copy, they must take more time. Government paper currency has embellished, detailed strokes and other designs for a reason. They are harder to copy accurately. They increase the forger's work and their chances of failing. These scrawled signatures of guys Grim met at work would backfire on them. Since they typically had inadequate letters and few squiggles, they eased a forger's task.

If you seriously want to own a forgery-proof signature, you can design it. But you will struggle keeping it. You are creating an alien signature. Since your personality imposes itself on your writing, it won't stand aside without some protest. It is determined to make you register *it* on the paper. You must concentrate harder to ensure the strokes differ from your customary style. Ironically, that makes you a forger too. You are forming a model to follow that was never yours, same as the forger faces. Through years of repetition and its servitude to personality, your normal signature won't submit gracefully.

"This commanding influence of personality on writing," Grim believes, "should oblige all questioned document examiners to learn handwriting analysis. They will realize why forgery is not easy, which will comfort them.

"How so?"

"They will know their work will be easier than maybe they thought. They will also see that making our signatures forgery-proof isn't easy. This should comfort them too."

"Why is that?"

"They will have more business."

Chapter 19

Alteration of Handwriting

The Jokester, the Make-over, and the Copy-Cat

Remember, when dealing with people we are not dealing with creatures of logic. We're dealing with creatures of emotion, bristling with prejudices, and motivated by pride and vanity.

Dale Carnegie, *How to Win Friends and Influence People*

We are at our personality's mercy. When we write, it is "boss of the household." They'll be no changes around here without its okay. If you attempt to roam with your strokes, be prepared for a smack upside your sorry hand.

Allan Grim

Things are not always as they seem. Toupées, tissue-stuffed bras, and Rock Hudson. And now, say it ain't so, Pluto. Yes, analysts face deceptions too. Times occur when handwriting analysts expect one piece of paper and they get another. On occasion when an analyst receives a paper with writing, it may have been changed from the writer's normal style. If a person realizes an analyst will assess their writing for personal qualities, fear may slip into their minds. To avoid an intolerable gash to their psyche, they scheme to improve their writing. They tweak strokes betraying drawbacks to ones showing virtues. They want an impressive analysis, not one that declares their raw, imperfect self.

Analysts know to be alert for the sham piece of writing. Every analyst has faced attempts to foil them in their duty to find truths of the writer, even the hurtful ones. Although it doesn't happen often, once is too many. Analysts want to keep their shaky standing from further abuse. For any fakery analysts have an advantage. The writer must know what the strokes mean and hope he is inserting the ones that make him look good. For each altered stroke the analysis declines but only gradually. With over a hundred strokes to review, a seriously flawed report takes several. Since the influential global factors, like slant and rhythm, can be altered too, the chances for successful deception increase for the globals. However, since each stroke has a global in it, the writer must concentrate harder. Where the analysis is for something serious, like a job applicant, the fallout can be troubling. Because of their impact bogus global strokes can fool the analyst. The altered style in a serious circumstance is the high crime and misdemeanor in handwriting analysis. This consoles analysts only in that they are not alone. Cheating also afflicts regular psychology tests and techniques. Of course it happens elsewhere too. We practice it when we go to church wearing cheerful smiles and spiffy clothes and acting pious as the choir boys and angels. After our good behavior we go home and resume our wretched, sinful selves again. Fortunately for analysts, since few people know the meanings of handwriting strokes, tinkered writings are scarce. The concern is that, as handwriting analysis becomes more prevalent in business, stroke-altering is likely to increase.

Most writing deceit occurs when the person changes his usual style. Occasionally an insecure writer will forego that for more drastic action. He steals the entire writing of someone else. Unless he knows all the trait-stroke meanings, that is taking a major risk. Assuming they know meanings, when they steal someone's identity, they are stuck with their drawbacks too. You wonder how they select the other writing. To do it right they must have an intimate knowledge of this other person and be convinced of their superlative virtues. It's been tried more than analysts are willing to admit. Sometimes it happened and the analyst didn't even realize he was fooled.

Once in a while outsiders toss analysts a stimulating inquiry. They wonder if a person's writing can be disguised beyond detection. A small sample of writing can hide some traits from the analyst. The larger the sample the less chance for tricking the analyst. The nerd who somehow got a date with the beauty queen can hide himself only so long. It may take time, but it will happen. Eventually his instinctive uncoolness betrays him. He lights up his filter cigarette at the wrong end. As he takes his coat off his arm catches in his sleeve. His insecurities rush in to smear him in dread, reddening his face and hipchecking him into stuttering and stumbling. He's been exposed and no more covering up. In graphology a longer sample ultimately should expose the dissembler. If presented with, say, only a brief sentence and a signature, a worthy analyst declines to review them for good reason. The smaller the sample the easier to disguise. A small sample is the nerd on his best behavior early on the first date. That is why the analyst will require at least a page or two of writing with a signature. Still, that won't completely eliminate disguise. To minimize further deceit, he asks the person to write in front of him. He also requests it be done spontaneously. If he keeps the writer's usual pace constant, it hinders them from penning false lines. False looks atypical and unnatural. Analysts want typical and natural.

No analyst can expose every disguise. Even insisting on a disguise-resistant sample, like a lengthy one or one done in front of the analyst, can be trouble. A clever person can take his script style and, by radically altering the strokes, create some marked differences, even in front of the analyst. Grim grabs a pen and quickly draws on a blank pad some light, backslanted writing with tight spacing between narrow letters. Assume this is the writer's real style, the one he fears to reveal. Grim turns to a new sheet of paper and draws a heavy, forward-slanted sentence with wide ligatures linking bloated letters. Though changing only four areas of the writing, the analyst may be hoodwinked enough to miss the substance of this individual's personality. True, plenty of other strokes remain, but mammoth distortion has disfigured this individual's portrait. He may win this furtive extreme make-over because the areas of change were vital to an accurate report.

Although radical stroke changes can be effective as disguise, they can backfire on the scamster. The writing can look suspicious, making the deception easier to spot. The analyst can flush it out himself. He can insist on genuine examples from earlier times. If he doesn't trust the writer, he can try to get them independently. He refuses to allow the writer to bring the items to him. He might go to someone who had received an item from the writer, such as a letter or a note. Anything from another person should do if it has the writer's innocent, unaltered writing style on it.

Frequently, a writing method to fool an analyst is printing. Anonymous notes are rarely written in script. The Ramsey ransom note is printed writing. Of course most of these aren't writings prepared for analysis. But the wicked writers instinctively know they may be analyzed for comparing to their normal script style or personality. That's one reason they print them. Actually, since the letters are unique, printing may be easier to expose. The challenge is finding other writings of suspects where they printed, especially if they customarily write script style. As with script, people will use patterns within their printing. This can weaken printing as a disguise. Although in school we learned printing before script, we lack a model to follow as we have for script. Who can recall the style for each letter of printing? With the splurge of fonts in computer software, many typefaces appear in items we read. Yet it's tough to recall details, particularly when composing small letters with serifs. Whatever the devious individual chooses, their styles will be roughly alike. For full disguise some tricksters try printing with all capitals. Usually we see normal writing with capitals only on formal words or at the head of a sentence. Thus, all caps can work better for these wrongdoers. You can only hope to find other examples of their printing with all capitals.

Time and again the inept amateur will betray themselves with tattling indicators. They can't think of everything because they don't know much of anything about handwriting. When they must write, analysts themselves will be sloppy enough despite their supposed knowledge. Too much to think about. Novice offenders will often flop in areas like vertical or almost vertical slant, mixed caps and small letters in one word, inability to render small letters (a, g, r, m, n, and p are tough to do), avoidance of serifs or flourishes, and over-sized capitals. Where the sample is suspicious and it is a moderate length, Grim will ask the suspect to write the same passage again. He will remove the first effort from view and request the second be written apace. No dawdling to allow time for thinking. Maybe have them do it one more time too. With so much writing and so little time, the writer is unlikely to repeat a strange scheme. If he fails, his status should change from mere suspect to accused.

Grim feels the analyst's pain at this finding. "The attempted deceit insults the analyst. He and his subject have been disrespected for their thinking they could put it over on us."

"Any consolations?"

"Yeah. This time my subject and I aren't embarrassed by an incorrect report."

At rare moments a new member of Grim's study group will bring a sample of writing to analyze. It will have no signature and reveal little about the person. It's natural for the group to want to hear at least something about the individual before they tackle it. Is this your boss? Somebody you want to get serious about? Things like that. Grim is okay with the initial secrecy. The analysis goes on untainted by bias. He calls it a "blind" analysis. When the new member offers the blind sample, the group exhausts its comments about the writing. The member confesses the writing is theirs. The analysts can just feel the irritation of the wool being pulled over their eyes. Grim says he himself is not usually fooled. He suspects it, clams up, plays along, takes on some guilt, and allows the member to complete what he calls the "sincere scam." Ironically it does elicit a purer analysis than the one where the analyst already knows the person being analyzed. Those suffer from the analyst's bias from his prior knowledge of the individual.

"It's a special problem with famous-people analyses," he adds. "They always rage with prejudice. What we know about someone inevitably colors the traits found in their writing."

"Will you do them?"

"I try to avoid them but if it's a big deal for someone, I will."

Many are only signatures anyway, loaded with image rather than reality. They are harder to get at the real person behind the celebrity. Having the rest of their writing is a bonus. Still, he likes to see how the public image compares to what the writing emits of their real selves. Have they been conning us all these years?

Celebrity or not, bias or prior knowledge of the writer can be foiled by requiring an analyst to justify his findings. Make them cite the strokes and their strength in the writer's make-up. Ordinarily Grim will politely ask for them. That won't be his only occasion for demanding proof. He keeps the evaluator honest. "Where do you see that in the writing?" he will insist. When an analyst says he sees "aggressiveness" in the writing he must specify where it is and how strong it is. A good classroom technique, it also enlightens the rest of the group. When no signature accompanies the writing, suspicion arises about the writer's identity. Suspicion shouldn't be automatic. Once in a while the sample lacks the writer's consent. It could be informal notes or personal writings where the writer has no reason to sign his name. Maybe they had no intention of sending it to someone else, like a to-do list. When the sample seems specially written for analysis, that's a strong clue it's the member's own writing. Some analysts think the "surprise" analyses are distasteful, to be discouraged, and even rejected. Maybe shoddy pool, if not dirty pool.

"I will put up with them," says Grim. "The member gets what they really desire—the straight story about themselves, frank and objective."

The risk is a volley of grapeshot from the group, exposing the writer's infirmities. If they want the truth from it, they get the truth because no one knows who it is. Hopefully they can handle it.

Practical jokers exist in most areas of our lives. With disrespect still heaped on handwriting analysis, chicanery remains a threat. Each analyst must be vigilant. Since history's judgment has not been kind to handwriting analysis, each analyst has little reputation to spare. The sneering contempt means standing is a sensitive issue. As the ancient proverb attests, good reputation can be destroyed by one incident. Grim warns students about it in his first class. Some analysts will analyze any writing, even one of uncertain pedigree. Failing to get consent for the analysis can be poor ethics. Aside from that, analyzing it can be foolish, like driving through an uncertain depth of water during a downpour. Luck can be a lady tonight, or a bitch. On occasion someone will thrust in their hand a sparse writing and ask, "What does this person's writing show?" This is a variation on the problem Grim's group seminar faces. Sometimes "this person" will be the one handing them the paper. As with Grim's group, a red-flag will be no signature. If the analyst fails to inquire further and blabs away with critical remarks, he can humiliate the writer and embarrass himself.

I ask, "What about confronting the one giving them the paper. Can't you ask who really wrote it?"

Grim says, "That may be futile. They still may lie about the true author."

Analysts who want to develop and promote their craft properly, Grim emphasizes, limit these petty plagues by confirming the right author. That is not always easy. When it wasn't done in front of the analyst the possibilities are limitless. A common one is that the person giving it wrote it but won't concede he did.

A quick and easy escape for the analyst is to dust off his ethics and decline this trouble-making analysis. Let the giver be shocked that analysts actually possess ethics. That's the refreshing price the analyst will pay to upset the giver for missing a free and prompt analysis. A Graphoanalyst has another way out. Put the blame elsewhere. Tell them the ethics code of his overseer IGAS doesn't permit an analysis without the consent of the writer of the sample. Most times either avenue should be sufficient.

———

Now and then a person clever of mind and mischievous of aim will test a busy analyst. The ploy is to submit writing under one name and soon after submit another sample of the same person's writing under another name. The actual content differs to prevent the analyst from recognizing the writing. Presumably the individual wants to see if the analyses are consistent. They're seeking a sly but informed judgment of the analyst's skills. Grim won't summarily deplore this tactic.

"Now and then it might be a good way to keep the analyst on his toes," he confesses. "I would rather the writer be more candid in his goal. If the analyst knows he's already done the person's writing, he can refer to the prior analysis to prepare the new one."

The writer might choose to wait until he is in some traumatic or life-changing situation when he can sit down and write his sample. Or right after if it passes. The analyst can dissect the writing for evidence of change in the writer. To focus the analysis, he might have the writer compose the very same words as the first sample (without it in front of him, of course, so he can't copy the strokes. This is the blind sample) Since each sample will have the same letters, any changes in the strokes will be striking.

At times someone will approach Grim and remark something like this: "I guess my writing is useless for analyzing. It's not really my writing. I copied the style from a friend I admired in school. You can't use it. Right?" Not true, says Grim. Our first model in school, The Palmer Method, we copied although we were ordered to do it. That's why it's hard to analyze the writing of children who have just learned it. When we left second grade and ultimately flopped into the chaise longue of our own methods, we had to erect them from somewhere. We didn't capture them from the sky above. We copied them as well. On the surface we chose lines that felt good to us and looked good to us. Our hands and our eyes are the two ways we perceive handwriting. The style impressed us either consciously or non-consciously. We had seen the design somewhere. Maybe you selected a few parts from hither and other parts from yonder. Maybe a curled ending stroke from a celebrity's style in a magazine and a flamboyant t-bar from a yearbook writing. As to the non-conscious, you never really thought about it; you just did it, as Nike told you. You didn't create a fresh genre of writing. Grim maximizes, "There are no new ideas—only old ideas re-arranged." This is the routine we all use in selecting strokes for our way of writing.

"Does this mean what you chose is not you?" I ask.

"No, it really is you," Grim responds. "We believe in the theory that, no matter what sources you choose, you make your strokes from your uniqueness as a person. And the reason is deeper than you realize. It wasn't random or happenstance or indirectly linked to just anything. You selected your strokes because it satisfied your mind's regular act of echoing your personality."

This all sounds familiar. It's handwriting analysts' theory become their gospel. They are sure that brain impulses order your hand to maneuver your pen to follow your personal features. It may have been conscious. Or maybe deeply non-conscious. Most of the time it was probably non-conscious. Although we may be consciously aware of our strokes' fountain, they probably flooded the paper without our studied awareness of their look. We just started writing and the result on paper is actually us despite our borrowing it from others. Which ones we borrow are choices. We took only the ones our personalities sent us for take-out. They had us order only attributes that gratified them through the strokes we made.

"We are at our personality's mercy," Grim stresses. When we write, it is "boss of the household. They'll be no changes around here without its okay. If you attempt to roam with your strokes, be prepared for a smack upside your sorry hand."

If you can't accept this explanation of the brain's mastery over our hand, do this. Grab a friend and tell them you are giving them some new strokes for their handwriting. They may think, okay, not a problem. Let me have them. Make them really different from how your friend usually writes. When they start drawing them, they'll feel uncomfortable, tense, irritated. When you think about it, having to do it should be no big deal. Just concentrate and it's a snap. It turns out *not* to be. Grim says this inherent tug surfaces when he analyzes someone whose customary mode is printing. Usually he will ask the person to add something in cursive. That gives a rounder picture of their character. Some haven't written in cursive for years. They react as if being asked to take their first skydive from a plane. When you are forced to adopt unfamiliar strokes, you squirm. It will upset you and stress you. You will labor although it may be more subtle than anything. You won't succeed without your psyche balking.

Grim says he scuffles for a fitting analogy to convey our personality's hold over our pen marks. He tries what happened in junior high science class. When you tried putting those two magnets together at the same magnetic poles, they didn't want it to happen. Neither does your personality when you reform your writing. It is a ceaseless battle. Your personality has tensile strength like spiders with their amazing webs or that bamboo in Asia. Each is hearty but flexible. Although your personality is dynamic and changeable, when challenged it resists bending. If it ultimately accepts those new shapes, invisibly it kicks and silently it screams all the while. Will it be that good little boy mommy likes and stop this nonsense once and for all? No, unless your personality itself changes to line up with the new strokes. Good luck with that.

Chapter 20

Printing

The Inscrutable Epidemic Sweeping the Nation

Can it be analyzed?   Why do we print?
Are printers different people?

A few years ago Grim was invited by his local high school to take part in a Career Day. He had a booth set up for handwriting analysis as a career. A cloudburst of students and teachers approached him with a downpour of questions about the subject. Grim seized the occasion to survey them about their writing habits. Several wrote samples for him. He had heard how common printing is among young people. One more time these local students bolster it. It still shocked him. Since then the grapevine informs him that printing cracks and rumbles like a lawless forest fire among young people and a surprising number of adults. Everyone including analysts wonders why printing is so widespread today. Actually a more frequent question trumps that issue—Can printing be analyzed? What does it mean when someone prints? Possibly the answer to the first issue lies in the other two.

Printing is the first method of writing we learn in early grade school. With the regression in school penmanship, it's the only kind some children learn. Printing is the first writing we see when our parents read to us and when we learn to read since all our books use printed type faces. When you get a head start at home before learning penmanship in school, your mom will start you with printing. It may end there too. Where it prospers most is with the young. Many schools teach it and don't progress to script. A portion teach script, then install printing later anyway. Now a major phenomenon, printing must be confronted.

"Some analysts speak more glibly about the meaning of printing than they should," Grim asserts. If there is much scientific study for it, he hasn't seen it or even read or heard about it. He believes it should be studied in depth to determine the preliminary issues it raises. Do we apply a different set of principles for evaluating it? Do printers have different personalities from scripters?

Now we have many questions to resolve. Before those issues are reached, an important first query. What is printing anyway? That is not as simple as you might think. Some would define it as merely script writing without connections between the letters. Others would say you need another element. The upper loops (those strokes rise above the small letter area in the b, h, k, l, and f) and the lower loops (those that descend from the small letters in the f, g, j, p, q, y and z) must both be absent. These letters can have upstrokes or downstrokes, usually simple vertical lines. They just can't have loops, which are oval or rounded enclosures that cross themselves near the baseline. This view wants printing to emulate typewriter or, more recently, word processor letters, aka manuscript writing. Some describe printing as simply manuscript writing. Aside from those basic types, others describe printing as, at minimum, disconnected letters with other notable features: all capital letters; letters that otherwise look like script except the connections between letters are missing; letters that have upper and lower loops but are otherwise disconnected; and some more. A few theorize that each of these features would have to be evaluated separately.

Next, Why is the person printing in the first place? Grim thinks you should ask when they started printing. Was anything eventful occurring, like a soul besieged by crisis? Some of us, particularly in recent decades, began with print style and never got to script. What's interesting for Grim is the individual who learned printing, then graduated to script (most of us took these steps, especially the oldsters), and finally reverted to printing in adulthood. Most of these lapses into printing occur in the teen-age years. If you ask many of these people, they will tell you they reverted to printing because they wanted to make their writing clearer. Or their writing was sloppy and unreadable and they wanted to make it readable, or less sloppy. These motives may be similar. In contrast, several others switched to printing when their script style was legible. If they felt no compulsion to escape, why did they do it?

What really mystifies Grim is why adults shift to printing after loyalty to script from second grade. He questions their true motive. Unwittingly those adults utter only surface reasons, he believes. The real reasons lie deeper, in that great inscrutable area everyone seems to know about but can't tell you what or where it is. It's called the unconscious. You will have to hold that heavy thought for the moment. Grim is convinced the real basis for switching comes from rhythm, a principle from IGAS doctrines. "Unreadable" writing is not part of the analyst's lingo. Or at least it shouldn't be, as Grim emphasizes in his classes. In the early moments of the first class he startles them with this: An analyst doesn't care if a piece of writing is readable, legible or even sloppy or messy, scribble, scrawl, or chicken scratch. Those words should be banished from the analyst's glossary. Whether it can be read or not, any writing can be analyzed. The reason is that it has strokes, which are only parts of letters. Each stroke has meaning as a separate trait. Every letter has at least a few strokes in it. Some have potentially many, such as the letter t. Where the t-bar is placed will give you a series of them. How it is made—thick, thin, long, short, upswinging, downswinging, and like that, can yield many more. Whether the letter itself is clear doesn't matter. The stroke discloses the meaning for a trait. This is all Graphoanalysis, which believes that strokes matter and global factors matter, and that they should unite to matter even more in erecting a complicated structure called personality. This is Grim's school of thought and he's sticking to it. He is joined by other graphologists who will look at the branches of those trees (letters) in arriving at personality. Gestaltists claim to approach the writing only part way till they reach the outline of the writing found in the large portions (groves of trees), which Graphoanalysts call global factors (appearing in every tree like the trunk's thickness and the tree's size). Gestaltists say the strokes inside letters should be shunned, except they pollute their certainty with exceptions. Some of those are so numerous that the Lilliputians have taken over Gulliver. Forgive me my trespasses for what is really a review from earlier chapters. Emphasis sometimes must trump repetition.

By themselves most letters do not mean anything. However, analysts impart special meaning to certain letters. For example, capital letters tell how the writer values himself in society. Where looped the letters t and d can reveal sensitivity. The buckle portion of a k can show defiance. Whether the letters appear readable or not, strokes have a familiar enough look that they can be unraveled for trait meanings. That's all the analyst needs. Strokes can stray as if in a drunken stupor. It doesn't matter. Analysts still learn to recognize them and give them a trait slot. When he teaches or gives a speech, Grim points out that scribble is only for practicing pre-schoolers and prosperous businessmen. He scrawls a word on the board, thrashing about so it can't be read. He asks if anyone can read it and of course no one can. He wants to show that since illegible letters have strokes, no matter how bizarre, an analyst can glean traits from those strokes. Letters may contain many strokes and thus many traits. Even letters otherwise unreadable may contain several identifiable strokes. Your girlfriend may care if your gushy letter to her is readable. If she has taken it to an analyst to see if she should marry you, that analyst won't care if it is readable. As long as it has strokes, he can analyze it. For your sake you will hope it is readable. An unreadable love letter may be grounds for her questioning your affections and commitment. Illegibility alone does not prevent an analyst from doing his work.

The analyst may be dismayed to see these wild strokes but for other reasons. To understand why is also to understand why someone whose script was unreadable lapsed into printing. Besides the presence of strokes, another reason unreadable writing can be analyzed is the "rhythm" of its strokes. This is one of those global factors analysts deem important in any analysis. It's also one of those eye-glazing concepts that Grim despises but readily admits is crucial to understand his topic. Global factors are not strokes as such but aspects of writing that are found in all strokes. As global factors these larger aspects also disclose key data about the writer's personality. Since they are broad they give very important information. To locate them the analyst steps back and gazes at the whole writing. This is that gestalt concept in handwriting "rearing its splendid head," as Grim expresses it. He elaborates by asking the class to visualize the entire writing sample (hopefully at least a page or two) as a vast forest. (You may have heard this before. This time maybe it will sink in.) The trees are the individual letters.

Paragraphs are groves of trees and a sentence is a tree line. Within each letter are the strokes, which are branches of those trees. Global factors go beyond letters and exist everywhere in the writing. Every tree is composed of them. They are how all the trees are constructed. Thus, every letter has them but you pull back from the writing to distinguish them and consider them in their totality. Graphoanalysis recognizes five of them: the slant, thickness, size, rhythm and the fifth is the three zones as one.

Rhythm is the feng shui of writing strokes. An analyst deploys it to gauge the writing's harmony, balance, uncluttered paths (between strokes), and unseeable natural forces (like your personality's tug on your strokes). As an aspect of writing, the rhythm of the writing can be observed from afar. In fact it is more discernible from a distance. You want to see the forest for the trees. It also illuminates personality even though the letters themselves may be illegible. How this happens is that an analyst surveys the writing as a whole and sees that it might be "unreadable." What makes it so in his wilderness laboratory is that the stroke patterns appear irregular. As a concept, rhythm is what you probably thought it was. Before you entered this laboratory. As a layperson you saw rhythmic writing as maybe harmonious, or that it flows well, or looks pleasing to the eye. Analysts technify these into weighing the strokes' constancy through their repetition. What you saw innocently is what they are describing. Everywhere strokes recur in patterns the analyst appraises their regularity. For example, do the strokes reach the baseline consistently? If they do, they are regular. Is the spacing between letters roughly equal? If so, they are regular. Is the height of the small letters similar? If yes, they are regular. Anyplace common strokes repeat, the analyst determines patterns. If most of these patterns are consistently regular, the whole writing has good rhythm. Some people can't make their common strokes repeat, leaving irregular patterns. A layman views frenzied strokes as sloppy handwriting. Not the analyst. He only cares if the strokes are regular or not. If they are erratic, he calls the writing disrhythmic, or more simply, poor or chaotic rhythm. It will look illegible but that is what the layman sees. Remember when your mom said you wet the bed? (Okay, it was your brother.) Your doctor wasn't seeing weewee on the sheets. He was diagnosing enuresis and looking for why you (he) did it. In like manner the analyst seeks to know how regular the strokes are and what they mean for your personality.

A prime step in any analysis is gauging the strokes' regularity. If they make regular patterns, this is solid or regular rhythm, the mode we were all taught. You could say that we were actually taught to write from an ideal template. Most of us write with sturdy, reliable writing that is fairly consistent. This shows a durable, steady individual succeeding against life's storms and droughts. Where the writing deviates from good rhythm and its yardstick regularity, the analyst sees signs of trouble in the personality. Writing that wanders here and there away from the school model constitutes chaotic or poor rhythm. It may in fact be unreadable. This chaotic writer suffers an emotional pounding. They've been trying to drive through life but can't help knocking over those orange cones. Inconsistent writing betrays uncertainty, doubt, and confusion. The writer cannot function effectively as an individual. Writers with very poor rhythm can't conform their strokes to the standard of steadiness. The consequence to their personality is behavior that wavers and stumbles in the face of society's demands. Rhythm can be drawn on a continuum to tableau its forms. In the middle is good rhythm, which is regular but not overly so. This is the ultimate—graceful and harmonic. On the opposite end from the chaotic rhythm is writing where the strokes are *too* regular. It looks painfully rigid. The person strains to obey society's dictates. The writing looks stiff and mechanical, void of any agility and appeal. It seems to reflect just what its writer is—uptight.

Armed with disrhythm, analysts can take any printed sample and make sense of it. Even if all the letters and strokes are disrhythmic, the writing can be explored for personal qualities. In general the more disrhythmic the writing, the fewer positive qualities you are likely to find. The next step is to consider the upstrokes and downstrokes in the printing. Most printing will have many downstrokes to the baseline but few upstrokes. Analysts see the downstrokes as what they call "control" strokes and upstrokes as "release" strokes With many downstrokes the writer seeks control of the sloppiness (poor rhythm) to make it readable (good rhythm). What is going on underneath is that the person is trying to re-gain control of his stormy emotions, as he can't conquer them. The upset remains and it won't go away. Hence, the person reverting to print mode is trying to escape his riotous feelings and calm his life. He couldn't manage them and printing creates the firewall from their threat to his well-being. Where they go is for psychology to assess. This is where your concept of the unconscious part of our minds may be as good as anyone else's.

Ever ready with his gaudy images, Grim suggests, "Maybe the printer's feelings are consigned to a third floor closet in his mind. They bang on the door pleading to be released, only to renew their torment. For now they will have to stay to allow their possessor, the writer, to survive as an individual."

A plausible enough description for what happens to the emotions. For many, it would win by default. Thoughtful theorizing it is for Grim to embrace this view. He is not alone; many other analysts join him in it. These analysts are filling the vacuum of thinking and research on the issue. That is only where it is at the moment—a serious and conceivable guess for why an adult will take up printing after living with script since Palmer or his cronies in grade school. Until it is scientifically tested, it will remain an enticing opinion.

Grim has approached some of these printers and asked about their lives when they switched from script to printing. They confess to lives then of emotional disorder. A common one was the teen-ager whose parents were splitting up when they suddenly felt the impuse to print. He is careful to appraise the teen-age stories. They could easily have dredged up anything that sent them reeling in those fitful years. Everyone will have a story. Of course not everyone changed from script to printing at the time.

Some people have lived with script writing that was *satisfactory* when they decided to go to printing. Presumably since the rhythm was fine, there was no emotional upset to confront and avoid. A few analysts suggest their motive was escape from allowing others to know them. They create another version of that mask Grim uses to distinguish our public and private selves.

Grim doubts this theory and instead suggests, "If the writing is conventional, the writer himself should be sound emotionally and adjusting fine to his existence. If you are seeking a person who feels no need to hide his true self, the traditional style is your model. Therefore, no mask is necessary."

He is willing to say, however, these people may have felt the ball peen hammer of psychic turbulence jarring their stolid lives. When you're not used to upset, the effect can be agonizing. When bad things happen to good people, they suffer mightily because they don't expect it and aren't used to it. Printing may be their acceptable drug since smothering emotions is legal and often *de rigueur* for conformists. When they became comfortable in printing style, they decided why discard what's keeping them on keel. Temporary relief becomes permanent addiction through their cheap, new drug of choice called printed writing. *De rigueur mortis* sets in.

Analysts can shuttlecock back and forth over those preferring print instead of script. This sidesteps the more basic issue. If printing's role is a finger in the dike against intolerable feelings, can it still be analyzed for personality? Grim's tentative view is that it can be, with lawyerly qualifications. A typical script style has upper loops, which rise above the small letters that inhabit what is called the mundane or middle zone. Script also has lower loops, which descend from the baseline on which rest the small letters. Those lower loops are the site of the lower zone. In first grade we were given a sheet of blue or red lines on that tablet of thick, cheap paper engrained with wood chips. Since no baselines exist on unlined paper, an analyst must create one as an invisible line. The baseline is The Olde Homestead for strokes. It is the place from which all strokes begin and to which all strokes return. Or at least they are supposed to when you draw strokes with the school model. Some analysts prefer the baseball icon and call it home base or more properly home plate. With printing, analysts are often faced with upper and lower extenders, strokes that rise above the small letters (like l) or go below the baseline (like y). In printing they are customarily drawn without loops. They may consist of single lines going up or down, as your word processor gives you with manuscript style on the monitor screen. Loops are very important for analysts. They can be made several different ways. Each interval of degrees mark a separate personality trait. Without loops the analysis slips in its accuracy. By the same token, a few people who print still make loops in their extenders. The writing looks almost like printscript, which is just cursive style minus the clotheslines between the letters. It is an odd style and obviously rare.

Printing lacks some other important pieces that hamper a good analysis. Analysts pursue an important area called the middle or mundane zone containing circle-form letters. As a naked circle letter, the small letter o is the prototype. Others with wrappings are a, b, c, d, g, p, and q. Although they can have other strokes, they all have a circle of some kind resting on the baseline confined to the mundane area. Printers typically draw them without any lead-in stroke and without any lead-out stroke. In script, as we connect strokes between letters, our personal styles often invade the circles with added strokes. The lead-out stroke may even leave the circle from within it. These encroachments form loops and other strokes inside the circle. Writers draw these strokes in several ways. Each way they do reveals a different trait of personality. Those inside strokes are important to analysts as they tell how honestly we convey personal information. Some analysts see them as key indicators of honesty. A natural conclusion but that over-simplifies their role, which is still important as a tile in the integrity mosaic. Since printing separates letters from each other, thereby omitting lead-in and lead-out strokes, analysts cannot easily determine that honesty. With upper and lower extenders missing loops, and circle letters missing potential inside strokes, this printing method won't be complete, and accuracy fades.

Some people choose to print with all capital letters. This seems to remove the three zones, global factors crucial in any analysis. The lower zone is below the baseline, the middle zone is from the baseline to the top of the small letters. The upper zone is from the top of the small letters up. Using all capitals suggests the writer has one big middle zone covering the space of all three zones, although presumably the bottom of a capital letter sits on the baseline. That is one of the problems. Besides missing several strokes, like upper and lower extenders, the analyst doesn't know what zones are being made. Some analysts suggest capital letters create all three zones, supposedly because the letters are usually large. We can't tell without lined paper. However, people who use all caps use lined paper once in a while just like the rest of us. Usually it's an official form of some kind. Most of the time the writer will keep all the caps on or above the line. Since no one has resolved how many zones printed capitals make, printing with all capitals seriously impairs a good analysis.

Grim also wants to know if printing is the writer's normal style. If you print your grocery list or fill out a form, and your normal style is script, a good analysis is not impossible. Just unlikely. It depends on the script style. Some people's script is close to their printing. Simply remove the letters' linking strokes and notice the similarity. Some analysts request two samples: the printing style they profess is their customary one and a script style, however they make it. When Grim requests script from people who normally print, many agonize over it. If they haven't written script in years, some will balk, as if they were asked to roller skate after not skating since childhood. Usually the writer can handle it. However, when the person is struggling with the script and it happens to look disrhythmic, Grim's theory on people turning to printing seems to bear out. He may be forcing them to re-visit a time in their life when events bumper-carred them about and the guy running the funhouse ride left to get a burger. To relieve the emotional anguish displayed in their restless script style, they exchanged it for the balm of printing. Have they been enjoying that comfort ever since? If yes, this seems to prove his absorbing theory.

Another scenario exists—those who have always printed and continue to do so. Grim hasn't resolved his view on this. This is a large group and it's mostly young people. A few never learned script, so they say. Others blame teachers for demanding they print since it presumably made their writing legible. When Grim requests they also provide a script sample, some of them pause as if dazed. Like the previous group, they strain to begin the switch. This astounds Grim. Despite their short experience with it, script should be a snap. Their confused face suggests you've asked them to draw an item on paper they've never seen. Most of them ease through it. Typically the writing looks like their usual printing style with the letters connected.

Grim has seen little compelling authority on what is at work with printing and printers. One expert he respects has had years of experience with schoolchildren and penmanship. She also happens to be a veteran Graphoanalyst. Eileen Page, with a Masters in Graphoanalysis, lives in Newton, Massachusetts, and has been an elementary school educator for several decades. A member of the IGAS Advisory Board, she has authored somber, cerebral volumes on handwriting and handwriting analysis. She has observed youngsters writing back to when writing was cool and blackboards were black. Hardly any students printed then, except for their first penmanship. She laments the status of handwriting. Printing has flooded our society with a new ice age of stale, chilly, forbidding glaciers of writing. She believes this stems from several factors: a more diverse and mobile culture, extended families, de-personalizing technology, simplified lives, increasing speed and needed clarity in rushed lives, and longed-for detachment from our unsettled emotions in this squirming society. She judges that most individuals who print began, not because it is faster, but because it is more comfortable for them. Sounds familiar to Grim. Are they different from scripters? Yes. Printers tend to handle their lives differently. They are logical, structured, orderly types. Their choice is to avoid dealing with their tempestuous feelings. They harness them by printing's profusion of downstrokes (control strokes) and dearth of upstrokes (release strokes).

Printing and script are only step-brothers. Their parentage and their varied look seem so far apart. Grim wonders if printing should be analyzed from an independent set of rules. For those who print as their usual style, does that alone suggest their personalities differ? As mentioned, his colleague Eileen Page suggests they do. Grim is unaware of any studies on this alluring point. His anecdotal experience varies. In fact, script style evolved in the early Middle Ages from, would you believe, printing? Before script, monks had labored over hand-printed manuscripts in all capital letters. Time and tedium told them that connecting the letters enabled them to write faster. Thus the birth of small letters. They transformed the capital letters into smaller letters to accommodate lead-in and lead-out strokes. By taking less time than capitals, small letters also were proficient in other ways. We know these stylistic changes as part of our modern forms. Little has changed except for sleeker, plainer fancy script models that we learn in school. Writing progressed further when its slant leaned more to the right, thus smoothing the run of the strokes. Amazingly, those elegant manuscript flourishes of patient monks endured to the twentieth century. They were edgetrimmed by education pressuring for a more efficient and less stressful method on students' hands and wrists. As we know, Palmer and the others retained some curlicues, mostly in the capitals. Modern models deleted these wasteful and inefficient strokes.

Despite the fall of flourishes, many writers still fashion them. This, however, does more than make Grim glare at them for their foolishness. It goads him to offer it as another exhibit for graphology's acceptance. When people go back to Medieval writing with their printing, their needless flourishes, their all-capitals styles, their upright slant and other reactionary ways of writing, these are all signals of personality wailing for recognition.

"Why else would a person persist in these modes of writing?" Grim demands to know. "Because they just prefer the romantic appeal of these wasteful elements?

"Why not." I say. "Many people seem to prefer these decorations. Then you have the people who like doing Calligraphy."

"Not likely. It must relate to the inner power of their personalities. Probably a romantic nature is already part of these personalities. This would justify them doing it."

Grim has surveyed numerous people who print as their customary way of writing. He's stunned how many report they print because they can write faster than with script. We know many changed to printing when they had to take notes in school. We all know note-taking requires speed to keep up with the instructor. Grim wants to set these people straight. He thinks those Medieval monks would chant their approval. Printers misunderstand what happens when they print in lieu of connecting letters with script. Since printed letters have space between them from their separation, printing is not faster than script. It won't do the job you are hoping for. You wonder what in the monastery was the hurry, but those monks started connecting printed letters to speed up their manuscripts. Script will be faster since the pen does not have to jerk up and down with the constant pen lifts. Barely noticeable is each lift—that's probably why most people are fooled by them—they keep the letters from linking up. Script will flow more smoothly and inevitably quicker by letting it run on without breaks. Aside from the connections, where printers misperceive the speed of printing is in the stroke designs. Many writers solder extra strokes on their letters, intending to clarify their identity. Instead, they are merely adorning their letters. The fewer strokes in a letter, the quicker the sample is done. As all they do is decorate a letter, serifs, those tiny outcroppings from letters, aren't needed either. However, they apparently have a purpose. Type font and reading experts will tell you letters with gentle serifs are easier on the eyes.

Many printers should spend their time purging their needless strokes, especially in their capital letters, says Grim. Those letters are notorious for lavish waste. Since they are large and often separated from their other letters, people are impelled to creative heights. Actually any embellishment could be considered wasteful. If you call any stroke not essential to a letter an embellishment, it is. Then you ask what is essential and you could say any stroke that makes the letter readable as that letter and no more.

Against the benefits of efficiency, Grim thinks capital letters too long have desolated the countryside like a damsel-seeking dragon. Capitals are made larger than the rest of the letters and are placed at the beginning of a formal word and each sentence. In signatures they are the lead-off letter of each name. In these positions they are often scribed with no tie to the rest of the word. This isolation frees these beasts for spreading their immense wings, whipping their savage tails, and flame-throwing their breaths wherever they choose. And that is the problem. The flourishes flaunted may be dazzling but they are never frugal. If you want your writing to be efficient all around, reduce or delete them.

A major step for efficiency, says Grim, is to choose a proper general style of writing. Take that Italics lettering seen on your old typewriters or your current word processors. *It looks like this.* As manuscript-Italic style, its svelte letters look slimmer and more natural. It is the health nut of letter fonts. It contains virtually no wasted strokes, such as embellishments and other creative but unneeded lines. Yes, some serifs appear but jut out only far enough to soothe the eyes. It contains only proficient strokes, those that can be made swiftly, with no drop-off in readability. The pen will shweeeen across the page. Like a New York taxi, Italics rarely tangos, sambas or brakes before reaching its stop. Hence, if students want better notes in class, adopt Italics style. It is faster, simpler, more efficient and just as readable. Disconnecting the letters won't improve their writing. It will take longer than Italics to write the same words. In addition, after a lengthy read our eyes stress and fatigue. With Italics' smooth economy, your eyes stay fresh longer.

Chapter 21

Doctors' Writing

Why Can't They Write like You and Me?

Phillip Crozer was selected as one of the student speakers for his high school Commencement. At this majestic event he was at the lectern and began reading from handwritten notes. As he glanced up and down between his notes and the audience he wavered, then spoke. "I owe almost all my success to my mother." He paused again, then read haltingly from his text. "By her marvelous example as a single parent, she was my shining star giving me the ability to do great things." Another pause. The emotion of his tribute seemed to overcome him. He stared down at his paper. A few seconds later he looked up, leaned forward, and focused his eyes into the audience. Suddenly he barked, "Mom, you really have to do something about your handwriting!"

No, Mom is not a doctor. But we know that might have been among your thoughts as you howled at this amusing incident. Doctors and their handwriting have become a LettermanLeno national joke. Except 1.5 million people each year don't think it's funny. According to the Institute of Medicine, that's how many people are harmed by drug errors each year. Many involve doctors and their handwriting. Some of these people die.

As part of their duties doctors have to give orders and directions, some at serious risk to our lives. They must also prescribe medicine, treatment, and other items for their patients. They must keep records of their treatments and other activities. Since lives are at stake they must record and retain data on what they have done and what they order or request be done. When doctors order prescriptions or request other important steps that might affect us, these steps must be in writing. Traditionally, most of these have been in their handwriting.

With the threat of serious consequences, including death, readability is critical. All of this has become a major issue today because the public perceives that the handwriting of doctors is messy, illegible, unreadable, awful, poor, bad, horrible, sloppy. At least that is the list of adjectives the public grumbles to analysts, mostly in jest. If you recorded the questions analysts hear most, the Doctor Question is near the top. It is—Why do doctors have such (your adjective here) handwriting?

Grim claims to have given this much thought. His opinion will surprise most people—

"They don't."

"What do you mean?" I ask.

"They don't have bad handwriting," he states matter-of-factly.

We demand he elaborate. He says he is glad to but asks for patience again as you gave him for printing. Yes, you did. Radical opinions take time to explain.

He has his own way of framing the issue. "As a group, doctors don't write any worse than the rest of us." He continues: "If you took a hundred doctors out of the hospital and a hundred people off the street, the doctors' writing wouldn't be any more unreadable or illegible or messy."

"Whose would be better?"

"Frankly, the doctors' would probably be better than the rest of us. That's really what the question relates to."

Grim interjects that he knows of at least two studies on the issue. Both appeared in the British Medical Journal. Each went their separate ways. The one that said there is no significant difference used people to determine legibility. The one that said doctors have worse writing used a computer. The one with no difference confined its comparisons of doctors' writing to other health care professionals. Interestingly, they also compared their writing to health care executives and found their writing worse than doctors. The doctors'-worse study had them write their signature, the alphabet letters and the numbers in a blank.

"That methodology, for starters, is flawed. I don't think much of either study."

"Why is that?"

"They don't really understand how graphology and personality affect handwriting's look. They don't seem to know also the multiple factors that can affect handwriting's legibility. Any of those could skew an evaluation of legibility."

To grasp Grim's view you must know the conditions he applies to it. Fairness to doctors demands it, he insists. Ideally handwriting should be evaluated only under optimum conditions. This is whether or not it involves doctors' handwriting. Although desirable, he understands it isn't always possible. If the two groups (doctors versus you and me) are writing under what he calls the most favorable conditions, namely, relaxed but spontaneous pen movement (see the chapter The Analysis), the two groups should be similar. Add to the desirable conditions a solid table to write on, a comfortable chair to sit on, and a decent pen to maneuver.

First consider what's implied if we say doctors *do* write worse than we do. Handwriting reveals personality and, as rhythm told you, illegibility is the quality that makes the two groups differ. As an aspect of the writing, rhythm is crucial, and unless you realize this, you won't understand Grim's reasoning. He attempted to clarify illegible writing and rhythm in the chapter on printing. Based on what illegibility means, to declare doctors' writing different means they are different as persons. As stated in the section on printing and rhythm, illegible writing equates to disrhythmic writing, which suggests emotions and actions creating havoc in the writer's life. His feelings are in distress. His insecurities come out to play and they don't play well with others. He wants to act properly but his insecurities rule his conduct. As a result he can't conform to what society says is normal behavior. Doctors are not being described here as a group or else our illnesses wouldn't get better. With so many emotional issues doctors wouldn't get their work done or done competently. Most of doctors' writing should be classified as fairly conventional. Of course some doctors have their problems with coping. In the main, however, doctors do comply with society's standards, for which we are thankful. Thus why the writing is illegible at all comes from elsewhere.

What Grim calls the "fallacy" about doctors and their handwriting comes from several factors that only doctors experience. As we all need some medical treatment at times, doctors occupy our lives by necessity. Therefore, we all seem to have had personal episodes involving doctors, or ones we learned from the media, where doctors wrote unreadable orders or prescriptions. We share in the shock of someone dying because they overdosed from a misread prescription or a similar situation. In medicine, errors are magnified because people can die. If you misread yours spouse's grocery list and bring home rye bread instead of raisin bread, presumably no one dies. (Other consequences in your household may occur, which we try to avoid imagining.) All of us sense the impact because none of us can avoid doctors. It can happen to any of us. Although none of the people you know may have died or suffered adverse reactions from any misreading, we have all seen poor doctor's writing. At least we think we have. Next time we or someone we care about could be a victim. Thus we could swear that doctors write worse than we do because we have heard the horror stories. The potential for harm to us is immediate. Every so often we see another example of jumbled writing, a sudden death and the stark headlines. Someone dies from a drug overdose because the pharmacy couldn't understand the doctor's writing on the prescription. Or whoever administered the drug misread the order. We also witness for ourselves and our family and friends instances where a doctor's action or statement was questionable. They are not perfect in their professional lives and in their personal conduct. All of this has an emotional impact on us. But the actual episodes of doctor error are much smaller than our emotions realize.

Grim grants that doctors write illegibly on many occasions. That doesn't mean it is their usual custom. Often doctors are in a hurry or they are distracted or busy or stressed or just impatient or under pressure or tired or even indifferent. Maybe they wrote as they were standing up or walking down the hall or in some other unusual position. The writing will suffer. When you have paper in your lap or somewhere away from a table or any solid surface, writing quality suffers. If you look at the writing on a golfer's scorecard, it often looks weak and grouchy. If they're not keeping it on the spot meant for it on a motor cart, on the hard surface in the middle of the steering wheel, most golfers will fill in the scores while holding it in their free hand and maybe walking from a green to the next tee. Or the card is held in the scorekeeper's lap while sitting on a bench.

A small portion of doctors will write to make it readable for only those familiar with their writing. They may believe it makes the writing harder to forge. Doctors with heads grown too big for their bill–less blue caps may do it to command respect. Others may do it from arrogance, broadcasting that they...are...a...DOCTOR and you... are...NOT.

Some want it to look like no others because it is a doctor's. Grim sees these as similar to what other haughty men of science often do with their words in a diagnosis or description in their discipline. They keep their special knowledge to themselves by hiding it in dense phrasing occupied by abstruse words (like abstruse). They believe they belong to a class with power, prestige and privilege. They want only those anointed to understand them. The rest can kneel and be impressed. Therefore, readable but obscure words can have the same purpose as unreadable writing. That's one reason for doctors to do it. Whichever explanation for writing applies to your doctor, each alone can provoke illegibility. Since these are common circumstances with doctors, they provide the excuse, if not the justification, for doctors appearing to have worse writing than their patients. Among those patients would be you and me. Also, these reasons will occur often, certainly more than they should. Consequently, if you measure doctors' handwriting by *actual* frequency, doctors have bad handwriting. But then, with all the moofafala in our lives, so do we. Physician, heal thy handwriting. Patient, get real with *thy* handwriting.

The causes may be many; the need has been grave; the problem chronic; the years long. The medical community has recognized it and tried to correct it. Finally in the 1990's the American Medical Association directed a message to doctors to resolve it. Instead of telling them to reform their handwriting, it read: "Doctors' poor handwriting is legendary. Nearly one in fifteen patients in the hospital in American suffers an adverse reaction directly related to errors by doctors or other hospital staff members. Excluding surgery, script errors are the leading cause of such problems." It is recommended that "doctors with poor handwriting, either print, type, or use a computer."

The impetus for action was a steady surge of incidents, lawsuits, and headlines. Malpractice claims have forced the leaders in medicine into remedies. Hospitals, insurance companies, litigating attorneys and the legislature have all worked toward an acceptable remedy. The medical establishment had conceded the problem exists and they took partial stabs at it. Serious attempts to resolve the handwriting problem were reached only in the 1990's. Varied solutions had been tried. Getting doctors to print rather than using script was an early one. Handwriting classes have been run and not just for doctors. They still occur but few doctors have taken the time from their rounds at the hospital and at the country club. With computers becoming more agile, more doctors are either trying them or being compelled to use them.

Finally, better writing is gaining traction in the hospitals and the doctors's offices. Readability is better. However, the doctors' own writing may not be the source of the improvement. Medicine has initiated an organization called the Institute for Safe Medical Practices. Dr. Michael Cohen, its President, who is from Huntingdon Valley near Philadelphia, has taken on the problem as part of his organization's mandate. In an interview with National Public Radio on July 2, 2003, he offered some useful and revealing perspective on it. He thinks one useful step is to put the purpose of the medication on the prescription or order. If the reader can see why it is being used, identity is sharpened.

Attacking the problem at its core, penmanship classes for physicians have been tried for several years. Dr. Cohen believes they are mostly ineffective, without explaining why he or his cohorts think so. For their own reasons, analysts would concur with that. Trying to alter handwriting is turning the plane into a fierce headwind. How anyone writes occurs for a reason, which can't easily be changed merely by new passages for their strokes. (Remember disrhythm and what it means?) Whether Doctor Cohen is familiar with handwriting analysis and the force of personality is unknown. Nevertheless, doctors who should be taking the handwriting classes are lying on the Caribbean beaches and flying down those Colorado slopes in droves. Computers have been a solution for a small but growing segment. Some hospitals and their insurance companies have dragged doctors to the monitor and rubbed their up-raised noses in it. A key step forward has been the computer programs that include a hand-held device. However, it is costly and most doctors still resist. Nevertheless, it seems the wave of the future.

Achieving legible writing is only part of the objective. Too many drugs are similar in spelling or sound. The doctor can mis-identify them and a pharmacist or nurse can misread them. Dr. Cohen acknowledges the AMA Journal has published a finding that one-third of doctors have unreadable writing. Grim would like to know the basis for the results. For instance, where did they get the samples? Working doctors or a special session with them? Cohen adds that some nurses and pharmacists could improve their writing too. Cohen is not aware of any study that has shown doctors writing to be more unreadable than other kinds of people. However, that statement came after the British Medical Journal studies and Grim wonders why he didn't mention them.

"I was glad to hear Cohen's comments. He appears to be frank and realistic about the issues. But he should have a better understanding about graphology and personality."

Why does Dr. Cohen think doctors have such bad writing? He doesn't really know, although he cites a few elements that match Grim's. Despite Cohen's head being in the right position about this issue, Grim thinks his head is in a dark place on vital handwriting principles. Based on only the interview, Cohen has no professed knowledge of either handwriting's source in our minds or its relation to personality.

"With no working acquaintance of that," Grim emphasizes, "Cohen and his medical group can't fully appreciate the doctors' problem. Therefore, until they do, they are unable to adequately resolve them."

"Well, what is your solution?"

"If they are not going to submit to a full understanding of graphology, then they should use technology devices that eliminate handwriting from recording and conveying medical information. Learning and applying our subject would become unnecessary."

Whatever Doctor Cohen and Grim think about handwriting classes for doctors, some outsiders want to help. In Portland, Oregon, two handwriting specialists, Inga Dubay and Barbara Getty have been doing something about it every January 23rd since 1989. That bleak, wintry day happens to be John Hancock's birthday. Arguably his signature is the most famous in American history. The timing has been intentional. Legend says he wanted to insure King George III wouldn't miss it on the Declaration of Independence. It *was* the largest signature and readable too. Mission accomplished for this one "traitor" to the Crown. If we had lost he may have been hanged the highest and with two loops around his neck. To foster good handwriting, the ladies have been holding free handwriting classes for three hours on a Saturday morning. They have successfully filled hundreds of seats at their sessions. They teach Italics writing. "Excellent choice of handwriting method," concurs Grim. Anyone who writes is invited to attend and improve their writing. Doctors and lawyers come, as do others, some ear-pinched there by determined secretaries and spouses. Many hope to lose their pathetic scrawls.

Dubay and Getty aim to help people overcome their deficient writing along with encouraging good penmanship. In particular, they want to disabuse adults of using that Palmer Method so many learned in grade school. They consider its "loopy style tormenting to both hand and eye." They read about the business losses from poor handwriting and the human losses from doctor's scribbles. The Postal Service reports that millions of letters go to its dead-letter office each year. Your stamps work to reduce that pile. It has developed devices to read addresses. In 1980 when the ladies published their first book, *Italic Handwriting Series,* it couldn't be delivered because the printer's handwriting was illegible. (Should a form of the word "irony" appear in this last sentence. You decide.) After their 1991 book *Write Now* was recommended in the *American Medical Association News,* they began workshops at local hospitals. From there the movement for medical people expanded to the current target of all those caring about their readers' eyesight and conveying their written messages.

These spirited ladies endorse Italics style as it has fewer pen lifts and more natural wrist movements. Besides, it just flows better than the rigid strokes of grade school. By having them use its graceful serifs, they get participants to bond the letters into cursive writing. They snub loops as you might find on top of an h or l. They take too long and encourage more clutter. If someone practices tracing the letters for ten weeks, they should see a "complete transformation," says DuBay.

Grim wonders what graphology's role is for this. The ladies believe that your peculiar lines before your "transformation" should return eventually. Really? That sounds like, I do believe, correct me if I'm wrong, Matilda, graphology.

"That's because those ladies know whereof they speak," Grim tweet-tweets and almost swoons. "They know that personality is a force that will not be denied."

What about the future, ladies? Will the classes be cancelled for lack of need from handwriting's death? Getty doesn't fear for that dire prospect. In spite of computers and other technology, "There's a Latin quote '*Littera scripta manet,*' which translates 'The written letter remains,'" she affirms.

Chapter 22

Writing on the Edge

One person–several styles, the moody writer, lefthanders, perfectionist writing, and the weird guy who writes with a ruler

A man walks into a psychologist's office and says to him, "You know, sometimes I really get down and depressed. Other times I get really upbeat and ecstatic. I don't suppose you can figure out what I've got since I'm different from moment to moment."

The psychologist replies, "I can diagnose what you've got but it will be double."

The man winces. "All of a sudden I don't feel so good." "You have depression, the psychologist fires at him. That will be $150.00 for this visit."

"Oh, thanks. I am so glad I saved the extra fee. I feel great about things now. I think I'll leave."

"You are also a man with…—oh, never mind," starts the psychologist, catching himself.

And the man hustled out.

Once in a while someone will approach Grim and tell him they don't know how he can analyze their writing. One day they write a certain way and the next day another. Occasionally someone else says their writing varies by the moment. They write one style in their initial sentences, a different style later in the same piece. Sometimes a writer rocks back and forth between script and printing styles. Can any sense be made out of these variations? Is it possible to analyze these contrasting styles? Grim has heard all of them and they are more pervasive than you might think.

"Each situation is different," he starts. "Some people say they write differently all the time. They say they have no consistent style but rather a mixture of them. None of us is a mechanical robot. By degrees we fluctuate every time we write, some wildly, more barely."

"This statement sounds vapid," I complain. "That hardly enlightens. Aren't human beings really shifting and fickle no matter how predictable they seem? Isn't this fact a basic problem for analysts?"

"True, we are dynamic beings," he responds. "Some alterations are so slight and are not important to an analyst. If many occur, they can be meaningful. With massive changes the meaning multiplies. Graphoanalysts examine over a hundred strokes in any full-fledged analysis. Many of these really don't change much. Most of the time changes aren't significant enough to matter," he explains.

Where changes occur in what he terms "major" strokes, he can still evaluate the sample. Writing that tos and fros presents a challenge, Grim admits. It is not that common. When it occurs the writer's strokes will often undulate in the same sentence or paragraph. Incredibly some will jump from script to printing and back again. Grim calls this "Jekyll and Hyde" writing. The meaning for analysts is akin to what psychologists face when a person is sometimes really down and depressed and other times really up and jubilant. That is the well-known disorder older folks knew as Manic-Depressive, now called Bi-Polar. It's the same principle. A person whose strokes are inconsistent, erratic, heaving from here to there—Grim sees that as a person struggling with their identity. They don't know who they are, and don't know where they are headed. Uncertainty and doubt about abilities, confusion about their role in society, and indecisiveness in their important decisions all batter them. Unstable, they can't act in a disciplined, steady manner. When people run into this individual, they don't know if they'll get a greeting or a grating. Even friends experience it. The cursed individual is anguished as they don't fathom their actions from minute to minute. They can't control how they behave, and they don't know why. As for the unchanged strokes, they still confer their customary meanings, although now the analyst must assess them in light of the contrasting strokes. Analysts know they will be important because they are both unusual and powerful. Even when laymen see the strokes they must sense that something odd occurs. At the very least, phenomena like this confirm again that handwriting is not accidental. Since the handwriting seems to mirror this unique behavior, analysts view this trait-stroke association as another exhibit in their informal evidence to convince the authorities.

———

Generally we all have personal foundations composed of rows and rows of sunken pilings commonly known as traits. Any changes usually occur only after long duration or a short but wrenching experience. As a rule, the changes are minor. We are vibrant beings, not automatons. Superficial changes can and do happen all the time. Most changes occur when we face sudden disturbances, such as the loss of a family member, firing from a job or an assault from a mugger. They can be life-changing and force us to adjust our behavior. We may look at ourselves and others differently.

Occasionally changes in our personalities occur while other traits may conceal them. They will not be evident to others. In handwriting all the traits blaze on its high-definition screen clear and pure. Let's say you have deep resentment, a personality element divulged in your handwriting. In contrast, you may have strong traits of pride, dignity, conservatism and tact. These also appear in the writing. They can drag the resentment into a protective casserole, hiding it from your friends and family. It might surface only when trouble dominates your life. Grim warns his students and fellow analysts to be wary of resentment as a trait. It can be very powerful, as it festers from the time the person was deeply imposed upon. As it refuses to disappear, the memory of bitterness lingers and rankles everywhere he goes. Although the writing reveals the resentment, it won't disclose its source. How the stroke is made will tell how painful the resentment is. An extra thick stroke shows deep resentment. Believe it or not, the analyst can determine roughly how long it has lingered. The resentment stroke is a stiff lead-in line that begins at or below the baseline. It can start below that baseline and the farther below it does, the longer the resentment has persisted. Although the analyst can't tell the specific cause, usually the writer knows since it possesses him. Grim finds the resentment stroke often in writing samples. When he sees it in a signature, it is more potent and usually more certain.

A few times Grim has given a talk to his church Confirmation group about resentment's kinship to his religion. With Christianity as the context, Grim portrayed resentment as the inability to forgive. As Christianity stresses heavenly forgiveness, he thought it appropriate to discuss it and relate it to handwriting analysis. Many people retain anger about incidents occurring years ago. Actually they can't exorcise it as it strangles them emotionally. Usually the memory is a major incident, like losing your daughter in a car accident by a drunk driver. Your anger toward the driver may embed itself and harden. Sometimes the bitterness is long and deep, like your parents forcing you to work as a child in their business and losing so many youthful experiences. Recently a movement has arisen where people still bitter over horrific events in their lives are counseled to put them behind them. It's for their own physical and mental health. Many people won't let go because they will feel guilty for not carrying the memory long enough or strong enough. This especially occurs when the grief is over a family member. Society demands they feel sad for so long as their personal duty. Regrettably, if they don't get on with their lives, the emotional cancer can devastate if not destroy them. As Carrie Fisher (Star Wars actress Princess Leia and author) described it: "Resentment is like drinking poison and waiting for the other person to die." The movement wants you to forgive the other person but not to forget the situation. That's simply because they can't. If you've lost a family member or other dear person, it's natural that you won't anyway.

After the Jekyll and Hyde personality and the Bi-Polar personality we visit their kin, the moody personality. Burdened by emotions that are volatile and unpredictable, his feelings gyrate. We all have our ups and downs. This person has them too often and too extreme. He is predisposed to act improperly no matter what the occasion. He can be glum and sullen; he can be lively and cheerful. We never know from moment to moment. He is not really someone whose behavior changes all the time. All this changeability is an integral part of his being. He is just considered a changeable personality. That is who he is. Thus we can classify and describe this portion of his personality. Since changeability is part of him, we interpret his strokes just as we do for the Jekyll and

Hyde and Bi-Polar. Although he won't sit still for his handwriting picture, that doesn't mean we can't analyze his writing. From time to time he is difficult to figure. But that is his nature. His type has been with us throughout history, including centuries before Christ. It was in China. Referring only to the slant of this type's writing, Confucius once said, "Beware of the man whose writing sways like a reed in the wind." Consider this statement's significance. He spoke in Ancient China on the other side of the world and around 500 BC. This soothsayer from 2,500 years ago demonstrates that handwriting is universal and timeless. Today at the copy machine we would say the same thing about that guy in the third partition down whose writing meanders like the Mississippi. Analysts have writing signs to distinguish this personality type. As with the other two types, the writing will show it despite their irregular actions. His behavior is somewhat like the Bi-Polar personality but much less extreme. A bounty of people occupy this group but they don't usually behave so erratically to need treatment.

—---

We all know lefthanded people. How many exist vary with your abacus. People are lefthanded for some actions but not others. Estimates differ but seem to cluster around 13% of the population. We are also unclear why people are left- or righthanded. Most people seem to do it as a natural act from birth. Others seem to begin from life circumstances. If you surveyed your community, virtually everyone would guess that lefthanders have personalities no different from righthanders. When they each grab a pen and begin writing, a different story erupts. In the way they hold the pen and the paper, lefties swerve visibly. They turn their paper, crook their hands, and hold the pen—all oddly. They top off their oddness by using their left hands to hold the pen. To righthanders, that may be the oddest act of all. Righthanders wonder why they write as they do.

According to handwriting analysis, everyone's writing should yield the same information about them. Lefthanders seem to upset beliefs about handwriting and personality. Should we apply other rules for lefties? In view of items like slant, isn't that mandatory? As we all know, lefties slant their letters more backward than righties. Since slant is a major aspect of handwriting analysis, must we re-draft its rules for lefties? Only a small percentage of righties backslant, probably about 5%. We are all sure that more lefties backslant their writing. Some of us would even say that lefties who backslant predominate. For lefties do we ditch slant and its meaning for handwriting analysis? After all, slant is fundamental as a global factor identifying the writer's emotional structure. Fortunately IGAS has studied this disparity in slanting between righties and lefties to see the impact on its slanting principles. It approached the issue by first testing the common view that lefties backslant much more than righties. A survey of handwriting samples of leftiess and righties revealed that lefties *do not* backslant any more than righties. Scratch one large myth. The results were also a relief to handwriting analysis by further confirming its rules about slant of the letters. It could continue to assert that they are universal and apply to lefties and righties alike. For the record, backslanted writing demonstrates a person who keeps their feelings inside and needs to know they are secure before letting people into their intimate selves. They are not easy to get to know. They hold back their feelings. If lefties did backslant their writing more than righties, this would mean they have different personalities from righties. It would mean lefties are more emotionally withdrawn than righties. As far as we know they are not and there is no reason they should be. Experts seem to believe that the source of lefthandedness is a horde of factors with genetics the leading reason. No expert would cite the person's emotional reserve as a cause or an effect of being lefthanded.

This notion about lefties' backslant has been a Methusala myth. But we still want to know why many lefties hold their pens, wrist, hands, and the paper goopiloptic ways. The most credible reason is to move left to right across their bodies. Righties don't need to. Still, and here is the hard part to grasp, none of that actually affects their lines drawn on the paper. Thus the beliefs about lefties, as with doctors' messy handwriting, are urban and rural folktales. They are really no different from you and me. The surveys did discover one modest difference. When lefties crossed their t's, they drew them right-to-left more than righties. Otherwise, no difference in the strokes. This research on the backslant of writing adds convincing weight to the handwriting-reveals-personality argument.

Actually, writing with a backslant is not that easy. Try it, you righthanders. When you do it, your pen drags. Imagine spending all your time writing class notes or a long letter with backslanted strokes. In due course it will exhaust you. No good reason exists for wanting to do it. Do you wish to jog in your galoshes? Forward slant enables the writer to glide across the page. The person who backslants as their customary way of writing must be doing it for a psychological reason, one related to their personality. Why else would they do it?

The thought is sobering. Personality impels us to slant our letters backward, straight up, or forward based on our emotional make-up. No one would consciously, intentionally backslant that severely. Their personality made them do it. It's pitiful for those who must do it since it is awkward and wasteful. As presented before, graphology says those who do it can't help it. Actually they can, but they don't try. Backslanters know it's not right. When you suggest changing to an upright or slightly forward slant, most will just nod. When you ask them why they backslant so steeply, they are puzzled. They've never known what analysts can readily tell them. When they hear it they still don't believe it and don't seem to get it. People with emotions frozen inside spend much time worrying about themselves without knowing themselves. They can't easily convey their plight to others as they fear being hurt. No one backslants on purpose. But simply altering their writing to a forward slant is hurling themselves against the rampart of their barricaded feelings. IGAS founder Milton Bunker emphasized that important aspects of a person's make-up like slanting were not good for subjects to change in an instant. Since it reflects the person's emotional footing, it shouldn't be attempted lightly. It is too deep in their constitution merely to change from the stroke of a pen.

Palmer's name was the Google of penmanship in twentieth century America. If personality exhibits itself through handwriting, any penmanship instructor should be aware of its force. What did Palmer know about handwriting analysis? According to Bunker, Palmer claimed he allowed the student's uniqueness to assert itself.

Bunker quoted Palmer in his Graduate Course: "It has been proved through at least two generations, that the copybook kills individuality and makes freedom of movement impossible."

But Palmer declared that *his* copybook method was different. "Pupils practicing from these lessons acquire the general style of the copies, but at the same time there is left to them the possibility of developing their own individuality."

In evaluating Palmer, Bunker wrote: "Palmer recognized that this individuality tended to assert itself in writing; it had to be given consideration in penmanship instruction."

Whether this also meant he believed this uniqueness reflected the writer's personality is another question. Bunker doesn't say. If Palmer wouldn't concede that we write differently after a while because of our personality, he may be splitting nibs.

"What else is individuality when you come down to it?" Grim poses. "As we used to say in the law, that may be a distinction without a difference."

Palmer created an iconic way of writing that schoolchildren have followed for so many years. It's lost its prominence in the last several decades. In many scattered schools students still learn it. Since handwriting reflects personality, say analysts, Grim wonders if the model writing style and personality relate in meaning. If students use the Palmer Method, does this suggest that its strokes comprise the writing of the ideal person? Is this Palmer personality one we all should aspire to? How should the writing of a perfect person look?

Like Gregorian monks, analysts drone that handwriting follows personality. If Palmer meant for children to learn his system, was he telling them you will be the model citizen if you do?

"Palmer's intent was directed at comfortable, readable and efficient writing. It was not to foster the ideal personality the writing might demonstrate," says Grim.

His system unwittingly created the ideal person as a by-product. The actual traits revealed in Palmer's strokes are fairly close to this model, but not perfect. In fact, every penmanship model reflected some of the qualities of the person whose style it fosters. Milton Bunker studied all the master penmen and their individual styles.

He remarked, "Skill [in penmanship] does not lessen the individuality of the writing...[D]espite highly developed artificial styles of handwriting the writer cannot conceal his character and personality traits from an experienced Graphoanalyst."

With society's norms as the ideal, Palmer gave us an exalted peak to climb. If anything it might have injected some graphotherapy into rowdy children, guiding their handwriting strokes into those of a dutiful child. Whether that changed them into a better person at the same time is the question. (Graphotherapy is discussed in depth in the chapter on Other Uses for graphology)

Graphoanalysis lists a trait known as "perfectionism." It is a general style in which the handwriting looks precise, faultless, and perhaps beyond human creation. Actually it is more than a trait or maybe not even a trait. It seems more like those global factors that Grim promotes. Since it appears in every stroke of the writing and you can't find it in any specific stroke, you could say it is one. Although Graphoanalysis presents it as a trait, Grim thinks it should be designated as a global factor. He sees it as a sub-heading under rhythm, which is one of the global factors IGAS identifies. It is a type of rhythm. Using his continuum, rhythm runs from chaotic, mediocre, solid, perfect, and finally rigid. Palmer's style is under the perfect category. Grim finds that non-IGAS books in graphology do discuss perfectionist-style writing. It doesn't have to appear as they learned in school. No one can recall each of the school model strokes anyway. Hither and yon people exist who seem to strive for that supreme status. Grim calls it the "Martha Stewart" personality. Many people are flawed but they have a mindset to excellence, if not perfection. That is Stewart. Grim saw her handwriting on TV as she wrote a note to an apprentice she had just dismissed from her reality show. The writing is not copybook nor close to perfect. Nevertheless, he finds it exemplary and showing someone steady and disciplined with some adaptability. She has said she is a perfectionist but confesses she is not perfect.

When you ask a perfectionist what their faults are, they hesitate. You can see the discomfort. The most dominant aspect of their lives is image, looking good to the rest of us, and at all costs. They agonize over what people think of them. Eventually they may confess to a few weaknesses to remove the impression they're a snob. Probably the qualities they cite won't topple them from their exquisite pedestal because their admitted flaws will be minor. Can we stipulate that no perfect individual exists and we know that without having met everyone in the world? I knew you would agree. Nevertheless, Grim says some writers as people place themselves far along on that continuum toward the ideal. As a consequence they have a writing style close to the Palmer model. Most are women. It won't necessarily resemble Palmer or any of the other school models. It will be nearly faultless in its own way.

Since a human being drew it the actual writing will not be perfect. Some peoples' writings are what Grim calls "virtually perfect." They come darn close. But they have their own style, sometimes not even resembling Palmer at all. They do it by adding starch to their lines. Hence, it appears rigid. Analysts call this "persona" writing from the Greek word for mask.

Life is a boombangian ordeal for these writers. Their constant striving is an strenuous burden as they seek to emulate society's ultimate person. Just as their writing is done with extreme care, they won't tolerate sloppiness or mediocrity around them. Second best is not good enough. Like a tattoo artist inking a Hell's Angel, they are cautious and meticulous while under constant stress. They're obsessed with trivia and their discipline can upset themselves and others. Many have a papier-mâché-over-clay foundation. They are afraid of being exposed as not that great. They need perpetual approval and if it doesn't come, they may crumble into a pitiable heap. To keep their pretense alive they construct an especially airtight, armor-plated, hatch-battened suit of personality. Think of Nixon in his suits but try not to think of his imperfections. They fear someone will penetrate it or remove it before their eternal Halloween is over. Living under unrelenting pressure to do everything just right, they hope to prolong it. If they can, no one can criticize them and everyone will praise them. Their image may be undeserved but it will be intact.

Since Palmer is not the only school of penmanship, how would the others compare in reflecting the ideal personality? The older ones pale because they are festooned with an unctuous display of lines desperately seeking attention. Grim sees Italics, which is gaining ground, as a superb benchmark. Those who use it differ from Palmer by being less concerned how they look, more interested in proficiency, more practical in their efforts, smarter and more agile of mind, yet more rushed in life's race to Nevernevergonnagetthere Land.

Besides our lawyer and doctor and repairmen we surely don't want anyone or expect anyone to aspire to perfection. What should the writing of the virtually-but-not-perfect individual resemble if we won't require them to be Martha Stewart? To descend from perfectionism to a more realistic, less uptight person, the writing would need a makeover.

"I would like to see some waviness in the baseline and other strokes. This shows they can be flexible to consider alternatives to deal with life. They wouldn't be so focused on image" Grim offers.

Perfectionists tend to be inflexible as they fear it lowers their status. When they try to change and aren't as terrific as they hope people think they are, they are disgraced. They cannot allow that to happen. With the softening of the writing strokes the individual morphs into someone real and tolerable. Thus the writing will show some variations, such as in the baseline, which will gently rise up and down rather than appear ruthlessly straight. The baseline can't vary too much as that will segway into instability and confusion. Once the baseline approaches the roller coaster look the meaning has evolved from resilience to erratic behavior. The person changes too much, which translates to unpredictability and insecurity. This person has lost the rudder and the keel of their ship and the rambling wind and the harrying currents of life are his fate. Therefore, for the perfectionist writing to overcome its fatal perfectness, the writing must thaw its rigidity. The same goes for whoever wants to escape from the perfectionist prison. Let go of your obsessive behavior. Whichever comes first, the corrective actions or the altered writing, the one will affect the other. Analysts believing in graphotherapy affirm that one will lead to the other, regardless of the order.

A troubling offshoot of this lofty writing is the person who must use a ruler to make straight baselines under their letters. Yes, there are still people who do this. Everyone seems to know one of them. Thankfully few practice this grotesque ritual. Why do they do it?

"I see it as someone compensating for an irrational fear that they can't hold themselves together emotionally."

"Why do they feel that way?" I want to know.

"That's a question for a psychoanalyst. And they do need one."

"Well, what do you think is at work.?"

"I think they're trying to quell an obsession that their inner unrest will spiral into chaos. In a strange way this further demonstrates handwriting's link to personality," Grim adds.

When you consider it, why should a person care if their baseline isn't perfect (except perfectionists)? Why do they need to use a ruler to ensure it? Can't they persevere without this radical step? Grim thinks they do it from submission to their sorry personality.

"Otherwise, they shouldn't want to do it because it is just *weird.*"

Chapter 23

Handwriting and the Law

Confessing without your Miranda Rights
and Hidden in Plain Sight,
Invasion of Privacy, Defamation,
and Copyright Infringement

Y ou're a wonderful young lady and you think you've found your
soul mate. You have dated him for some time now and you await
an engagement ring. Instead you get a Dear John letter calling off the
relationship. When you seek a reason why, he stonewalls. Eventually
you learn through the grapevine he had obtained an analysis of your
handwriting. You were jilted by your handwriting?

You're a great guy who applied for a superb job with a solid
company. You think you're well-qualified and that the employment
interview went well. You get a letter from human resources informing
you someone else was hired. You ask why and they tell you it was
close but the other guy did better in the handwriting analysis. The
difference was your *handwriting?*

Two upset people. In the old days they sulked for a time. The
lady went out and found a new love of her life. The guy put it behind
him and applied elsewhere for a job. Today you aren't sulking. You're
door-slamming torked and you won't stand for it. What's up with
this handwriting nonsense? You have rights, you are sure. Who's that
lawyer you met at the barbecue who said he "knocks down walls for
the little man?"

Handwriting is the source of detailed knowledge about people.
The average person doesn't know how it can rummage through your

private life and assemble features about you as a person. It's special as it is you telling the world if you want the lowdown on me just check my writing. I'll tell you anything you want to know and I won't realize I just did it. Your handwriting is your confession without being read those Miranda rights. It doesn't use rubber hoses, hot lights, or promises of a light sentence. You don't get hounded with hours of questions from a bat-breath, spitting, vein-straining accuser in a cold, grubby room. You get no call to an attorney either. When you realize its power you figure you must have legal rights. You lost the guy of your dreams or the job of a lifetime. But do you? Did they need your okay before analyzing your writing? Was it an invasion of your privacy? Is there some law that protects a job applicant against this? Or a spurned lover?

The first legal issue people raise and want to know most about is this: Does an analysis invade your privacy? By its nature handwriting analysis invades your privacy or else it wouldn't be doing its job. Is it then a *legal* invasion of your privacy? Can it be stopped or damages awarded if it has occurred? Are there other laws it violates? If you want to know, sit still for the explaining. You will learn what the law says and why it does. Relax, you might even find it digestible and tasty.

The right to privacy is a topic that broad_____-------__ jumped into the limelight in the whirlwind 1960's. It's even bigger today. With geometric advances in technology, our private lives have become more available to everyone, not just nosy strangers. Both the public and the government have seized these advances to obtain information on people who may not want others to have it. Tiny cameras, bugs, the internet, the press, TV cameras, cell phones, and video cameras bring you muchclosertoothers. Although handwriting analysis has been around a long time, it hasn't changed in recent times. It does what it's always done. It takes your personal method of writing and probes it for meaning about your virtues and your failings. It's no more meddling than it was before. With the evolution in privacy rights and technology, has our ardor for privacy caught up to handwriting analysis? Should it be curtailed for its exceptional ability to expose your intimate self? Should an analyst be required to get your consent before an analysis is done?

The right to privacy is really the right to be left
alone.

If you scan the U.S. Constitution for its express language, you won't find it. In the 1960's the U.S. Supreme Court went through the august document with a fine-tooth comb and said it found it. Not *in* the document. It was in the sky. They did it by borrowing a spelling bee word from astronomy called "penumbra." When an eclipse of the sun occurs, on its circumference the sun emits a ghostly glow around the moon, which otherwise hides the sun. The bright ring it creates is a "penumbra." Meanwhile back on earth, the Supreme Court reeeeeeaached its decision by finding the right of privacy on the "penumbra" of a few Constitutional provisions. They meant "edges" but were just using creative symbolism to say the right of privacy is implied, not expressed in the Constitution. One edge they cited is in the Fourth Amendment, which says that you and I should be secure in our persons, papers and effects. The government is not permitted to get into items you own or possess, such as your home or car, or even your body, like taking a blood sample, unless it has some reasonable basis. If we won't let them, it can ask a judge, who then issues a search warrant, which we know gets the authorities in.

The U.S. Supreme Court didn't create privacy as a right. It had been around as the common law in most states and is enshrined in ten of their constitutions. Generally the rules the various states have followed are slightly different from the U.S. Supreme Court's but may amount to the same idea. They will say that a person's privacy has been invaded where the activity was "highly offensive to a reasonable person." Or that it amounts to an "unreasonable intrusion upon the person's seclusion." In general everyone seems to get the same idea of what needs protecting. But let's stipulate that it's a broad concept in need of narrowing.

Since the Supreme Court's decision in the 1960's, privacy as a concept has become less nebulous only from evolving facts of the cases kneading it into shapelier mush. These involved activities where individuals believed the government should bud out, such as using contraceptives, having abortions (as in *Roe vs. Wade*), and home-schooling children. These are all unique but socially explosive personal issues. In 1973 the Supreme Court finally got a case about handwriting. In *United States vs. Mara* it held handwriting in general wasn't entitled to privacy protection.

The Court declared that "Handwriting, like speech, is repeatedly shown to the public and there is no more expectation of privacy in the physical characteristics of a person's script than there is in the tone of his voice."

The case was not about handwriting analysis. The issue was whether someone can be forced to turn over a sample of their writing to be examined, as in a forgery case. The principle is still there. Handwriting is everywhere and often seen by the public. It has no special niche that should keep it from the prying government or private parties. In a later decision the Court equated handwriting to our bodies themselves, calling it "an identifying physical characteristic." In the 1977 decision in *U.S. vs. Euge*, a taxpayer was ordered by the IRS to produce exemplars of his signature to verify it on documents. In *U.S. v Rosinsky* a federal appeals court sharpened its statements on the privacy invasion of handwriting.. The Court declared that "What someone's handwriting looks like is considered public information—similar to, for example, how someone dresses or their body language, and the psychological analysis that can be extracted from the information is not considered an invasion of privacy."

This is only a general principle. Handwriting analysts glibly cite cases like this to assert they can seize anyone's writing and dive into it. They are misguided. A court can say someone's privacy is wrongly invaded in appropriate circumstances. To understand how privacy can affect the analysis of our handwriting, some more background should help. We have other privacy issues in our daily affairs that bother us more than our handwriting. These will lead us to concerns about our handwriting being analyzed. One issue is the government and private persons intruding on our personal space. As a rule courts have been reluctant to prevent your fellow citizens from looking into what you do as a person. We live in a civil society where we often have close contact with each other. We may not always want people near us but that is customary in our social communities. The law is liberal in allowing what you might consider unwanted actions in public areas. If you're strolling on the sidewalk or shopping in a store, someone can take your picture. You may be thinking of those sneaky, outtamyface paparazzi. Too bad but it's a public area. The logic is—If you choose to be there, other people can see you and be next to you or walk by. The camera is merely the extension of its holder, recording what the holder or anyone else sees with their eyes. The view of you is just permanent on a photo or videotape. If you're also talking to a friend, the sound of your voice can be recorded too. It's a public area where strangers can hear you as you pass them on the public sidewalk. Same principle. The recorder just picks up what that stranger could hear anyway. Either way, you know the other person doesn't have to cock his ear to hear you or put the recorder close to record you. Now that you are armed with this, you can record that blabbing cell phone user. Maybe that will get him to press the hang-up icon and keep walking.

This right to meddle in people's public lives has limits. Courts limit both government and private intruders by the rule of what is reasonable to the person who feels the intrusion. That could be you or me. If you are on the sidewalk and speak softly to a friend to avoid others from hearing, that should be protected. Whispering is even better. Hence, if you intended to keep your conversation private, a court will say someone else can't record it. If they already did record it, a court would stop its being used. However, if you're committing a crime, you wouldn't be protected.

Your indoor communications should also be safe from invasion. Telephone conversations are notable for enjoying privacy. We have laws that prevent recording of a telephone conversation without both speakers' consent. When you talk to someone on the phone you don't expect a third person to hear your conversation. Years ago we had party lines where it was unavoidable. That private call today between you and your friend or relative has an exception. If there is a reasonable basis for it, such as possible criminal activity, the police can get a warrant from a judge to listen in on a phone conversation. They can record it as well. This is the familiar act you hear about when some crime probe is in the news. It's called wiretapping. They don't need the beeper and they don't need to tell you or your friend they're listening. But they need the warrant in hand, which of course you won't see. That is legal. If the criminal would see it first, he wouldn't even make the call.

Outside of speaking, similar standards of what's reasonable protect your privacy. You must do your part to expect your activity to remain private. If you leave a stash of cocaine on your dining room table easily seen from outside your window, a neighbor could snap a picture of it and hand it to the police. You can blame yourself for leaving the curtains open. The drugs were in plain view. Same with the marijuana pipe you left in the console when the cop looked in your car window from outside. No search warrants needed and it can be seized and used to convict you of a crime.

When we venture into other areas outside our everyday world, the privacy rules are still based on reasonableness. What does the individual reasonably expect to be kept from eavesdroppers? If you provide your doctor with a list of your prior illnesses and drugs you take, you expect he will keep the writing from anyone else. He may show the list to his staff and other people who need to know the information for your proper treatment. That is okay. You want him to do that as best for your care. But not to others.

With handwriting, the privacy rules are similar. We send cards and letters, complete forms and applications, write notes to others, show our writing to friends and acquaintances, fill out and sign checks and other items. In view of our writing's typical wide display, the Supreme Court says looking at writings is not invading your privacy. Just as we speak loud enough that we know strangers can hear us, so we usually expect our writing to be seen by others. That's the general rule. However, if you pen an amorous note to your girlfriend, you don't intend anyone else to see it, least of all the government (okay, maybe her father). If you didn't consent and your girlfriend took your letter to an analyst, you may have a privacy claim against your girlfriend and the analyst. Although not a large civil claim, it should be enough to get you into court. If you consent to her showing it to an analyst to determine if she should marry you, don't get upset when you get a bad review from the analyst. Your consent gave up any privacy right you had.

Privacy is generally about the substance of the thing invaded, not the form. When you talk on the phone you don't care so much about your voice being heard. It's the words you say in your conversation. With the love letter it's the same idea. You want the amorous words hidden from view, not your writing style. *How* you write isn't important to intruders. It's *what* you write. Your concern is the content of the message. You reasonably expected only a certain person would see it. You could say the form of the writing is also being invaded because it is seen. But what is the harm? Why does that need to be protected? It doesn't. Nevertheless, since the form creates the substance and it's impossible to excise the strokes (the form) from the actual words written (the substance), a court will protect the entire writing from the public.

What is special about privacy and handwriting analysis is that your writing style *is* the substance. Your attorney might argue that point in your privacy claim involving a handwriting analysis. He will contend the strokes reveal information about you that you want to keep private. The analyst will reply that's silly. Everyone knows your handwriting. Moreover, if handwriting analysis is not a scientific technique for gleaning personality, the analyst gets nothing from your writing. So what's the beef? What harm do you suffer if you believe handwriting analysis is junk in the first place? You must believe in handwriting analysis to complain of an analysis of your writing. If the court is willing to accept your reasoning, shouldn't you have to show that handwriting analysis is scientifically valid? What a turnaround. That is the basis anyway. It does appear to give handwriting analysis a worthy defense, but it amounts to arguing that graphology is unworthy as a technique. Apparently this argument has never come up in court. By the same token, no analyst has ever been shown to violate a writer's privacy, as an applicant for a job or otherwise.

Time and again an analyst will be presented a sample of writing of a celebrity or other famous person and asked to analyze it. Consent is typically unattainable unless you have a way to get through to Harrison Ford or Barry Bonds or the late Jackie Kennedy. Privacy principles still apply but are an unlikely problem for analysts. Well-known individuals are unlikely to refuse analysis of their signatures or other writing. Most take time *giving* their signatures through autographs. Probably few have even thought about it. If they did, how many would be upset? Their agents and PR people would encourage releasing one more juicy item about them to the adoring, lick-chopping public. The opposite is more likely—they will madly-gladly distribute reams of their autographs and other writings. In this instance they don't reasonably expect to keep their writing hidden from the public. However, if a renowned person had sent or delivered a contract letter to his agent or attorney or sent a love letter to his girlfriend, and somehow it was stolen or misdirected to the public, that writing would be treated differently. Yes, he may be a public figure but as his private document, he did not intend to share it. A court would prevent its analysis. If the analysis has already been done without consent, the court would allow some damages. It would be an invasion of the famous person's privacy. Yes, they have those rights too. The damages in most of these cases wouldn't be very large. They would relate to the impact on the hurt feelings of the celebrity mostly from the embarrassing details of the writing's content.

Where sweat drips more over privacy is in business. A prospective employee wants and needs a job. Losing out on it can ripple with effects. Money, jobs, family lives, and status are at stake. Hence, a privacy suit over handwriting analysis is more likely in employee hiring. If a person applies for a job and must fill out an application, he normally expects only those who need to see it will see it. The hiring manager, his potential boss, and the head of the company are expected to see it. Today another person that should be added to the list is a handwriting analyst. More companies are doing that. Applicants are not used to that, however. Therefore, to protect the analyst and the employer, the company should tell the applicant his writing will be analyzed by an outside individual. That is certainly the fair and ethical step to take. The employer should supplement that by asking the applicant to sign a consent and waiver to an analysis of his handwriting. This is a legal agreement whereby the applicant acknowledges that he willingly agrees to the analysis. As a result he gives up any right to sue the employer from a handwriting analysis and a resulting written report. The agreement should also include a clause that he can refuse an analysis and still be considered for the job. Another provision will help the employer. It should acknowledge that the analysis is one and only one factor the business will consider in its hiring decision. This will lower the probability the analyst and the employer will be sued for invasion of privacy and other actions attorneys might try to initiate. If the applicant declines to sign the consent, the company can do the analysis without it. The applicant is on notice it will be analyzed. When they hand over the sample they know it will be reviewed by an analyst.

"I had no choice," the applicant will insist. "I would have been rejected on the spot."

"That's not so," the employer will respond. "We're just being prudent. Besides, you can go elsewhere for a job.

"What about my right to work *here*."

"You don't have that right. Ask your own attorney."

No court has ruled on whether an applicant's privacy was invaded where his writing was analyzed without his consent. As with any agreement, courts can deny a consent is valid where duress, coercion, or undue influence is shown. However, where the company told the refusing applicant they can reject his application because of his refusal to sign a consent, no court has held against the employer. Apparently in that context an applicant doesn't have a right to a job.

To lessen the chance of court action, the company can take other steps. Confine the writing and the analysis to only the select group in the company that needs to see them. It's what people expect when they hand over their sample. Although it may be wearing suspenders along with a belt, asking *every* applicant for a sample may aid the employer. This deflects the separate issue of discrimination, although it doesn't eliminate it completely. (More on this shortly) Everyone knows it's typical to fill out an application form. Consent for that form is unnecessary. But where the employer asks for a separate writing and says it will be analyzed, getting the consent is wise.

Handwriting analysts prepare written reports to outline the personality and character of the individual. They are supposed to tell the truth as revealed in the writing strokes. Since we all doomp around loaded with imperfections, some adverse remarks will appear in these reports. The traits found and the conclusions drawn can blemish the person analyzed. An upset applicant may want to run to an attorney, especially where they were rejected for a good job. They might try asserting traditional legal remedies, along with claims under recent federal laws. Where the person claims his reputation was smeared, he might sue for traditional defamation. His attorney will tell him to sue at least the company and the analyst, maybe the HR officer too. For oral statements it's slander. For written ones it's libel, which includes anything recorded, like audio and videotapes and computer disks. And handwriting analysis reports.

Thus far no cases have held against the analyst or the employer. The threat of a legal claim remains because of two combustible items. We used to be a nation of laws. We are now a nation of law suits brought by lawyers in suits, depositing another layer of soot on our civil skyscraper. Libel in handwriting is an unfamiliar outback. Whether a claim would succeed probably will revolve around the set of facts.

If the employer is sued, to pacify a judge partial to the applicant, the employer should follow some guidelines. Initially it should use only an analyst certified by one of the renowned organizations. When preparing reports, analysts should skip the most harmful comments, especially about the applicant's reputation qualities. Omit discussing their flawed integrity. Mention the individual and sensitive items like integrity only in direct oral conversations with senior people in the organization. Convey the findings in private to the immediate manager. Limit the eyes on the report, and write on it "Personal and Confidential" and keep it that way. If it's being faxed, call the faxee to confine it to one person.

The analyst wants to make clear he is not interfering in the applicant's effort to form a relationship with the employer. The analyst is providing an objective report of his findings on the applicant's features for a specific position. He does not recommend or suggest hiring the person. That is for the company to decide. All these steps are bricks in the wall of business protection. They won't ensure no lawsuit will be filed and won't ensure the employer will win one. But they will achieve laudable goals—reduce the chance of a lawsuit, the risk of one succeeding, and the size of any verdict for damages against the company. Against these steps is the issue that won't go away. Graphology can face it in any court claim. A rejected applicant might argue that since handwriting analysis hasn't been found scientifically valid, an employer using it acts in an unreasonable manner. So far this hasn't worked.

Under defamation law, which includes libel and slander, the employer or other party obtaining an analysis also has a defense. It's called truth. The analyst must know the trait conclusions are true or at least have reasonable grounds to believe they are true. Otherwise, an applicant has a possible claim. With handwriting analysis the target, the absorbing question is how the judge will measure truth. He may deem the analyst competent and honest as an expert in his field. Is that enough or must he review the status of the subject to determine how legitimate the analysis is? A claimant will argue that the "truth" the analyst delivered to shame him had no empirical basis. If the science is poor the report is giddleemajibbilee. The analyst's comments had no reasonable basis. The analyst might be personally convinced of the individual's poor character from his review of the writing and his knowledge of handwriting analysis principles.

If the court wants to be strict, that may not be enough. It could rule that the science of it must have been accepted by the expert community, such as the American Psychological Association. Otherwise the opinion of the analyst isn't reasonable. That's a plaintiff's argument anyway. For the record, this esteemed group neither accepts nor rejects handwriting analysis.

"We don't have a position on that, the APA doesn't take sides," says Mara Greengrass, a public and member communications official at the APA.

That is significant for handwriting analysis, not because the group has no official position but because it has no official *opposition* to handwriting analysis. Thus, no active steps to pursue graphology. It also means the APA has not felt compelled to develop an official position against it, perhaps suggesting graphology isn't so bad after all. Maybe this would have an impact on a judge.

The analyst can summon other deterrents. Specify that the report's findings are based solely on principles of handwriting analysis. Emphasize to the client that the hiring should occur only after weighing several factors. Foremost is that the analysis is one and only one factor they should consider. Although analysts believe their work is a crucial step, the company shouldn't broadcast this high regard. If a rejected applicant learns he was denied a job where an important criterion was a doubtful technique, he may be inflamed to sue.   In Pennsylvania and some other states, an employer has an additional defense. The law gives it a "qualified privilege" to take customary hiring steps if it operates in a professionally reasonable manner. The privilege arises from the employer's legitimate interest in finding the right people to further its business. Their human resources people have a duty to speak candidly to management and even seek outside aid (like analysts) and counsel on hiring. The privilege would seem to allow the employer to do a handwriting analysis on a potential worker. They must do it properly and discreetly.

Analysts often take the writing of famous people and analyze it. Virtually all of that occurs without permission of the person. Besides privacy issues, it might raise questions of copyright violations. The law prohibits someone from taking a writing or other document and presenting it to the public as his own work or creation. Typically a famous person will not seek a copyright for his signature or his handwriting. No analyst is trying to take the writing and declare that it's his item. He's only borrowing it to discover and reveal to the public the writer's personality. Although the design of the strokes is important, he is not stealing the document. Nor the content, which is irrelevant for an analysis. He doesn't claim he himself wrote the passages or the signature. He acknowledges someone else's authorship. Therefore, an analyst should be free from a copyright or trademark infringement claim for those signatures. If they're folded into a trademarked logo, like Eddie Bauer or Lord and Taylor, the answer is similar. The analyst is not trying to lift it from the ad and adopt it his own or from the person who holds the copyright or trademark. He is interested only in examining it for personality characteristics.

The typical situation for analysts should be explained further. When you send a letter you have created a document that, by itself, copyright law will protect. It's a fixed record (writing) of a creative (no matter how slight) expression of an idea. Even after it is received by the addressee, your rights continue. The recipient acquires ownership of the physical letter itself. The recipient may do what they want with it but if they sell or give it to someone else, your copyright is still protected. What can you sue for if the letter is taken to an analyst who charges to have it analyzed? If the copyright owner, the writer of the letter, has not registered the letter in Washington with the Copyright office, he can sue for damages but he must prove actual losses from the infringement by the current owner of the letter. Damages would likely be minimal if that is all that was done with the letter. They wouldn't get their attorney fees either. However, formal copyright registration of the letter enhances any claim dramatically. If you have registered the letter (not very likely unless it was special) with the U.S. Copyright Office, you can get statutory damages between $750.00 and $30,000.00 based on how serious the infringement was. You can also get reasonable attorney fees for having to bring the suit. There is also a separate provision allowing up to $150,000 for a *willful* violation of the copyright laws.

To be awarded the special damages granted by the statute, you must register the copyright within 90 days of your work being published or at least before it is infringed by the wrongful party. You can also get a court order preventing further use of the letter without your permission.

If the letter had been registered and the analyst does an analysis for free and gives it to a client and that is all that happens, the court would likely award minimal damages, but attorney fees would be covered. Courts generally don't give them the full amount of attorney fees claimants are seeking as they believe attorneys overcharge. However, if the analyst or their attorney is being obstructionist and uncooperative in the law suit, a court could give full attorney fees. For statutory damages the analyst can readily argue that he hasn't used the letter as his own creative idea (which is what the law is really trying to protect). He seeks only to look at the strokes for their meaning in personality. Thus, the damages as to an analysis are minimal to that extent.

A court will apply certain factors to evaluate how serious the infringement is. One is how much of the protected work (the letter or signature) is taken to use. In the typical case it's the whole item, which would seem to be a problem. But since the letter is only a vehicle for gleaning personality from strokes, this factor shouldn't be applied so heavily against the analyst. Other factors are the purpose of the use, the nature of the work being taken, and the effect on the potential market for the work, and its value. As they are not taking the strokes for their own, they are just conveying what they might mean for their personality. The nature of the work taken also seems to have little impact on what is done with it. Their writing isn't really valuable as such. It is common, especially their signatures. Yes, it has market value where it is a celebrity or famous figure. But typically there are many of them and none has any special value unless they are rare (being dead will raise it) or are on a unique document. As to the effect on a potential market, or the work's value in a market, we aren't detracting from them or siphoning away what they might achieve if they themselves would circulate their writing for profit. Perhaps if their writing was not generally available to the public, it would have an inflated value.

Within copyright law is a doctrine that might further aid analysts. "Fair use" also allows someone to comment on the work, such as a critic reviewing a film. That argument alone should be cogent. As to the purpose, analysts aren't trying to steal it to make it their own, which seems to be the essence of copyright protection. They don't care about the content, only the form in the strokes.

Chapter 24

Discrimination and Disabilities

Keeping the Analyst out of Court

Today the more serious and likely threat to employers may come from your Uncle Sam's getting loose from his Washington, D.C. asylum. He has paid an unwelcome visit to American business offices. In particular Congress has enacted statutes to protect civil rights of certain classes of people. You recall the civil rights laws from the 1960's involving public places, voting, and others. We now have laws banning workplace discrimination for race, sex, and religion, and age (over 40). Some attorneys suggest that handwriting analysis might run afoul of these federal laws enacted in the late twentieth century. Later provisions expanded the coverage to persons with disabilities. An employer can't deny them a job out of hand. If he otherwise qualifies they must hire him and reasonably accommodate his disability to enable him to do his work. Till now no courts have ruled if these laws apply to handwriting analysis.

Outside handwriting as a hiring issue, this legislation has generated schools of fishy lawsuits. Employers feel like a Columbia River salmon having to resist the cold, rushing water in their gills from these laws. All they want to do his hire the best workers to vault their business upward in the stream of commerce. Some wording in the statutes is ambiguous and these beleagured businesses think courts have construed them beyond Congresses' intent. Where ambiguous laws, possible large damages, and legal fees to the claimant meet, it won't be New Orleans, but you will find lawyers gone wild. They hardly need a camera pointing at them to lift their dark blue vests. They hope juries will toss their clients money to buy their wives expensive pearl necklaces to take on their vacation break.

The law addresses discrimination against the protected employees in hiring steps. One traditional step is asking applicants to take tests, like psychology tests. If an employer requires it, the test must not create an unfair disadvantage against him as a member of the protected group.

"Well, handwriting analysis is not even a test," I say.

"Some attorney with a disgruntled client may argue that it is," Grim answers. "You pull out all the stops if there is a good cause of action to pursue."

"Has any court done that?

"No court has decided the issue."

"It's not a skill or intelligence test, is it?"

"Right, it isn't. Graphology insiders acknowledge it might be part personality assessment test and part psychology technique.

"But if it's a *test*, where are the questions?"

"The analysis report identifies personal qualities of the applicant from information in his handwriting. Thus, supposedly the applicant 'answers' the 'non-questions' about his personality."

"How?"

"Merely by writing. Because the answers are contained in the writing strokes."

"But aren't the strokes disclosing information that is innocent and unconscious."

"Actually they may also be responding to nothing, except for a request to write in their natural style."

"So where is the test there?"

"Since the writer gives information about themselves as a person, it is a personality test. That would be the applicant's argument."

"Yeah, but if you ask for someone's handwriting, that doesn't show any intent to give answers, let alone intent to discriminate."

"Good point. But they say whether the employer intended to discriminate shouldn't matter.

"What do you mean?"

"What's done with the handwriting can *result* in discrimination. That should be enough, so they contend."

"That's a stretch."

Unfortunately, the U.S. Supreme Court has heard these contentions and agreed to the stretch. An unintentional act to discriminate occurs where the consequences of the company's action alone will support a claim. Thus, whether the employer meant for their test to cause unfair results on a protected group is irrelevant, said the Court. If the actual effect is unfair, that's enough. The Equal Employment Opportunity Commission (EEOC), the enforcer of these federal laws, promoted these arguments. It has said that any hiring step that might have "a disparate impact" on any protected group is illegal discrimination. ("Disparate"—ah, one of those "eye-glazers." They probably mean "different" or "unequal") Psychology tests or techniques are considered hiring steps. Analysts assert they can't tell any of those protected individuals from handwriting. Otherwise, some tentative favorable news has come from the EEOC. Its staff has confirmed in a letter to analysts that the Commission is not aware of any evidence that handwriting has that adverse "disparate impact" on the protected classes.

Plain experience and formal surveys reveal that most people can tell whether a person's writing is male or female about two-thirds of the time. The venerable forensic document examiner Albert Osborn concurred it could be done "with varying degrees of certainty." Analysts contend that this is due to women having nicer general qualities (think feminine), which are reflected in their writing strokes. You could also say women attend more to the form of their strokes whereas men seem more interested in the content. Men, especially boys, seem more energetic and aggressive in their writing. They want to get it over with and move on. With women's slower, measured pace, their more refined taste seems better displayed in their aesthetic writing strokes. For now in the courts and in the federal government, handwriting has survived any charges it adversely affects anyone applying for a job. This is because no court has directly decided the issue.

Grim points out that analysts have a counter argument if gender becomes a court issue. Advocates contending sex discrimination on a foundation of science, "should be hoisted on their own petards. It's easy, they say, to tell if the writing is a woman's. Really? With an error rate of 33%? In science that will get you a door in your face."

Every rule has exceptions, even those federal discrimination laws, the giant octopus that keeps employers on edge in their employee screening. The prospects for employers aren't all bad. If handwriting is an important function of a job, the employer may treat that requirement differently. It is not discrimination to require a secretary to have good handwriting. It's job-related. But businesses can't fabricate a work task to make it seem a focal part of the position. They must justify it as necessary to that position.

This recent disabilities protection for applicants has triggered an avalanche of litigation. As stated before, if the individual can handle the important part of the job, the employer must reasonably accommodate him and allow him to attempt the work. Many cases are about what a disability is and what employers must do to accommodate the worker. Although no handwriting case has been litigated, lawyers can be creative with the right facts. If you think the disabilities law relates only to people in wheelchairs or the blind, you are misinformed. Take handwriting itself as an aspect of a job. Someone with no hands, or just unable to write with their hands, must be accommodated. Therefore, the employer can't require a writing sample from them.

Disabilities law also extends beyond physical problems at work. It shields people with mental and psychological impairment too, including depression, bipolar, obsessive-compulsive, and other personality disorders. No, businesses don't have to let every maniac or drug addict in the plant. Exceptions were carved out for illegal use of drugs, compulsive gambling, and others. These originate voluntarily and violate our morality. A compassionate employer can even get into trouble. If the employer views the applicant or a current worker as having a mental or physical problem, they are *deemed* to consider them disabled. They must hire them, or keep those already there, and allow for their difficulty. Thus analysts are cautioned about describing the mental, or physical health of the applicant in their reports. Emotional health is included within that mental health. A liberal judge could consider areas within the term "emotions" as disabling. Analysts must focus reports on an applicant's behavior and relate it to the job. Referring to employee infirmities as emotional or psychological can only force a business to comply with these pushy discrimination laws.

The EEOC itself has been troubled about personality tests. It views them as virtually skirting what the law requires. Most questions have been too broad and astray. They mistake proper attributes for a specific job. It insists the tests measure the job-relevant skills of the applicant. If they don't, the skills should be needed in the business. Since handwriting analysis could be considered a personality test, it remains in the line of its ire and its fire. A recent federal appeals court case in Illinois addressed the coverage of personality tests, allowing them where they measure personality traits like honesty and sociability. When they attempt to go into areas like depression, hypochondria, hysteria, paranoia, and mania, the court held they violate the disabilities act. The law forbids a medical test for hiring if it's designed to identify mental disorders or impairments. These tend to draw out the applicant's disabilities. The result is discrimination. The employer can overcome this by showing it was necessary for the business (called necessity) or the qualities relate to the particular job being filled (called relatedness). Apparently the burden for employers isn't as tough even before showing either necessity or relatedness. The court experience of employers has been good based on their experience with hiring the kind of protected claimant. If a discrimination claim is raised, the employer does not have to show the test was valid. It only has to show that it has been 80 per cent successful in hiring the protected group members.

To help employers and analysts with these federal discrimination laws, experts recommend the employer give the analysis to all applicants. That may be overly cautious. Others would limit the analysis to all applicants for similar positions, like executives. It isn't easy deciding which are similar. Perhaps the safest move is to give the analysis to all potential employees. Some cynical critics of handwriting analysis see harm from that. They contend that's discriminating against *all* applicants. It's also important to shape the analysis around qualities related directly to the position. Determining qualities that relate can be difficult, especially for a management slot. You can argue that virtually every quality known is important to their work.

Also, in his report an analyst should discuss only traits directly related to the job at hand. At the very least he should omit anything that might affect differently the protected classes of people. No surveys have been done on how handwriting analysis might do that. Analysts have long asserted they can't tell your sex, age, race, religion, and national origin from handwriting.

The biggest threat for employers and their retained analysts under these discrimination laws is not the ones just described. Instead, it's the beast of burden—of proof, that is. Forget about discrimination laws, litigation and criminal attorneys must tangle with this sinister animal their whole career. In every court case it's the difference between a claim going to a final decision and a claim being dismissed before a final decision. In every criminal and civil case the law tells the parties who must go first in court and prove the claim. This is the burden of proof. In most cases the party who started the case must go first and establish probable cause (that means show they have a reasonable basis for being in court). If the evidence doesn't at least show probable cause, the judge dismisses the case without a decision on the overall claim. Why waste the court's time if you can't establish facts that minimally support your claim? That is the reasoning. If the inadequate claim would qualify for a jury, that group never gets to render a verdict. In these discrimination cases the important burden of proof is reversed. The applicant simply testifies to facts showing what he thinks is discrimination and the burden is thereby shifted. Now the employer, and thus the analyst himself, must justify their use of the analysis.

With this burden on the employer and thus back on the analyst, the scientific problem returns to haunt it. Excuse the tangle of nots, but it's tough to express this. A court can hold that, since it's not yet scientific, it can't prove it isn't discriminatory. Since recent court decisions held intent doesn't matter, the important criterion becomes the effect of the analysis. A claimant might contend that analysts cannot prove their report hasn't a "disparate impact," the magic language the EEOC uses for test consequences. Since handwriting analysis cannot prove it doesn't discriminate in the consequences, it violates the federal law. That is the argument anyway. The critical burden is thus on handwriting analysis, not the federal government or the upset applicant. No handwriting analysis studies have been comprehensive enough to evaluate this question of the effects on these protected groups. From their vast experience, to a man and woman, analysts are convinced it doesn't discriminate. Until the comprehensive research on both handwriting analysis and its effects has been completed, these discrimination laws are potential obstacles to handwriting analysis in pre-employment screening.

Timid analysts and employers can quail from potential lawsuits. Or they can march ahead trying what elsewhere has worked superbly in the workplace. More businesses are turning to handwriting analysis, especially since the lie-detector test was banned by federal legislation. The law retains the right to use the lie detector for security and some governmental positions. Handwriting has been a blessing to businesses in hiring good people for the right position. Some swear by it though are uneasy discussing it publicly. Others open up, like Hal Cross, human resources Vice-President of Fike Corporation, a manufacturer of valves. One of 325 employees of Fike, he spoke after nine years of using it and not one complaint.

"You can be overly cautious and choose not to do anything, but then you end up being too afraid to move. I feel that when you have an excellent and accurate assessment tool at your disposal then you should use it." He says they administer it fairly and consistently with all applicants. In that way they think they minimize any legal or other fall-out.

Chapter 25

Handwriting Analysts as Experts

Getting the Analyst into Court

If those forgery fellows can testify in court as experts, can graphologists?

A common inquiry from the public is the role of handwriting analysis in the legal system. It wants to know if an analyst can testify in court. For many centuries experts called questioned, forensic or disputed document examiners have been allowed to testify in court. They are asked to review a specimen of writing, such as a forged signature on a will or contract. Their role is commonly confined to determining whether the signature is the actual signature of the person whose name appears on the document. The trial could involve more than a signature. Maybe it's an entire will written in longhand or an anonymous ransom note. The issue might be whether the person whose name appears at the end in fact signed it or wrote the words before it. These experts do this primarily by comparing the writing and signatures to other known specimens of their writing called exemplars. In the old days their work aids were magnifying glasses and, later, miscroscopes. Today their devices and technology will excite CSI fans. On occasion evidence is vital about when the writing was done. It could help determine if the writing is real. Today devices can date the ink, the paper, and the typing. Often someone will write a document with several pages. At issue may be whether the second page is a phony. Maybe someone replaced the actual second page and changed the wording on it. When the first page sits on top of the second, impressions can be made on the second by pressing on the first. Sensitive devices now can record impressions on pages several layers down on a pile of sheets.

Unlike forensic document examiners, handwriting analysts, limited to personality in writing, are barred from testifying in court about a writer's personality. A common misnomer is that they can. It might be confusion with forensic expertise, which has been allowed for centuries. Many people think that personality analysts can, for example, testify whether someone had the personality or at least the ability to commit the crime charged. Or they think they should be able to. Handwriting has not advanced far enough for that. The scientific community still scorns the handwriting-equals-personality connection. That remains a giant barrier.

Before reaching that scientific threshold is another one just as fundamental. Consider a criminal proceeding. Why any person will commit a crime can be complex and uncertain for any expert, let alone an analyst. This applies whether handwriting is involved or not. Courts won't let a person testify as an expert whether they believe someone committed a specific crime or could have committed such a crime. Even a wife or a mother who may have lived with the accused for many years can't testify that their husband or son could not have committed the crime. Of course that doesn't stop them from blubbering it outside the courtroom to the media. Despite their knowing all about the accused, no testimony. The rationale is that no one can know by observation over the years if he did *this* particular act. They may have a sound idea if they are capable of any particular crime. They may even know if they are strongly liable to commit a crime or not very likely to commit a crime. That's not enough. The correlation is not close enough between someone's tendencies found in personality traits and specific offenses. These opinions are considered too speculative. The law requires as proof more certainty than that. Besides, many people have strong motives to break the law but don't. Others have broken the law several times but we can't tell for sure they did *this* time. The facts themselves should sustain his guilt. Then there are people who do break the law and we are stunned.

You may be thinking you could swear people have testified in court about a person's behavior and that is related to personality. Despite the ban on experts in court on personality issues, some other witnesses can offer testimony on personal features of a party in court. Lay witnesses of course can testify about behavior they observed involving the crime being committed. Experts also testify about specific parts of the case, like cause of death, insanity, DNA, and others. In a civil case (like an auto accident where negligence of a driver is alleged) the jury need find only a preponderance of the evidence to find for the plaintiff against the defendant. Many facts have some connection to a specific crime and the person accused of committing it. Some of it is hearsay, some not material enough, and the rest not adequate enough to cover the issues at hand. If a driver who drinks a lot is involved in an auto accident, testimony of his problem drinking won't be admitted in the civil case. It would be limited to his drinking in the hours before the accident. Even showing he is an alcoholic, has been in rehab, and attends AA won't be enough. The intoxicating effect of the alcohol must have a direct relation to the cause of the accident. For handwriting analysis the court won't allow it even though it might show a variety of ills the driver has. The ills must connect in a more exact, significant way to the behavior that made him drink and drive recklessly. That really can't be established. We can't reliably predict if he drank and drove merely because he was insecure and shy. Even alcoholics could be driving and be in an accident when they were cold sober. Unless they were negligent at the time, they are not liable in a civil case or guilty of DUI in a criminal case.

What about character witnesses? Don't handwriting analysts know character from handwriting? Yes. The courts won't allow them to testify on that issue either. In effect every criminal case is an attack on the character of the accused. People of good character supposedly do not commit crimes. With certain crimes the law specifically considers character an element of the crime itself. Those kinds of offenses usually involve some kind of deceit or falsity, such as forging a check or defrauding an investor. Courts have allowed people to testify about someone's reputation in the community for good character where character is an element of the crime itself. Anyone who does so must have good knowledge of that reputation from his own information and talking about him with others in the community. They are not expressly saying he did the crime charged, only that his character was considered good in the community. This shows some evidence that he probably didn't do it. Is this the kind of case where a handwriting analyst might testify? You would think perhaps this limited role is general enough to allow the testimony. The answer is still no. The chronic flypaper of poor scientific credibility prevents it.

You may have heard of another exception that allows people to testify in court involving the personality of the defendant in a criminal case. If they have good reason anyone can testify the person had a motive to commit a crime. Where a wife has been charged with murdering her abusive husband, a friend or child could testify that the deceased was abusive to his wife. They are testifying as an eyewitness to the abuse. But no one can give an *opinion* if they believe she actually did kill him. They must have been an eyewitness or have some other partial compelling evidence they present. Perhaps they saw the wife with blood stains on her hands a few minutes after her husband was found dead.

Now we know experts or other witnesses can't offer overall opinions on guilt in criminal cases or liability in civil cases. Even this rule has an exception. Courts allow testimony about the criminal suspect's pattern in prior similar offenses to prove the one now at issue followed that pattern. Let's say a criminal defendant has already been convicted of prior burglaries where he came in through a window and took only silverware. If he is now on trial for a burglary where the perpetrator went in a window and stole silverware, testimony of those prior similar actions (sometimes called Mode of Operation, or MO for short, as crime buffs recognize) will be allowed. This may seem prejudicial to the defendant because he is not being tried for those prior offenses. Since it also shows he has been a criminal, won't this bias the jury against him? It will. Still, the courts have ruled that the link is so close from *specific similarities* that their value as proof is high, not just speculative. They're too coincidental to ignore these prior bad acts. The testimony is also not an opinion about his patterns of prior similar conduct. It's their existence as a fact. It is not given by an expert either. The witness may be a clerk from the criminal records office merely reciting previous crimes from the public record.

Some courts have accepted handwriting analysis for personality in a limited way in criminal cases. This is after the defendant has been convicted. At sentencing the standard of proof for defendant's punishment is not as strict. The defendant has already been convicted and what is proper now isn't as important. The right to cross-examine any witness on this is also more liberal. Evidence, often weaker than in the trial itself, still remains for any side in the case. The court may hear from a variety of sources to determine what this defendant's sentence should be. Victims will speak, a probation officer might give a report, friends and family will speak to support the defendant, and others. The hearing is less formal and more relaxed in the evidence allowed. A few courts have allowed handwriting analysis to supplement the traditional testimony in fitting a sentence to the crime and the criminal. Some judges have allowed handwriting analysis to be included in a probation report in recommending the sentence and any probation as part of it. The analyst will see what the individual is like as a person to aid the court in its deciding what's good for this defendant and the community. Of course what the analyst says is only one of several factors. A judge in Colorado regularly refers handwriting of juveniles to an analyst to help him in his juvenile cases. Although he uses other sources too, he uses handwriting analysis to help decide whether the offender should be put on probation, restricted in freedom, or directed to a vocational setting. It has also helped prison authorities in places like Kentucky to evaluate convicts for rehabilitation. In each instance the judge or other court official has been personally convinced of the value of graphology.

Despite the ban on personality testimony from experts *during the trial*, graphologists have testified in trials for limited purposes. They have been allowed to testify as experts to establish a person's state of mind at a certain time, such as when they might have gotten violent, or were contemplating suicide, or were under extreme stress. In those situations the contemporary writing reflected their actions in those circumstances. Although some trial courts have permitted analysts to provide this limited testimony, the reason is not clear. The appellate courts (who tell the trial courts what the law is) have uniformly denied handwriting analysts from testifying at trial on *any* issue of their personality expertise. The basis is that someone's mental state is directly related to their general personality features. Trial courts are supposed to follow the law as the appellate courts define it. Thus no testimony about personality aspects of someone's behavior from their handwriting. Apparently in those cases where the analyst testified, no appeal was filed. Why these lower courts allowed the testimony is a mystery in view of the longstanding rule. An example where a trial court seemed to properly follow the appellate court rulings is the New York case in *Cameron v. Knapp*. A party tried to have an analyst testify that a surgeon's shaky hands stemmed from his mental condition revealed in his handwriting strokes. The trial court allowed no testimony on the doctor's mental or physical condition based on his handwriting. The court held that no current evidence exists that handwriting analysis is held reliable by the medical or scientific community.

—

Handwriting and fingerprints have a kinship of close pedigree. Maybe like brothers. They both involve the hands. They both result from imprints on paper. They both supply information that allows you to identify and distinguish one person from another. Both have been allowed in court for a long time. Fingerprint experts, such as the FBI crime lab people, have always enjoyed a singular standing in forensic evidence. For over a century fingerprint testimony has been allowed in courts all over the world without serious question. The same for handwriting experts involved in questioned documents such as forgeries and anonymous writings. That standing has been shaken after the 1993 U.S. Supreme Court decision known as the *Daubert* case. Although neither handwriting nor fingerprint evidence was involved, the resounding impact of the case applies to them. It was about experts and their testimony. The Court ruled that the party presenting expert opinion evidence must first establish its scientific validity. Determining if the scientific standards have been met is the role of the judge himself, the "gatekeeper," as lawyers call him. He reviews the scientific status of the subject (as presented by the parties in the case) and decides himself if it meets the standards. It is not for the authorities in the specific area to do it even though judges are not scientific authorities themselves. But judges are guided by those authorities in deciding to allow expert testimony. To make that initial finding, the Court suggested some items the judge should consider in determining the scientific basis for the expert testimony. They include—

1.   Hypotheses tested

2.   Peer review and publication in scientific journals

3.   Error rates established

4.   Approved methodologies

5.   Acceptance by peer group in general.

This decision might seem to raise no new standards for expert evidence. Expert opinion for handwriting analysis always needed some scientific foundation to be admitted in court. So did any expert opinion for other subjects. However, it does create new challenges for U.S. lawyers needing experts for their cases. In its younger days in the nineteenth century, American justice hadn't seen much scientific surveying. Science and schools were not advanced like today. People became experts often by informal study in their field. Schoolchildren learn about how Abraham Lincoln became a lawyer through reading law by the fireplace in his home. Many scientific-sounding doctrines uttered by scientific-acting witnesses were getting by on scientifically-weak foundations. Some had been accepted for years from the accumulated weight of their prior court acceptance. Experts' reputations were earned by the straps of their boots. In many areas expert evidence had never faced the cool, rigorous scrutiny of science's emerging standards of objectivity, validity, reliability, peer review and the rest.

The scientific method that students learn as they fight boredom in chemistry or psychology is also important to the law. A longtime leading area that had been accepted is fingerprints. To the shock of most, there has never been a comprehensive scientific study of fingerprints. That particular issue hasn't yet reached the U.S. Supreme Court in the wake of *Daubert*. Of course, fingerprinting has an advantage over handwriting. It is physical evidence, a superior kind for establishing scientific proof. It doesn't easily change. Yes, handwriting is also physical. But its interpretation can be deemed subjective or psychological. Handwriting can also easily change at the whim of the writer himself. Thus, after a comfortable, lengthy past, fingerprinting found itself on boggy legal ground. Of course handwriting already rests on a swamp if you ask the psychology authorities. The courts are guided by these authorities.

Plenty of cases, mostly criminal, with fingerprint evidence have hot-coalwalked through the courts since *Daubert* in 1993. Defense lawyers have dutifully argued against the evidence, thus leaving it up in the air until the U.S. Supreme Court gets a direct case on fingerprint evidence. Can you believe it, fingerprints and handwriting share a common defect for satisfying *Daubert*—the lack of comprehensive study of their scientific merit. Up until now handwriting analysis has generally avoided the legal question of its validity because proponent's lawyers didn't bother offering it in a court trial to demonstrate personality issues, with one exception. As stated shortly before, courts allowed it for only the mental condition of the writer, such as mental capacity or undue influence from a stronger-willed person. Still, the thrust of *Daubert* may work in favor of handwriting analysis. The Court allows the *trial judge* to decide the scientific value, not the outside authorities. It may be a judge would conclude it has been through a lot and held up well despite the authorities thrashing it. A good omen for it is the fate of fingerprinting after *Daubert*. Since it was announced in 1993 it has fared well with the trial courts. Yet it doesn't have the scientific grounding that courts should compel to let their handwriting experts on the stand.

The other area of court evidence for handwriting is questioned documents (QD). As discussed before, this area is limited to non-psychological, visual comparisons of writing, such as forgeries and the like. As also stated previously, that kind of testimony has been allowed in court over the centuries. That evidence has the same problem as fingerprints—no prior overall scientific surveying. With scientific opinion evidence under siege, those experts don't want to weaken their standing any further. One way it is threatened is their association with handwriting analysis. The stigma of the pseudo-science reputation of handwriting analysis continues to taint any questioned document expert who wants to testify in court. To their credit some of these experts have also studied handwriting analysis. In truth, some of them studied it first. It's a natural transition to move between the two of them. Analysts take a treasure of knowledge with them. Analysts learn about each little stroke and each major aspect (like slant). With these as background, they know they are all important to show uniqueness in writing styles.

To qualify as an expert in court, QD experts omit handwriting analysis study in their Curriculum Vitae. They do it to avoid trouble in being qualified to testify as an expert. They won't say they ever had any involvement in it, whether training, experience, schooling or practice. If it's exposed, their questioned document expertise might be compromised. That gloomy stain of handwriting analysis' lack of credibility follows them into court. They want to erase that stain even though they may be a faithful analyst. A survey found somewhat more than half of document examiners were also handwriting analysts.

Including handwriting analysis in the QD examiner's credentials does not disqualify him as an expert. It just leaves him vulnerable to a derisive attorney cross-examining him in the initial stage about his expert qualifications. When he pins you to that "unscientific junk," you are branded as guilty by association. Because you performed handwriting analysis won't disqualify you as a QD expert either. But with a meager background in QD, it may lower your chances of being qualified in court as a QD examiner. In addition, you can bet your Sacajawea dollar the other side's attorney will hammer to the jury in his closing argument that this expert's valid testimony came from a "so-called expert who practices that discredited party, carnival, parlor, boardwalk, fortune-telling exercise called handwriting analysis." If that attorney and that jury only knew.

Now they do.

NOTES

Chapter 1
Starting from Scratch

22   In the 1990's a type-written document surfaced that showed a secret trust set up by John Kennedy: "Caslon analytics profile, forgery, fraud & forensics," website: caslon.com.au/forgeryprofile1.htm

29   Grim says it's easier to comprehend if you look at from the perspective of the esteemed Czech analyst, Robert Saudek: Huntingdon Hartford, You Are What You Write, (New York: MacMillan, 1973), page 12

25   "Most self-expression is too fleeting" Gordon W.Allport and Philip E.Vernon, Studies in Expressive Movement, (New York: MacMillan 1933)

30   Someone calculated that the odds of two signatures of one person alone written freehand: John Rodden, "Is Handwriting Analysis Making the Transition from Séance to Science?" Today, The Philadelphia Inquirer, April 16, 1978, page 33

Chapter 2
Brainwriting

34   Bart Baggett has a website that is heavy on promoting his thriving internet handwritinganalyisisbusiness:BartBaggettwebsite:handwritinganalysis101. com/FAQS

34   Barnard Collier, who is called a Director of Graphology Consulting Group and Graphotechnology, asserts: Website graphologyconsulting.com/main/home

40   "I can't imagine how acupuncture works" Elise Hancock, Ideas into Words (The Johns Hopkins Press, 2003)

40   In a few weeks Dianne Kalal was to become a bride: Rose Matousek, The ABC's of Handwriting Analysis (Hinsdale, Illinois: Self-Published 1985) pages 10–12

41   "Simple experiments with individuals writing in the air": Eric Singer, A Manual of Graphology (New York: Crescent Books 1974) page 27

41   In mid-twentieth century Germany a farmer: Singer, page 27

43   the strokes of the psychotic surprisingly run close to normal: Barry l. Beyerstein and Dale F. Beyerstein, The Write Stuff, Evaluations of Graphology—The Study of Handwriting Analysis (Buffalo: Prometheus Books 1992) page 150

43   Some research was instituted by a few analysts to see if alcoholics: David Lester, The Psychological Basis of Handwriting Analysis (Chicago: Nelson-Hall, 1981) pages 105–107

45   Grim points out one study that analyzed the writing of thirty convicted embezzlers: Handwriting Institute, Inc.

47   Veteran Graphoanalyst Kathy Urbiha…has surveyed the writing of actual prison convicts: Sheila Lowe, The Vanguard, April–June 2001, page __

52   …the director of A. N. Palmer Company once told Milton Bunker: M. N. Bunker, Handwriting Analysis, The Science of Determining Personality by GRAPHOANALYSIS (Chicago: Nelson-Hall 1969) page 178

52   Bunker himself thought that not one in ten thousand: Bunker, ibid., page 178

51   D'Nealian was introduced into the schools in the 1960's as a more simplified cursive: Lesson One, The IGAS Instruction Department, The Graduate Course in Graphoanalysis (Chicago: IGAS 1985), page 51

51   Don Neal invented it to ease the transition from manuscript to cursive writing: Website for Zaner Bloser Penmanship Company, zanerbloser.com

Chapter 3
History

57   The oldest piece of writing comes from about 5,500 years ago: Many contributors, The Last Two Million Years (Pleasantville, New York: The Reader's Digest Association, Inc. 1997) page 302

58   Middle-East eventually began making impressions: Ibid. page 302

58   To the southwest Egypt developed a better surface: Ibid. page 303

59   China sandaled on some different paths: Ibid. page 303

63   Meantime, papyrus was losing its luster from scarcity and cost: Huntingdon Hartford, *You Are What You Write*, (New York: MacMillan, 1973), pages 19-21

61   Chinese governments adopted his principles of moral character: *The Last Two Million Years*, page 305

61   The Chinese use individual characters: "The Power of Writing," *National Geographic*, November, 1999, page 23

Editor's Note: The history of handwriting analysis appears in many volumes, most of them incomplete and sketchy, some now very old. Much of it is common knowledge among analysts as are Lindbergh and the Hindenburg to aviation historians. This chapter is not an attempt to be comprehensive either. It is an attempt to relate the important events more completely than before and to note significant signposts in graphology's progress. Some of the specific sources for this history are also sources elsewhere in this book for other citations related to other topics. These primary sources for the history are Roman, *A Key to Personality*, Singer, *Manual of Graphology*, deSainte-Colombe, *Grapho-Therapeutics*, Lowe, *Idiot's Guide*, Casewit, *Graphology Handbook*, Hartford, *You Are What You Write*. For full citations go to the point these authors first appear in this book.

62   Aristotle was a teacher whose ideas were recorded and still inspire us: several sources

68   It's 1879 and you're in Leipzig, Germany: Robert S. Feldman, *Essentials of Understanding Psychology* (New York: McGraw-Hill, 1989) page 14

69   Hippocrates…had suggested we are made up of four humors: Feldman, page 14

69   Descartes…thought our nerves were hollow tubes: Feldman, page 14

71   One man in Italy, Fra Moretti studied around 50,000 samples of handwriting: Norman Werling, Certified Master Graphoanalyst, "Graphoanalysis: Who Made the Rules?" monograph

74   Beginning in the nineteen-teens the staple of American periodicals carried articles and features of the topic: Tamara Plakins Thornton, *Handwriting in America, A Cultural History* (Yale University Press, New Haven, 1996) pages 119-120

77   France and England used handwriting analysis to screen soldiers for placement and ability: John Rodden, "Is Handwriting Analysis Making the

Transition from Séance to Science?" *Today, The Philadelphia Inquirer*, April 16, 1978, page 41

75 Doodles seem specially attached to us: Robert Reisner, *Graffiti* (New York: Cowles, 1971); Lowe, *Idiot's Guide*, pages 303-310

76 An experiment was conducted with the handwritings of Michelango: Clara Roman, *Handwriting, A Key to Personality* (New York: Pantheon Books, 1952)

77 "A person who actually pursued that in earnest is Alfred Kanfer" Robert Backman, "Retrospect: Robert Kanfer," The Vanguard, October-December 2005, page 8

82 Mark Hopper, head of Handwriting Research Corporation...declares that his organization: Bill Leonard, "reading employees," *HR Magazine*, April, 1999, page 69

80 Bibliographies of Research Studies: Sheila Lowe, author of the *The Complete Idiot's Guide to Handwriting Analysis*, at page 392 cites her Annotated Bibliography of Research in the United States Since 1970 to be found on her website writinganalysis.com. Her e-mail address is Sheila@sheilalowe. com. The International Graphoanalysis Society has a booklet entitled An Annotated Bibliography of Studies in Handwriting Analysis Research, last revised in 1994 by James C. Crumbaugh, Ph.D and John O. Steele. E-mail to Greg Greco, President, at greg@igas.com. Also from the Handwriting Research Corporation, which indicates it has a library of studies and database of materials and has done its own since 1979. Check its Website at HRC.com. David Lester, *The Psychological Basis of Handwriting Analysis* (Chicago: Nelson-Hall, 1981) also cites various studies throughout his book limited of course to pre-1981 studies. The website of analyst Iris Hatfield Holmes with her organization HuVista International and her Human Graphics Center lists several studies. The website is huvista.com. She also mentions a volume of James H. Miller called *Bibliography of Handwriting Analysis: A Graphological index* (Troy, New York: The Whiston Publishing Company 1982). The International Graphology Colloquium has a website igc-grapho.net with a link to their academics and research.

81 Handwriting Research Corporation's has issued data on the current state of handwriting analysis: Handwriting Research Corporation's Website handwriting.com/facts/history

Chapter 4
Milton N. Bunker, Dogged Detective, Reluctant Trailblazer

The sources for this chapter were these volumes: Bunker, *Handwriting Analysis, The Science of Determining Personality by Graphoanalysis*, Chapter One, supra.; M. N. Bunker, *What Handwriting Tells You* (New York: The World Publishing Company 1951) Chapter One; M. N. Bunker, *Secrets... your handwriting reveals about you* (Chicago: International Graphoanalysis Society 1995) Chapter One; June J. Speer and Royce L. Smith, *The Early Years of Milton Newman Bunker, founder of International Graphoanalysis Society* (Garden City, Kansas: Elliot Printers, Inc. 1977)

Chapter 5
Pedagogue

99   It's about a dog and a baby and a prince from the 13th Century. This tale derives from a poem written by William Robert Spencer entitled "Beth-Gelert, Or, The Grave of the Greyhound" appearing in various compilations, such as *The Best-Loved Poems of the American People*, selected by Hazel Felleman (New York: Garden City Books, 1936), as updated, page 215-216

Chapter 6, 7 and 8
None

Chapter 9
Word Stories

158   Sometime after the murder a national periodical called on him to evaluate: Don Gentile and David Wright, "Jon Benét Breakthrough, Mom's Secret Uncovered," *National Examiner*

161   A few years ago the Phoenix, Arizona, area was in turmoil: Segment on Dateline NBC, _____2005

182   [Barry Beyerstein] says there must be at least five million other people in the U.S. who are also stubborn: *Dateline NBC*, March 23, 1997; Beyerstein and Beyerstein, *The Write Stuff*, supra., page 365

176   An example: "I am more outgoing than shy" has been replaced: Erin White, "Interviewing your personality, Workplace," Careerjournal.com, as stated in *The Week*, November 24, 2006

178   One gaining notice is the Assessment Center Technique: "Personality Profile Plus," *New Yorker*, September 20, 2004, page 43

183   Beyerstein impugns another technique that has gained ground: Larry Reibstein with Karen Springen, "Spotting the Write Stuff," *Newsweek*, February 17, 1992, page 44

169   Critics contend that you and he will both scour your present and past to confirm that you have it: Beyerstein and Beyerstein, supra., *The Write Stuff*, supra., page 27

168   Psychologists and others have used The Rohrschach Inkblot Test since the 1920's: Beyerstein and Beyerstein, *The Write Stuff*, supra., page 294

186   "Daddy, can I have a drink of water" Copyright 2005 Satellite XM Radio, Inc., Comedy Channel

188   Five years later his infant son was kidnapped from his New Jersey estate and murdered : There are many sources for the facts and speculation about the Lindbergh kidnapping and murder and Bruno Hauptmann's guilt, including recent television documentaries on Court TV Channel, Arts and Entertainment Channel, and The History Channel

188   After Hauptmann was convicted and still refused to admit anything, the founder of Graphoanalysis, M. N. Bunker, reviewed the [Hauptmann ransom] note: Bunker, *What Handwriting Tells You*, supra., pages 163–166

189   Klara Roman, the transplanted Hungarianpsychologist,...supposedly developed the word from the Italian word pasta: Lowe, *The Idiot's Guide*, page 173

189   Distinguished analyst Shirley Spencer did employment screening:, "Profile" Shirley Spencer, *The New Yorker*, December 24, 1949, page 34

Chapter 10
Science

171   Doctor A.A. Roback, Psychology Professor at Harvard: Curtis Casewit, *Graphology Handbook* (Rockport, Massachusetts: Para Research, Inc., 1980) page 5

Chapter 11
The Analysis

212   One prominent analyst was analyzing samples from a group of people: Maurine Moore, "Signatures, The face we present to the world," *The Journal of Graphoanalysis*, April 1982, page 7

200   A man shows that he is open and honest but he also shows he is passionate and weak-willed: De Saint-Colombe, *Grapho-Therapeutics*, page 4

220   A prominent example is the signature of Richard Nixon: Curtis Casewit, *Graphology Handbook* (Rockport, Massachusetts: Para Research, Inc., 1980) pages 132–133

221   If personality can change over years, and the writing follows suit, what about over a few days?: *Case and Comment*, _____page 6

221   Henry Hawksworth wrote a book called *The Five of Me*: Matousek, *The ABC's of Handwriting Analysis*, supra., pages 33–34

222   People in altered states have been asked to write to see the effects: Eric Singer, *A Manual of Graphology* (New York: Crescent Books 1969) page 15

228   More was learned just in the 1990's than the entire history of psychology and neuroscience before: Antonio Domasio, Neuroscientist, *Scientific American*, December, 1999

230   A. N. Palmer, the master penman, once said it as simply a mechanical procedure: Thorton, *Handwriting in America*, page 103

230   Other skeptics have granted its uniqueness among persons but explain it as just "physiological idiosyncracy.": Thorton, *Handwriting in America*, page 103

Chapter 12
Member in Good Standing National Guilt-by-Associaton

232   The U.S. Department of Justice became so alarmed about the implications of the Daubert case, Diana Diggs, "Handwriting Analysis Gets A Boost As Forensic Evidence," *Lawyer Weekly USA*, July 22, 2002, page 15. Adam Liptak, "Prosecutors Hope New Study of Handwriting Analysis Will Silence Skeptics," *The New York Times*, _____ 2002, page __

239   For a few years now West Coast analyst Sheila Lowe has been selling her *Sheila Lowe Handwriting Analyzer*: Sheila Lowe, *Idiot's Guide*, supra., pages 376-384

240   Mark Hopper, President of Handwriting Research Corporation in Arizona has built probably the biggest handwriting company in the world: Handwriting Research Corporation website handwriting.com

Chapter 13
Status

254   Professor Barry Beyerstein of British Columbia is a consultant and executive committee member of the Committee for the Scientific Investigation of the Paranormal: Beyerstein and Beyerstein, *The Write Stuff*, supra., page 489

258   Handwriting analysis evolved from this idea of "sympathetic magic": Beyerstein and Beyerstein, "The Origins of Graphology in Sympathetic Magic," *The Write Stuff*, supra., Chapter 9, page 163 et seq.

258   Our imagination falls into this mental trap, which has an eye-glazing name, "pareidolia": Beyerstein and Beyerstein, *The Write Stuff*, supra., pages 173-175

261   From psychology Beyerstein deployed a theory that freshman read about in their introductory textbooks. It's called "cognitive dissonance": Beyerstein and Beyerstein, *The Write Stuff*, supra., page 216,364 and 366

264   Dr. Rowan Bayne is a psychologist with the British Psychological Society. He thinks it should be ranked with astrology: Johnathon Duffy and Giles Wilson, "Writing Wrongs," *BBC Newsmagazine*, February 1, 2005, Website: Wikipedia.org/graphology

262   During the Presidential Campaign for the 2000 Election Grim was asked by Dickinson College: Allan K. Grim, Jr., "SHOWING THEIR HANDS," *Dickinson Magazine*, Fall 2000, page 48

263   One he cites is a newspaper article quoting Joseph Horn, a University of Texas-Austin Professor of Psychology: Robb Todd, "Handwriting's Hidden Secrets," *Knight Ridder News Service*

266   In a handwriting analysis article in the national science magazine *Psychology Today* McNichol was asked: Scanlon, Mathew-Mauro, James, "The Lowdown on Handwriting Analysis," *Psychology Today*, November-December 1993, Page ___

269   Osborn's book was the first comprehensive treatise on the subject: Albert S. Osborn, *Questioned Documents* (1929; Second Edition re-printed New Jersey: Patterson Smith, 1978)

269   Terming it "pseudo-science" here and " occult" there and " intuitive"down there: Osborn, supra, page 436-438

269   Some have claimed it can tell of disturbances in the bowels, diseases of the stomach, love of young animals, and male or female sterility: Osborn, supra., page 437

269   Too many outside factors and its "fundamental defect": Osborn, supra., page 438-439

270   Curiously, he mentions more ways it doesn't reek: Osborn, supra., page 436-437

270   efficient, incompetent, passionately accurate, and if he is a bungler: Osborn, supra., page 421

270   Osborn concedes handwriting can tell to a degree when you were born: Osborn, supra., page 437

271   Just as Osborn has done, Barry Beyerstein has also conceded some attributes handwriting might reveal about a writer: Barry Beyerstein, "How Graphology Fools People" August 20, 2006, Website: Quackwatch.org,

241   The Library of Congress re-classified Handwriting Analysis in 1980: Library of Congress BF889-BF 905

242   Around 1990 some legislators in Rhode Island and Oregon tried to ban it as an employment step: Julie Spohn, "The Legal Implications of Graphology," *Washington University Law Quarterly*, Volume 75, Number 3, Fall, 1997

242   Mark Seifer, who testified before their legislative committee: Letter to Rhode Island Legislative Committee May 3, 1990, from Mark Seifer, Ph. D, *The Journal of The American Society of Professional Graphologists*, 1991, page 5

246   Harley-Davidson makes motorcycles. Right?: Tom Peters, Re-Imagine! Business Excellence in a Disruptive Age _____

250   The position of the American Psychological Association on handwriting analysis is significant: Melinda Kohn, Seth Pittman, "Merits of handwriting analysis spark a lively debate," *Eastern Pennsylvania Business Journal*, March 25-31, 2002, page 22

Chapter 14
Handwriting and Penmanship

280   Surveys indicate 90% of job applications are filled in handwritten: Linda Templeton, "Is Technology Erasing Penmanship?" *USA Today*, _____

280   School work is roughly 95% with those young hands: Lisa Kozleski, "Perfect penmanship pays off," *The Morning Call*, July 15, 1999, page B6

282   This continues to appall etiquette's Miss Manners: Miss Manners: "Putting ink on paper is still most proper manner of communicating," *The Morning Call*, July 10, 2005

283   Actually if she hears about That's Gratitude, a Baltimore company: Sheila Lowe, *The Vanguard* (as noted in *Newsday*), April-June 2006, page 11

283   Miss Manners has heard the question about satisfying the thank-you e-mail: Miss Manners, supra., *The Morning Call*

283   Marsha Egan, a leadership coach from Reading, Pennsylvania, took a column: Marsha Egan, Coach's Corner, "Handwritten notes gain in value as they become rarer," *Eastern Pennsylvania Business Journal*, July 4-10, 2005

278   A man returned to his car to find his hood and fenders smashed: Ken Macrorie, *Telling Writing* (New Rochelle, New Jersey: Hayden Book Company. 1970) page 39

284   Miss Manners underscores that a handwritten letter shows you are sincere: Miss Manners, supra., *The Morning Call*

273   Bill Crossman is a philosophy and English professor at Vista Community College: Christian Berg, "Out There, Reading and Writing Obsolete," *The Morning Call*, January 1, 2001

279 5 states have their own standards for testing high school students: Templeton, "Is Technology Erasing Penmanship?" Templeton, supra.

279 The brief experience with the written portion of the SAT: Margaret Webb Pressler, "The Handwriting Is on the Wall, Researchers See a Downside as Keyboards Replace Pens in School," *Washington Post*, October 11, 2006, Page AO1

281 ...the classic fountain pen has developed its own niche, Nancy Herrick, "A Pen for All Seasons," *Milwaukee Sentinal Journal*, May 5, 1998, page 3

278 One of those has been word maven William Safire: William Safire, *On Language* (New York: Times Books, 1980), page 50

274 Susan Bowen of the International Pen Association thinks the "true culprits" aren't computers: Susan Bowen, "Handwriting: A Key to Literacy," *Pen World International*, Vol. 17, No. 3, 2003

275 Family psychologist John Rosamond thinks few schools teach handwriting because it involves drill: *The Morning Call*, April 20, 2006, page___

275 Margaret Webb Pressler, "The Handwriting Is on the Wall, Researchers See a Downside as Keyboards Replace Pens in School," *Washington Post*, October 11, 2006, Page AO1

275 Experts believe after fourth grade it is probably a slim hope to correct faulty penmanship: Christina Hoff Sommers, "The Write Stuff," *The American Enterprise Institute for Public Policy Research*, July 1, 2001

Chapter 15
Personal Uses

287 In th'early pahwt of the 20th Cen'ry in the South Geohge Wawshington Carveh had a thang for peanuts: National Peanut Board Website, nationalpeanutboard.org

290 Chief Justice William Rehnquist reflected: William Rehnquist, George Mason University Commencement Address, as reported in *Chicago Tribune*, June _ 1993

291 One group of analysts was approached by a couple whose son had been playing Little League baseball: handwriting sample presented to Pennsylvania Chapter of IGAS, 1996

292   Consider the child who writes with robust straight lines and angles: Rose Matousek, *The ABC's of Handwriting Analysis, supra.,* page 20

293   If the child draws pleasing rounded strokes resembling sweeping clouds: Rose Matousek, *The ABC's of Handwriting Analysis, supra.,* page 20

276   Several studies of handwriting and school students found that where the content was similar: Christina Hoff Sommers, "The Write Stuff," *The American Enterprise Institute for Public Policy Research, Short Publications,* July 1, 2001

293   A survey estimates that in young boy-girl relationships: Doctor Phil, *Doctor Phil Show,* CBS-TV, 2006

294   TV's Doctor Phil says that life is a series of choices, Doctor Phil, *Doctor Phil Show,* CBS-TV, 2005

296   One analyst had a memorable occurrence with a client who contacted him while using a dating service: Curtis Casewit, *Graphology Handbook, supra.,* page 1

Chapter 16
Business Uses

300   Where many organizations apply it, largely for help in selecting employees, they are reluctant to admit they do: Lerry Reibstein with Karen Springen, "Spotting the Write Stuff," *Newsweek,* February 17, 1992, page 44

299   Tom Payette is a hard-nosed car dealer in Louisville, Kentucky: Alessandra Bianchi, "The Character-Revealing Handwriting Analysis," *INC. Magazine,* February 1996, page 77

300   Handwriting Research Corporation puts the number that currently use it at around 5,000: Handwriting Research Corporation Website: handwriting. com/facts/history/html

300   In Israel the estimate is about 90 to 95%: Nadia Lerner, "HANDIWORK-Are your loops and squiggles the window to your identity?" *Reading Eagle/ Reading Times,* Lifestyle A17, 1999

300   Handwriting Research Corporation confines its use percentage to 80% of the large corporations in France and Switzerland: Website: handwriting. com/facts/history/html

301   In a sixteen-year study conducted by psychologist Herb Greenburg, President of Marketing Research and Survey Corporation:, Website: Handwriting Research Corporation, handwriting.com/facts/history.html

304   Also fifty per cent of the employees hired don't last six months: "Write That Resumé Right," *San Diego Union-Tribune*, January 29, 1996, Section C-1

386   They will say that a person's privacy has been invaded where the activity was "highly offensive to a reasonable person.": These rules are codified in a volume courts throughout the United States apply as the general common law for torts and other areas of law. For privacy principles see *The Restatement of Torts 2d*, Section 652 (1977)

303   Insurance companies especially like to use it to select sales people: John Rodden, "Is Handwriting Analysis Making the Transition from Séance to Science?" *Today, Philadelphia Inquirer*, supra., page 35

303   Here are some for hiring the wrong person: David Tuller, "What's New in Employment Testing," *The New York Times*, February 24, 1985

304   The most prevalent motivation for workplace violence is personality conflicts: Website: dsda.com/CM/News/Violence

303   According to Peter Drucker, "One third or more of all hiring decisions: Website:astrategicperformance.com/consulting

305   A study on resumes by Avert, Inc.: Noami Goldin, "The Business of Ethics, Kit and Kaboodle," *Cornell Daily Sun*, October 25, 2006

307   Most people leave from problems with their boss: Survey by Challenger, Gray and Christmas, an outplacement firm with offices in 16 US cities

307   70% of workers said they have a "toxic boss"according to Monster.com: *The Week*, July 29, 2006

307   Organizational consultant Ken Siegel thinks corporate America's "ranting bosses": *The Week*, July 29, 2006

307   A 2006 Washington Post article said that about 70% of major corporations: Amy Jacobs "Workplace, Interviewing your personality," *The Washington Post* as stated in *The Week*, November 24, 2006, page 48

308   Sharon Stockham, Senior Vice-President of Human Resources at Exchange Bank in Rosa, California: Bill Leonard, "Reading Employees," *HR Magazine*, April 1999, page 69

309   At the Fike Corporation, an industrial products manufacturer in Blue Springs, Missouri: supra., page 69

309   The big tax company H & R Block has been using it for years: David Tuller, "Passing the Penmanship Exam," *The New York Times*, February 24, 1985

309   Michael Henke is market sales manager of Humana Care Plus: Tuller, "Passing the Penmanship Exam," supra.

309   Northwestern Life Insurance Company of Milwaukee has a Tampa, Florida branch: Tuller, "Passing the Penmanship Exam," supra.

312   Grim cites a survey about why most salespeople failed (either let go or quit): Shirley Hawe, Portland, Oregon, Master Graphoanalyst Presentation to Pennsylvania Chapter of IGAS, Spring, 1993

Chapter 17
Other Uses

315   Years ago a young mother left her new-born baby on the steps of a church: J. J. Leonard, "That's Write!" *Parade*, June 7, 1992, pages 16–17

315   Israel has been fighting for its life ever since its founding in 1948: *The Journal of Graphoanalysis,* _____ page 14

317   Carl Belfiori, a longtime analyst from and HR man from Michigan: Allan K. Grim, Jr., Interview with Belfiori, October 29, 2005, Niagara Falls, Ontario, Canada.

317   Helene Keller, an accomplished veteran analyst from Harrisburg, Pennsylvania; Allan K. Grim, Jr., Interview with Helene Keller, September 17, 2005, Reading, Pennsylania

317   Ruth Holmes, enjoys the interplay with the students: *Pennsyl-points*, Pennsylvania Chapter of IGAS newsletter from online discussion of post-prom experiences, May, 1997, page 5

320   Alice Weiser has been an analyst since 1976: Randall Patterson, "Reading between the Lines," *The Houston Post,*_____

321   Maurine Moore, from Cheyenne, Wyoming, has been a jury consultant since 1973: Faye A. Silas, Graphoanalysis—"Choosing jurors by penmanship," *American Bar Association Journal*, November, 1983, page 1609

325   One of these is sexual abuse: Suzy Ward and Judi Johnson, "Research of Sexual Abuse Indicators in Handwriting," Presentation to Handwriting Analysts, Inc., Graphological Forum, April, 1991; Royce Smith, "Indications

of Sexual Abuse in Writing (Females)," Presentation to Pennsylvania Chapter of IGAS, May 22, 1993

326   Some studies have been done of common stroke patterns of those with compulsive eating disorders: Royce Smith, "Handwriting Characteristics--Compulsive Eating Disorder," Presentation to Pennsylvania Chapter of IGAS, May 22, 1993

327   The earliest formal steps to investigate [graphotherapy] began in 1910: Paul de Sainte Colombe, *Graphotherapeutics* (Hollywood: Paul de Sainte Colombe Foundation, 1972) page 13

327   More efforts by University of Paris psychologist Raymond Trillat were featured in a 1956 *Time* article: "Pen & Pencil Therapy," *Time,* April 23, 1956, page____

327   The success of these American pioneers was advanced by a naturalized American, Paul de Sainte Colombe: Colombe, *Therapeutics,* supra, back cover

328   A 1970 Time article heralded Colombe's accomplishments: "Pen-and-Pencil Therapy," *Time,* September 21. 1970, page____

328   One who experimented with the technique in the early 20th Century is the founder of Graphoanalysis, Milton Bunker: The IGAS Instruction Department, Graduate Course in Graphoanalysis, Lesson 3, (Chicago: IGAS, 1987), pages 3-13

324   Some of the markings are not just anonymous shrieking: Scott Kraus, "Gang Scrawl sprawl," *The Morning Call,* November 13, 2006, page B4

Chapter 18 and 19
None

Chapter 20
Printing

361   Eileen Page, with a Masters in Graphoanalysis, lives in Newton, Massachusetts: Eileen Page, Oral Presentation to Congress of IGAS, October 29, 2005

Chapter 21
Doctors' Writing

365   Philip Crozer was selected as one of the student speakers at his high school Commencement: Lee Silber, *Self-Promotion for the Creative Person* (New York: Three Rivers Press, 2001), page 72

366   Grim interjects here that he knows of least two studies on the issue: Doctors not worse— "The truth about doctors' handwriting: a prospective study," British Medical Journal, Volume 313, December 21, 996, pages 1657-1658. Doctors worse— "Legibility of doctors' handwriting: quantitative comparative study," British Medical Journal, Volume 317, December 26, 1998, pages 863-864

371   In Portland, Oregon, two handwriting specialists, Inga Dubay and Barbara Getty have been doing: Susan G. Hauser, "Italic-Writing Missionaries Make a Convert," The Wall Street Journal, February 10, 2000, page ___

Chapter 22
Writing on the Edge

376   As Carrie Fisher (Star Wars actress Princess Leia and author) described it: Mike Sager Interview with Carrie Fisher, "What I've Learned," *Esquire*, January 2002

377   People are lefthanded for some actions but not others: alt.lefthanders Frequently Asked Questions, Lefthanders' Website: faqs.org/faqs/lefty-faq

378   Fortunately IGAS has taken steps to review this disparity in slanting: "The IGAS Seminar, An Investigation, Handedness and Graphoanalysis," *The Journal of Graphoanalysis*," February, 1975, page 5-7

380   Milton Bunker studied all the master penmen: Lesson One, The IGAS Instruction Department, The Graduate Course in Graphoanalysis (Chicago: IGAS 1985), page 55

379   According to Graphoanalysis founder Milton Bunker, Palmer claimed to allow: Ibid., page 48

Chapter 23
Handwriting and the Law

386   In the 1960's the U.S. Supreme Court went through the august document with a fine-tooth comb: the case was *Griswold v. Connecticut*, 381 U.S. 479 (1965), in which the Court held that a state law banning the purchase of contraceptives by a married couple was unconstitutional.

386   In 1973 the U. S. Supreme Court held handwriting in general wasn't entitled to privacy protection: *U. S. v. Mara*, 410 U.S .19, (1973)

387   In a later decision the court equated handwriting to our bodies: U.S. v. Euge, 444 U.S. 707 (1980)

387   In U.S. v Rosinsky a federal appeals court: U.S. v Rosinsky, 547 F2d 249 (4th Cir. 1977)

386   It has been around as the common law in most states and is enshrined in ten of their constitutions: Kimberli R. Black, "Personality Screening in Employment," 32 *American Business Journal* 69, 1994), page 93

394   The law gives it a "qualified privilege": Spohn, , IV. POSSIBLE CAUSES OF ACTION RELATING TO GRAPHOLOGY IN EMPLOYMENT DECISIONS, A. Defamation, *Washington Law Review Quarterly*, Notes 64-76

394   For the record, [the American Psychological Association] neither accepts nor rejects handwriting analysis: Seth Pittman, "Merits of handwriting analysis spark a lively debate," *Eastern Pennsylvania Business Journal*, March 25-31, 2002, page 22

Chapter 24
Discrimination and Disabilities

397   In particular Congress has enacted statutes to protect civil rights of certain classes of people: Title VII of the Civil Rights Act of 1964, *as amended*, 42 U.S.C. § 2000e *et seq.*

The Age Discrimination in Employment Act of 1967, *as amended*, 29 U.S.C. § 621 *et seq.*

The Americans with Disabilities Act of 1990, *as amended*, 42 U.S.C. § 12101 *et seq*

399   Letter of February 28, 2001, from Assistant Counsel Dianna B. Johnston in response to request for opinion to EEOC whether it was legal to use handwriting analysis as a pre-employment screening tool

399   Plain experience and formal surveys reveal that most people can tell whether a person's writing is male or female: Beyerstein and Beyerstein, *The Write Stuff*, page 46

400   The EEOC itself has been troubled about personality tests: The Commission elaborated on this point in its March 1997 Enforcement Guidance on the ADA and Psychiatric Disabilities, stating that "[t]raits and behaviors are not, in themselves, mental impairments, although they may be linked to mental impairments." Such personality traits include stress, irritability and anger management, chronic lateness, poor judgment, integrity, teamwork, and prejudice. Questions or tests designed to determine whether an applicant exhibits any of these traits, behaviors or temperaments would not be considered medical and must be done during the pre-offer stage. As noted above, such tests would not become "medical" examinations solely because a psychologist administers and interprets them._____ **ADA: Disability-Related Inquiries and Medical Examinations, Staff Advisory letter,** August 6, 2001

411   A survey found that somewhat more than half of document examiners were also handwriting analysts: Beyerstein and Beyerstein, *The Write Stuff*, page 50

401   A recent federal appeals court case in the Seventh Circuit in Illinois addressed the coverage of personality tests: *Karaker v. Rent-A-Center, Inc.*, 411 F.3d 831 (2005 CD Illinois)

401 If a discrimination claim is raised, the employer does not have to show the test was valid: See the website aptitude-testing.com/brogdon.htm Martin Green, PRE-EMPLOYMENT TESTING...When is a test "valid" enough?

403 Others open up, like Hal Cross, human resourses Vice-President of Fike Corporation: Leonard, *HR Magazine*, supra., page 69

Chapter 25
Handwriting Analysts as Experts

408 A judge in Colorado regularly refers handwriting of juveniles: Casewit, *Graphology Handbook*, supra., page 151-152

408 An example where a trial court seemed to follow the appellate court rulings: *Cameron v. Knapp*, 520 NYS2d 917, 137 Misc.2d 373 (NYSup Ct 1987)

394 For the record, this esteemed group neither accepts nor rejects handwriting analysis, Pittman, "Merits of handwriting analysis spark a lively debate," *Eastern Pennsylvania Business Journal*, supra, page 22

411 Since it was announced in 1993 these two areas have fared well with the trial courts: See, for example the summary of court decisions compiled by questioned document examiner Hanna McFarland on her website at write-exam.com/case-law.htm

Photo and Other Credits

Chapter 1, Elementary schoolroom photo, Our Lab School, Kutztown University Presents the Lab School Reunion Program 2005; Chapter 2, Writing of Dianne Kalal, Rose Matousek, ABC's of Handwriting Analysis, 1985; Chapter 3, Confucius drawing, Josh Wilker, Confucius, Teacher and Philosopher, Franklin Walts, Division of Groler Publishing, New York, 1999; Aristotle drawing, Encyclopedia of World Biography, 2d Edition, Gale Research, Detroit, 1998; Chapter 4, Milton Bunker photo, M.N. Bunker, Handwriting Analysis: The Science of Determining Personality by Graphoanalysis, Nelson Hall, Chicago, 1955; Chapter 5 and 7, Grim photos, Grim family collection; Chapter 9, Patricia Ramsey writing of Ramsey ransom note, International Appraisers, Inc., 2002; Chapter 10, photos of Lindbergh, Hauptmann, and ransom note, George Waller, Kidnap, The Story of the Lindbergh Case, The Dial Press, New York, 1961; Chapter 11, Richard Nixon signatures, Ruiz and Amend, Handwriting Analysis, The Complete Basic Book, Newcastle Publishing, North Hollywood, 1980; Chapter 13, photo of P.T. Barnum, Barnum's Own Story, Waldo R. Browne, Dover Publications, New York, from Barnum Museum; Chapter 14, Handwritten note of doomed miner, Associated Press, 2005; Chapter 15, children's writing, Crises in Human Development, International Graphoanalysis Society, Chicago, 1983; Chapter 17, scene from Twelve Angry Men, United Artists, 1957; Chapter 18, Article with signatures of locals from Philadelphia Magazine, January 2008

Thanks to Tom Moore for his not trivial time and perceptive comments; and thanks to fellow Graphoanalyst Martha Murphy for reviewing the text and providing extensive worthwhile input; finally, thanks to Ryan Grim, Virginia Grim Follweiler and Ruth Grim Leestma for their valued suggestions and support.